Fixed-Income Analysis for the Global Financial Market

Fixed-Income Analysis for the Global Financial Market

Money Market, Foreign Exchange, Securities, and Derivatives

Giorgio S. Questa

John Wiley & Sons, Inc.

New York • Chichester • Weinheim • Brisbane • Singapore • Toronto

This publication is designed to provide accurate and authoritative information in regard to the subject matter covered. It is sold with the understanding that the publisher is not engaged in rendering professional services. If professional advice or other expert assistance is required, the services of a competent professional person should be sought.

Library of Congress Cataloging-in-Publication Data:

Questa, Giorgio.
    Fixed-income analysis for the global financial market : money
market, foreign exchange, securities, and derivatives / Giorgio S.
Questa.
    p.   cm.
    Includes bibliographical references and index.
    ISBN 0-471-24653-0 (alk. paper)
    1. Money market.   2. Foreign exchange.   3. Derivative securities.
4. Options (Finance)   I. Title.
HG226.Q84   1999
332'.042—dc21   98-44947

Printed in the United States of America

10   9   8   7   6   5   4   3   2   1

Contents

19. Modeling the Yield Curve

Preface

The purpose of this book is to explain in a user-friendly way the pricing and risk analysis of fixed-income securities and derivatives. It is therefore appropriate for a wide range of finance professionals, MBA students, and advanced undergraduates majoring in finance or financial economics. The structure of the book has been carefully planned to facilitate self-study and to provide maximum flexibility to both practitioners and instructors. The layout is very modular to make life easier for those who need a reference manual. Professionals studying to take qualifying examinations for the securities industry (such as the CFA and the NASD/NYSE exams in the United States, and the SFA tests in the United Kingdom) should find this book a useful complement to the standard study materials.

A deliberate effort has been made to use mathematics lightly, pursuing simplicity of statement, to make things easier, not harder. Most successful finance professionals and capable MBA students do not have a strong mathematical background; their needs should be adequately served. Fixed-income analysis is a quantitative discipline, and this is not a watered-down manual. On the other hand, more than 99% of the activity that goes on in everyday financial life lies comfortably within the coverage of this book and can be analyzed with elementary mathematical tools. From the point of view of prerequisite mathematical knowledge, this book should be well within the reach of those who have passed the GMAT test for admission to U.S. business schools.

The emphasis, throughout, is on how to build mainstream operational knowledge from the ground up. There are more than 300 exhibits, mostly based on relevant market data. Nearly all graphs include some of the numerical data on which they are built in order to allow easy checking and replication of the results. This helps the reader to gain familiarity with the world of finance; conceptualizing is a predominantly context-sensitive effort.

Financial activity has witnessed a phenomenal development in the 1980s and 1990s. There has been a parallel growth in the number of practitioners who need a clear and operational understanding of modern fixed-income analysis. These include those who work in banks, securities dealers, institutional investors, accounting and consulting firms, financial departments of nonfinancial corporations, banking and securities industry regulators, governments and other public entities, and so on.

A serious knowledge of finance cannot be restricted to a relatively small number of highly mathematical product specialists steeped in the arcana of their discipline. The well-publicized problems that occurred in 1994–1998, due to trading in securities, derivatives, and hybrids, speak volumes about the need for a much better diffusion of updated financial know-how. Finance has become a well-established discipline. It has benefited from the seminal contributions of a number of outstanding economists, such as Keynes, Samuelson, Hicks, Arrow, and Debreu. Some authors have been rewarded with the Nobel Prize in economics for their pathbreaking work in finance: Franco Modigliani, William Sharpe, Merton Miller, Harry Markowitz, Robert Merton, and Myron Scholes.

We now have a wealth of highly mathematical and rigorous research monographs and scientific journals. These publications are cutting edge but are often loaded with very complex mathematics and cater only to a relatively small number of highly trained academics and specialists, referred to, only half-jokingly, as rocket scientists.

There is, however, a real discontinuity, a fault line, between the abundance of scientific works and the unfortunate paucity of books aimed at the nonmathematical specialist to allow him or her to get a firm grounding in the quantitative methods of modern finance. In a way, this book was born out of a sense of frustration at this unsatisfactory state of affairs. The relative scarcity of books on fixed-income analysis has also made it necessary for a number of well-known authors to add summaries on fixed income to their works on investments, international finance, or corporate finance; the result is a proliferation of necessarily incomplete analyses.

A true global financial village is emerging, heavily dependent for its operations on real-time international telecommunications networks. "Over the past decade or so, the world economy has changed profoundly: it has become a truly global system . . . international flows of money have grown explosively . . . interest rates in one economy affect investments in others. Capital roams freely around the world" (*The Economist,* 1995). In the world we now live in, it makes sense to consider the international dimension as an integral part of the analysis. Consequently, the focus of this book is on fixed-income instruments that can be freely traded internationally, usually without controls, taxes, or other restrictions. Global is taken to mean the U.S. market plus the Euromarket.

This level of globalization is by no means something we should take for granted, a permanent feature of the international economy. Nor is it something that necessarily will go on existing irrespective of intelligent efforts to maintain and improve economic cooperation among nations. The many setbacks that had to be overcome on the way to a single European currency provide both a cautionary tale and a reason for optimism. The Euro became a reality on 1 January 1999.

This book devotes a considerable space to derivatives, including equity options, that are a quasi-fixed-income product.

- First, financial derivatives have registered an impressive growth in the 1980s and 1990s. The outstanding volume of over-the-counter derivatives totaled over $47 trillion at the end of March 1995 (Central Bank Survey of Derivatives Market Activity, BIS Feb 96). The Central Bank survey is conducted every three years and only the preliminary results of the 1998 survey were available at the time this book went to press. Exchange-traded financial derivatives totaled more than $9 trillion as of the end of 1997. As a reference measure, the GDP of the United States totaled less than $9 trillion in 1998. No serious finance professional can choose to turn a blind eye on these financial products that now permeate business activity.
- Second, the set of tools developed to analyze derivatives is now an integral part of risk-return management in banks, asset managers, securities dealers, non-financial corporations, governments, and other public entities. Derivatives are also commonly used for the practical implementation of the risk-management process itself.

In some MBA and professional courses, derivatives are taught as a stand-alone subject. This approach has its drawbacks. Derivatives are, in fact, much easier to understand within the context of the assets on which they are based. It is hard to analyze fixed-income derivatives without an operational knowledge of fixed-income products. Furthermore, most trading, hedging, and investment strategies are based on the combined use of both cash and derivative products.

Reader's Guide

This book has been planned with a view to make it as user-friendly as possible. The reader's time should be considered for what it is: a scarce and valuable resource. The following outlines some of the steps that have been taken to improve the presentation.

APPLYING THEORY TO REAL-LIFE CASES

The focus of this book is on the fundamentals of fixed-income analysis. There is no way one could cover the myriad of products and of trading and hedging strategies that have been created, Lego-like, by combining in clever and original ways (often tax- or regulation-driven) a limited number of basic building blocks.

If you get a real grip on the basics, you will find it easy to understand and price structured products, whereas trying to distill structural knowledge from a huge set of applications is a next-to-impossible task. To develop an operational and lasting familiarity with fixed-income analysis, you cannot limit yourself to reading and understanding. You have to make time for trying out the application of tools and techniques. Therefore this book contains a very large set of market data–based exhibits and examples that constitute a hands-on guide to practical implementation.

There are more than 250 analytical exhibits, complemented by some of the numerical values on which they are based. This will allow you not only to visualize the behavior of the relevant functions, but also to replicate the results, thereby truly mastering the relevant concepts.

Practical experimentation is made easier by FinCalcQ, a collection of simple, spreadsheet-based functions. You are therefore encouraged to have a personal computer available as you read this book and to experiment on your own, getting ideas by reading the financial pages or looking at data screens (Bloomberg, Reuters, Telerate, etc.).

BUILDING ON RESULTS

The structure has been planned to maximize the stepping-stone effect. This should also make this book easier to use as a reference manual for more experienced professionals. Short-term money-market securities and transactions are analyzed in Part 1 as they constitute the essential foundation for a clear understanding of long-term instruments that are covered in Part 2. Forwards and futures are analyzed in both Part 1 and Part 2, to link their analysis to that of the relevant cash instruments. Forwards and futures are close substitutes for cash transactions and are also much easier to understand within this context. Pooling these instruments in a derivatives section usually makes things harder, not easier.

Options are covered separately in Part 3 because of their nonlinearity when compared to cash instruments. Their analysis is unified by the need to use a coherent set of statistical concepts and tools.

A number of tools and techniques that are usually covered within the context of long-term securities are analyzed in Part 1 with reference to short-term money market instruments (e.g., the uses and limitations of the exponential notation for continuous compounding, the term structure of yield rates, cash-and-carry arbitrage, etc.). This approach is justified by two main facts:

- First, money market and foreign exchange operations have become quite sophisticated (and are now attracting a lot of attention from institutional investors which used to consider them in a rather "residual" way).
- Second, a number of concepts are in fact much easier to grasp within the context of simpler short-term securities. Once the basic knowledge is firmly in place, extending the analysis to more complex cases becomes relatively simple.

Containing Mathematical Complexity

Modern finance, like engineering, is an essentially quantitative discipline (the expression "financial engineering" is in fact gaining ground). Its purpose is to allow professionals to make accurate choices among alternative actions in funding, liquidity management, securities trading and hedging, and asset management. It is therefore useless to try to come to grips with this subject without a serious commitment and a good facility with numbers. Beware of finance books that promise "no mathematics." This sort of promise is about as reliable as politicians' campaign pledges.

The decision to place an upper limit on the prerequisite level of mathematical sophistication means that some more advanced topics could not be covered in full analytical detail (continuous-time finance is a powerful development but does require a good level of mathematical knowledge). There are a number of ways in which mathematical complexity has been contained without impairing the completeness of the analysis.

Mathematical "proofs" have been kept as intuitive and easy as possible, adopting a step-by-step approach. Most of the proofs in this book would not make the grade when examined with the standard of rigor that characterizes modern mathematics. Why bother then, you could ask. The answer is that some familiarity with elementary algebra manipulations of financial equations is extremely helpful in developing a hands-on knowledge.

Numerical and graphical examples are systematically used, both for clarity and to anchor the concepts to their real-life analysis. Whenever a result is intuitively evident, we can rely on a numerical example and/or a diagram, dispensing with mathematical proofs. Many such proofs would be mathematically trivial while requiring a lot of algebraic manipulation. To facilitate understanding and insight, it is essential to clear away as much clutter as possible.

The widespread availability of computing power is of great help. We can do away with the sometimes cumbersome mathematics necessary to solve problems numerically (approximate methods to compute the yield to maturity, linear interpolation within the yield book, approximation of functions through expansion in series, etc.).

A minimum level of mathematical background is assumed. If you need to refresh your knowledge, plenty of excellent and straightforward introductory texts are available. Therefore you will find no summary of calculus in this book. You will find instead two chapters dedicated to an introduction to elementary probability theory for financial applications. There are of course many books on statistics and probability, but they are usually not tailored to the needs of a finance professional.

Mathematical Symbols

I have simplified symbology by choosing to work with real-life cases (e.g., instead of introducing a symbol to represent the foreign-exchange (FX) spot rate between two currencies, one can conduct the analysis in terms of, say, the ¥/$ rate). Rather straightforward and simple problems should not be obfuscated with layers of difficult-to-memorize symbols.

I have also taken the approach of using symbols that can be easily read also by those who do not enjoy a 20/20 eyesight. The main change from the traditionally used symbols concerns the notation for the continuously compounded rate (using R instead of r) and for the exponential function, indicated as $\exp(X)$. This notation is in line with the $\ln(X)$ format and is a lot more readable. The added bonus is that in most spreadsheet and programming applications the exponential function is indicated as $\exp(X)$.

Streamlining the Book

This book has been kept as concise and compact as possible. A long-winded style tends to make things harder by interrupting the necessary concentration. (There are of course subjects, such as financial history, where a more eloquent style is in fact functional to a better understanding of the relevant issues.)

The practitioners of finance work in a fully computerized environment where data are available on-screen in the form of tables and charts. I have tried to adopt a similar style of presentation. This approach makes things easier and more intuitive. The human brain is endowed with large areas dedicated to recognizing and processing images, rather than words or algebraic symbols. Condensing information into a visually structured form is therefore a powerful conceptualizing aid. Moreover, you should be well at your ease when reading the on-line quotes (Bloomberg, Reuters, etc.) as well as those provided by the financial newspapers (*Financial Times, The Wall Street Journal*, etc.).

A certain degree of familiarity with the terminology of finance and the institutional framework is assumed. However, a wealth of manuals are dedicated to the institutional framework. I would like to cite the various training manuals available for those taking the Securities Industry examinations (such as the well-known Series 7, General Securities NYSE/NASD Registered Representative). The global banking and investment-banking scenario is analyzed in great depth by Smith and Walter (1990), Smith (1993), Mishkin (1995), Levich (1998), Grabbe (1996), and Solnick (2000). The recent book by Bodie and Merton (1998) provides a clear and comprehensive introduction to finance.

There is no discussion of subjects that traditionally fall into the scope of economics, such as utility theory, dynamics of market-clearing prices, optimal monetary policy in an open economy, term structure of interest rates, determinants of foreign exchange parities, and the like.

Large portions of economic analysis, both at the micro and macro level, are extremely relevant to the activity of the finance professional (and most banks and investment banks have well-developed economic intelligence capabilities). The would-be financial professional is well advised to get a firm grounding in economics. There is, however, a relative abundance of excellent textbooks on economics, and I felt that including half-baked summaries would increase the size but not the usefulness of this book.

The country-specific legal fiscal and regulatory constraints imposed on borrowers and investors are not covered in this manual. The analytical tool kit developed here should prove useful in analyzing optimal financial strategies under regulatory constraints. The same exclusion is applied, with some exceptions, to the effects of taxation, that is often extremely relevant to financial decisions. A considerable amount of ingenuity has been displayed to optimize funding costs or portfolio returns within country-specific fiscal frameworks.

The bibliography is also quite limited and concentrates on books that are both up to date and easily available. Very complete bibliographies can be found in Duffie (1996); Campbell, Lo, and MacKinlay (1997); and Levich (1998).

Acknowledgments

My greatest debt goes to M. Van Biema (Columbia University Business School, New York), who has followed this project from inception to publication. I have shown and discussed parts of the manuscript with the following: S. Bakovljef (CEO, ALNISTA Capital Management, London); D. Ballon (President, TT International Advisors Inc., New York); E. Barone (Professor of Finance, LUISS University, Rome); V. M. Borun (chair of the department of finance, Fordham Graduate Business School, New York); E. Derman (Goldman Sachs); C. Downton (CIO, Pareto Partners, London); G. M. Jabbour (Director, Master of Science in Finance Program, George Washington University, Washington D.C.); R. Layard-Lieshing (head of research, Pareto Partners, London); M. Levis (Director, Master of Science in Finance Program, City University, London); A. Medio (Director, Master of Science in Economics and Finance Program, Venice International University, Venice); E. Namor (head of research, SanpaoloBank, London); H. Ogilvie (Deutsche Morgan Grenfell, London); D. Perry (International Finance Corporation, Washington, D.C.); L. Polenghi (Invesco Europe, London); M. Polenghi (Birckbeck University, London); C. Ponticos (Pareto Partners, London); R. Ricciardi (CIO, Invesco Europe, London); Dominik Salvatore (chair of the faculty of economics, Fordham University, New York); L. Seef (Bloomberg, London); T. Sigeti (Bloomberg, London); R. Smith (Pareto Partners, London); B. Solnik (Finance and Economics Department, HEC, Paris); A. Tardy (Global Equity Derivatives Group, JP Morgan, London); D. Theobald (managing director of fixed-income research, JP Morgan, London).

I also gratefully acknowledge the help and encouragement I received from Pareto Partners.

Errors or shortcomings are, of course, my own responsibility.

In an early phase of the project I received help from Bloomberg London. I also wish to thank Myles Thompson, Mina Samuels, and Michael Detweiler (all of John Wiley) and the people at Impressions Book and Journal Services for their support and help.

Part 1

Short-Term Money Market Instruments

Chapter 1

Background and Terminology

This is an introductory chapter. If you have a background in finance, you should be able to browse through it rather quickly; however, do not skip it altogether, because some relevant features covered here are not easily found in other reference books.

The first four sections will introduce some of the basic concepts and terminology of fixed-income markets. The next two sections provide brief coverage of the two most pervasive short-term financial instruments, that is, bank deposits and short-term securities. Section 1-7 is an appendix dedicated to auctions, which are a widely used pricing and issuing mechanism (most government securities, including U.S. Treasury bills, notes, and bonds, are sold this way). Before we plunge into the subject matter of this chapter, it will be useful to spend a few words on terminology.

- The word securities is often used to indicate financial instruments, such as derivatives, that in fact are not securities.
- *Coupon* is a term originally associated only with bonds and notes, which, until book-entry securities became the norm, were printed carrying the appropriate number of coupons, one for each interest payment. Currently the word coupon also indicates periodic interest payments from fixed-income instruments that are not bonds, such as interest-rate or currency swaps; see Chapter 10.
- The word coupon is also used as a shorthand expression for coupon bonds and/or notes. The expression *U.S. Treasury coupons* will therefore indicate T-bonds and T-notes, both of which pay interest semiannually.

1-1 QUOTATIONS, BID-ASK SPREAD, AND TRANSACTION COSTS

A number of important developments in modern finance are analyzed with reference to a frictionless world (zero transaction costs, continuous markets, identical lending and borrowing rates). This is justified by the necessity of presenting core ideas without the cumbersome mathematics that can be necessary to deal with a non-frictionless financial world. In real life, however, transaction costs play an important role.

Most fixed-income and foreign exchange instruments trade over the counter (OTC), with market makers quoting two-way prices that are disseminated through computer networks. Deals are normally transacted over the phone, and their confirmation in writing can take place in a variety of ways, whenever possible taking advantage of some specialized infrastructure, such as Fed Wire, Trax, or Swift. As a rule, OTC market makers keep a taped record of telephone deals.

The most noticeable exception to OTC markets is represented by financial futures and options exchanges, some of which are committed to open-outcry trading, such as the Chicago Board of Trade and the Chicago Mercantile Exchange. The quotation mechanisms for futures and options exchanges will be examined within the appropriate context.

The market rules examined in this paragraph should be sufficient to convey a basic understanding of the quotation mechanism in OTC markets. Further quotations systems will be covered in the relevant sections of this book. We operate in a very sophisticated and highly computerized environment. Yet a number of old, and often irrational, pricing and quoting traditions survive and are regularly utilized in everyday activity. Outdated as they might be, they are part of the terrain and must be clearly understood. An interesting example is the foreign-exchange quotation of the U.K. pound (£ or GBP), always in the form of foreign currency unit per 1 £, which still reflects the days in which the pound did not follow the decimal system and it was therefore inexpedient to quote a £ price for 1 unit of foreign currency (the same quotation applies to the Irish punt, I£, which, however, will soon disappear because the Republic of Ireland has joined the Euro).

These quirks are by no means confined to old instruments. Forward rate agreements (FRAs) and exchange-traded interest rate futures are both quite recent (the 90-day T-bill future was introduced in 1976 and FRAs in 1984), but their quotations follow different rules (see Chapter 4). The following terminology is commonly accepted:

Bid price = the price at which the market maker stands ready to buy
Ask (offer) price = the price at which the market maker stands ready to sell
Midprice = the arithmetic average of bid and ask prices
Bid-ask spread = gross revenue margin for the market maker

The quantities to which the bid-ask prices apply are subject to both lower and upper limits. Market makers usually do not deal in retail size. They also introduce upper limits to avoid being caught off-guard by large orders in moments of price volatility. Most of the quotations are only indicative for large volumes and have to be confirmed over the phone before a trade is finalized.

Bonds and Notes

Most fixed-income securities are quoted in terms of price (the bid is obviously lower than the ask), with reference to a face value of 100 currency units. In the United States, this quotation is known as *dollar price*. Prices are usually quoted *clean*, that is, without accrued coupon, which is paid on settlement over and above the clean price; see Section 1-2. There are, however, some oddities, the best known of which is represented by U.S. Treasury bonds, notes, and strips. For these securities the fractional number, separated by a colon or by a hyphen, is expressed in 32nds of 1% (see Exhibits 1-1 and 1-2).

Exhibit 1-1 World Bank $ Global Bond: Trade = 3 July 1996, Mty = 21 July 2005

Coupon = 6-3/8, payable semiannually

Bid = 95-3/4; Ask = 95-7/8; Spread = 1/8 = 0. 125

Source: Financial Times/ISMA International Bond Service

Exhibit 1-2 U.S. T-bond: Trade Date = 20 February 1998, Mty = 15 February 2025

Coupon = 7-5/8, payable semiannually

Bid = 122:19 = 122 + 19/32 = 122.59375

Ask = 122:25 = 122 + 25/32 = 122.78125

Spread = 6/32 = 0.1875

Source: The *Wall Street Journal*

Short-Term Discount Securities

Discount securities, such as Treasury bills (Exhibit 1-3) and commercial paper, do not carry add-on interest (coupon) and are issued and traded at a price that is lower than their redemption value (face value or maturity value). The interest paid by the issuer, over the time span from issue to maturity, is therefore equal to the difference between purchase price and face value. These securities are usually quoted in terms of the percent discount rate that is utilized to determine their price (also known as bank discount basis, see Section 1-6). In this case, due to the inverse relationship between price and discount rate, the bid rate is going to be higher than the ask rate. A common piece of jargon in the money market is *basis point* (bp), that is, 1% of 1% = 0.01%.

Quoting Bid-Ask Rates on Deposits

Quotations are expressed in terms of the interest rate. The bid rate, which the bank is willing to pay on deposits (buy deposits), is obviously lower than the ask (offered) rate at which the bank will lend money (sell deposits). The *Financial Times* follows the London rule of quoting the offer rate first (see Exhibit 1-4). Note that live quotes on screens are now generally expressed in decimal form and that the bid-ask spread is usually lower than 4/32 of 1%.

Exhibit 1-3 U.S. Treasury Bill: Mty = Thursday 7 January 1999

	Rate	Price	
Bid	5.04	95.5480	Settlement = Mon 23 Feb 98
Ask	5.02	95.5657	Days to Mty = 318
Spread	0.02	0.0177	Price = 100 - Rate * Days / 360

Source: The *Wall Street Journal*

Exhibit 1-4 US$ 3M Deposit: Trade Date 16 March 1998

Offer	5: 21/32	5.6563	Offered (Ask) Rate
Bid	5: 17/32	5.5313	
Spread	0: 4/32	0.1250	

Source: Financial Times

Foreign Exchange

Foreign exchange (FX) quotations will be examined again in Chapter 4. For the moment let us note that there is a potential source of ambiguity: Buying $ against ¥ is the same transaction as selling ¥ against $.

Spot sale of ¥ against $ = Spot purchase of $ against ¥

To identify the bid and the ask, we must define, on a conventional basis, which currency is considered to be bought/sold. The most widespread quoting rule in FX trades involving the $ is to consider the U.S. currency as the object of purchase or sale. Therefore ¥/$ = 124.30/39 means that the FX dealer is buying $ at ¥ 124.30 (bid) and selling $ at ¥ 124.39 (ask, offer). We have seen that the £ is quoted in terms of units of currency per £. A $/£ quotation of 1.6328/38 entails that the market maker is willing to:

- Buy £ at $1.6328 (= sell $ at 0.6124 £ per $)
- Sell £ at $1.6338 (= buy $ at 0.6121 £ per $)

Transaction Costs

Transaction costs are commonly defined in terms of a *roundturn*, that is, buying a financial instrument and then selling it. For market-maker quotations, the cost of a roundturn equals the bid-ask spread—you open the position at the ask price and then you close it at the bid. In markets based on the open outcry system, each transaction has the same price for the buyer and for the seller, but both pay a commission to the broker(s) for executing the trade. The roundturn cost is simply the sum of the buy and sell commissions. In the futures markets, where open positions often have a very short life, brokers often quote commissions on a roundturn basis. The important concept of *market liquidity* is also defined in terms of transaction costs. A liquid market allows you to deal in volume, in a short time span, at low transaction costs. Thinking of transaction costs in terms of roundturn is usually accurate considering that, in most cases, investments are not held to maturity. When determining portfolio adjustments and switches between securities, you must factor in transaction costs.

Example: You are an asset manager and you own $5 million, face value of the World Bank 6⅜% global bond, maturity 21 July 2005 (bid-ask = 95.75 − 95.875 on 3 July 1996). A securities dealer proposes a switch to bonds that yield a few basis points more and that are of the same quality (maturity, coupon, liquidity, high credit rating, etc.). In deciding whether to accept the advice of the broker/dealer, you should verify the yield advantage considering that you will be selling the World Bank bonds at the bid price and buying the proposed bonds at the ask.

Exhibit 1-5 Settlement for $10 million, 5.02%, U.S. T-Bills, Mty = 318 days

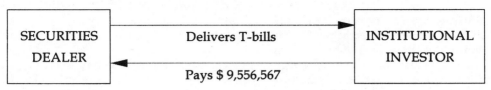

Selling a bond to buy another bond (one that presents more desirable risk/return characteristics) was traditionally called a *bond swap* in Wall Street jargon. This can now be confusing because, since the beginning of the 1980s, swap has come to indicate a specific and very widely used derivative product. A new term, *bond switch*, is now being used as a substitute for bond swap. You should remember, however, that bond swap is still very much alive in Wall Street–speak.

If you are a market maker, you face much lower transaction costs on the securities and instruments in which you are active. You can easily build up inventory by buying at the bid and waiting before selling. You are also at an advantage in selling short because you can go directly to your customers to borrow the necessary securities; see Section 1-3.

1-2 TRADE, SETTLEMENT, AND MATURITY DATES. ACCRUAL RULES

The settlement of fixed-income transaction hinges on a large set of market conventions. They are the province of operations and clearing specialists, and full coverage of their intricacies would require a separate book. In this section we shall therefore examine only those rules and examples that are necessary to build a satisfactory level of insight and to understand how to carry out fixed-income calculations.

Trade Date

The trade date is the date on which a commitment is made (to buy, sell, lend, borrow, swap, write an option, etc.). When securities are bought at an auction, the trade date coincides with the day on which the results of the auction are known and the bidders are told their allotments and invoice price(s). When securities are bought by members of an underwriting group (a common practice for corporate bonds and for Euromarket issues), the trade date coincides with the date on which the allotments are finalized by the lead manager(s) of the underwriting group.

Settlement Date and Fail to Deliver

The settlement date is the date on which the contract is fulfilled. The concept is better understood with reference to a few examples (see Exhibit 1-5).

Spot Sale of Securities. Settlement date is when the buyer pays the price and the seller delivers the securities. Usually this takes place through some clearing organization, such as Fed Wire, Depository Trust Corporation, Euroclear, Cedel, and others, to guarantee *delivery versus payment* (DVP).

When the seller cannot deliver the securities in due time, we have a *fail to deliver*. A complex set of rules governs fails-to-deliver in different markets and for different instruments. A common consequence, however, is that until the securities are delivered, the buyer does not have to pay for them, and therefore the seller loses the interest that would have accrued on these moneys. Fails that occur on a Friday are particularly disliked by sellers of securities (and liked by buyers) because they entail the loss of a minimum of three days of accrued interest.

U.S. Treasury securities settle *regular way* on the first business day following the trade date ($T + 1$ in settlement jargon). Corporate bonds and international bonds settle on the third business day after the trade date ($T + 3$). The $T + 3$ rule went into effect in mid 1995; before that, the rule was $T + 5$. In the U.S. Treasury market it is not uncommon to agree on *cash settlement,* that is, settlement on the trade date (this is made possible by the high level of efficiency of Fed Wire).

When a security is first issued, the settlement date is usually a few business days after the trade date (e.g., 13- and 26-week U.S. T-bills are auctioned on Monday and settle on the following Thursday).

Time Deposits, such as Euromarket Deposits. Settlement means the delivery from the lender to the borrower of the contracted amount. Settlement in the Euromarkets is usually $T + 2$. The contracting parties can agree, however, for settlement on the trade date (e.g., overnight deposits) or on the first business day following the trade date (e.g., for overnight deposits starting the day after the trade date—in jargon, TOMNEXT = *tomorrow next*). An overnight deposit settling ($T + 2$) is known as SPOTNEXT.

Foreign Exchange. Spot transactions settle regular way like Eurodeposits, that is, $T + 2$. This involves two-way flows, as shown in Exhibit 1-6. The currency flows are in the form of sight deposits. Forward transactions settle on some contractually specified future date. A 3-month forward FX transaction will have the same two-way flows as a spot transaction, but these will take place 3 months after the settlement date of the spot transaction.

Maturity Date; Days from Settlement to Maturity

A number of fixed-income instruments (such as time deposits, T-bills, commercial paper, repos, FX swaps, zero coupon bonds, etc.) have only one maturity date, and day-count calculations are performed with reference to this single date. Other instruments (such as coupon-paying bonds, swaps, etc.) have more than one maturity date (in the case of a bond, the dates of the coupon payments plus the final maturity date when the bond is redeemed; the last coupon is usually paid on final maturity).

Days from settlement to maturity (DSM) is obviously important for both interest accrual and present value and yield calculations. The generally accepted rule is that days are counted from the day of settlement (included) to the day of maturity (excluded). The logic underlying this rule is that payments have to be made early enough

Exhibit 1-6 Purchase of $1 million Against JPY, ¥/$ = 110.60

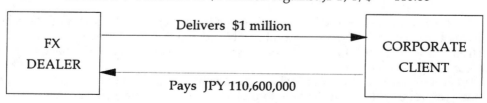

Exhibit 1-7 The Bank Method

Eurodollar deposit		U.S. T-bill, $100,000	
Trade date	Wed-3-Jul-96	Trade date	Fri-20-Feb-98
Settlement date	Fri-5-Jul-96	Settlement date	Mon-23-Feb-98
Maturity date	Fri-4-Oct-96	Maturity date	Thu-7-Jan-99
Days	91	Days	318
Offer rate	5.625%	Asked rate	5.02%
Interest	$1,421.88	Discount	$4,434.33
		Purchase price	$95,565.67

in the day to allow the receiver to use the funds to make other payments or to deposit them into a bank account, earning interest for the day. The settlement payment made by the buyer must therefore give him the right to any interest maturing on the fixed-income security on settlement day. The payment on maturity to the buyer gives him the availability of the funds for the maturity date and therefore must exclude interest accrual on the security for that day. You can compute DSM in two different ways.

1. DSM = the actual number of days elapsing between settlement and maturity. This method is usually referred to by the abbreviation ACT (for actual). This is by far the most widely used method.
2. The 30/360 rule, according to which every month is assumed to have 30 days, and consequently the year has 360 days. This method is utilized in some very large markets such as U.S. corporate bonds, and U.S. municipal bonds, but can be somewhat inaccurate at month's end (you add 2 days at the end of February and subtract 1 day for 31-day months).

Days from Coupon to Settlement

Coupon securities are usually quoted clean. Accrued interest is paid to the seller over and above the clean price. When we add the accrued coupon to the price of a bond, we obtain the *invoice price,* also know as the *gross price* or *dirty price*. We must therefore count the days from coupon to settlement (DCS)—the days between the first day of the coupon period (included) and the settlement date (excluded).

The date on which a coupon is paid is excluded from the day count and is the first date of the following coupon period. Note that the parties in a securities trade can agree on a *flat price* because the payment of interest is uncertain—that is, when the issuer of the bond is in default.

Three Commonly Adopted Accrual Rules

Determining DSM or DCS is only the first step; you must also know which of the three main accrual rules is applicable:

The Bank Method. Refer to Exhibit 1-7. The actual number of days (DSM = ACT) is divided by 360 instead of by 365 (or 366 in leap years); this method is also indicated as ACT/360. This rule is utilized to compute interest on Eurodeposits, which means

Exhibit 1-8 ACT/ACT Basis for Coupon Accrual U.S. T-bond, 7½%
Maturing 15 November 2016

trade date	Thu-11-Jul-96
regular-way settlement	Fri-12-Jul-96
next coupon payment	Fri-15-Nov-96
1st date of coupon period	Wed-15-May-96
DCS	58
days in coupon period	184 (15 May incl., 15 Nov excl.)

The semiannual coupon accrued to the seller equals $(3.75\% \times 58/184)$
and will be added to the purchase price.

that interest is a little higher than the quoted rate. A rate of 6% on a 365-day deposit would yield interest in the measure of 6.0833%. Note that for deposits and loans denominated in £ and in Belgian francs, the accrual rule is DSM/365. The bank method is also applied to discount securities, such as T-bills and commercial paper. The discount is calculated, however, on the face value instead (*bank discount basis*) and not on the amount invested.

The ACT/ACT Method. Refer to Exhibit 1-8. The actual number of days is divided by the actual number of days in the year (366 in leap years). It is adopted in a number of very important coupon-paying bond markets, such as the government bonds of the 11 countries that have adopted the Euro, and U.S. Treasury notes and bonds. When the ACT/ACT rule is applied to semiannual coupon payments (e.g., U.S. Treasuries) the actual number of days from coupon to settlement is divided by the number of days in the relevant half-year.

The 30/360 Rule. Refer to Exhibit 1-9. The 30/360 rule is an approximation of the ACT/ACT method. It accrues a yearly coupon over 1 year (and a semiannual coupon over 6 months) but can be inaccurate at month's end. Prices and yields adjust to take this anomaly into account, as we shall see in Section 7-3. This method is adopted both in the U.S. corporate bond market and in some sectors of the Eurobond market.

The Dated Date and Ex-Dividend Prices

It can happen that a coupon-bearing bond or note is issued after the first accrual date. The 100-yr Walt Disney note (see Exhibit 7-1) had its first accrual date on 15 July 1993, while the issue date was 21 July 1993. In this case the bond is issued with accrued coupon (dirty price). The first accrual date is also known as the *dated date*. Within the first coupon period, days from coupon to settlement will always be computed with reference to the dated date. In some markets, coupon bonds trade ex-dividend (which means ex-coupon) starting a certain number of days before the coupon payment date (this practice, similar to that which is widespread for shares, does not appear to be very rational in a world of $T + 3$ settlement). When a bond trades ex-dividend, the invoice price is adjusted with a negative coupon accrual from settlement date (included) to the payment date of the current coupon (excluded).

Exhibit 1-9 30/360 Coupon Accrual: U.S. Corporate Bond and $ Global Bond

Coca Cola 8. 50% (semiannual coupon), 1 Feb 2022

Trade date	Thu-11-Jul-96	
Regular-way settlement	Tue-16-Jul-96	T+3
Previous coupon payment	Thu-1-Feb-96	
Next coupon payment	Thu-1-Aug-96	
DCS	165	
Days in coupon period	180	(6 months)
Accrued coupon	$3.8958	$4.25 x 165/180

World Bank, $ global bond, 6. 375 % (semiannual coupon), 21 Jul 2005

Trade date	Mon-8-Jul-96	
Regular-way settlement	Thu-11-Jul-96	T+3
Previous coupon payment	Mon-22-Jan-96	
Next coupon payment	Mon-22-Jul-96	
DCS	169	
Days in coupon period	180	(6 months)
Accrued coupon	$2.9927	$3.1875 x 174/180

Usually Eurobonds carry annual coupons. Global bonds usually carry semiannual coupons to conform to the U.S. domestic market tradition.

1-3 LONG AND SHORT POSITIONS; SHORT SELLING SECURITIES

The issues relating to long and short positions in interest rate and foreign-exchange instruments lie at the heart of hedging and risk-management strategies. In this section we shall explore only a few preliminary concepts relative to securities, deposits, and FX positions. The necessary extensions of the analysis will be covered later in this book.

Long and Short Securities Positions

The definition of a long securities position is quite straightforward. You are long a security when you own it. Accordingly, if you are long, you gain if the security price goes up and you lose if it goes down. This connection (long ⇒ gain, if the price increases) holds for all financial instruments, including derivatives (in fact, the quotation system of derivative instruments, such as futures, has been designed in such a way as to preserve this relationship). Owning a security does not necessarily imply *possession* and *control* but only that you have contracted to buy it at a predetermined price. In other words, the buyer is long the securities beginning with trade date, or time-0, irrespective of the settlement date.

 You have a short securities position when you have a commitment to deliver a security and you do not own it. In most cases, being short a security means that you have borrowed the security to sell it to a third party. The sale of a borrowed security is indicated as a short sale. Generally, securities are sold short in the belief that the price will decline and that it will be possible to make a profit buying back the security at a lower price to return it to the lender.

> *Example:* If on 3 July 1996 you had shorted the World Bank global bond (6⅜% mty 21 July 2005) at 95.80, you could have bought it back on 8 July 1996 at a price of 94.25, thereby realizing a profit of 1.55% on the face value of the bond. (This profit figure is calculated assuming a frictionless financial system—no bid-ask spread; the bond is bought/sold at the mid-price—and zero borrowing costs.) The drop in price was due to the announcement on Friday, 5 July 1996, by the U.S. Labor Department that employment was booming (239,000 jobs had been created in June) and that wages were rising at a record-setting rate. The potential overheating of the economy made a rate increase by the Federal Reserve Board likely. Bond traders dumped inventory, sending the price of the benchmark 30yr Treasury bond plunging and driving the yield to 7.15%, up from 6.93% on Wednesday.

Usually, short sales are made when the short seller has already borrowed the securities or is reasonably certain that the securities can be borrowed in time for regular settlement (if it turns out that the short seller cannot borrow the shorted securities, this will result in a fail to deliver). A securities dealer can, however, be temporarily short a certain quantity of a given security if she has sold it without having it in her inventory and has not yet bought it to cover the short. Given the stringent settlement rules, this temporary short can be kept for only a very limited time without seriously risking a fail to deliver.

In theory, you could short a security without having to borrow it by contracting a forward sale. In practice, this is not common. An exception to this rule is when U.S. Treasuries trade on a *when-issued* basis (wi) after the announcement of the auction and must be delivered on issue date (see Section 1-7).

Long and Short Positions in Money-Market Deposits

You are *long a deposit* when you have borrowed funds for a certain time, at a given interest rate; in money-market jargon, you have *bought a deposit*. You are *short a deposit* when you are the lender (you have *sold the deposit*). The price of a time deposit is its contract rate (say LIBOR plus 10 basis points). Therefore, when the rate goes up, the longs gain and the shorts lose. Conversely, when the rate goes down, the longs lose and the shorts gain.

You gain (lose) if you have secured borrowing at a rate that is lower (higher) than the current market rate. This gain (loss) can, therefore, be measured by the amount of interest saved (lost). This entails that the term of the deposit is quite important. The longer the term, the larger the gain (loss) given a market rate movement.

Note that this is only a first approximation. Interest is paid at maturity and therefore should be discounted back to obtain a really accurate measure. Exhibit 1-10 shows that (due to the importance of term to maturity) a long and a short position do not necessarily compensate each other. If a bank funded itself buying a 90-day deposit to fund a 270-day loan, it would register a profit if rates decrease and a loss if they increase. This is a very simple example of the *duration* issue and of its importance in hedging.

Long and Short FX Positions

Determining net FX exposure is easier than doing so for interest rate securities. A nearly one-to-one relationship exists between FX rate movement and exposure. If a

Exhibit 1-10 Gain (Loss) on a Long and a Short $1 million Deposit

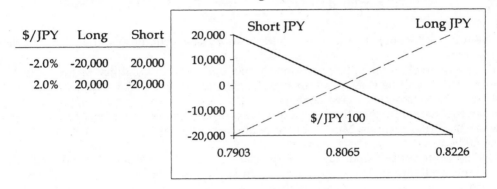

Rate change	90 days long	270 days short
-0.50%	1,250	-3,750
0.50%	-1,250	3,750

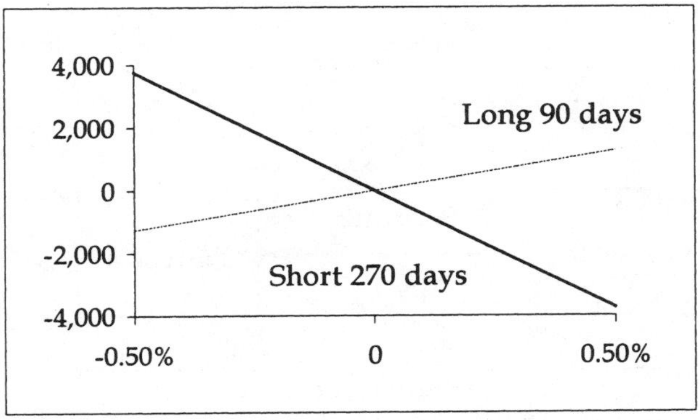

Exhibit 1-11 Gain (Loss) on a Long and a Short of JPY 124 million

$/JPY	Long	Short
-2.0%	-20,000	20,000
2.0%	20,000	-20,000

U.S. firm is long ¥ 124 million (equivalent to $1 million, at 0.8065$/100 ¥), it will gain or lose in direct proportion to the $ value of the ¥; see Exhibit 1-11. If you have a series of long and short positions in a currency, you can easily prepare a currency balance sheet just by taking their algebraic sum.

In computing its FX position, a firm (nonfinancial corporation, asset manager, bank, broker/dealer) will, as a rule, utilize its home currency as a base. A ¥ asset (e.g., a loan to a customer) will entail an FX exposure for a U.S. firm. Conversely, a $ asset will represent an FX exposure for a Japanese corporation.

Short Selling Securities

In most cases, securities are not sold for forward delivery. A short position is therefore implemented by a regular sale of borrowed securities. As a general rule, which does admit some exceptions, when you borrow securities you must post collateral to mitigate the credit risk for the lender of the securities. This collateral is always higher than the market value of the borrowed securities to provide a cushion against their appreciation. The market value includes accrued interest in the case of coupon bonds or notes. In a frictionless economy where you can borrow or lend at the same riskless rate without posting collateral, a short sale generates cash for the short seller (the

Exhibit 1-12 Securities Lending Flow Chart

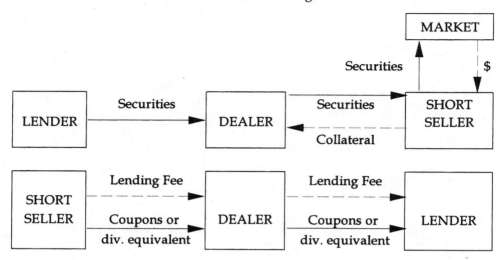

revenue of the sale). In the real world, a short sale usually absorbs cash or other collateral.

The overcollateralization margin is dependent on the volatility of the securities borrowed. It will be very small for U.S. T-bills and quite high for long-term bonds or stocks. The borrowing agreement usually provides for an increase of the collateral when the market price of the securities increases (*margin call*) and a release of collateral when the price declines. Most short sales are organized through a securities dealer, as visualized in the flow chart (Exhibit 1-12).

The lender of the securities is compensated with a fee that will depend on market demand and supply. When a security is in short supply relative to the demand for borrowing it, it is known as a *special* and commands a higher lending fee. The lender is also entitled to receive the dividends or coupon payments that accrue during the lending period. This means that the short seller will have to make equivalent payments to the lender because the real dividends or coupons are paid to the *holder of record*.

Note that the securities lender may well be subject to an unfavorable tax treatment on, say, dividend payments. In this case, lending stock to a borrower who enjoys a lighter tax burden could generate a tax advantage, the so-called *coupon/dividend washing* tax loophole.

The practice of short selling securities is often regulated and restricted. The best-known example of this regulation is the U.S. stock market, where the Securities and Exchange Commission has established the following:

- Every short sale (and reversal of short sale) must be declared as such on the trade ticket. Market transparency is therefore enhanced by the availability of data on short interest, that is, the outstanding amount of stock of each corporation that is borrowed for short selling.
- Short sales cannot be executed when the price of the stock is declining. A short sale can therefore take place only on an *up-tick* (when the price has increased at least one tick) or on a *zero-plus-tick*, that is, at the price of the last trade(s), but at least one tick higher than the last price that was not equal to the price of the short sale. The uptick rule is based on the assumption that short sellers could

exacerbate the situation for a declining stock, causing panic to manipulate the market. Most finance experts, however, believe that this rule is not very useful, especially in a sophisticated market such as the U.S. stock market; see Sharpe (1995).

1-4   ARBITRAGE-FREE PRICING AND THE LAW OF ONE PRICE

Arbitrage is usually defined as the possibility of locking in a riskless profit by simultaneously buying and selling in different markets. *Arbitrage-free* pricing implies that a set of prices that allows arbitrage will not last long because financial intermediaries and sophisticated investors will spot arbitrage opportunities and trade to exploit them. This in turn will quickly eliminate the arbitrage windows by:

- Increasing demand in the relatively cheap market(s); this will drive up prices, making it more expensive
- Increasing supply in the more expensive market(s), exerting a downward pressure on prices and making it less expensive.

A security (or a portfolio of securities, derivatives, or both) will provide a set of future payments, identified by the times at which the payments are due and the states of the world on which they are contingent (*time-state claims*). This is known as the *time-state paradigm*, and its initial development is associated with Kenneth Arrow and Gerard Debreu, two Nobel laureates in economics. Within this framework one can say that an arbitrage provides a positive net payoff in at least one time and state and no negative net payoff in any time and state.

Another well-known way of referring to arbitrage-free pricing is the *law of one price*. With reference to the Arrow-Debreu time-state paradigm, we can say that two securities (or two portfolios) that are characterized by the same time-state claims must have the same price. This leads naturally to the concept of *replicating portfolio*, defined as a portfolio that replicates the time-state claims of the security or derivative that we want to price.

The arbitrage-free approach is extremely important in pricing securities and derivatives (pricing based on the law of one price and on replicating portfolios). Arbitrage pricing theory is also one of the building blocks of mainstream modern investment theory. The arbitrage theory of capital asset pricing was pioneered by S. Ross (1976). The general concept of arbitrage is relatively straightforward—some would say downright obvious. Its applications can be rather complex, however. A number of examples of arbitrage-free pricing will be analyzed throughout this book, with reference to specific contexts. In this section we shall examine only some very general concepts, to help build a clearer insight into this fundamental tool of modern finance.

Transaction Costs and Arbitrage-Free Prices

When observing live quotations on trading screens (Reuters, Bloomberg, etc.), we can often detect small deviations from arbitrage-free prices. However, if we tried to take advantage of these small price misalignments, transaction costs would offset the *riskless profit*. The markets are therefore said to be *trading within transaction costs* or *transaction costs close*. To simplify the analysis, most arbitrage-free pricing equations are expressed assuming that there are no transaction costs and that securities and other financial instruments can be bought/sold at the midpoint between bid and ask prices.

You will often find references to *arbitrageurs* as a specific group of market partici-pants. Remember, however, that most arbitrage trades are done by dealers that are in a very favorable position to lock in arbitrage profits. They have the necessary human and computational resources to spot price misalignments as soon as they appear. They also incur much smaller transaction costs because most often they do not have to pay the full bid-ask spread on their trades. Moreover, since different market makers may have different transaction costs, it may be possible for some, but not all, to exploit arbitrage opportunities.

Bid-ask market-making spreads cannot be considered as riskless arbitrage profits; if they were, then the bid-ask spread would collapse to zero. The spread is both fee revenue, for providing a service to clients, and compensation to market makers for the risks they incur in holding inventory. In the case of *credit-risk-sensitive* products (money-market deposits, forward FX transactions, swaps, etc.), the spread must also compensate for the credit risk incurred by the financial intermediary.

Market prices are therefore nearer to arbitrage-free prices whenever the imple-mentation of an arbitrage strategy implies relatively low transaction costs. The U.S. Treasury bonds market is a good example of this state of affairs. Coupon bonds can be broken down into a series of zero coupon bonds (also known as *Treasury STRIPS* or T-STRIPS), and an appropriate series of T STRIPS may be reconstituted to form a coupon bond or note. Stripping and reconstituting involve negligible transaction costs, no credit risk is involved, and there are no capital adequacy requirements. This insures that the pricing of Treasury coupons and T-STRIPS is very close to arbitrage-free.

Arbitrage and Capital Adequacy Ratios

Exploiting certain arbitrage possibilities can well imply a regulatory capital absorption that may not be sufficiently compensated by the arbitrage profit. A number of arbitrage possibilities relate forward prices to spot prices. The riskless profit can often take the form of a borrowing rate lower than the current market rate, or a yield rate on a riskless asset that is higher than the riskless rate. These arbitrage opportunities can imply setting up a complex position (*replicating portfolio*) and keeping it on your books for some amount of time; this is where capital adequacy ratios come into play.

Full Arbitrage and Path Arbitrage

Full arbitrage involves setting up a trade (either spot or with forward components) with the purpose of locking in a profit, net of transaction costs. Path arbitrage occurs when a firm has, say, two or more different ways of carrying out the same financial transaction and chooses between the alternatives depending on current market prices. A typical example occurs in FX transactions.

> *Example:* A U.S. firm needs to have the availability of ¥ 1 billion, in 3 months' time, to make a payment to a supplier. The firm has the necessary $ amount currently available, and it wants to lock in the forward $/¥ exchange rate to avoid FX risk. The firm has two options:
> - Buy forward the ¥ and invest for 3 months the necessary $ amount.
> - Buy spot ¥ and invest them for 3 months at the current ¥ rate.
>
> Choosing between the two possibilities does not represent a full arbitrage. Path arbitrage does not incur in extra bid-ask spreads and therefore is available to non–market makers.

Necessity of a Market-Clearing Mechanism

The law of one price requires the presence of an adequate market mechanism that will allow arbitrage to take place. If there is no such market mechanism, we can have

Exhibit 1-13 Theoretical and Actual $/ECU Exchange Rates, 18 April 1997

	Amount	FX rate-$	$-Value
German Mark (DEM)	0.62420	1.713	0.3644
French Franc (FRF)	1.33200	5.771	0.2308
British Pound (GBP)	0.08784	0.613	0.1434
Italian Lira (ITL)	151.80000	1693.000	0.0897
Dutch Guilder (NLG)	0.21980	1.925	0.1142
Belgian + Lux. Franc (BEF+LUF)	3.43100	35.320	0.0971
Spanish Peseta (ESP)	6.88500	144.520	0.0476
Danish Krone (DKK)	0.19760	6.532	0.0303
Irish Punt (IEP)	0.00855	0.644	0.0133
Greek Drachma (GRD)	1.44000	270.030	0.0053
Portuguese Escudo (PTE)	1.39300	172.230	0.0081
Theoretical ECU $-Value			1.1441
Actual ECU Market Rate			1.1394

Source: Bloomberg

apparent violations of the law of one price. In Chapter 12 we shall examine one of these possible violations in the context of the *put-call parity* for options. There are, however, many other interesting examples, some of which we shall now succinctly survey.

A closed-end mutual fund can trade at a discount to its book value, that is, at a price that is lower than the aggregate value of its investment portfolio. This obviously means that the market does not have a high opinion of the fund managers, who in fact are considered as a *shadow liability*. There is an apparent violation of the law of one price because the fund is valued at less than its assets, contradicting the principle of value additivity. An obvious arbitrage would be to buy the fund and liquidate it, thereby unlocking the value represented by the difference between the fund's market capitalization and its *net asset value* (NAV). This arbitrage, however, is costly, time-consuming, and conditional on a variety of legal requirements. This is why the financial pages are graced by a number of below-NAV quotations for closed-end funds.

The concept of management as a liability can apply to conglomerates that have a stock-exchange capitalization that appears to be lower than the value that would be fetched by the different firms included in the conglomerate if they were self-standing entities. This is known as *conglomerate discount*. The arbitrage strategy is quite complex, time-consuming, and expensive. It often involves a hostile takeover bid on the conglomerate to spin off its assets. The best-seller *Barbarians at the Gate: the Fall of RJR Nabisco* by Burrough and Helyar (1990) provides a gripping description of the takeover of RJR Nabisco by the leveraged-buyout firm of Kohlberg, Kravis, and Roberts.

One last interesting example of apparent violation of the law of one price was provided, on a macro scale, by the FX market. The ECU was defined as a fixed basket of currencies after the Maastricht treaty of 1992. The composition of the ECU is shown in Exhibit 1-13. The value of the ECU against a non-ECU currency, such as the US$, should therefore have always been equal to the value of the underlying basket (again, for the principle of value additivity). However, the two values did diverge (the spread was in the order of 3% in Q1-1996) because there was no mechanism for breaking down the ECU into its constituent currencies or for creating an ECU with the appropriate currency basket.

1-5 EUROMARKET TIME DEPOSITS AND LIBOR REFERENCE RATE

The explosive growth of international finance centers around a well-organized global OTC market for interbank time deposits, denominated in all the main freely convertible currencies. The growth of this market is of course connected to that of the foreign exchange market. This global market continues to be called the Euromarket because of its London origin in the 1960s. It now spans a number of financial centers (New York and Tokyo being the most important after London, which has managed to keep its leading role). The defining characteristic of this international market is that deposits are not subject to reserve requirements and that interest is usually paid without being subject to withholding tax.

Euromarket rates can change freely in time and are continuously broadcasted, with real-time updates, by the large information providers such as REUTERS and Bloomberg. The liquidity of this global OTC multicurrency market is also enhanced by foreign exchange and money-market brokers such as Cantor Fitzgerald, Tullet and Tokyo and others.

The importance of this free market has grown to the point that most domestic rates track the Euromarket rates, after the necessary adjustments for reserve requirements and taxation. Euromarket rates also serve as a pricing reference for a number of important and widespread financial products and derivatives (e.g., floating-rate notes and bonds, floating-rate loans, FRAs, swaps, futures, options). With reference to the London-quoted rates, the following terminology is now well established:

- LIBOR = London interbank offered (ask) rate
- LIBID = London interbank bid rate.
- LIMEAN = Average between LIBOR and LIBID (midpoint rate)

Reference rates fixed in other financial centers are designated with names that refer to the city where they are quoted, for example, PIBOR = Paris, FIBOR = Frankfurt, and TIBOR = Tokyo.

Banks operating in the main centers of the global market quote interbank bid-ask rates for wholesale deposits (minimum amount $1 million or equivalent) for different currencies and different maturities, usually from 1 day to 1 yr (see Exhibit 1-14). For maturities of up to 1 yr, interest is assumed to be paid at maturity. For the most important currencies, banks quote rates for multiyear periods; in this case, interest is paid annually, in arrears (in accordance with the Euromarket standards, where fixed-rate bonds usually carry annual coupons).

- Banks will make interbank deposits only to those banks with which they have an open credit line. The whole business of extending and reviewing money-market credit lines is a complex area of international bank management (money-market lines are also used for foreign exchange transactions and for money-market derivatives).
- Bid-ask rates are not cast in bronze. Banks that enjoy a very high creditworthiness are able to fund themselves at a cheaper rate. Conversely, banks that are not

Exhibit 1-14 Eurodeposit Rates, 28 October 1996

	USD		JPY		DEM	
ON	5.3750	5.4375	0.4688	0.5000	na	na
TN	5.2500	5.3125	0.4688	0.5000	2.9375	3.0625
SN	5.2500	5.3125	na	na	2.9375	3.0625
1W	5.2500	5.3125	0.4688	0.5000	3.0000	3.1250
2W	5.2500	5.3125	0.4688	0.5000	3.0000	3.1250
3W	5.2500	5.3125	0.5000	0.5313	3.0000	3.1250
1M	5.2500	5.3125	0.5000	0.5313	3.0000	3.1250
2M	5.3125	5.3750	0.5000	0.5313	3.0000	3.1250
3M	5.4062	5.4687	0.5000	0.5313	3.0000	3.1250
4M	5.4375	5.5000	0.5313	0.5625	3.0000	3.1250
5M	5.4687	5.5312	0.5313	0.5625	3.0000	3.1250
6M	5.5000	5.5625	0.5625	0.5938	3.0000	3.1250
7M	5.5312	5.5937	0.5625	0.5938	3.0625	3.1875
8M	5.5625	5.6250	0.5938	0.6250	3.0625	3.1875
9M	5.5937	5.6562	0.5938	0.6250	3.0625	3.1875
10M	5.6250	5.6875	0.6250	0.6563	3.1250	3.2500
11M	5.6562	5.7187	0.6250	0.6563	3.1250	3.2500
1yr	5.7187	5.7812	0.6563	0.6875	3.1250	3.2500
2yr	6.0000	6.1250	0.8750	1.0000	3.9375	4.0625
3yr	6.1875	6.3125	1.3125	1.4375	4.5000	4.6250
4yr	6.3125	6.4375	1.6875	1.8125	5.0625	5.1875
5yr	6.4375	6.5625	2.0000	2.1250	5.4375	5.5625

ON = Overnight deposit, for immediate settlement
TN = Tomorrow Next TOMNEXT, overnight deposit settling T+1
SN = Spot Next = overnight deposit with regular settlement T+2

Source: REUTERS

perceived to be solid may have to pay a premium over the offered rate. An interesting example is represented by the so-called *Japan premium*, which Japanese banks had to pay for a few months (Q3 of 1996) when a series of bad news about their credit losses made the markets less eager to fund them. Japan premium reemerged in 1997–1998 due to the bad news about the Japanese financial system and to the Asian financial crisis.

• Highly rated nonbanks can get rates that are similar to interbank rates. A role is played, however, by capital-adequacy ratios, which favor banks over nonbanks.

LIBOR Reference Rate

A number of forward-looking financial instruments are anchored to the future value(s) of some well defined interest rate(s) (see Exhibit 1-15). Due to the established role of both the Euromarkets and of London, a number of those instruments are based on

Exhibit 1-15 Floating Rate Instruments and LIBOR

Floating-rate loans	Interest-rate and cross-currency swaps
Floating-rate notes and bonds	Forward-rate agreements - FRAs
Floating-rate convertibles	Interest-rate futures

Exhibit 1-16 British Bankers Association LIBOR

RATES FIXED AT 11:00 LONDON TIME 20-FEB-1998

	USD	GBP	DEM	CHF	JPY	ECU
1WK	5.62500	7.37500	3.68750	0.81250	0.60156	4.34375
1MO	5.62500	7.50000	3.46875	0.81250	0.67578	4.34375
2MO	5.62500	7.56250	3.50000	0.89453	0.87891	4.34375
3MO	5.62500	7.56250	3.50391	0.96094	0.86328	4.34375
4MO	5.62500	7.56250	3.53125	1.00000	0.85156	4.34375
5MO	5.62500	7.56250	3.56250	1.03125	0.83203	4.34375
6MO	5.62500	7.56250	3.59375	1.06250	0.83594	4.34375
7MO	5.62500	7.56250	3.62500	1.07422	0.82031	4.34375
8MO	5.62500	7.54688	3.64844	1.10547	0.82031	4.34375
9MO	5.62500	7.53906	3.65625	1.12500	0.81250	4.34375
10MO	5.63672	7.53125	3.68750	1.14844	0.80859	4.34375
11MO	5.65625	7.52734	3.71875	1.18750	0.80859	4.34375
12MO	5.66797	7.52734	3.75000	1.18750	0.80859	4.34375

Source: Bloomberg

LIBOR. But LIBOR is a continuously changing rate; furthermore, different banks can quote, at any time, different bid-ask rates.

To have a reliable yardstick on which to base financial commitments, most contracts adopt the British Bankers Association (BBA) daily LIBOR reference rate. BBA-LIBOR is determined as the average offered rate, quoted at 11:00 A.M. London time, by the most active banks for the currency in question. The procedure calls for an ideal number of 16 banks; the 4 highest and the 4 lowest rates are excluded, and LIBOR is defined as the arithmetic average of the remaining 8 rates. BBA-LIBOR rates are officially disseminated by Dow-Jones Telerate at page 3740 for the main currencies (see Exhibit 1-16) and at page 3750 for other currencies.

1-6 SHORT-TERM DISCOUNT SECURITIES

US T-bills are the most important short-term securities in the international financial markets. They are backed by the full faith and credit of the United States Treasury and are considered virtually exempt from credit risk. Their outstanding volume is substantial, and they are widely held by non-U.S. residents, including central banks that utilize them as a liquid investment for their $-denominated reserves.

Their importance lies also in the fact that they are one of the instruments of the Federal Reserve's intervention in the money markets to control the level of interest

Exhibit 1-17 Marketable Interest-Bearing Debt of the U.S. Treasury, in $ billions, End of Period

	Bills	Notes	Bonds	Indexed notes (*)	Total
1991	590.4	1,430.8	435.5	n.a.	2,456.7
1992	657.7	1,608.9	472.5	n.a.	2,739.1
1993	714.6	1,764.0	495.9	n.a.	2,974.5
1994	733.8	1,867.0	510.3	n.a.	3,111.1
1995	760.7	2,010.3	521.2	n.a.	3,292.2
1996	777.4	2,112.3	555.0	n.a.	3,444.7
1997	715.4	2,106.1	587.3	33.0	3,441.8
Q2-98	641.1	2,064.6	598.7	50.1	3,354.5

(*) The US Treasury first issued inflation-indexed notes in Q1-1997.

Bills, notes and bonds represent nearly 100% of the marketable, interest-bearing debt of the U.S. Treasury.

The decline of the total interest-bearing debt of the Treasury reflects the federal budget surplus of the U.S. economy, which is projected at $76 billion for fiscal 1998.

Source: Federal Reserve Bulletin

rates. The T-bill market is very liquid and the bid-ask spreads are quite narrow. The bid-ask spread for T-bills is expressed in basis points of discount rate and can appear to be rather large for bills maturing in a short time. In fact, when the bid-ask spreads are translated into $ prices, they are quite small.

T-bills are issued in book-entry form; the bills are not paper certificates but are represented by records in the computers of the Federal Reserve (in accounts held by banks that are members of the Federal Reserve System). In secondary-market transactions, T-bills *settle regular way* on the business day following the trade date ($T + 1$) (see Exhibits 1-17 and 1-18). T-bills are issued through auction, where primary dealers (recognized as such by the Treasury) submit their competitive bids, expressed in terms of discount rate (see Section 1-7). On any given date, there will be T-bills maturing every week for the following 6 months and every 4 weeks for a further 6 months.

- Thirteen-week and 26-week T-bills are auctioned every week, normally on a Monday, and issued on the following Thursday. Maturity is usually on a Thursday. When Thursday is not a business day, the issuing or maturity date will be the first business day after Thursday (such as Friday, 5 July in Exhibit 1-18). This means that the supply of 3M bills is increased by 6M initial maturity bills with 13 weeks to maturity. The amounts to be auctioned are ordinarily announced late in the afternoon on the Tuesday preceding the auction.
- One-year (52-week) T-bills are issued every 4 weeks. The auction takes place on a Friday and the bills are issued on the Thursday of the following week. Every 4 weeks, the supply of 13-week T-bills is increased by an old 1yr bill with 13

Exhibit 1-18 Selected T-bills, Trade = 10 June 1996, Settlement = 11 June

Maturity	Term	Bid	Asked	Asked Price	Spread $ (**)
Thu-13-Jun-96	2	5.19%	5.09%	99.97	6
Tue-18-Jun-96 (*)	7	5.18%	5.08%	99.90	19
Thu-20-Jun-96	9	5.15%	5.05%	99.87	25
Thu-27-Jun-96	16	5.09%	4.99%	99.78	44
Fri-05-Jul-96	24	4.99%	4.89%	99.67	67
Thu-01-May-97	324	5.50%	5.48%	95.07	180
Thu-29-May-97	352	5.54%	5.52%	94.60	196

Italics indicate the maturity dates of one-year original maturity bills.

(*) The bill maturing on June 18 (not a Thursday) is a cash management bill.

(**) $ Bid-Ask spreads relate to $1 million face value transactions.

Representative OTC quotes based on mid-afternoon transactions of $1m or more.

Source: The *Wall Street Journal*

weeks to maturity. The amounts to be auctioned are ordinarily announced late in the afternoon on the Tuesday preceding the auction.

- Cash-management bills are issued at irregular intervals with maturities ranging from a few days to almost 9 months. Typically, they are issued to fund government spending peaks, and they usually mature shortly after one of the major midmonth tax-receipt dates (March, April, June, September, and December). Most of the time, cash-management bills mature on a Thursday so that they become interchangeable with normal bills. There are exceptions however; see Exhibit 1-18, where the T-bill maturing on Tuesday, 18 June 1996, is a cash-management bill.

U.S. Commercial Paper

U.S. commercial paper (USCP) is short-term unsecured debt issued by domestic and foreign corporations in the U.S. market. The maximum maturity is 270 days (beyond 270 days, the securities would have to be filed with the Securities and Exchange Commission [SEC]). De facto, maturities tend to be a lot shorter, such as 30 days, and commercial paper is utilized mainly for short-term liquidity management by both the issuers and the buyers.

Commercial paper is also considered an exempt security, that is, freely tradable by U.S. banks, which were severely limited in their ability to underwrite corporate debt and equity by the Glass-Steagall legislation. Some very large issuers have their own sales force that places the corporate commercial paper with wholesale investors (*directly placed commercial paper*). Most issuers, however, find it expedient to utilize the professional services of banks and broker/dealers that specialize in commercial paper placement (*dealer-placed commercial paper*) (see Exhibit 1-19).

Exhibit 1-19 USCP Outstanding, in $ billions, End of Period

year	Financial dealer	Financial direct	Financial total	Non-financial	All issuers
1991	213.0	182.5	395.5	133.4	528.8
1992	226.5	171.6	398.1	147.6	545.6
1993	218.9	180.4	399.3	155.7	555.1
1994	223.0	207.7	430.7	164.6	595.4
1995	275.8	210.3	486.1	188.3	674.4
1996	361.1	229.7	590.8	184.6	775.4
1997	513.3	252.5	765.8	200.9	966.7
May-98	569.1	274.5	843.5	210.5	1,054.0

Dealer = Dealer-placed   **Direct** = Directly placed

Source: Federal Reserve Bulletin

Financial companies now account for over 80% of the market. These issuers include special-purpose companies established by large industrial corporations that produce consumer durables to provide consumer financing to their customers (such as General Motors Acceptance Corporation [GMAC]). Non-U.S. issuers also tap the USCP market and represent over 20% of the dealer-placed market. The USCP market is very liquid and provides issuers with a large degree of flexibility. Well-known and highly rated issuers can tap the market for large amounts on a very short timetable. Corporations have issued in the USCP market to bridge-fund mergers and acquisitions. Three interesting examples are:

- American Home Products raised $8.4 billion in 1 day in November 1994 to bridge-fund the acquisition of American Cyanamid.
- In March 1996, Walt Disney raised $8 billion for its acquisition of Capital Cites/ABC and Lockheed Martin raised nearly $7 billion to acquire Loral.

Euro Commercial Paper

Euro commercial paper (ECP) first appeared in the 1970s, much later than USCP, which dates back to the last century. It is a relevant component of the Euromarkets but has never achieved the size or degree of liquidity comparable to those of the USCP market. One of the reasons for this lack of importance resides in the fact that other financial instruments (such as Euronotes) are more flexible and are not limited by regulatory constraints (the USCP market growth is attributable in part to regulatory issues such as the exemption of commercial paper from SEC registration and Glass-Steagall limitations). An interesting feature of ECP is the possibility of issuing it in several currencies, as shown in Exhibit 1-20.

1-7   AUCTIONS

Many fixed-income instruments are created and issued through bilateral OTC negotiation (term deposits, commercial paper, FX spot and forward transactions, repos,

Exhibit 1-20 ECP Outstanding, $ million Equivalent

CCY	Dec 1995	%	March 1997	%
$	54,772	62.9	65,934	59.4
DEM	9,106	10.5	10,101	9.1
GBP	5,643	6.5	9,990	9.0
CHF	7,484	8.6	8,436	7.6
AUD	3,564	4.1	3,774	3.4
ECU	1,590	1.8	2,220	2.0
JPY	2,135	2.5	5,883	5.3
Other	2,787	3.2	4,662	4.2
Total	87,081	100	111,000	100.0

Source: JP Morgan, Global Commercial Paper

forward rate agreements, and swaps). This issuing flexibility is greatly facilitated by the existence of standardized *master agreements* that define the legal profile of the transactions. Securities issues tend to be somewhat more formalized and can take place through well-regulated auctions or through syndicated placements.

Auctions tend to be utilized by governments to issue treasury securities, whereas syndicated placements are adopted by corporations and other issuers. Both auctions and syndicated placements can take many different shapes in accordance with market practice and regulatory framework. The theory of auctions is also a budding field of economic research. The involvement of economists in designing optimal auction procedures hit the news when radio bandwidth was auctioned in the United States in the 1990s.

An in-depth analysis of auctions and syndicated placements is clearly beyond the scope of this book. We shall therefore provide an extremely concise description of the auction of treasury securities in the United States. Not only is the U.S. treasuries market the largest homogeneous fixed-income market in the world, but its issuing mechanisms are considered to be at the cutting edge of market practice and increasingly are being adopted by other countries. If you are interested in learning more about U.S. treasury auctions, you are advised to read the relevant chapter in Sundaresan (1997).

The description of U.S. treasuries auctions is based on a circular of the Department of the Treasury entitled "Sale and Issue of Marketable Book-Entry Treasury Bills, Notes and Bonds" (published 5 January 1993, effective 1 March 1993). Book-entry security means a security the issue and maintenance of which are represented by accounting entries or electronic records and not by a paper certificate. This circular reflects some changes in the terms and conditions governing treasuries auctions, which were proposed by the Department of the Treasury in 1992, partly in response to the problems that emerged in 1991, when Salomon Brothers was caught violating the auction rules (this was considered a serious breach and led to the resignation of Salomon's chairman, president, and other senior managing directors).

Auction Calendar for U.S. Treasuries

Treasuries are divided into the following three classes:

Exhibit 1-21 Issuing Calendar for U.S. Treasuries

13-week and 26-week bills	Auctioned every week on Monday, for settlement on the following Thursday
52 week bills	Auctioned every four weeks on Monday, for settlement on the following Thursday
2-year and 5-year notes	Auctioned toward the end of every month, for settlement on the last business day of the month
3-year note 10-year note 30-year bond	Auctioned every quarter for settlement on the 15th of February, May, August, or November. Semiannual coupon and principal payments are also aligned on the 15th of those months.

1. Bills, which are short-term discount securities with maturities of up to 1 year
2. Notes, which are coupon-bearing securities (semiannual coupon) with original maturities up to 10 years. Notes are issued with terms of 2, 3, 5, or 10 years.
3. Bonds, with initial maturities of up to 30 years (semiannual coupon). As a rule, bonds are issued only with a 30-year maturity.

Treasury securities are auctioned according to a well-defined calendar, which helps in maintaining an orderly and liquid market (see Exhibit 1-21). Note that for bonds and notes, the auction announcement does not fix the coupon rate. The coupon will be determined by the Treasury on the basis of the weighted average yield of the winning competitive bids. The coupon, fixed in increments of 1/8 of 1%, is usually set to be immediately smaller than the weighted yield, so that the bonds and notes are issued slightly below par.

- *Reopening* means the auction of an additional amount of an existing security. In this case the auction announcement obviously indicates the coupon rate.
- *Dated date* means the date from which the interest accrues. The dated date and the issue (settlement) date are the same, except when the dated date is earlier than the issue date. In the case of reopening, the dated date can be several months before the settlement date.
- *Settlement date* means the date of final and complete payment for securities awarded in an auction. Settlement amount means the par value of the securities awarded, less any discount amount and plus any premium amount and accrued interest (from dated date to settlement date).

Bids can be submitted by *primary dealers* (the 40 dealers who are authorized to deal directly with the Federal Reserve) on their own account or for the account of large institutional investors. Customers can submit bids through either primary dealers, who submit bids directly to a Federal Reserve Bank, or via intermediaries, who in turn route them to a submitter (see Exhibit 1-22).

Exhibit 1-22 Bidding Flow Chart for U.S. Treasury Securities

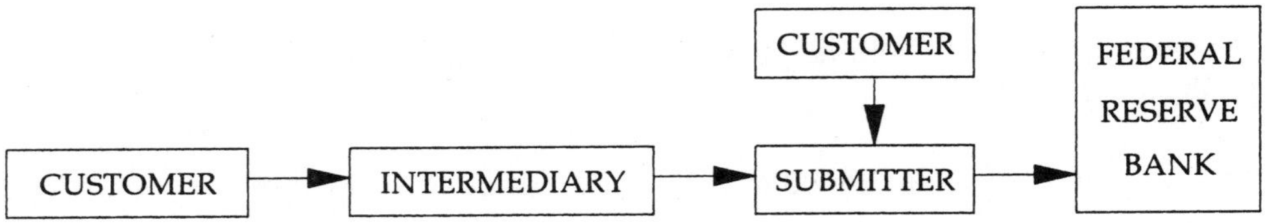

```
                                    ┌──────────┐        ┌──────────┐
                                    │ CUSTOMER │        │ FEDERAL  │
                                    └────┬─────┘        │ RESERVE  │
┌──────────┐    ┌──────────────┐    ┌────▼─────┐        │  BANK    │
│ CUSTOMER ├───►│ INTERMEDIARY ├───►│ SUBMITTER├───────►│          │
└──────────┘    └──────────────┘    └──────────┘        └──────────┘
```

Multiple-Price (Discriminating Price) Competitive Auctions

Each competitive bid must indicate a quantity of securities (expressed as face value) and an annual yield (or annual discount rate in the case of T-bills). Yields and discount rates must be expressed with two decimals, for example, 5.73%. After February 1995 bids on notes and bonds can be expressed with three decimals, that is, in 10ths of a basis point of yield. Note that each bidder can submit multiple competitive bids, obviously at different yields. The Treasury allots the securities that are being auctioned beginning with the lowest yield and then moves to the next best bid, continuing in this manner until all the securities are allotted.

Within the same auction, securities can be sold at different prices to different bidders, and also to the same bidder if that party has submitted multiple bids, some of which turn out to be winning. Multiple-price auction means an auction where each successful bidder pays the price equivalent to the yield rate that it bid.

When bids at the highest accepted yield (or discount rate for T-bills) exceed the available amount, bids are prorated by the Department of the Treasury. Depository institutions and dealers, whether submitters or intermediaries, are responsible for prorating awards for their customers at the same percentage announced by the Treasury.

Noncompetitive bids are also allowed, and they are allotted the full amount of the bidded securities. They are bids to purchase securities at the weighted average yield or discount rate of awards to competitive bidders. There are certain restrictions on noncompetitive bids, to make sure that most securities are in fact awarded to competitive bidders.

- A bidder bidding competitively for his own account may not bid noncompetitively for his own account in the same auction.
- A bidder may not bid noncompetitively for more than $1 million in a bill auction or for more than $5 million in a note or bond auction.

The success of an auction can be measured, albeit imprecisely, by its *bid/cover* ratio, which is the ratio of the bids received to the amount awarded. The level of uncertainty about the auction outcome is usually measured by:

- The yield spread of winning bids (highest yield minus lowest accepted bid)
- The *tail of the auction,* which is the difference between the weighted average yield or discount rate of the auction (applicable to noncompetitive bidders) and the lowest accepted bid

Uniform-Price Auctions

With uniform-price auctions, all the winning bids pay the price corresponding to the highest winning yield (lowest winning price). This seems to entail that the proceeds from the auction will be lower than with the discriminating-price mechanism because a number of winning bidders will get securities at a price that is lower than what they were willing to pay. Things are in fact less simple. Multiple-price auctions can in fact produce lower bids than uniform-price auctions because of the so-called *winner's course,* that is, placing a winning bid at a price materially higher than that offered by other winning competitors. Therefore, we have a complex situation. The uniform price auction will give back part of the bids, that is, the difference between all winning bids and the lowest winning bid price. However, the bids could prove to be higher, therefore more than offsetting the give-back effect.

When-Issued Trading

A well-known characteristic of the treasury market is *when-issued* trading (wi), which starts when the issue is announced and continues until the securities are issued (all wi trades settle on the issue date). In the case of new treasury coupons, wi trades are done on a yield basis until the coupon is announced by the Department of the Treasury and on a price basis after the coupon announcement (there is obviously no wi trading in the case of reopening).

Chapter **2**

Interest, Discount, and Compounded Yield

This chapter is somewhat technical and covers some of the basic building blocks of fixed-income analysis. If you already have some knowledge of the mathematics of finance (also known as *bond mathematics*), you will be able to browse through it quickly and with very little effort. However, you are not advised to skip it, because it contains some useful materials that you may not find in other manuals. Some concepts can be deceptively simple. In fact, they are sometimes explained with a less than satisfactory level of accuracy.

To make things easier, we shall distinguish, as neatly as possible, between interest rates and yields. Whenever feasible, we shall restrict the term *interest rates* to indicate those rates that are used to contractually determine the amount of interest that accrues on a fixed-income instrument (e.g. deposit rate, bond coupon rate, swap rate, etc.). Conversely, *yield* will be used to indicate those measures of *intensity of interest* that take into account not only the contractually relevant rates but also the market price and the redemption value of fixed-income instruments; a bond that is priced below par will yield more than its contractual coupon rate.

This distinction between rates and yields cannot be made as clear-cut as desirable because of market conventions (an example is the well-known internal rate of return [IRR], which is clearly a yield and not a rate measure). Moreover, you are likely to come across several publications where the two terms are used somewhat interchangeably and sometimes are also assigned the same symbols.

2-1 INTEREST RATE, DISCOUNT RATE, AND SPOT YIELD

The following equations summarize, with reference to the simple context of time deposits, some of the concepts and symbols that we shall use throughout this book. Exhibit 2-1 provides step-by-step examples of interest calculations, with reference to Eurodeposits, in four different currencies.

Exhibit 2-1 Interest Calculations for Eurodeposits, Trade Date = Friday, 20 February 1998; Settlement = Tuesday, 24 February 1998

ccy	$	DEM	JPY	GBP
Term	3M	3M	6M	6M
Mty	Mon-25-05-98	Mon-25-05-98	Mon-24-08-98	Mon-24-08-98
DSM	90	90	181	181
T	0.250000	0.2500000	0.5027778	0.495890 (*)
BBA-LIBOR	5.6250%	3.5039%	0.8359%	7.5625%
PV	1,000,000	1,000,000	1,000,000	1,000,000
I	14,063	8,760	4,203	37,502
FV	1,014,063	1,008,760	1,004,203	1,037,502

(*) The accrual rule for the GBP is DSM/365

Box 2-1 Money-market calculations

PV = Principal (amount invested), also known as present value

I = Amount of interest ($, DEM, JPY, etc.)

i = Yearly interest rate

T = Term, in years

FV = Future value, that is, principal + interest

$I = PV \cdot i \cdot T$

$FV = PV + I = PV \cdot (1 + i \cdot T)$

PV is the discounted value of FV = the value that we must invest to obtain FV.

$$PV = \frac{FV}{1 + i \cdot T} \Rightarrow i = \frac{FV - PV}{PV} \cdot \frac{1}{T}$$

Bank Discount Basis and Discount Securities (T-bills, Commercial Paper, etc.)

Discount securities carry no coupon and are issued and traded at a price lower than face value (FV). According to a time-honored but not very rational tradition, these securities are usually quoted following the *bank discount basis*—that is, the discount rate d is applied to FV. The discount rate quotation is usually based on T = ACT/360. The spread between bank discount rate and money-market yield increases with the spread between PV and FV, and therefore with both d and T. Discount rates should be used only as a market-quotation mechanism and nothing more. It is therefore always necessary to compute the equivalent money-market yield (also known as CDY). The return on a discount instrument is a computed yield and not a rate (no contractual interest accrues on it) (see Exhibit 2-2).

Exhibit 2-2 Money-Market Yield as a Function of *T* and Discount Rate

Days	*T*	4%	5%	6%	7%	8%	9%
90	0.25	4.04%	5.06%	6.09%	7.12%	8.16%	9.21%
180	0.50	4.08%	5.13%	6.19%	7.25%	8.33%	9.42%
270	0.75	4.12%	5.19%	6.28%	7.39%	8.51%	9.65%
360	1.00	4.17%	5.26%	6.38%	7.53%	8.70%	9.89%

Box 2-2   Bank discount basis and money-market yield

d = bank discount rate

$PV = FV \cdot (1 - d \cdot T)$

The discount rate is computed on FV and, since $FV > PV$, d will always be lower than the money market yield i, which, applied to PV, yields FV.

$$PV = FV \cdot (1 - d \cdot T) = \frac{FV}{1 + i \cdot T} \quad \text{for } \{d,i,T > 0\}$$

$$(1 - d \cdot T) = \frac{1}{1 + i \cdot T} \Rightarrow (1 - d \cdot T) \cdot (1 + i \cdot T) = 1$$

$$d \cdot T + d \cdot i \cdot T^2 = i \cdot T \Rightarrow d = \frac{i}{1 + i \cdot T} \Rightarrow d < i$$

Price Value of One Basis Point of Discount Rate

The price value of one basis point of discount rate (*PVbp*) measures the $ change in *PV* due to a 0.01% change of the discount rate. Exhibit 2-3 shows clearly that *PVbp* rises linearly with *T*. The level of discount rate *d* has no influence on *PVbp*. The important issue of the sensitivity of the price of a security to a change in yield (also known as *duration analysis*) will be further developed in Chapters 6 and 7.

Exhibit 2-3 *PVbp* for a $1 million T-bill

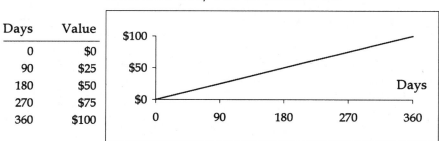

Days	Value
0	$0
90	$25
180	$50
270	$75
360	$100

Box 2-3   Price value of one basis point of discount rate (*PVbp*)

$PVbp = [FV - FV \cdot d \cdot T] - [FV - FV \cdot (d + 0.01\%) \cdot T]$

$FVbp = -FV \cdot d \cdot T + FV(d + 0.01\%)T = FV \cdot T \cdot 0.01\%$

For $T = 1$ (360 days to maturity), $PVbp = \$100$ for a \$1 million face value T-bill.

U.S. Bond Yield Equivalent for T-bills

Exhibit 2-4 includes a column, *bond-yield equivalent* (BEY), which is normally quoted in order to compare U.S. T-bills and other discount securities to U.S. Treasury bonds and notes (*coupon securities*).

For maturities of up to a half year, BEY is defined as CDY, annualized, however, with days/365 (to reflect the fact that Treasury coupon securities accrue interest based on days/365). Therefore, BEY > CDY.

When maturity exceeds 6 months, BEY is calculated using the compounded yield equation (see Sections 2-2 and 2-3).

Exhibit 2-4 U.S. T-bills: Trade = Tuesday, 3 March 1998, Settlement ($T + 1$)

Mty	Days	Ask	Price	BEY	CDY
Thu-5-Mar-98	1	5.04%	99.9860	5.11%	5.04%
Thu-12-Mar-98	8	4.64%	99.8969	4.71%	4.64%
Thu-19-Mar-98	15	4.89%	99.7963	4.97%	4.90%
Thu-26-Mar-98	22	4.79%	99.7073	4.87%	4.80%
Thu-2-Apr-98	29	5.02%	99.5956	5.11%	5.04%
Thu-9-Apr-98	36	4.98%	99.5020	5.07%	5.00%
Thu-16-Apr-98	43	5.28%	99.3693	5.39%	5.31%
Thu-23-Apr-98	50	5.21%	99.2764	5.32%	5.25%
Thu-30-Apr-98	57	5.18%	99.1798	5.30%	5.22%
Thu-7-May-98	64	5.01%	99.1093	5.13%	5.06%
Thu-27-Aug-98	176	5.10%	97.5067	5.30%	5.23%
Thu-3-Sep-98	183	5.11%	97.4024	5.32%	5.25%
Thu-17-Sep-98	197	5.13%	97.1928	5.35%	5.28%
Thu-15-Oct-98	225	5.12%	96.8000	5.35%	5.29%
Thu-12-Nov-98	253	5.16%	96.3737	5.40%	5.35%
Thu-10-Dec-98	281	5.15%	95.9801	5.40%	5.37%
Thu-7-Jan-99	309	5.12%	95.6053	5.38%	5.36%
Thu-4-Feb-99	337	5.16%	95.1697	5.43%	5.42%
Thu-4-Mar-99	365	5.14%	94.7886	5.42%	5.42%

Quotations: The *Wall Street Journal*

Interest-at-Maturity Securities

Interest-at-maturity securities (such as certificates of deposit) carry only one coupon, payable at maturity. Their analysis is quite similar to that of discount securities, but certain adjustments have to be made to adopt the familiar $(PV \Rightarrow FV)$ equations:

- First, FV includes the coupon payment, determined as simple interest on the par value (PAR), taking into account the time between issue and maturity.
- Second, PV must take into account both the price of the security and any accrued interest at the time of purchase. You will recall that price + accrued interest is known as dirty price or invoice price.

Interest-at-maturity securities provide a first example of the necessity of distinguishing clearly between rates and yields. In fact, these securities have both a contractual interest rate, which determines FV and C, and yields, that depend on their market price.

Box 2-4   Interest-at-Maturity Securities

$FV = PAR + CPN$

$CPN = PAR \cdot i \cdot TIM$

$CPN = $ coupon

$PAR = $ par value (usually \$100), also known as face value or redemption value

$i = $ coupon rate, equivalent to the interest rate i on time deposits

$TIM = $ time between issue and maturity

$PV = P + AI = $ dirty price, also known as invoice price or gross price

$P = $ price, clean price

$AI = PAR \cdot ci \cdot TIS = $ coupon accrued, accrued interest

$TIS = $ time between issue and the settlement of the security's purchase

$TIS + T = TIM$

$$CDY = \left(\frac{FV}{PV} - 1\right) \cdot \frac{1}{T} = \left(\frac{PAR + CPN}{P + AI} - 1\right) \cdot \frac{1}{T}$$

2-2   COMPOUNDING AND INTERNAL RATE OF RETURN

Compounding can be deceptively simple and requires a little extra attention to get it right from the start. The effort is time well spent; compounding is the most basic building block of fixed-income analysis. Both interest rates and CDY are quoted in terms of yearly rates. This useful convention is clearly insufficient when comparing investments over different time horizons. To complete the picture we must introduce *compounded yield* (Y) that is, interest on interest.

Time-horizon differences are clearly more important for medium- and long-term instruments. Market practice recognizes this by using consistently (well, sort of) compounded yield for maturities of more than one year (6 months in the U.S.). For short-term money-market instruments, CDY is the standard, and Y is utilized only for special calculations.

Exhibit 2-5 Y as a Function of X and R

X	R = 6%	R = 7%	R = 8%	R = 9%
1 Annual	6.0000%	7.0000%	8.0000%	9.0000%
2 Semiannual	6.0900%	7.1225%	8.1600%	9.2025%
4 Quarterly	6.1364%	7.1859%	8.2432%	9.3083%
12 Monthly	6.1678%	7.2290%	8.3000%	9.3807%
365 Daily	6.1831%	7.2501%	8.3278%	9.4162%
Continuous	6.1837%	7.2508%	8.3287%	9.4174%

Box 2-5   Compounded Yield

Let us start with a 1-year investment at 6%, with semiannual compounding. After 6 months the value per $ invented equals $(1 + 3\%)$ and this amount will in turn be reinvested for a further 6 months.

$FV = (1 + 3\%) \cdot (1 + 3\%) = 1.0609 \Rightarrow Y = 6.09\%$

Increasing the frequency of compounding we get:

$(1 + 1.5\%)^4 = FV$ per $ invested, quarterly compounding; $Y = 6.136\%$

$(1 + 0.5\%)^{12} = FV$ per $ invested, monthly compounding, $Y = 6.168\%$

In general, indicating the yearly nominal yield with R and the compounding frequency with X we obtain:

$$Y = \left(1 + \frac{R}{X}\right)^X - 1$$

Say we want to compare rates for 6-month and 1-year Eurodollar deposits to determine whether to invest for 1 year, or to invest for 6 months and then roll over the investment for 6 more months. We cannot ignore the fact that the semiannual alternative will allow us to reinvest interest at the end of the first 6-month period. Let us assume that the rate at which we can reinvest equals the rate for the first 6 months (this assumption is only a useful starting point; we shall deal explicitly with its limitations in Chapter 4). Exhibit 2-5 shows that the gain from compounding $Y - R$, as a function of the compounding frequency, for different levels of R

• Increases with the frequency of compounding
• Increases more than linearly with the increase in R

Exhibit 2-6 Compounded Interest Calculations, $Y = 6\%$

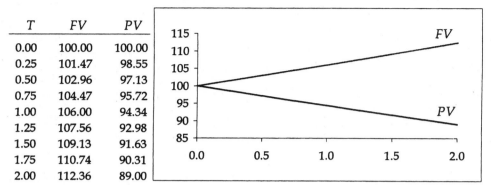

T	FV	PV
0.00	100.00	100.00
0.25	101.47	98.55
0.50	102.96	97.13
0.75	104.47	95.72
1.00	106.00	94.34
1.25	107.56	92.98
1.50	109.13	91.63
1.75	110.74	90.31
2.00	112.36	89.00

A Word of Caution

Compounding is a meaningful (although not perfect) way to compare rates that apply over different time spans. It should, however, be used with caution. If we invest in 6-month Eurodeposits at rate i, this does not imply that we will be investing for 1 year at i compounded semiannually. In fact, given the variability of interest rates, it is almost certain that our reinvestments after 6 months will be at a rate different from the present 6-month rate. Assuming that the present level of LIBID is 5.6%, the overall result will be

$$FV = \left(1 + \frac{H1}{360} \cdot 5.6\%\right) \cdot \left(1 + \frac{H2}{360} \cdot LIBID_X\right),$$

where $H1$ and $H2$ are the number of days in the two half-year periods (e.g., $H1 = 182$; $H2 = 183$), and $LIBID_x$ is the unknown level of the bid rate on Eurodeposits, in 6 months' time.

Daily Compounding and Continuous Compounding

Let us now, however, take a nominal rate R compounded daily. This allows us to derive the equation to use the *annual compounded yield* to compute interest and discount for arbitrary periods that can be expressed with an integer number of days (such as 92 days, 274 days, etc.). This is obviously important. First, a number of securities and other financial instruments are issued with an initial life that includes a fraction of a year. Second, securities and other financial instruments, issued for an integer number of years, are traded on the secondary market when their residual life includes a fraction of year. We used a nominal rate, compounded daily, to determine Y, PV, and FV for any arbitrary number of days. The same identical result could have been reached using a nominal rate compounded several times a day, or better still, a continuously compounded nominal rate. Using a continuously compounded nominal rate is important because it provides the basis to formulate compounding in the useful logarithmic format (see Box 2-7).

Box 2-6   Daily Compounding

$$FV = PV \cdot \left(1 + \frac{R}{365}\right)^{DAYS} = PV \cdot (1 + Y)^{\frac{DAYS}{365}}$$

The right-hand term of the equation allows us to forget about R, the nominal rate compounded daily, and to use directly the yearly compounded rate. The proof straightforward:

$$1 + Y = \left(1 + \frac{R}{365}\right)^{365} \Rightarrow (1 + Y)^{\frac{DAYS}{365}} = \left(1 + \frac{R}{365}\right)^{\frac{365 \times DAYS}{365}}$$

Term could, of course, be expressed as a fraction of year $T = DAYS/365$:

$$FV = PV \cdot (1 + Y)^{T} \Rightarrow 1 + Y = \left(\frac{FV}{PV}\right)^{\frac{1}{T}}$$

Examples:

1. A 92-day, $1 million loan at 5.5% is equivalent to an annual compounded yield of

$$FV = 1{,}014{,}055.56 = 1{,}000{,}000 \times \left(1 + 5.5\% \frac{92}{360}\right)$$

$$1 + Y = \left(\frac{1{,}014{,}056}{1{,}000{,}000}\right)^{\frac{365}{92}} = 1.056938 \Rightarrow Y = 5.6938\%.$$

The nominal rate R equivalent to Y on a daily compounding basis can be easily computed with the following equation, but in facts this computation is not necessary to determine Y.

$$1 + Y = \left(1 + \frac{R}{365}\right)^{365} \Rightarrow R = 365 \times [(1 + Y)^{\frac{1}{365}} - 1] = 5.5380\%$$

2. Determine what FV you must get on a 274-day, £1 million deposit to obtain an annual compounded rate of 7%.

$$FV = 1{,}000{,}000 \times (1 + 7\%)^{\frac{274}{365}} = 1{,}052{,}102.27. \qquad (R = 6.7665\%)$$

Box 2-7   Continuous Compounding

The annual yield Y corresponding to a continuously compounded nominal rate R is given by the following equation:

$$(1 + Y) = \lim\left(1 + \frac{R}{X}\right)^{X} \quad \text{for } X \to \infty$$

Expressing term as a fraction of year ($T = days/365$) we obtain

$$FV = PV \cdot (1 + Y)^{T} = PV \cdot \left(1 + \frac{R}{X}\right)^{XT}.$$

Given Y, the value of R under continuous compounding would be a fraction of a basis point lower than the value of R under daily compounding.

Exhibit 2-7 Compounded Yield and LIBOR; Trade Date = Monday, 28 October 1996; Settlement = Wednesday, 30 October (*T* + 2)

Mty	M	Days	$ LIBOR	$ Y	JPY LIBOR	JPY Y
Mon-2-Dec-96	1	33	5.3125%	5.5202%	0.5313%	0.5399%
Mon-30-Dec-96	2	61	5.3750%	5.5748%	0.5313%	0.5398%
Thu-30-Jan-97	3	92	5.4687%	5.6607%	0.5313%	0.5397%
Fri-28-Feb-97	4	121	5.5000%	5.6810%	0.5625%	0.5714%
Mon-31-Mar-97	5	152	5.5312%	5.7001%	0.5625%	0.5713%
Wed-30-Apr-97	6	182	5.5625%	5.7195%	0.5938%	0.6029%
Fri-30-May-97	7	212	5.5937%	5.7386%	0.5938%	0.6028%
Mon-30-Jun-97	8	243	5.6250%	5.7571%	0.6250%	0.6344%
Wed-30-Jul-97	9	273	5.6562%	5.7758%	0.6250%	0.6342%
Mon-1-Sep-97	10	306	5.6875%	5.7930%	0.6563%	0.6657%
Tue-30-Sep-97	11	335	5.7187%	5.8117%	0.6563%	0.6655%
Thu-30-Oct-97	12	365	5.7812%	5.8615%	0.6875%	0.6970%

Source: REUTERS

Compounded Yield and Simple Interest

When we want to compute continuous compounding within a money market context, we must remember to transform the ACT/360 daycount in ACT/365 before applying the preceding equations (see Exhibit 2-7). The last equation in the box can be rewritten as follows:

$$(1 + Y) = \left(\frac{FV}{PV}\right)^{\frac{1}{T}} = \left(1 + i \cdot \frac{ACT}{360}\right)^{\frac{365}{ACT}}$$

Spot Yields and Internal Rate of Return

Up to now, we have examined compounded yield and compounded discount for fixed-income instruments characterized by a very simple cash flow pattern. You invest *PV* at time-0 and you get back *FV* at maturity, the so-called *point-input point-output* cash flow. Securities with this kind of cash flow are known as *pure discount securities* (e.g., T-bills, commercial paper, zero coupon bonds, etc.). The yields associated with such pure discount securities are also known as *spot yields*, because they refer to time horizons that begin immediately, that is, with a spot transaction (e.g., deposit, purchase of T-bills or commercial paper, etc.). As you can easily see, spot yields are usually different for different maturities (e.g., the compounded spot yield on the USD was 5.52% for 1 month and 5.86% for 1 year).

A large number of fixed-income instruments, however, pay interest throughout their lives (e.g., coupon bonds), and some repay principal in several installments (e.g., sinking fund bonds). It is common practice in the financial markets to associate a single yield measure to such cash flows. This yield measure is known as *internal rate of return* (IRR). When this measure is applied to securities it is usually called *yield to maturity*

(*YTM*) or, somewhat less frequently, *redemption yield*. Collapsing all the different spot yields into one single yield indicator *YTM*, presents several drawbacks that we shall examine in more detail in the following chapters. However, this single-number *YTM* is still widely used as a quotation mechanism because of its great practicality.

> *Example.* For the most important currencies, banks quote *forward rate agreements* (FRAs; see Section 4-3), which allow you to lock in the future value of Euro rates for up to 2 years. If you lock in 6-month ask rates over a 2-year time horizon, you can determine what amount of interest you are going to pay, semiannually in arrears, after 6, 12, 18, and 24 months. You can now compute the *YTM* over the 2-year period. This will collapse the four rates into one single rate, which must be regarded as a sort of "average" between the four rates. By doing so you gain in practicality (one single rate), but of course this single rate does not convey any information on the slope of the term structure:
>
> - *YTM* is higher than the lowest spot rate and lower than the highest. This result is self-evident when you consider that the *YTM* is a sort of average between spot yields.
> - The preceding payments take into account the ACT/360 rule but do not adjust for leap years and for payment dates falling on non–business days (one semester = 182.5 days) (see Exhibit 2-8).

Box 2-8   Yield to Maturity

PMT_K = Amount of the kth payment

T_K = term of the kth payment (in years)

We can now compute a single yield measure that will give *PV* when used to discount all the payments.

$$PV = \frac{PMT_1}{(1 + YTM)^{T1}} + \cdots + \frac{PMT_N}{(1 + YTM)^{TN}} = \sum_1^N \frac{PMT_K}{(1 + YTM)^{TK}}$$

The preceding equation can be used to compute:

- *PV*, knowing *YTM* and the payments

- *YTM* given *PV*. In general, the value of *YTM* must be determined with numerical methods (see the following example), which are readily available both on PC spreadsheets and on the screens of information providers.

2-3   U.S. Bond Yield Basis and the Treasury Method

In the U.S. bond market, yields are quoted as if they were capitalized twice a year. The historical origin of this peculiar convention reflects the fact that, in the United States, bonds traditionally pay interest twice a year. Therefore, when the bond trades at par, its yield to maturity equals the coupon rate (see Chapter 7). The U.S. bond yield basis (also known as *bond basis*) really means that instead of quoting an annual compounded yield, we quote a semiannual compounded yield. From an analytical point of view, the two methods are equivalent, and we can adopt one or the other provided that we first make the necessity adjustment. From now on, we shall indicate the U.S. quotation with Y_{us} for spot yields and with YTM_{us} for yield to maturity (see Exhibit 2-9). The preceding symbols become *USY* and *USYTM* in the exhibits.

Exhibit 2-8 Computing *YTM* on Forward Rate Agreement (FRA) Rates,
Trade = Monday, 16 December 1996

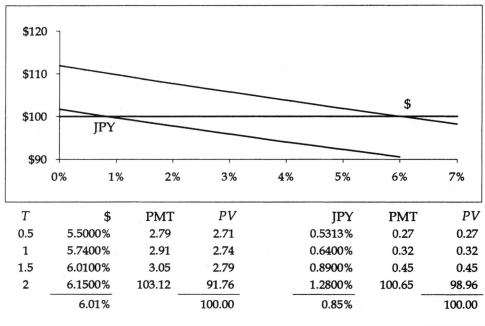

T	$	PMT	PV	JPY	PMT	PV
0.5	5.5000%	2.79	2.71	0.5313%	0.27	0.27
1	5.7400%	2.91	2.74	0.6400%	0.32	0.32
1.5	6.0100%	3.05	2.79	0.8900%	0.45	0.45
2	6.1500%	103.12	91.76	1.2800%	100.65	98.96
	6.01%		100.00	0.85%		100.00

Source: REUTERS

Exhibit 2-9 Euro (ISMA) Yield and U.S. Bond Yield

Y	USY	USY	Y
5%	4.9390%	5%	5.0625%
6%	5.9126%	6%	6.0900%
7%	6.8816%	7%	7.1225%
8%	7.8461%	8%	8.1600%
9%	8.8061%	9%	9.2025%
10%	9.7618%	10%	10.2500%

Box 2-9   U.S. Bond Basis

$$1 + Y = \left(1 + \frac{Y_{us}}{2}\right)^2 \Rightarrow Y_{us} = 2 \cdot (\sqrt{(1 + Y)} - 1)$$

When computing *FV* or *PV* using the U.S. bond basis, we must express term in semesters and fractions of semesters *H*, which is roughly equivalent to multiplying *T* by 2.

$$FV = PV \cdot \left(1 + \frac{1}{2} Y_{us}\right)^H \Rightarrow Y_{us} = 2 \cdot \left[\left(\frac{FV}{PV}\right)^{\frac{1}{2T}} - 1\right]$$

Exhibit 2-10 T-bill Example

Maturity	Days	Ask	Price	BEY	CDY
Thu-7-Jan-1999	309	5.12%	95.6053	5.38%	5.36%

Exhibit 2-11 SIA Day Count for a 309-Day T-bill

Days in H1	Days in H2	Da = 309 - H2	Da/H1	Term	*PV* at *Y* = 5.38%	*Y* at PV= 95.6053
184	181	128	0.6957	1.6957	95.5990	5.372%
183	182	127	0.6940	1.6940	95.6032	5.377%
182	183	126	0.6923	1.6923	95.6075	5.382%
181	184	125	0.6906	1.6906	95.6118	5.388%

We have seen that for T-bills, the U.S. securities industry makes a distinction between maturities of less than 6 months (money market yield is used, with ACT/365 accrual) and maturities over 6 months, when compounding, U.S. style, is the rule. In this second case the bond equivalent yield is usually indicated as BEY. Let us consider the example in Exhibit 2-10. A quick and widely used way to proceed is to determine *H* by dividing the number of days to maturity by 182.5 (average half-year).

$$Y_{US} = 2 \cdot \left[\left(\frac{100}{95.6053} \right)^{\frac{1}{H}} - 1 \right] = 2 \cdot \left[(1.045967)^{\frac{182.5}{309}} - 1 \right] = 5.38\%$$

The method adopted by the Securities Industry Association (SIA) is more laborious in the determination of *H* but gives a result that, in the case of T-bills, is usually very similar to that obtained with the shortcut method. Days to maturity would be split into two segments:

- One whole virtual semiannual coupon period to maturity, that is, to 7 January 1997 (we call this a virtual coupon period because T-bills do not carry coupons). We can indicate the number of days in this period with *H2*.
- A first incomplete virtual semiannual coupon period, from settlement to the beginning of the virtual semester to maturity. We shall indicate the number of days in this half-year with *H1*. Term would then be set at one full semester plus the relevant fraction of the first semester (actual days divided by the number of days in the notional first semester).

The difference between the SIA method and the shortcut method is depicted in Exhibit 2-11. Notice that the more laborious SIA method gives a result that depends on the calendar days in the two semesters; this explains why most investment houses apply the 182.5-day approach, that is both simpler and more consistent.

The Treasury Method

In some books and research documents, you are likely to come across a complex-looking (but in fact simple) equation to determine BEY for T-bills. This is due to the fact that in the United States there are two methods for computing bond yields when the term to maturity includes an incomplete half-year. The SIA method applies continuous compounding over the whole term to maturity in a way similar to that adopted by the International Securities Market Association (ISMA), except for the use of semiannual compounding. The Treasury method consists of applying simple interest to the incomplete semester.

Box 2-10   U.S. Treasury Method for T-bills

For a T-bill with maturity of more than 182 days and less than 1yr we have the following equation:

$$PV \cdot (1 + Y \cdot Ta) \cdot \left(1 + \frac{Y}{2}\right) = 100,$$

where Ta = the incomplete semester, expressed as a fraction of a year.

$$(1 + Y \cdot Ta) \cdot \left(1 + \frac{Y}{2}\right) - \frac{100}{PV} = 0 \Rightarrow \frac{Ta}{2} Y^2 + \left(Ta + \frac{1}{2}\right) Y + 1 - \frac{100}{PV} = 0.$$

The preceding equation is a straightforward quadratic:

$$Y = \frac{-b \pm \sqrt{b^2 - 4ac}}{2a} \quad \text{where } a = \frac{Ta}{2}; \; b = \left(Ta + \frac{1}{2}\right); \; c = 1 - \frac{100}{PV}$$

From a financial point of view, the only meaningful solution is the positive one. At the current level of interest rates, the Treasury and SIA methods produce nearly identical results. The preceding equation can be used only for T-bills and for T-STRIPS in their final year to maturity. In all other cases the solution must be found with numerical methods.

2-4   INFLATION AND REAL YIELDS

Without a doubt, inflation is one of the most important subjects in economics. A lively debate goes on in the economic profession as to its causes, accurate measurement, consequences, and remedies. Some of this research effort focuses on issues that are directly relevant to finance, such as the effect of inflation on the level of interest rates, on foreign exchange parities, and on stock market returns. In this section we shall set ourselves the more modest task of examining inflation-adjusted interest rates and yields.

Real Interest Rates

Several inflation statistics are currently in use, such as the consumer price index (CPI), the wholesale price index, and the gross national product (GNP) deflator. When it comes to measuring real interest rates, the most widely used indicator is the CPI.

The CPI expresses inflation in terms of compounded annualized rate of growth of the index. Therefore, we often read statements such as "In the 1st quarter of 1998 (Q1-1998), consumer price inflation, expressed as a compounded annual rate, equaled 2.7% in the United States versus 1.9% in France." We can therefore use the following equations.

Box 2-11   Inflation Rate and Consumer Price Index

$CPI_T = CPI_0 \cdot (1 + \pi)^T$

CPI_0 = consumer price index at the beginning of period T

CPI_T = consumer price index at the end of period T

π = annualized inflation rate

T = time horizon (usually month, quarter, half-year, year)

$\pi = \left(\dfrac{CPI_T}{CPI_0}\right)^{\frac{1}{T}} - 1$

Box 2-12   Real Inflation-Adjusted Yields

$\dfrac{FV}{CPI_T} = \dfrac{PV(1 + Y)^T}{CPI_0(1 + \pi)^T}$

Setting $CPI_0 = 1$ we obtain

$PV\left(\dfrac{1 + Y}{1 + \pi}\right)^T$ = inflation-adjusted future value.

And therefore, indicating the real inflation-adjusted yield (annual compound rate) with IAY we obtain

$IAY = \dfrac{PV\left(\dfrac{1 + Y}{1 + \pi}\right) - PV}{PV} = \dfrac{1 + Y}{1 + \pi} - 1.$

You will find that real interest rate is often indicated as

$IAY \cong Y - \pi.$

The following equation shows that the simplified formula is acceptable, provided that π is relatively small. With double-digit inflation (as you are likely to find when examining financial instruments of some emerging markets), the approximation clearly overestimates the real interest rate because it does not divide $(Y - \pi)$ by the divisor $(1 + \pi)$.

$\dfrac{1 + Y}{1 + \pi} - 1 = \dfrac{Y - \pi}{1 + \pi} < Y - \pi$

To determine the real interest rate, we must compare the change in purchasing power over a given period.

The realized real yield for a given period (for example, Q2-1998) should be measured after the end of the period, when the change in the CPI is known from official statistics. We should also utilize a meaningful yield on a fixed-income instrument maturing at the end of the period under observation (e.g., 3-month LIBOR for Q2-1998).

Sometimes real interest rates are calculated for a future period based on estimated inflation. Sometimes the real interest rate is computed with reference to a daily interest

Exhibit 2-12 Inflation and Realized Real Yields

| | CPI | CPI | | 3M LIBOR | |
	Q2-98	Q3-98	π	Q2-98	RY
USA	163.00	163.60	1.48%	5.6250%	4.08%
JAPAN	102.20	102.10	-0.39%	0.7969%	1.19%
GERMANY	120.00	119.90	-0.33%	3.5313%	3.88%
U.K.	163.40	164.40	2.47%	7.7344%	5.14%
FRANCE	116.40	116.10	-1.03%	3.9375%	5.02%
ITALY	108.10	108.30	0.74%	5.0469%	4.27%

LIBOR is adjusted for daycount and ACT/360 accrual

Source: Datastream

Exhibit 2-13 Pre-Tax Yield Needed to Obtain a 2% Real, After-Tax, Return (tax rate = 30%)

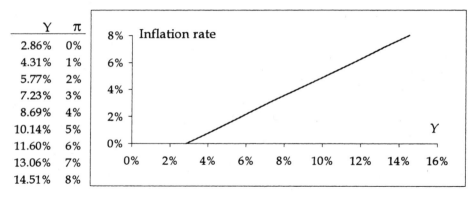

Y	π
2.86%	0%
4.31%	1%
5.77%	2%
7.23%	3%
8.69%	4%
10.14%	5%
11.60%	6%
13.06%	7%
14.51%	8%

rate, such as the federal funds rate in the United States—for example, "Many economists who believe U.S. economic growth is about to slow to a more sustainable pace have pinned their hopes on the historically high level of real interest rates. Recently, they note, the federal funds rate (the interest rate paid by commercial banks for overnight money) has been about 2.25% or 225 basis points above the consumer price index." (*Business Week*, 30 September 1996). See Exhibit 2-12.

Inflation, Taxation, and Real Interest

Taxation of fixed income instruments is usually determined on the basis of money income without adjustment for inflation. Real after-tax results are therefore equal to

$$FV_{RAT} = PV \frac{1 + (1 - \omega) \cdot Y}{1 + \pi},$$

where FV_{RAT} = inflation-adjusted after tax future value, and ω = the tax rate.

$$Y_{RAT} = \frac{1 + (1 - \omega) \cdot Y}{1 + \pi} - 1,$$

where Y_{RAT} = real after-tax interest rate (see Exhibit 2-13).

2-5 YIELD SPREADS ON SHORT-TERM DOLLAR SECURITIES

The most important short-term dollar yields are those on Eurodollars and U.S. T-bills (and near-to-maturity treasury bonds, notes, and strips; see Chapters 6 and 7). Federal Funds rates are obviously very relevant, but Fed Funds are predominantly overnight deposits and can be traded only between banks that must keep zero-interest reserves with the Federal Reserve Bank.

The U.S. commercial paper (USCP) rates are also important, but maturities are mostly much shorter than the legal limit of 270 days. Moreover, the different credit ratings of the issuers make USCP rates less homogeneous than those of bills and Eurodeposits. The *Federal Reserve Bulletin* publishes statistics relative to USCP rates for terms of 1, 3, and 6 months as an average of offering rates on commercial paper placed by several leading dealers for firms whose bond rating is AA or the equivalent.

Yield Spread Between Euro$ and U.S. T-bills

When comparing Eurodollar deposits and T-bills, we must make sure that we are comparing homogeneous yield measures. The most appropriate choice is the money-market yield, or CDY (working with R yields would be a lot simpler from a mathematical point of view, but this would not be in line with market practice).

We must also compare the bid rate for Eurodollars with the ask rate for the T-bills (which are the relevant rates for an investor). After we have made all the necessary adjustments to obtain comparable values, we still find that the Eurodollar yields are noticeably higher than those on T-bills. This is known as *TED spread*, from the ticker symbols of the IMM futures contracts (see Exhibit 2-14) (see Chapter 4). The difference between the two rates is attributable to the following main factors, which explain yield spreads for different fixed-income securities with the same maturities:

Exhibit 2-14 CDY on Eurodeposits and T-bills, 14 November 1996

Days	T-bills ask rate	T-bills CDY	$ LIBID
30	4.92%	4.94%	5.31%
90	5.02%	5.08%	5.44%
180	5.06%	5.19%	5.50%
270	5.08%	5.28%	5.56%
360	5.12%	5.40%	5.63%

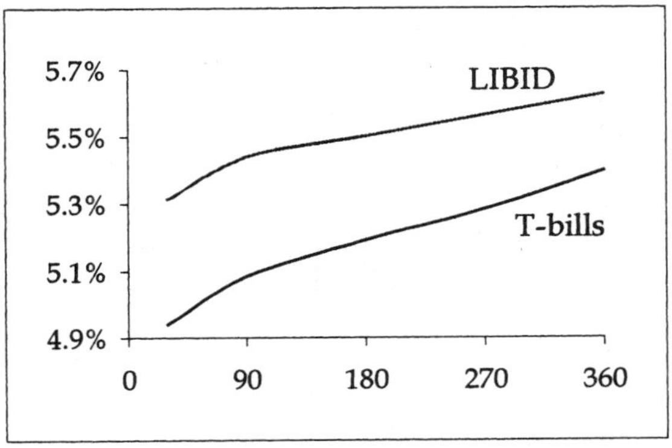

Source: Bloomberg

Exhibit 2-15 Yield Spread Between 3M Euro$ and 3M U.S. T-bills

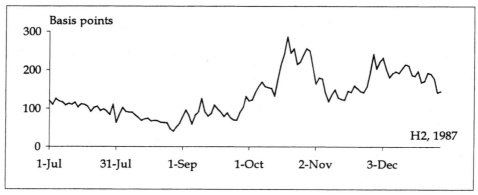

Source: Bloomberg

Exhibit 2-16 Yield Spreads: Bills and Near Maturity Bonds, 14 November 1996

The graph shows a linear interpolation of the CDY for bills and near-to-maturity bonds, notes and strips.
A scatter diagram would have been less legible.

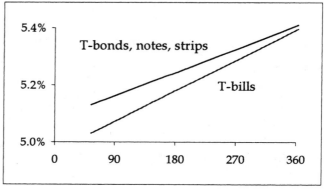

Source: Bloomberg

- *Liquidity.* T-bills are readily negotiable and can be sold in size, in a very short time, with negligible transaction costs. A Eurodollar deposit is for a fixed term and is therefore much less liquid (it is, of course, possible to extinguish it before maturity, for example, with an offsetting transaction, but this is more costly and requires more time). From a regulatory standpoint, this difference in liquidity also means that a number of financial institutions can count U.S. T-bills as part of their minimum liquidity reserves, while interbank term deposits would not qualify.
- *Taxation.* For non–tax-exempt U.S. investors, T-bills present a tax advantage because the income from Treasury securities is exempt from state and city taxes in the United States. T-bills are also exempt from withholding tax, which is an attractive feature for foreign investors.
- *Capital adequacy requirements.* For banks, under the Basle rules, U.S. T-bills do not require any capital absorption, whereas deposits with another bank require regulatory capital in the measure of 1.6% of the amount deposited (1.6% = 20% of 8%).

- *Credit risk.* U.S. Treasury securities are considered safer than the safest banks (Treasuries are backed by the full faith and credit of the U.S. government).
- *Eligibility.* A number of institutional investors are severely constrained in their ability to utilize time deposits as short-term fixed-income assets.

The interaction of the preceding factors means that the spread between the two rates does not remain constant in time. When markets become worried about the solidity of banks, the spread becomes wider. A typical example was October 1987, when the U.S. stock market crashed (on a single day, Black Monday, 23 October, the index lost 23%), followed by sizable downward corrections in almost every stock market in the world. This created some anxiety regarding the solidity of financial institutions, and consequently the TED spread increased by well over 100 bp. (The anxiety turned out to be unjustified; due to the prompt reaction of the Federal Reserve, which pumped liquidity into the system, the dreaded domino effect never materialized.)

You should also notice that before the time of the crash, the yield spread between Eurodeposits and U.S. T-bills was much wider than it is today (Exhibit 2-15). In 1987, banks were considered much less creditworthy than they are currently, in 1998 (in the early 1980s, many internationally active banks had been severely affected by the debt crisis of developing countries, with Mexico and Brazil the largest debtor countries to have declared a moratorium on their debt-service payments).

Yield Spread between U.S. T-bills and Near-to-Maturity Bonds, Notes, and Strips

Liquidity considerations play a role, albeit a relatively small one, in determining a yield differential between U.S. Treasury securities within the same range of maturities. As you can see in Exhibit 2-16, T-bills, being more liquid, command a slightly lower yield than near-to-maturity bonds, notes, and strips.

Chapter **3**

The Exponential Notation

3-1 THE EXPONENTIAL NOTATION FOR CONTINUOUS COMPOUNDING

Continuous compounding and discounting can be expressed with the natural exponential function (base $= e =$ base of natural logarithms). In the following equations R is the continuously compounded nominal annualized yield, and T, as usual, stands for term-to-maturity expressed in years. For a proof, see the Mathematical Appendix.

$$FV = \exp(R) = (1 + Y),$$

$$R = \ln (1 + Y) \Rightarrow Y = \exp (R) - 1.$$

Note that this is merely a different notation for compounding—more powerful and compact from a mathematical point of view and therefore utilized in most works on derivatives and in all scientific work on continuous-time finance. There is a one-to-one relationship between Y and R; they are simply different mathematical ways to express compounded yield. This straightforward equivalence is sometimes misrepresented. You are likely to find statements that can be misleading, such as "Eurobonds pay annual coupons, U.S. treasuries' coupons are semiannual, and GNMAs make monthly payments. As the coupons become more frequent, it becomes more accurate to assume exponential continuous compounding." GNMA is a common way of referring to bonds issued by the Government National Mortgage Association, an agency of the U.S. government.

Using the following equations, we must be careful to remember that Y is a yearly compounded yield or *effective annualized yield* (EFF), while R is a *nominal yield* on *annual percentage rate* (APR) that, continuously compounded, gives $1 + Y$ (see Exhibit 3-1).

$$1 + Y = Exp(R) \Rightarrow (1 + Y)^T = Exp(R \cdot T),$$

$$\frac{1}{(1 + Y)^T} = Exp(-R \cdot T).$$

Exhibit 3-1 Values of R and Y

R	$\exp(R)$	Y	Y	R
4%	1.0408	4.08%	4.00%	3.92%
5%	1.0513	5.13%	5.00%	4.88%
6%	1.0618	6.18%	6.00%	5.83%
7%	1.0725	7.25%	7.00%	6.77%
8%	1.0833	8.33%	8.00%	7.70%
9%	1.0942	9.42%	9.00%	8.62%
10%	1.1052	10.52%	10.00%	9.53%

$$Exp(R \cdot T) = \frac{FV}{PV} \Rightarrow R = \frac{1}{T} Ln\left(\frac{FV}{PV}\right)$$

When we use Y to move from a higher to a lower value, such as in discounting, this is done dividing by $(1 + Y)$. In fact, a negative rate equivalent is implicit in the ordinary compounded yield approach:

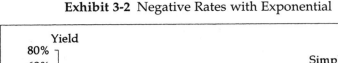

$$1 - Y_Q = \frac{1}{1 + Y} \Rightarrow Y_Q = \frac{Y}{1 + Y}$$

The $\exp(R)$ format automatically produces a negative value of R when used for discounting. This means that $R < 0$ when FV is smaller than PV. Say you want to measure the return on a stock that has lost you money. If the price declined from \$100 to \$90 in six months ($T = 0.5$), you obtain

$$R = \frac{1}{T} Log\left(\frac{FV}{PV}\right) \Rightarrow R = \frac{1}{0.5} Log\left(\frac{90}{100}\right) = -21.0721\%.$$

The preceding negative yearly rate has the same absolute value of the positive rate you would obtain if your volatile stock climbed back to \$100 (see Exhibit 3-2).

Exhibit 3-2 Negative Rates with Exponential

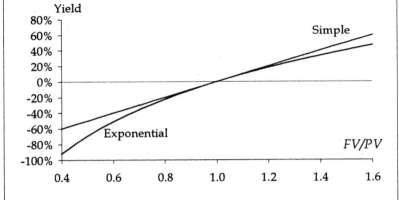

Exhibit 3-3 Time-Sequence with Simple Yield

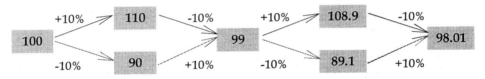

$$R \;=\; \frac{1}{0.5}\, Log\!\left(\frac{100}{90}\right) \;=\; 21.0721\%$$

You can, of course, work with negative rates using simple interest/discount y. The problem here is lack of time consistency. For example, a 10% increase followed by a 10% decrease does not return to the initial value, as shown in Exhibit 3-3.

Internal Rate of Return

The exponential format can be used to determine the internal rate of return (IRR) of a cash flow. The equation is a straightforward adaptation of that analyzed in Section 2-2 (see Exhibit 3-4).

$$PV \;=\; \frac{PT_1}{\exp(IRR\cdot T_1)} \;+\; \cdots \;+\; \frac{PT_N}{\exp(IRR\cdot T_N)} \;=\; \sum_{1}^{N} \frac{PT_J}{\exp(IRR\cdot T_J)}$$

IRR = Internal rate of return

PT_J = Amount of the Jth payment ($J = 1, 2, \ldots, N$).

T_J = Term of the Jth payment (in years)

3-2   PERIOD RETURN AND LOGS OF PRICE RELATIVES

The analysis in Chapter 2 assumed that securities and other fixed-income instruments are held to maturity. This approach is obviously very important because yield measures convey important information when you must choose among securities. Furthermore, some instruments are usually held to maturity (such as term deposits and commercial paper). If you want to look at things from the point of view of the issuer, then most instruments are "kept" to maturity.

We must now consider the case when the return on a fixed-income instrument (or a portfolio of fixed-income deposits, securities, and derivatives) is computed for a shorter time span, also known as *investment horizon*. There are two very good reasons for this kind of analysis.

1. A number of securities and derivatives are often sold before maturity (T-bills, with their active secondary market trading, are a case in point, and so are futures, with an average holding period of a few days).
2. Most institutional holders (institutional investors, banks, investment houses, mutual funds, etc.) must mark to market their securities positions at predetermined intervals (daily, in most cases) and are, of course, interested in computing their performance at each mark-to-market date.

Exhibit 3-4 Computing IRR on Forward Rate Agreement (FRA)
Interest Payments

T	R	$	PV-$	R	JPY	PV-Yen
0.5	5.8370%	2.79	2.71	0.8438%	0.27	0.27
1	5.8370%	2.91	2.74	0.8438%	0.32	0.32
1.5	5.8370%	3.05	2.79	0.8438%	0.45	0.45
2	5.8370%	103.12	91.76	0.8438%	100.65	98.96
			100.00			100.00

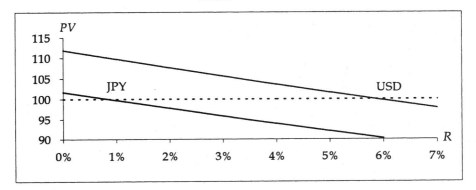

The return over a time horizon will clearly depend on the value of the security, or the derivative, at the beginning (PV_0) and at the end (FV_T) of the period.

$$FV_T - PV_0 = \$ \text{ return over the investment horizon}$$

$$\frac{FV_T}{PV_0} = value\ relative, \text{ also known as } price\ relative$$

Both *PV* and *FV* must include accrued interest (in the case of coupon bonds, this is known as dirty price or invoice price). You must also take into account any interest received (or paid) during the period, normally adding it to FV_T. In the case of futures, daily settlements must be treated in the same way. When the interest amount is large and it is received many days before the end of the period, you should compute interest on interest. When the financial asset, or derivative, is denominated in foreign currency, its return should be computed adjusting for foreign exchange (FX) changes.

Dealing with horizon returns requires two different yield measures. The use of a simple interest/discount rate is necessary for applications such as computing the return on a portfolio as a function of the returns on the individual assets that compose it.

The use of the exponential rate *R* is instead required for problems such as computing the average yield over a succession of investment horizons. It is useless to say that we require two different measures, because each of the two methods gives inconsistent results when used for the inappropriate class of applications.

Exhibit 3-5 Horizon Yield, World Bank 6⅛ Bonds, Mty 21 Jul 2005

	Trade date		Dirty price	Clean price	Accrued coupon	Settlement
Buy	Mon-8-Jul	PV=	97.3677	94.3750 ask	2.9927	Thu-11-Jul
Sell	Tue-16-Jul	FV=	99.0094	95.8750 bid	3.1344	Fri-19-Jul
FV/PV = 1.0169				CDY = 76.93	Y = 114.44	R = 76.28

Positive Horizon Return

When the horizon return is positive, you can easily compute annualized yield as follows (see Exhibit 3-5):

$$CDY = \left(\frac{FV_T}{PV_0} - 1\right) \cdot \frac{1}{T}; \quad Y = \left(\frac{FV_T}{PV_0}\right)^{\frac{1}{T}} - 1; \quad R = \frac{1}{T} \cdot \ln\left(\frac{FV_T}{PV_0}\right)$$

Compounded yield measures are also utilized in a number of contexts that are unrelated to fixed-income calculations. The most common example is represented by the monthly inflation data, which are often quoted in terms of both the monthly increase and the corresponding annualized rate. In the financial press you can read statements such as "In June 1996 the consumer price index (CPI) rose by 0.4% at an annualized rate of 4.91%."

Negative Horizon Return: Simple Interest/Discount Measure

A first way of dealing with the problem of computing negative horizon yields is to use simple interest/discount:

$$y = \frac{FV_T - PV_0}{PV_0} = \frac{FV_T}{PV_0} - 1 = \text{horizon simple interest/discount rate}$$

$$y \cdot \frac{1}{T} = \text{annualized simple interest/discount rate}$$

This method has the important advantage of producing a negative rate when the horizon return is negative. It is used very widely, and not only for fixed-income securities. In the financial press you can read statements such as "On July 15th the Dow Jones industrial average (DJIA) declined by 161 points, or 2.9%, to 5,450" (*The Economist*, 20 July 1996. The U.S. stock market had reacted negatively to a rise in long-term interest rates).

Another standard use of this discountlike measure is in FX quotations, to indicate whether a forward currency price is lower or higher than its spot price, as in the rates taken from the *Financial Times* of 18 March 1998 (Exhibit 3-6). The percentage annualized change (% PA) is given as a positive number when the forward trades at a premium versus the spot (such as the JPY).

Time-Sequence Consistency with Exponential Rates

In some cases the simple discount method can be somewhat inadequate. If you are examining a time series of returns (prices, foreign exchange rates, etc.), you will often

Exhibit 3-6 FX Forward Premium (Discount) — Simple Interest

ccy	Spot	Three months		Six months	
		Rate	% PA	Rate	% PA
Japan - JPY	129.210	127.575	5.10%	122.805	5.00%
Greece - GRD	318.815	323.765	-6.20%	335.435	-5.20%

need to obtain the same rate (absolute value) moving from, say, 100 to 110 and from 110 to 100. This time-sequence consistency is quite important in the case of options analysis, when we want to examine the time path of a stochastic process. We have already seen that under simple discount, a 10% increase followed by a 10% decrease will not bring us back to the starting point (the same applies to a 10% decrease followed by a 10% increase).

Another way of stating this problem is to observe that given a series of simple interest/discount period returns (e.g., the yearly returns of an investment fund, the quarterly returns of an investment in the S&P 500, etc.), their arithmetic average is higher than the average compounded yield, unless all returns happen to be equal. This is a consequence of the fact that the average compounded yield is a geometric average, and a geometric average is always smaller than the corresponding arithmetic average when its terms are not all equal.

By using the exponential rate you solve the issue of time-sequence consistency because the average rate equals the average of period rates; see Exhibit 3-7. This useful characteristic of the exponential rate is easy to prove.

$\bar{R}$ = arithmetic average of rates
R^* = average rate
FV_K = future value after K periods $\{K = 1, \dots, N\}$

$$\bar{R} = \frac{1}{N} \cdot \left[\ln\left(\frac{FV_1}{PV_0}\right) + \dots + \ln\left(\frac{FV_N}{FV_{N-1}}\right) \right]$$

$$\bar{R} = \frac{1}{N} \cdot \ln\left[\left(\frac{FV_1}{PV_0}\right) \cdot \left(\frac{FV_2}{FV_1}\right) \cdot \dots \cdot \left(\frac{FV_N}{FV_{N-1}}\right) \right] = \frac{1}{N} \cdot \ln\left(\frac{FV_N}{PV_{01}}\right) = R^*$$

FX quotations provide another interesting example of the unsatisfactory results of simple rates when dealing with time-related issues. The exchange rate between the \$ and the JPY can be expressed either in terms of JPY per \$ or in terms of \$/JPY. Say the JPY appreciates or depreciates against the \$. Using simple interest/discount you will get two different measures, depending on whether you use the JPY/\$ rate or the

Exhibit 3-7 Average Rates on a 4-period Investment Horizon

T	0	1	2	3	4	
Values	100	110	100	90	100	Average
Simple rate	n.a.	10.00%	-9.09%	-10.00%	11.11%	0.51%
Exp. rate	n.a.	9.53%	-9.53%	-10.54%	10.54%	0.00%

Exhibit 3-8 Asymmetry Between FX Quotations with Simple Rates

	JPY appreciates against the USD	JPY depreciates against the USD
$/JPY	1.0000 ———▶ 1.2000 20.00%	1.2000 ———▶ 1.0000 -16.67%
JPY/$	100.00 ———▶ 83.33 -16.67%	83.33 ———▶ 100.00 20.00%

Exhibit 3-9 Symmetry of FX Quotations with Exponential Rates

	JPY appreciates against the USD	JPY depreciates against the USD
$/JPY	1.0000 ———▶ 1.2000 18.23%	1.2000 ———▶ 1.0000 -18.23%
JPY/$	100.00 ———▶ 83.33 -18.23%	83.33 ———▶ 100.00 18.23%

Exhibit 3-10 Average Simple Yield of a Portfolio

	Weight	PV	FV	y	Wgted - y
Security-A	60.0%	60	72	20.00%	12.00%
Security-B	40.0%	40	36	-10.00%	-4.00%
Portfolio	*100.0%*	*100*	*108*	*8.00%* =	*8.00%*

$/JPY quotation. This problem, however, disappears if you use exponential rates (see Exhibits 3-8 and 3-9).

3-3   CONVEXITY OF THE LOG-RATE FUNCTION

The discount method is appropriate when you need to compute the return on a portfolio given the returns on the individual securities. The average yield is, in fact, equal to the weighted average of the yield rates (see Exhibit 3-10).

$$W_A = \frac{PV_A}{PV_P}, \ W_B = \frac{PV_B}{PV_P},$$

$$PV_P = PV_A + PV_B.$$

Exhibit 3-11 Average Exponential Yield of a Portfolio

	Weight	PV	FV	R	Wgted - R
Security-A	60.0%	60	84	33.65%	20.19%
Security-B	40.0%	40	24	-51.08%	-20.43%
Portfolio	*100%*	*100*	*108*	*7.70%* >	*-0.24%*

$$W_A \cdot \left(\frac{FV_A}{PV_A} - 1\right) + W_B \cdot \left(\frac{FV_B}{PV_B} - 1\right) \equiv \left(\frac{FV_P}{PV_P} - 1\right),$$

$$FV_P = FV_A + FV_B.$$

We cannot use the exponential rate to find the average yield of a portfolio because the portfolio yield would turn out to be larger than the weighed average yield of the component securities (see Exhibit 3-11).

$$\ln\left(\frac{FV_P}{PV_P}\right) > W_A \cdot \ln\left(\frac{FV_A}{PV_A}\right) + W_B \cdot \ln\left(\frac{FV_B}{PV_B}\right)$$

$$R(P) > W_A \cdot R(A) + W_B \cdot R(B)$$

The inequality is a direct consequence of the fact that the ln function we use to determine R is concave. In Exhibit 3-12 the x-axis represents the future value of the portfolio for all possible linear combinations of the two securities. The $60 value corresponds to a portfolio 100% invested in the loss-making asset B, whereas the $140 value corresponds to a 100% allocation to the outperforming asset A. The R-yield of the portfolio is a concave function of FV and therefore lies above the linear function that represents the weighted average of the R-yields for the two securities. Take a portfolio composed of 50% asset A and 50% asset B. Its future value will be $100.00, and $R(P) = 0\%$, while the weighted average of $R(A)$ and $R(B)$ is -8.72%.

$$-8.72\% = \frac{1}{2}(-51.08\% + 33.65\%)$$

An interesting special case of convexity correction (which plays a major role in option pricing) is when you have a two-security portfolio with equal weights. If you set $PV = 1$, you can describe any possible outcome over a short time span h with the following equations:

$$FV_A = \frac{1}{2} \cdot \exp(\kappa + \sigma)$$

$$FV_B = \frac{1}{2} \cdot \exp(\kappa - \sigma)$$

where κ is the average of the two exponential rates and σ is the standard deviation of the outcomes of the two securities (see Mathematical Appendix, for a simple proof). Due to the convexity correction, the future value of the portfolio will be higher than that entailed by the average yield rate

Exhibit 3-12 Average Yields

WA	$ FV(P)	y	R(P)	Average-R
0%	60.00	-40.00%	-51.08%	-51.08%
10%	68.00	-32.00%	-38.57%	-42.61%
20%	76.00	-24.00%	-27.44%	-34.14%
30%	84.00	-16.00%	-17.44%	-25.66%
40%	92.00	-8.00%	-8.34%	-17.19%
50%	100.00	0%	0%	-8.72%
60%	108.00	8.00%	7.70%	-0.24%
70%	116.00	16.00%	14.84%	8.23%
80%	124.00	24.00%	21.51%	16.70%
90%	132.00	32.00%	27.76%	25.17%
100%	140.00	40.00%	33.65%	33.65%

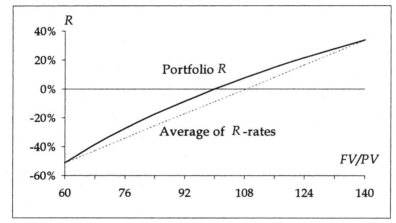

$$FV_P = \frac{1}{2}\left[\exp(\kappa + \sigma) + \exp(\kappa - \sigma)\right] > \exp(\kappa).$$

If the values are such that σ is small, say, less than 1%, you have

$$FV_P = \frac{1}{2}\left[\exp(\kappa + \sigma) + \exp(\kappa - \sigma)\right] \cong \exp\left(\kappa + \frac{\sigma^2}{2}\right).$$

3-4   EXPONENTIAL RATE AND TIME SERIES

The logs of value relatives approach is quite useful when dealing with the stochastic process followed by a time series. We shall do this with reference to the wave in the JPY/$ quotation, whereby the Japanese currency rose by over 20% against the USD in the first few months of 1995 and then began a multiyear slide. The first step is to take the values of the time series at the desired intervals, weekly in our example, and then compute the value relatives and their logs.

$$\frac{V_1}{V_0}, \ldots, \frac{V_K}{V_{K-1}}, \ldots, \frac{V_N}{V_{N-1}} \quad \{1.00227, \ldots, 0.9911\}$$

$$R_K = \ln\left(\frac{V_K}{V_{K-1}}\right) \quad \{0.27\%, \ldots, 2.24\%\}$$

The sum of R_K equals the log of the overall price change. For example, if the sum is zero, then the price has not changed over the period, irrespective of intraperiod fluctuations.

$$\sum_{K=1}^{N} R_K = \ln\left(\frac{V_N}{V_0}\right) \quad 0.22\% = \ln\left(\frac{0.9998}{0.9976}\right)$$

$$\bar{R}_K = \frac{1}{N}\sum R_K \quad 0.006\% = \frac{1}{37}\, 0.22\%$$

The average of R_K equals the average change, and therefore you can meaningfully compute statistical measures of dispersion, such as variance and standard deviation (see Exhibit 3-13).

Exhibit 3-13 $/·Yen in the 1995 FX "Tsunami Wave"

	$/100 JPY	FX rel	R	Sum(R)	Average(R)
2-Jan-95	0.9976	n.a.	n.a.	n.a.	n.a.
9-Jan-95	1.0003	1.0027	0.270%	0.270%	0.270%
16-Jan-95	1.0157	1.0154	1.532%	1.802%	0.901%
23-Jan-95	1.0022	0.9867	-1.342%	0.460%	0.153%
30-Jan-95	1.0157	1.0135	1.342%	1.802%	0.450%
6-Feb-95	1.0058	0.9902	-0.980%	0.821%	0.164%
13-Feb-95	1.0127	1.0068	0.676%	1.498%	0.250%
20-Feb-95	1.0272	1.0144	1.428%	2.925%	0.418%
4-Sep-95	1.0241	0.9911	-0.895%	2.618%	0.075%
11-Sep-95	0.9998	0.9763	-2.398%	0.220%	0.006%

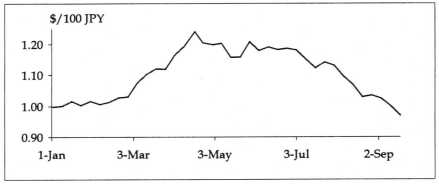

3-5   MATHEMATICAL APPENDIX

Proof of the Exponential Notation for Continuous Compounding

The exponential function has a domain that spans the real line while its range is limited to the set $(0, \infty)$; the dependent variable is always positive, irrespective of the value of the independent variable. The exponential function is continuous and differentiable.

$$y = e^X = \exp(X)$$

The irrational number ($e = 2.718282\ldots$) is the base of natural logarithms and of the standard exponential function. Readers who are amused by historical curiosities may be interested to know that the base of natural logarithms was modestly named e by the great Swiss mathematician Leonard Euler (1707–1783).

We have defined the continuously compounded yield in terms of R, a nominal rate compounded an infinite number of times:

$$(1 + Y) = \lim_{M \to \infty} \left(1 + \frac{R}{M}\right)^M \Rightarrow (1 + Y)^T = \left[\lim_{M \to \infty} \left(1 + \frac{R}{M}\right)^M\right]^T$$

We therefore only need to prove that

$$e^R = \lim_{M \to \infty} \left(1 + \frac{R}{M}\right)^M.$$

A standard result from calculus is

$$e = \lim_{X \to \infty} \left(1 + \frac{1}{X}\right)^X.$$

Introducing the continuously compounded nominal yield R, we get

$$e^R = \left[\lim_{X \to \infty} \left(1 + \frac{1}{X}\right)^X\right]^R.$$

Let us now define M as

$$M = X \cdot R \Rightarrow \frac{M}{R} = X \Rightarrow \lim_{M \to \infty} (X) = \infty \ \{R > 0\}.$$

We can therefore write

$$\left(1 + \frac{R}{M}\right)^M \equiv \left(1 + \frac{R}{X \cdot R}\right)^{X \cdot R} \equiv \left[\left(1 + \frac{1}{X}\right)^X\right]^R,$$

and therefore

$$(1 + Y) = \lim_{M \to \infty} \left(1 + \frac{R}{M}\right)^M = \left[\lim_{X \to \infty} \left(1 + \frac{1}{X}\right)^X\right]^R = e^R.$$

Therefore, R equals the natural logarithm of $1 + Y$, and we get negative rates when discounting or when $FV < PV$.

$$\frac{1}{1 + Y} = e^{-R}, \; R = \ln\left(\frac{FV}{PV}\right)$$

Expanding the Exp(R) Function in Taylor Series

The number e has the useful property of having an infinite number of derivatives, all equal to the primitive function

$$f(x) = e^X \Rightarrow f'(x) = e^X \Rightarrow f''(x) = e^X \Rightarrow \ldots \Rightarrow f^{(n)}(x) = e^X.$$

In order to have these properties, the number e has to be chosen in such a way that its derivative evaluation at the point $(x = 0)$ equals 1.

$$\frac{d}{dx}(e^X) = \lim_{h \to 0}\left(\frac{e^{X+h} - e^X}{h}\right) = e^X \lim_{h \to 0}\left(\frac{e^h - e^0}{h}\right)$$

$$\frac{d}{dx}(e^X) = e^X \Rightarrow \lim_{h \to 0}\left(\frac{e^h - e^0}{h}\right) = 1$$

The values of the exponential function are readily available on all spreadsheets. Examining the series expansion is useful, however, because such expansion is used in a number of proofs you are likely to come across in finance. Using zero as a point of expansion, the standard equation is as follows:

$$f(X) = f(0) + \frac{X}{1!}f'(0) + \frac{(X)^2}{2!}f''(0) + \ldots + \frac{(X)^N}{N!}f^N(X) + E_N$$

$$e^0 = 1, \; \frac{d}{dx}(e^X) = e^X$$

$$Exp(X) = 1 + \frac{X}{1!} + \frac{(X)^2}{2!} + \ldots + \frac{(X)^N}{N!} + E_N$$

Proof of the Special Case of the Concavity Correction

$$\frac{FV_P}{PV_P} = \frac{1}{2} \cdot (e^{\kappa + \sigma} + e^{\kappa - \sigma}) = e^\kappa \frac{1}{2} \cdot (e^\sigma + e^{-\sigma})$$

Now use the series expansion to obtain

$$\frac{FV_P}{PV_P} = e^\kappa \frac{1}{2} \cdot \left(1 + \sigma + \frac{\sigma^2}{2} + \frac{\sigma^3}{3!} + \frac{\sigma^4}{4!} + \ldots + 1 - \sigma + \frac{\sigma^2}{2} - \frac{\sigma^3}{3!} + \frac{\sigma^4}{4!} + \ldots\right)$$

$$\frac{FV_P}{PV_P} = e^\kappa \left(1 + \frac{\sigma^2}{2} + \frac{\sigma^4}{4!} + \ldots\right).$$

We can disregard terms with powers greater than 2, because they will be very small for a small value of sigma. For $\sigma = 1\%$ we have

$$\frac{\sigma^4}{4!} = 0.00000004\%.$$

Therefore we can write

$$\frac{FV_P}{PV_P} \cong e^\kappa \left(1 + \frac{\sigma^2}{2}\right).$$

$$\ln\frac{FV_P}{PV_P} \cong K + \ln\left(1 + \frac{\sigma^2}{2}\right)$$

A standard result of calculus is

$$\ln(1 + x) = x - \frac{x^2}{2} + \frac{x^3}{3} - \frac{x^4}{4} + \ldots \ (-1 < x \leq 1),$$

therefore

$$\ln\left(1 + \frac{\sigma^2}{2}\right) \cong \frac{\sigma^2}{2}$$

$$\ln\left(\frac{FV_P}{PV_P}\right) \cong \kappa + \frac{\sigma^2}{2}.$$

Chapter **4**

Spot and Forward Yields: FRAs, Repos, and Futures

In this chapter, we shall cover spot and forward yields, with reference to short-term money-market instrument. The analysis will be extended to foreign exchange (FX) transactions in Chapter 5, and to long-term securities, futures, and swaps in Part 2. The concept of forward yield is deceptively simple; in professional life you will frequently come across practices and interpretations that are at odds with an accurate understanding of modern yield-curve finance. We shall also introduce the concept of *local expectations hypothesis*, which is a straightforward extension of the law of one price (yields are prices).

Most finance professionals experienced an impulse of rejection when they first came across the subject of spot and forward yields. First, the symbology is somewhat heavy, because variables must have suffixes to indicate their time dimension. Don't let this put you off; the mathematics are in reality quite simple. Second, the subject can appear to be very abstract, with concepts, such as implied forwards, that sound far removed from real business life. Rest assured—forward yields are not a mere theoretical construction; we shall not be theorizing on how many forwards you can fit on the head of a pin.

Global financial markets are characterized by a wide range of forward-looking derivatives (such as forward rate agreements, swaps, repos, futures, and options) that allow to optimize hedging, trading, or investment strategies. Most of these instruments are actively traded, in large volumes, with limited transaction costs. Derivatives make it feasible to lock in arbitrage-free, transaction-costs-close forward yields, also known as *hedgeable yields*.

4-1 FORWARDS: ARBITRAGE-FREE PRICING AND CREDIT RISK

A forward contract, also known as *outright forward,* is a binding agreement to buy/ sell a well-specified asset, at a predetermined *contract price*, at a certain future *delivery date* or maturity. Forward contracts are extremely common and permeate economic life. The purchase of a commodity or a manufactured product with future delivery at a predetermined price is in fact a forward contract. Forward contracts originated over two thousand years ago to cope with harvesting cycles. Forwards are part of the universe of derivative products, that is, instruments that derive their value from that of some underlying financial (or real) asset.

Forward contracts lock in a future price (of a commodity, or foreign currency, or financial asset). As such, they eliminate uncertainty but certainly do not guarantee a better performance. If a U.K. firm that must make a future payment to a Japanese supplier buys the JPY forward, it could very well lose out if the Japanese currency depreciates against the £.

Forward Contracts and Arbitrage-Free Forward Pricing

When a commodity or a financial asset can be bought both spot and forward, the forward price will usually differ from the spot price. The difference between spot price and forward price is known as *basis*. In general, the relationship between spot and future prices for financial assets is determined by arbitrage-free pricing. Arbitrage consists in locking in a riskless profit by simultaneously entering different transactions in two or more markets—the spot and the forward markets, in our case.

- We have a *cash-and-carry* arbitrage when buying spot a commodity or a financial asset and simultaneously selling it forward allows you to lock in a riskless profit (arbitrageurs will buy spot and sell forward, thereby reinstating no-arbitrage price).
- We have a *reverse cash-and-carry* arbitrage when you can lock in a riskless profit by selling short the asset and covering your short position with a forward purchase (arbitrage-free pricing will be reinstated by the spot short sales and forward purchases).

When referring to cash-and-carry arbitrage, we must take into account all the costs and revenues deriving from the arbitrage, such as interest cost and yield on the asset. Buying spot and selling forward implies paying now and getting back the money at a later time. The interest paid to finance the position has to be deducted from the yield (interest or dividend) on the asset. This difference (interest cost − yield on asset) is known as *cost of carry*. When the interest cost is lower than yield, the cost of carry is negative, also known as *positive carry*.

$$\text{Forward price} = \text{spot price} + (\text{interest cost} - \text{yield})$$

$$= \text{spot price} + \text{cost of carry}$$

- When forward prices are higher than spot prices, we have a *normal market* (e.g., the forward ¥ and DM rates in Exhibit 4-1). The expression normal market comes from the fact that in normal conditions, forward prices in commodities and metal markets (e.g., gold) are higher than spot prices because there is no yield on the commodity, therefore (forward price = spot price + cost of carry). Another way to indicate a normal market is contango market.
- When forward prices are lower than spot prices, we speak of an *inverted market* (e.g., the forward ITL rate in Exhibit 4-1). Inverted markets are also known as *backwardation markets*. As the maturity of a forward contract approaches, interest

Exhibit 4-1 Spot and Forwards Against the $

	Spot	12M Fwrd
$/JPY	0.9044	0.9480
$/DM	0.6557	0.6717
$/ITL	0.6515	0.6367
$ per:	100 JPY	
	1 DM	
	1,000 ITL	

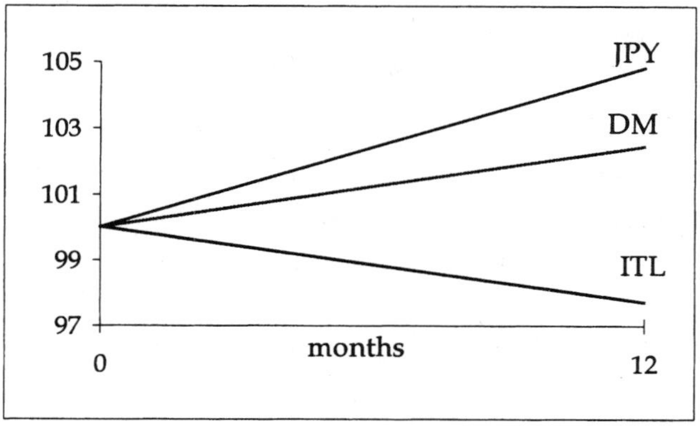

Source: Financial Times

cost and asset yield become less important, and therefore the forward price will converge to the current spot price.

Value at Maturity of Long and Short Forward Contracts

At time 0, the value of a forward contract is usually equal to zero, because the contract price is set with reference to the forward price prevailing at trade date. At maturity (delivery date), the contract will have a nonzero value whenever the contract price differs from the then-prevailing spot market price. You will remember that in the cash markets (securities, foreign exchange), being long means owning the asset. Being short means owing it.

The jargon and quotation system for forward-looking contracts (including exchange-traded futures) is designed to be consistent with that of the cash market. Being long a forward means having the right (and the obligation) to buy the underlying asset at some predetermined price. Therefore, a forward will appreciate if the price goes up and depreciate if it goes down. Being short means having a commitment to sell, and it works in the reverse. The expiration value of the forward therefore depends on the relationship between the *realization* of spot market prices (at maturity) and contract price.

> *Example:* Take a 1yr forward contract on 1 billion JPY, priced at $0.948 per 100 JPY, for delivery 4 July 1997. On the delivery date, the JPY had depreciated against the $, instead of appreciating as implied by the forward FX rate. Therefore, the contract had a positive value of $753,000 for the seller (= short the forward), who could buy JPY at the then-current market price of $0.8727 and sell them at $0.948 (see Exhibit 4-2).

$$\$753,000 = \frac{(0.9480 - 0.8727)}{100} \times 1,000,000,000$$

Mark to Market

When forward prices change, so will the value of existing forward contracts. The current value of a forward can be determined with reference to its expected value at

Exhibit 4-2 Possible Value at Delivery of a 1yr Forward on JPY1 billion

Spot rate at delivery	FV long $000	FV short $000
0.8532	-948	948
0.9480	0	0
1.0428	948	-948
0.9480 Contract Price		

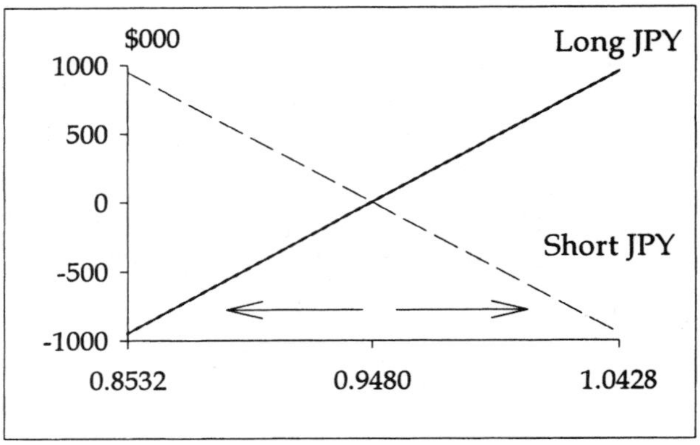

maturity, which in turn is a function of the contract price and of the current level of forward prices. Pricing a forward contract on the basis of current forward market prices is known as *marking to market*.

Let us use again our JPY example, with a forward price of $0.9480 for delivery on 4 July 1997. Take 31 March 1997 as the evaluation date. The forward price of the JPY, for delivery 4 July 1997, was then $0.8197, due to the noticeable depreciation of the JPY against the $. The mark to market, computed without discounting book from 4 July to 31 March, would be

$$\$1,283,000 = \frac{(0.948 - 0.8197)}{100} \times 1,000,000,000.$$

- If you were short the old contract, you could have bought ¥ 1 billion for delivery 4 July 1997 at $0.828, thereby locking in a $1,283,000 profit.
- If you were short the $0.9480 forward and your counterparty became insolvent, you would have to replace the forward with a new forward that would have cost you $1,283,000 more (also known as the *replacement value* of the contract).

At any given moment in time, there is a whole range of forward JPY contracts with the same delivery date but different mark-to-market values, depending on their contract prices. As we shall see in Section 4-5, the daily mark to market and settlement adopted by futures exchanges avoids this problem, so that all futures with the same delivery date will have the same price.

Mark-to-market value of a forward contract

Long = present value (current forward price − contract price)
Short = present value (contract price − current forward price)

Credit Risk in Forwards (Contingent Credit Risk)

Forward contracts are characterized by credit risk.

- If the contract has a positive value and you are long, then you will have a credit exposure to the short.

- If the contract has a negative value, then it is the short that is exposed to credit risk (the long could default on his obligation to buy at the contract price).

In traditional lending, only the lender incurs credit risk. In forward-looking contracts, there is no way of knowing, a priori, which of the two parties will be at risk. Forward-looking contracts are neither a claim nor a liability. They will take one shape or the other (*contingent claims* or *liability*) depending on the dynamics of market prices relative to the contract price. Exchange-traded futures were developed precisely in order to avoid the credit risk of forward transactions. In bank-speak, the aforementioned risk is referred to as *close-out risk* or *replacement risk*, with reference to the possibility of having to close out the forward if the counterpart becomes insolvent. Due to their contingent nature, forward-looking contracts are *off-balance-sheet items*. They must, however, be taken into account in monitoring credit risk and determining capital-adequacy requirements.

When determining their credit exposure to a client, banks take into account both the replacement costs of all existing forwards (also known as *current exposure*) and a probabilistic estimate of how these replacement costs could change in time due to market movements (also known as *potential future exposure*). The following excerpt from the 1994 annual report of BankAmerica Corporation (BAC) provides a neat summary of the concepts and terminology that we have been using:

> Risk of close-out loss arises from a counterpart's inability to perform under the terms of its contract and the necessity for BAC to replace that contract at current market value . . . BAC measures the close-out risk of all the foreign exchange and derivatives contracts it has with its customers. This measurement includes both current exposure and potential future exposure. Current exposure is the amount that BAC would have the right to receive if the foreign exchange or derivative contract was terminated on the date of evaluation. Potential future exposure is calculated based on the estimated change in the fair value of a contract over its remaining life.

Arbitrage and Credit Risk

One final word of caution: when we refer to riskless arbitrage profit, we are usually talking about price risk and not credit risk. Buying spot and selling forward could well lock in a small riskless profit after taking into account all costs. But this could still expose the arbitrageur to a certain amount of credit risk.

4-2 SPOT AND FORWARD YIELDS

A spot yield is defined as the yield on a fixed-income instrument, available for spot settlement, that will pay interest only at maturity (interest-at-maturity term deposit, pure discount security, etc.). A series of spot yields, for different maturities, defines a yield term structure (also known as the *spot yield curve*; see Exhibit 4-3).

The compounded-yield curve lies above the money-market curve because of both the day count difference and the effect of compounding (obviously greater for short maturities). For the 12-month maturity, the difference between Y and ask rate is entirely due to the difference in accrual rules: $5.86\% = 5.78\% \cdot (365/360)$. The yield curve is often computed in terms of money-market yield (CDY), of U.S. bond equivalent yield (BEY), and of continuously compounded nominal rate (R).

Forward Yields

Forward yields are the future spot yields implied by the current spot yields. For example, if the 1yr spot yield is 5.86% and the 6M yield is 5.72%, this entails that with

Exhibit 4-3 $-LIBOR and Compounded Yields, 23 October 1996

	LIBOR	Y
1M	5.3125%	5.52%
2M	5.3750%	5.57%
3M	5.4687%	5.66%
4M	5.5000%	5.68%
5M	5.5312%	5.70%
6M	5.5625%	5.72%
7M	5.5937%	5.74%
8M	5.6250%	5.76%
9M	5.6562%	5.78%
10M	5.6875%	5.79%
11M	5.7187%	5.81%
12M	5.7812%	5.86%

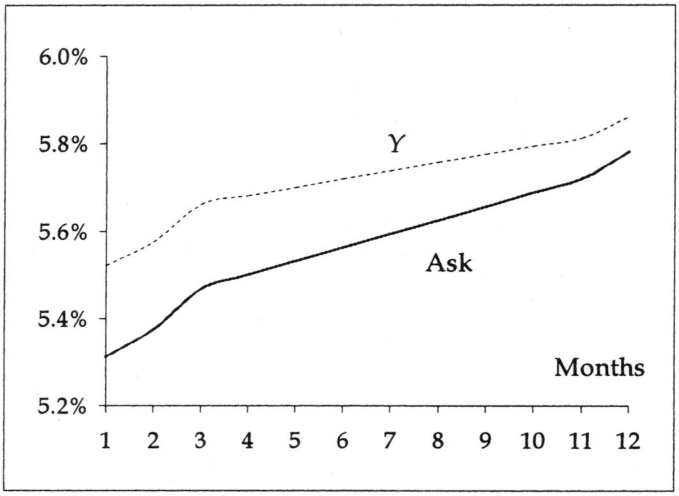

Y is computed assuming that all months have the same number of days

Source: REUTERS

a 1yr deposit, we are contracting to invest (borrow) at 6.00% in the second 6M period. This result follows from the fact that the 6M yield determines the future value after 6 months FV (0, 0.5), while the 1-year yield determines FV (0, 1). The derivation of forward yields from the spot yield curve is known as the *bootstrap method* (with reference to the joke about trying to lift yourself up by pulling hard on your own bootstraps, without any external fulcrum). You will often find the symbol $f(t,T_1,T_2)$ that indicates the continuously compounded forward rate, derived from the time t yield curve, spanning a finite time horizon:

$$[T_1, T_2 \mid t \leq T_1 < T_2].$$

By using the bootstrap method, we can determine forward yields only for time intervals that fall within the time span covered by our set of spot yields. Based on our 12M structure, we can therefore compute forward yields for time intervals ending within 1 year (see Exhibit 4-4). In real life, there is no discontinuity between the spot yield curve on money-market instruments (say, up to 1yr) and that for longer maturities. Spot and forward yields are usually quoted over multiyear time spans. The term structure of forward yields can also be summed up as a series of forward yields for back-to-back time intervals all of the same length. Exhibit 4-5 shows the series of 1M yields for the time intervals ending after (1, 2, 3, . . . , 12) months. As you can see, the 1M forward curve is a lot more irregular than the spot yield curve from which it is derived. This is intuitively evident when you consider that the forward yield must absorb in one month (we are now examining 1M forwards) variations in spot yield that affect FV over several months.

Exhibit 4-4 Selected, LIBOR-Based, Forward Yields

	Spot LIBOR	FV of 1 $	1 M Y	3 M Y	6 M Y	9 M Y
1M	5.313%	1.0045	5.52%	...	...	...
2M	5.375%	1.0091	5.63%	...	...	...
3M	5.469%	1.0139	5.83%	5.66%	...	...
4M	5.500%	1.0186	5.74%	5.73%	...	...
5M	5.531%	1.0234	5.78%	5.78%	...	...
6M	5.563%	1.0282	5.82%	5.78%	5.72%	...
7M	5.594%	1.0331	5.85%	5.81%	5.77%	...
8M	5.625%	1.0380	5.89%	5.85%	5.82%	...
9M	5.656%	1.0430	5.92%	5.89%	5.83%	5.78%
10M	5.688%	1.0481	5.96%	5.92%	5.87%	5.82%
11M	5.719%	1.0531	5.99%	5.96%	5.91%	5.86%
12M	5.781%	1.0586	6.41%	6.12%	6.00%	5.93%

All months have the same number of days = 365/12
The first number of each column (bold face) is the current spot yield

---

Box 4-1 Forward Yields

$H = T_2 - T_1$ = time horizon

$$Y(T_1, T_2) = \left(\frac{FV_2}{FV_1}\right)^{\frac{1}{H}} - 1$$

$$CDY(T_1, T_2) = \left(\frac{FV_2}{FV_1} - 1\right)\frac{1}{H}$$

$$R(T_1, T_2) = \frac{1}{H} \cdot \ln\left(\frac{FV_2}{FV_1}\right)$$

$$FV(0.5) = 100 \cdot \left(1 + 5.5625\% \frac{182.5}{360}\right) = 102.8199 \quad FV \text{ of 6-month spot deposit}$$

$$FV(1) = 100 \cdot \left(1 + 5.7812\% \frac{365}{360}\right) = 105.8615 \quad FV \text{ of 1 yr spot deposit}$$

$Y(0.5, 1) = 6.00\%, \ CDY(0.5, 1) = 5.84\%, \ R(0.5, 1) = 5.83\%$

A numerical example will clarify the issue. The 12M spot yield is $\cong$ 5 bp higher than the 11M spot yield; $\Rightarrow$ the *FV* of a \$100 investment will be $\cong$ 5 bp higher that it would have been if the 12M spot yield had been equal to the 11M yield. This 5 bp difference in *FV*, when attributed to a monthly yield, will result in a 60 bp difference in annualized yield (and in fact this is the difference between the monthly forward yield for the period ending in 12 months and the 11M spot yield). Another quite commonly used representation of the yield structure consists of showing the implied

Exhibit 4-5 Spot and 1M Forward *Y*

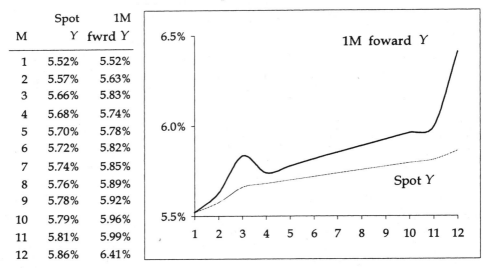

M	Spot *Y*	1M fwrd *Y*
1	5.52%	5.52%
2	5.57%	5.63%
3	5.66%	5.83%
4	5.68%	5.74%
5	5.70%	5.78%
6	5.72%	5.82%
7	5.74%	5.85%
8	5.76%	5.89%
9	5.78%	5.92%
10	5.79%	5.96%
11	5.81%	5.99%
12	5.86%	6.41%

spot yield curve computed at some future time. Our spot yield curve spans 12 months; it is therefore possible to compute the implied yield curve, as of 3 months into the future, and spanning a 9M horizon (see Exhibit 4-6).

It is also interesting to note that *FV* over a time span *T* can be expressed in terms of the compounding of a series of different yields (one for each subperiod *H*), thereby relaxing the unrealistic assumption of a single level of yields for the computation of interest on interest. We can think of the overall compounded yield as some weighted average of the yields for each subperiod. This is easy to prove using the exponential notation, and also when the time intervals are not of equal length.

Exhibit 4-6 Spot Yield Curve and Implied Yield Curve, 3M Forward

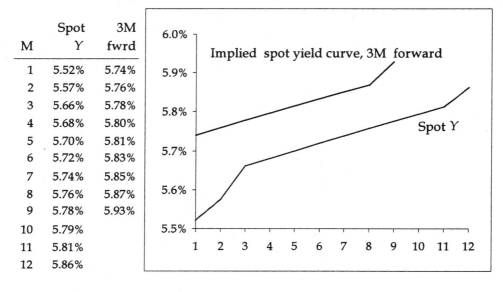

M	Spot *Y*	3M fwrd
1	5.52%	5.74%
2	5.57%	5.76%
3	5.66%	5.78%
4	5.68%	5.80%
5	5.70%	5.81%
6	5.72%	5.83%
7	5.74%	5.85%
8	5.76%	5.87%
9	5.78%	5.93%
10	5.79%	
11	5.81%	
12	5.86%	

Box 4-2   Compounding with a Set of Forward Yields

$$FV = PV \cdot \exp(H_1 \cdot R_1 + \ldots + H_N \cdot R_N)$$

$$FV = PV \cdot \exp(T \cdot \rho)$$

$$\rho = \frac{H_1 \cdot R_1 + \ldots + H_N \cdot R_N}{T}; \quad T = \sum_1^N H$$

Horizon Yields

Let us compare the yield, over an investment horizon of 90 days, of the two T-bills summarized in Exhibit 4-7. Forward rate analysis implies that both bills will produce the same 5.26% compounded yield over the initial 90-day horizon. The higher yield of the 363-day bill does not "percolate" in the first 90 days and is reflected only in the forward yield. Let us stress once again that this way of looking at things is not an abstract mathematical construction. A number of forward-looking derivatives, some of which we shall cover in the following sections of this chapter, enable you to lock in hedgeable forward yields. There is, however, an important difference between the two investment strategies:

- If you invest in the 90-day bill and hold it to maturity, both the $FV = \$101.27$ and the annualized yield (5.26%) are certain.
- If you invest in the 363-day paper, your return will equal the 90-day spot yield only if the realization of the 9M spot yield at the end of the investment horizon will be equal to the value implied by the time 0 yield curve. If the future realization of the 9M yield will turn out to be higher than expected, your return will fall short of 5.26%. Conversely, if the 9M yield will be lower than expected, you will do better than 5.26% (see Exhibit 4-8).

Both the short and the long bills will therefore produce an *expected yield* of 5.26% on the 90-day horizon; this is known as the *local expectation hypothesis*. (We shall cover more analytically the concept of expected yield in Part 3). We also know that, due to the fluctuations over time of market yields, the yield realization over the 90-day horizon of the long bill is almost certain to differ from the ex-ante expected yield. If you have a 90-day investment horizon, you should stick to the 3M paper unless you hold the view that interest rates are in fact going to decrease (the increase in volatility should be compensated by an increase in expected return).

Exhibit 4-7 US T-bills, Prices and Yields as of 14 November 1996

Maturity	Days	Ask rate	Ask price	Y(0, T)	FV(0, T)	Y(t, T)
Thu-13-Feb-97	90	5.02%	98.75	5.26%	101.3	.....
Thu-13-Nov-97	363	5.12%	94.84	5.47%	105.4	
Y (90, 363)	273	n.a	96.04	n.a	n.a	5.55%

Source: Bloomberg

68   *Spot and Forward Yields: FRAs, Repos, and Futures*

Exhibit 4-8   90-day Horizon Yield, when Investing in 363-day Paper

Future 9M Y	FV 273 days bill	3M Y
5.05%	96.3822	6.77%
5.30%	96.2110	6.01%
5.55%	96.0405	5.25%
5.80%	95.8707	4.49%
6.05%	95.7016	3.75%

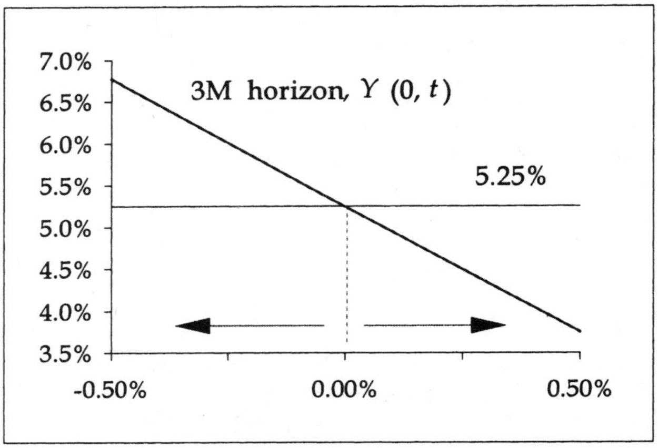

Exhibit 4-9 shows the opposite case, where you choose a 3-month investment with a 12-month investment horizon. You are now running a reinvestment risk that is justified only if you believe that interest yields are going to increase, thereby allowing you to gain from the possibility of reinvesting at a higher yield.

Financing Trading Positions

You may well come across the idea that holding a 1yr fixed-income security yielding, say, 5.5% while financing this position with 1M borrowing at a cost of, say, 5.2% will generate a profit equal to the positive carry. This idea is sometimes generalized when the yield curve is positively sloped (short-term yields are lower than long-term yields), it is potentially profitable to hold trading inventories of long-term securities, financing them with short-term money.

This is clearly a misconception. The result of this trading strategy will depend only on how the future level of long-term yields will compare with the level that is now implied by the spot yield curve. This invariance of the short-term implied yield holds

Exhibit 4-9   Investing First in 90-day, and then in 273-day Paper

Future Y	FV per $100	Realized Y
5.15%	105.15	5.18%
5.35%	105.30	5.33%
5.55%	105.44	5.47%
5.75%	105.60	5.63%
5.95%	105.74	5.78%

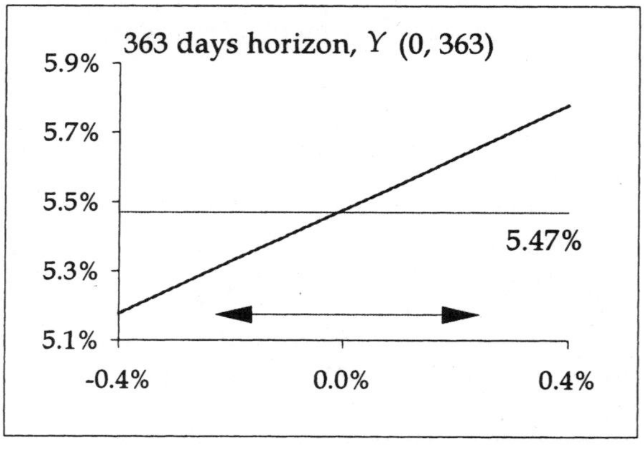

Exhibit 4-10 Eurodeposit Offered Rates, Monday, 23 October 1996

T	$	JPY	DEM	GBP	CHF
1	5.7812%	0.6875%	3.2500%	6.4375%	2.0000%
2	6.1250%	1.0000%	4.0625%	6.9375%	3.0000%
3	6.3125%	1.4375%	4.6250%	7.1875%	3.5000%
4	6.4375%	1.8125%	5.1875%	7.3750%	3.8750%
5	6.5625%	2.1250%	5.5625%	7.5625%	4.1875%

Source: REUTERS

also in a multicurrency environment (see Chapter 5). If the 1M $ yield is 5.2%, this is the implied hedgeable yield you will get investing in 1yr 5.5% paper and financing in with 1M JPY borrowing at 0.512%.

Spot and Forward Yields with Interest Payments before Maturity

Not all money-market instruments are pure discount securities (or interest-at-maturity deposits). We have already seen that for actively traded currencies, Eurodeposit rates are quoted for up to 5yr maturities. In this case interest, at a fixed rate, is assumed to be paid at the end of each year (see Exhibit 4-10).

To determine spot and forward yields, we must modify the bootstrap method to take into account the interest payments before maturity. This is quite a simple procedure. Let's take a 2yr deposit. Its *PV* must be equal to:

- The discounted value of the first interest payment (using the known 1yr spot yield)
- The discounted value of the principal and the second interest payment (using the unknown 2yr spot yield; see Exhibit 4-11).

Box 4-3   Bootstrap Method for 2yr Deposits

C = yearly interest payments (coupons) on 2yr deposit

$Y(0, 1)$ = 1yr spot compounded yield (known from 1yr rate)

$Y(0, 2)$ = 2yr spot compounded yield (to be computed)

$1 = amount of deposit

$$1 = \frac{C}{1 + Y(0,1)} + \frac{1 + C}{[1 + Y(0, 2)]^2} \Rightarrow \frac{1 + C}{[1 + Y(0, 2)]^2} = \frac{1 + Y(0, 1) - C}{1 + Y(0, 1)}$$

$$Y(0, 2) = \sqrt{\frac{[1 + Y(0, 1)] \cdot (1 + C)}{1 + Y(0, 1) - C}} - 1$$

Extending the analysis to more than 2 years is a relatively straightforward process. Once you have determined $Y(0, 1)$ and $Y(0, 2)$, you can easily determine the value of $Y(0, 3)$, and so on.

Exhibit 4-11 Spot and Forward Yields for 2-yr Deposits

	$	JPY	DEM	GBP	CHF
CPN =	6.2101%	1.0139%	4.1189%	7.0339%	3.0417%
Y(0, 1) =	5.8615%	0.6970%	3.2951%	6.5269%	2.0278%
Y(0, 2) =	6.2209%	1.0155%	4.1360%	7.0518%	3.0572%
Y(1, 2) =	6.5816%	1.3350%	4.9838%	7.5792%	4.0971%

Coupon APR is derived from exhibit 4-10, correcting for daycount

4-3   FORWARD RATE AGREEMENTS

Forward rate agreements (FRAs) were first introduced in 1984. Soon afterward, in 1985, the British Bankers Association (BBA) developed a standard contract for the new instrument (known as FRABBA). FRAs are (OTC) forward contracts on short-term interest rates, settled in cash and not by delivery. This product has been outclassed by interest rate swaps but is still actively traded in huge volumes and constitutes an interesting approach to the logic of forward-looking interest rate derivatives. As of the end of March 1995, outstanding FRAs totaled $4,597 billion, according to the *1995 Central Bank Survey of Foreign Exchange and Derivatives Market Activity.*

The buyer of an FRA locks in the current level of the forward borrowing rate, also known as the *contract rate.* The term buyer is consistent with the cash market jargon where the borrower is said to buy the funds. The seller of an FRA, short the FRA, locks in the current level of the forward lending rate. This lock-in of the borrowing rate is done with reference to:

• A defined amount of money, known as the *notional principal*
• A *reference rate,* usually BBA-LIBOR
• A defined maturity, *tenor,* for the *notional loan* (usually 3, 6, or 12 months)
• A certain *deferment period,* after which the notional loan is deemed to begin

Cash settlement means that the seller of the FRA is under no obligation to extend a loan to the buyer. The seller will:

• Pay the cash settlement to the buyer if the reference rate turns out to be higher than the contract rate (this amount will cover the extra interest cost due to LIBOR exceeding the contract rate, thereby hedging the buyer against the increase in the cost of borrowing)
• Receive the cash settlement from the buyer if the reference rate turns out to be lower than the contract rate (the FRA locks in the borrowing rate, and the buyer will not profit from a lower-than-expected LIBOR; see Exhibit 4-12).

Cash settlement, which allows a huge reduction in credit risk, is the main contract-design feature that assures the success of FRAs. All that the seller and the buyer of the FRA are risking is the (contingent) settlement amount. FRAs remain, however, a credit risk–sensitive product, but only to a very limited extent. This is confirmed by the data of the already cited *Central Bank Survey.* The $4,597 billion of FRAs notional principal outstanding had a gross market value (replacement value) of only $17 billion, that is, less than 0.4% of notional.

Exhibit 4-12 Cash Settlement of an FRA

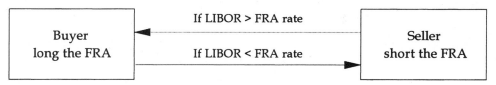

The decoupling of the interest rate lock-in from the actual lending means that banks don't have to commit to extend credit at a future date (at the end of the deferment period) when the credit rating of the corporation could have deteriorated. FRAs lock in market levels of borrowing rates, not borrowing rates for specific corporations.

Before the introduction of FRAs, banks used to extend fully committed forward loans (say, to lend for 3 months, forward 2 months). Such contracts, however, exposed the lending bank to the full credit risk on the loan principal. When banking supervisors, at both the national level and the G-10 level, began to insist on capital adequacy, forward lending contracts were regarded as outright lending for all intents and purposes.

The popularity of FRAs is due to the fact that they are very straightforward and easy to use. Being an OTC product, they are also quite flexible, as you can see from their wide range of maturities. Banks enjoy a competitive advantage in providing FRAs, not only in terms of having adequate trading desks but also because of the possibility of hedging a whole book of FRAs instead of just a few transactions. FRAs are not normally used by securities dealers and by asset managers to hedge short-term trading positions. Active FRA dealers quote bid-ask rates, but these quotations are applicable only to customers who have open credit lines with the dealer.

Box 4-4   Computing FRA's Settlement Amount

i_C = contract rate, fixed at dealing date (based on the forward value of LIBOR)

i_F = spot BBA-LIBOR on the fixing date, for the relevant currency and term

T = tenor of the notional loan (actual/360)

NP = notional principal

FRA = settlement amount

$$FRA = \frac{(i_F - I_C) \cdot NP \cdot T}{1 + i_F \cdot T}$$

Some Operational Details

The important dates in an FRA agreement are

- The trade date (or *dealing date*), when the FRA is contracted and the conditions (including the contract rate) are defined
- The *fixing date* (dealing date + deferment period), which is the date at which the reference rate is set
- The settlement date (the second business day after the fixing date, $T + 2$, in line with Euromarket standards).

Exhibit 4-13 Bid-Offer $-FRA Quotations, 23 October 1996

3M rates			6M rates			9M rates			12M rates		
1x4	5.56	5.59	1x7	5.65	5.68	1x10	5.76	5.79	1x13	5.88	5.90
2x5	5.59	5.63	2x8	5.69	5.73	2x11	5.81	5.84	2x14	5.93	5.95
3x6	5.60	5.64	3x9	5.71	5.75	3x12	5.85	5.88	3x15	5.98	6.00
4x7	5.64	5.68	4x10	5.76	5.80	6x15	6.00	6.02	6x18	6.12	6.14
5x8	5.68	5.72	5x11	5.81	5.85	9x18	6.14	6.17	9x21	6.25	6.27
6x9	5.74	5.78	6x12	5.87	5.90	12x21	6.26	6.29	12x24	6.35	6.37
7x10	5.80	5.83	7x13	5.92	5.95	15x24	6.37	6.40			
8x11	5.85	5.88	8x14	5.98	6.01						
9x12	5.90	5.93	9x15	6.03	6.06						
12x15	6.06	6.09	12x18	6.17	6.20						
15x18	6.18	6.21	18x24	6.36	6.39						
18x21	6.27	6.30									
21x24	6.37	6.40									

Source: REUTERS

To streamline the procedure and further reduce credit risk, the FRA's settlement amount is paid on the settlement date, which is at the beginning of the period covered by the notional loan, whereas LIBOR interest is paid at the maturity of the loan. To take this into account, the interest differential is discounted at LIBOR for the term (tenor) of the notional loan.

FRA Quotations and the Yield Curve

FRAs' maturities are usually shown on quotation screens with two numbers separated by a ($\times$). The first is the number of months between trade and fixing date (deferment period). The second represents the total life of the contract (see Exhibit 4-13). The difference between the two numbers is the maturity (tenor) of the notional loan. The quotation 4×7 refers to a 3M notional loan starting after a 4M deferment period. Rates are expressed in the usual bid-ask fashion. The spread is usually quite low (about 3 bp) when compared to that of deposits. We must remember, however, that we are referring to notional amounts, and the credit risk on an FRA's notional is much lower than on a deposit for the same amount.

FRA rates and spot rates define a set of hedgeable forward rates and a spot rate curve, stretching to 2 years into the future. These rates are, of course, transaction-costs-close to the spot rate curve and to the curve that can be obtained by the appropriate series (*strip*, in futures-speak) of exchange-traded futures (see Exhibit 4-14).

Example of a Successful FRA

The $ interest-rate dynamics of 1994 (see Exhibit 4-15) provide the scenario for an interesting case study of a multiple FRA transaction (strip of FRAs). In that year the Federal Reserve implemented a series of short-term interest rate hikes to control the inflationary pressures that were building up in the U.S. economy after many quarters

Exhibit 4-14 *Y* Term Structure Based on LIBOR and FRAs, 23 October 1996

M	3M FRAs	6M FRAs	9M FRAs	12M FRAs	LIBOR	LIBOR Spot *Y*	FRA Spot *Y*
1	...	...	...	...	5.31%	5.52%	5.52%
2	...	...	...	...	5.38%	5.57%	5.57%
3		...	...	...	5.47%	5.66%	5.66%
4	5.59%	...	...	...	5.50%	5.68%	5.72%
5	5.63%	...	...	...	5.53%	5.70%	5.73%
6	5.64%	...	...	...	5.56%	5.72%	5.75%
7	5.68%	5.68%	...	...	5.59%	5.74%	5.79%
8	5.72%	5.73%	...	...	5.63%	5.76%	5.80%
9	5.78%	5.75%	...	...	5.66%	5.78%	5.83%
10	5.83%	5.80%	5.79%	...	5.69%	5.79%	5.87%
11	5.88%	5.85%	5.84%	...	5.72%	5.81%	5.88%
12	5.93%	5.90%	5.88%	...	5.78%	5.86%	5.91%
13	...	5.95%		5.90%	...	...	...
14	...	6.01%		5.95%	...	...	...
15	6.09%	6.06%	6.02%	6.00%	...	...	5.99%
16	...	...	...	...	...	...	...
17	...	...	...	...	...	...	...
18	6.21%	6.20%	6.17%	6.14%	...	...	6.07%
19	...	...	...	...	...	...	...
20	...	...	...	...	...	...	...
21	6.30%	...	6.29%	6.27%	...	...	6.14%
22	...	...	...	...	...	...	...
23	...	...	...	...	...	...	...
24	6.40%	6.39%	6.40%	6.37%	...	6.22%	6.20%

The FRA spot yield curve is based on 3M FRAs

Source: REUTERS

of uninterrupted growth. We may add that this tightening of monetary policy proved to be a successful example of fine-tuning. The Fed defused inflationary pressures without choking growth, which in fact continued uninterrupted.

Consider a corporation that at the end January 1994 had the following floating-rate loan outstanding:

- Principal amount $10 million
- Maturity = Tue 31 January 1995
- Interest payable quarterly in arrears, at LIBOR + 60 bp

The rate of interest for each quarter is determined on the basis of the BBA-LIBOR quoted two business days before the first day of the interest period of the following quarter (in line with the *T* + 2 settlement of the Euromarkets). At the end of January

Exhibit 4-15 Daily Values of 3M LIBOR

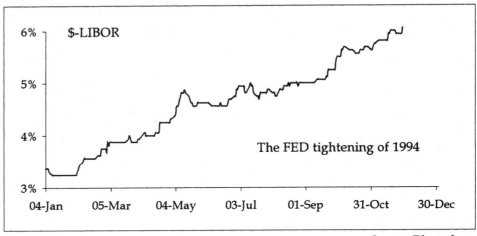

Source: Bloomberg

1994 the rate for the April payment had already been fixed (3.25% + 60 bp), but the future rates for the last 3 Qs were uncertain. To eliminate this uncertainty, the corporation could have bought three FRAs, thereby predetermining the level of LIBOR for the last 3 Qs of the loan (see Exhibits 4-16 and 4-17).

Replacement Value and Credit Risk in FRAs

Exhibit 4-17 shows that the market value (replacement value) of FRAs also tends to be quite small, as a percentage of the notional amount, when interest rates display a very strong level of volatility. This is because an FRA contract covers only one interest period (usually 3 or 6 months; sometimes 12 months). Consequently, the level of credit risk is minimal. At the trading date, the replacement cost of an FRA = 0, like all forward contracts when the contract rate is set equal to the market value of the forward

Exhibit 4-16 Spot Rates and FRA Quotations
Settlement Date = 31 January 1994

Interest payment date	DSM	Spot rates	(T-t)	FRA quotations	
Fri-29-Apr-94	88	3.2500%			
Fri-29-Jul-94	179	3.3750%	91	3×6	3.5000%
Mon-31-Oct-94	273	3.5000%	94	6×9	3.6875%
Tue-31-Jan-95	365	3.6875%	92	9×12	4.1875%

The positive slope of the FRA term structure shows that the market anticipated a rate increase, which, however, turned out to be much steeper than expected.

Exhibit 4-17 Quarterly Outcomes of the FRA Strip on $1 million

BBA-LIBOR fixing date	BBA LIBOR	FRA rates	Days	FRA $ settlement	% of notional
Wed-27-Apr-94	4.2500%	3.5000%	91	18,756.83	0.19%
Wed-27-Jul-94	4.8125%	3.6875%	94	29,010.46	0.29%
Thu-27-Oct-94	5.6875%	4.1875%	92	37,784.15	0.38%

Source: Bloomberg

rate. After the trading date, the market value of FRAs should be computed on the basis of the current market value of the relevant forward rate.

4-4 REPOS AND REPO RATES

In this section we will discuss repos and their role in forward transactions, such as short selling securities for hedging or speculative purposes. Repos are very popular in the U.S. and repo markets are continuing to expand worldwide, often encouraged by monetary authorities because repos contribute to a better liquidity and transparency of the markets (a recent example has been the introduction of an official repo market on treasury securities in the UK). The adoption of the Euro will, in likelihood, provide a boost for the repo market in the European currency.

A *sales-repurchase agreement*, or *repo* for short, is the sale of a security, or of a portfolio of securities, that the seller (*RepoCo*) has the right and the obligation to repurchase at a specified future date at a predetermined price. A repo is therefore a form of borrowing against collateral. The buyer therefore commits to sell back to RepoCo at the agreed-on date and price. When looked at from the point of view of the original buyer, whom we shall accordingly indicate as *ReverseCo*, a repo transaction is known as a *reverse repo*, or *reverse* for short. The interest paid by RepoCo to ReverseCo (at the repo rate) can be either incorporated into the repurchase price (repurchase price = sale price + interest) or computed separately and added to the contract price (see Exhibit 4-18).

The origin of repos predates that of financial futures, swaps, and FRAs. Repos were in fact used in the United States toward the end of World War I, when the Federal Reserve lent money to U.S. exporters, reversing bankers' acceptances. Repos have a very interesting, complex nature.

- They represent a special class of collateralized lending and borrowing. In fact, repos are more secure for the lender than lending against collateral. In the case of insolvency of RepoCo, the lender can just sell the securities that RepoCo cannot

Exhibit 4-18 Structure of a Repo Transaction

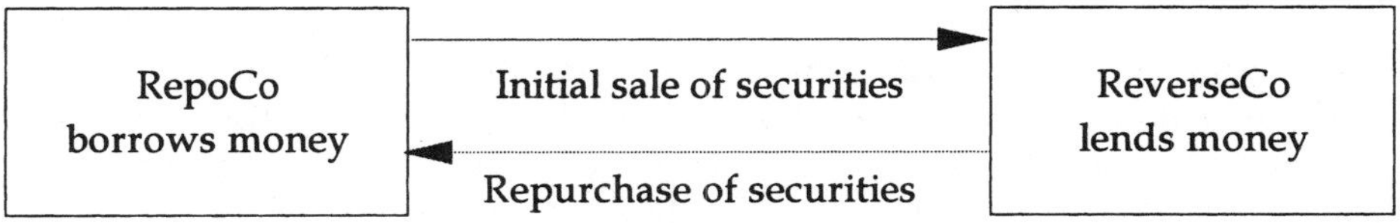

| RepoCo borrows money | Initial sale of securities → ← Repurchase of securities | ReverseCo lends money |

Exhibit 4-19 Repo Activity of U.S. Government Securities Dealers

	Jun 96	Dec 96	Jun 97	Oct 97	May 98
Reverse Repurchase Agreements	707	692	883	958	1,162
# Overnight and continuing	243	255	290	332	368
# Term	463	437	592	627	794
Repurchase Agreements	950	957	1,165	1,215	1,472
# Overnight and continuing	541	564	626	672	761
# Term	409	393	539	544	711

Average outstanding amounts, $ billions.

Source: Federal Reserve Bulletin

buy back. When you lend against collateral, the sale of collateral can be *stayed* by the court, and this can prove dangerous in volatile markets where the value of the collateral can decrease quite rapidly.

- They are a forward transaction and therefore a synthetic derivative contract. Due to the favorable level of the repo rate (which tends to lie somewhere between the rate on T-bills and that on federal funds) and to low margin requirements, repos can allow RepoCo to build up a fairly leveraged long-forward position in securities.
- ReverseCo is free to sell the securities it has acquired and therefore can set a highly leveraged short position for hedging or speculation. The repo buyer's right to trade the securities during the term of the agreement is due to the transfer of ownership, which does not occur in collateralized lending agreements.

The derivative-like interpretation of repos (and their widespread practical use) fully emerged in the 1970s. A securities house can also set up a *repo book*, doing both repos and reverses, thereby running both short and long forward positions. The importance of repos in the U.S. money market can be judged from Exhibit 4-19.

Development of the Repo Market in the United States

The commercial use of the repo became more widespread in the 1950s, when it provided cash-rich corporations with a safe way to place short-term money while allowing securities houses and banks to finance their inventories of government securities. The use of repos to create highly leveraged long or short securities positions emerged only in the 1970s, also as a consequence of the increased volatility of interest rates.

Like many relatively new financial products that facilitate leveraging, repos were not adequately understood by all market participants. It should be added that the treasuries market was, oddly enough, one of the less-regulated markets in terms of margins, short selling, mark-to-market procedures, and segregation of customers' securities. This led to a number of bankruptcies in the U.S. securities industry, whereby some firms used repos to place hugely leveraged bets on interest rates. Among the most noticeable cases we can cite are the following:

- Financial Corporation, which failed in 1975, causing a stir in the market but relatively limited losses to its lenders (in the order of $20 to $30 million)
- Drysdale Government Securities, which went bankrupt in 1982, causing large losses to many parties, including Chase Manhattan Bank. This situation prompted the Federal Reserve to take actions aimed at rationalizing the repo market, including lobbying Congress for a clearer characterization of repos in the bankruptcy code.
- Lombard Wall, which failed soon after Drysdale and created a serious political problem because a public entity, the New York State Dormitory Authority, lost money in the case

These debacles made market participants more aware of the necessary precautions and disciplines. To help in dealing with the legal issues, the Public Securities Association (PSA) produced a standard repo contract in 1984. At the same time, the Federal Reserve and the Securities and Exchange Commission (SEC) took the necessary steps to clarify the issues relating to the proper evaluation of collateral to the necessary capital-adequacy requirements for broker dealers running a repo book.

The Globalization of Repos

The globalization of repos began in the 1980s, by which time they were much better understood. This did not prevent the emergence of some problems, however. The Deutsche Genossenschafts Bank (the central institution of the German cooperative banking system) lost several hundred million DM on unauthorized bond trading that was covered up by a number of undisclosed repo transactions with some French banks.

The globalization of repos led the PSA and the International Securities Markets Association (ISMA) to produce, in 1992, a global master repurchase agreement (GMRA). A revised copy of the GMRA was published in 1995.

Repos as a Collateralized Lending Transaction

Usually, repos are done on Treasury securities. Their high credit rating, liquidity, and price transparency makes repos easy to unwind in case of insolvency. Most repos are 1-day transactions (often rolled over). If the original term for a repo is longer than 1 business day, the transaction is known as a *term repo*. Traditionally, the securities are sold and repurchased at a value that is somewhat lower than their market value (clean price + accrued interest for coupon securities). This is designed to protect the lender against the possibility of a price movement that could cause the collateral to be worth less than the amount lent. This margin, also known as *haircut*, is a function of the price volatility of the security utilized in the repo. It will therefore be quite small for short-term bills and somewhat larger for long-term bonds. In term repos, the contract usually allows ReverseCo (and, often, also RepoCo) to ask for a *repricing* of the securities if their value moves beyond safety levels.

There is an element of asymmetry in this application of haircuts. As in all forward contracts, repos represent contingent claims. You cannot identify a priori the party that will be incurring credit risk. Credit risk is contingent on market developments and on their influence on the value of collateral. If a ReverseCo goes insolvent holding collateral worth more than the loan to RepoCo, then it is the borrower who stands to lose.

Exhibit 4-20 Matched Repo Book

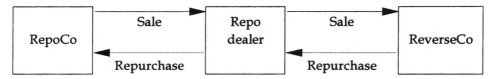

If RepoCo becomes insolvent, ReverseCo can promptly sell the securities. If the sales proceeds are higher than the amount lent (plus interest), this difference, known as *overage*, must be returned to the borrower. This was not always so. When Drysdale Securities went bankrupt, some of its counterparties actually gained by keeping the overage at the expense of the other creditors.

Securities dealers need to finance their inventories, but they also need to trade freely, thereby selling and delivering treasuries that they repoed out. Due to this need, many term repo contracts contain a clause granting RepoCo the *right of substitution* (i.e., to substitute the securities that it has sold with an appropriate amount of new securities).

Repos have been made safer and more flexible by the widespread adoption of *tri-party repos* (or *bank custody repos*). In these transactions, the securities are held by custodian banks (i.e., "held" in book-entry form with the Federal Reserve), and the movements between RepoCo and ReverseCo are carried out by the bank in a fiduciary capacity. When the securities are not explicitly held in safekeeping by a custodian, we have what is known as a *letter repo*. Letter repos can obviously create problems if the securities dealer that holds the securities against which it has borrowed goes insolvent.

Matched Repo Book

Securities dealers often run a *matched repo book* (MRB) as a profit center. A matched repo is simply a repo plus a reverse on the same securities or portfolio of securities. The profit on an MRB should come mainly from the spread between borrowing and lending rates (see Exhibit 4-20). Note, however, that the MRB is an instrument of choice with which to place bets on short-term interest rates (e.g., lending term money and borrowing overnight).

Repos and Securities Lending: Repo Rate on "Specials"

ReverseCo becomes the full owner of the securities it has repoed in. Therefore, it can sell them to create a short position. Repos are thus a widely used securities lending and borrowing method for Treasuries. In fact, a number of securities dealers have a Treasuries desk and a repo desk in order to have the in-house capability to carry out the interest rate–hedging activities that are a necessary complement to their trading activities on corporate bonds, municipal bonds, and mortgage-backed securities. The repo rate tends to be somewhere between the rate on federal funds and that on T-bills. The repo rate is a money-market rate and therefore interest accrues based on actual/360 (see Exhibit 4-21).

If you look at the live screens where brokers quote repo rates, you will notice that from time to time, for some specified security, the repo rate is a lot lower than the current overall market rate. This is because these securities are *specials*, that is, securities for which there is a high borrowing demand to cover short positions of securities

Exhibit 4-21 Repo Rates on U.S. Government Securities Compared to other $ Money Market Rates, 11 January 1999

	Bid Repo	Ask Reverse	Ask FED Funds	LIBOR
O/N	4.8700%	4.9000%	4.8700%	n.a.
1W	4.9400%	4.7000%	4.9375%	4.9431%
2W				
3W				
1M	5.0000%	4.8000%	5.0000%	5.0000%
2M				
3M	5.0000%	4.7800%	5.0000%	5.0378%

Bid-ask quotations are expressed from the point of view of the dealer that will do repos (borrow) and reverses (lend).

Source: Bloomberg

dealers or investment managers. If the supply of loanable securities is scarce when compared to the demand, would-be borrowers will be willing to pay a premium to obtain these securities; in turn, this premium will be deducted from the repo rate to obtain the repo rate on specials.

Repo Rate, Synthetic Forwards, Tails, and Implied Repo Rate

When you borrow at the repo rate to buy a security, you implicitly determine its future cost at the maturity of the repo, thereby setting up a synthetic long forward. In turn, this future cost determines the future yield to maturity on the security, also known as the *tail*. Computing the value of the tail (also called *figuring the tail*) is so straightforward that it requires only a simple numerical example (see Exhibit 4-22). The horizon return of your long forward will depend on the realization of the 3M bill rate in 3 months' time. The break-even cost of your synthetic long is 98.8255. If, in 3 months' time, the 3M bill rate will be lower than 5.09%, the market price of your bill will exceed the forward cost and you will gain. This requires, however, that the future realization of the 3M bill rate be lower than the rate implied by the time-0 spot curve; you are therefore betting on knowing better than the market what the market will do.

Exhibit 4-22 Repo Rate and T-bill Tail

	Term	CDY	Prices	
Repo	93	5.31%		
3M bill, disc. rate = 4.98%	93	5.04%	98.7135	Ask price of 3M bill
6M bill, disc. rate = 5.11%	177	5.24%	97.4876	Ask price of 6M bill
Repo-funded tail	84	5.09%	98.8255	Forward cost 6M bill

Source: Bloomberg

Exhibit 4-23 Repo-Based Arbitrages

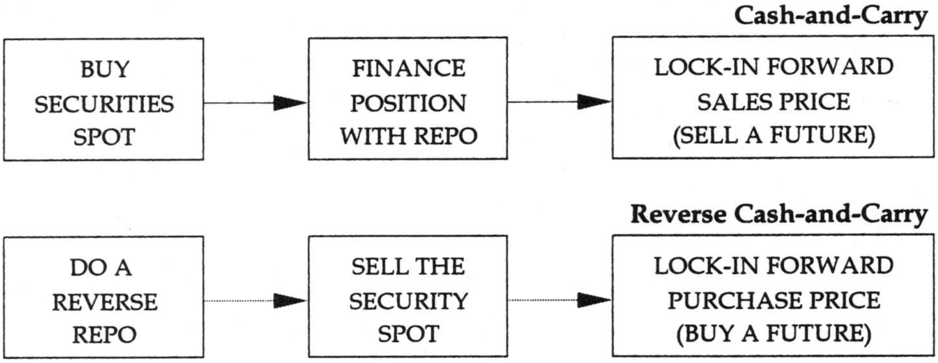

Cash-and-Carry

| BUY SECURITIES SPOT | → | FINANCE POSITION WITH REPO | → | LOCK-IN FORWARD SALES PRICE (SELL A FUTURE) |

Reverse Cash-and-Carry

| DO A REVERSE REPO | → | SELL THE SECURITY SPOT | → | LOCK-IN FORWARD PURCHASE PRICE (BUY A FUTURE) |

Assume you can lock in a forward sale price of the security that you have bought and repo-financed (usually by selling an exchange-traded future). You can easily compute the break-even repo rate on your transaction, known as the *implied repo rate*. If the market repo rate is lower than the implied repo rate, then you can lock in a riskless profit. This kind of arbitrage transaction is known as a *cash and carry* (this will be analyzed in more detail in the next section, drawing on the description of the U.S. T-bill futures traded on the IMM). A variation of the cash-and-carry is the *reverse cash and carry* (see Exhibit 4-23).

4-5 FUTURES

Whereas forwards are OTC products, futures trade on regulated exchanges that provide a well-organized and transparent marketplace. They allow the users to reap the economic benefits of forward contracts while avoiding the associated credit risk. It should be emphasized that the forward and futures markets expose investors and traders to exactly the same risks they would run in the cash market. In spite of this, one can find misleading representations, such as the following:

> The financial futures markets provide an investor with the ability to control a large position in a financial instrument without having to risk significant capital . . . Futures can be used to hedge either one position or an entire portfolio, thus allowing the investor to maximize upside potential while minimizing downside potential.

The standardization of futures markets and the daily settlement mechanism entail very low transaction costs and make futures an ideal instrument for short-term hedging purposes. This is clearly reflected in the ratio of daily trading to open positions for all the main financial futures contracts. The average life of most futures' contracts is just a few trading days.

Futures Versus Forwards and Daily Settlement of Futures

The distinction between forwards and futures is often obfuscated by definitions such as this one: "A futures contract is an agreement—originally between two parties, a buyer and a seller—to exchange a particular asset, for a set price, at a certain date in the future." This is somewhat misleading, because it happens to describe a forward rather than a future. A more accurate definition would be, "A futures contract is an exchange-traded instrument that performs the function of a forward (i.e., to guarantee a future price) by means of the *daily settlement mechanism*." Let us see how this works in practice and why daily mark-to-market and settlement was introduced by futures exchanges.

The standard long/short terminology holds for futures as well as for forwards. The buyer of a futures contract has a long position and stands to gain if the price of the asset goes up (and to lose if it goes down). The seller has a short position; her gains (or losses) are exactly the reverse of those of the buyer. When you buy or sell a future, you do so at a market-determined *futures price*, which tends to be close to the contract price (delivery price) of a *new* forward, with the same maturity, on the identical underlying asset. This is due to the law of one price. If at a given time t you compare a new forward and a future, both with maturity $T > t$, you will notice that

$F(t, T) \cong f(t, T)$
$f(t, T)$ = contract price (delivery price), at the market forward
$F(t, T)$ = futures price, at time t

Once a forward has been traded, its contract price remains unchanged throughout the life of the contract, thereby entailing the likelihood of a nonzero replacement value. Things work differently for futures, which are repriced (marked-to-market) daily at the *settlement price*, which is determined by the exchange on the basis of the prices prevailing at the end of the trading day.

The difference between the current settlement price and the settlement price of the previous day is settled in cash. This is known as the *daily variation margin* and as a rule must be paid within the morning of the next business day. Consequently, the replacement value of a futures contract is brought back to zero on a daily basis. The first daily variation margin payment for a new contract will take place on the first business day following the trade date.

Example: If on 17 March 1998 you had bought 10 June 1998 JPY contracts at $0.7814/100 JPY, you would receive a $4,375 settlement from the seller because the settlement price determined at the close of the trade date was $0.7849. Conversely, if you had bought at 0.7855, you would have to pay $750 to the seller. The $ values are easy to compute. The contract size is JPY 12,500,000 and the quotations are $ for 100 ¥; therefore

$$\$4,375 = \frac{0.7849 - 0.7814}{100} \times 12,500,000; \quad -\$750 = \frac{0.7849 - 0.7855}{100} \times 12,500,000.$$

The writer of a future (the short) has the option to wait until the maturity of the future in the delivery month. The delivery of a futures contract will then take place at the last settlement price before the expiration of the contract. This ensures that the futures price converges to the spot price at maturity. If this convergence does not take place, it will be easy to reap an arbitrage profit.

$F(T, T) \cong P(T)$
$P(T)$ = spot price at maturity of the underlying asset
$F(T, T)$ = last settlement price of the future

It is now easy to see how the daily settlement mechanism simulates the working of a forward contract. If the forward is held to maturity, there will be one single settlement payment; as a rule, no cash flows take place until the final maturity of the contract.

$P(T) - f(0, T)$ = gain (loss) of the long forward
$f(0, T)$ = delivery price of the long forward

For a future, the last settlement price will converge to the spot price. This entails that the algebraic sum of all the daily settlements in the time interval $(T - 0)$ must equal the difference between the future's price at time-0 and the realization of the spot price, at maturity, of the underlying asset. Unlike a forward, a futures contract will usually spin off daily cash payments to or from the buyer.

To sum up, the daily settlement of futures simulates quite effectively the functioning of a forward contract. This entails that futures and forward prices will be nearly identical, and this is well supported by statistical evidence. You should be aware, however, that small differences between futures and forward prices can be attributed to the difference in cash-flow patterns between daily settlement and settlement at delivery date. You will find a detailed numerical example, referred to a futures contract on the yen, in Chapter 5.

Liquidity Enhancement in Futures Markets

Exchanges have implemented a number of rules and regulations to foster liquidity, safety, and transparency of trading. Some of the most relevant features are listed here:

- The contract size is standardized; see Exhibit 4-24.
- Delivery dates are standardized (usually four dates per year) in order to have a sufficient concentration of homogeneous contracts; see Exhibit 4-25.
- A unit price movement is defined (*tick*), with a corresponding $ value for daily settlement purposes.

Settlement of Futures Trades—the Role of the Clearinghouse

The settlement mechanism reduces credit risk because the *replacement value* of all outstanding futures contracts is brought back to zero at the end of each trading day. If

Exhibit 4-24 Some CME FX Futures, 16 March 1998, Tick = $12.50

	Spot FX rate		Size	$ Size	Tick%
Japanese Yen	JY 100	0.7719	12,500,000	96,488	0.01%
Deutschemark	DM	0.5491	125,000	68,638	0.01%
British Pound	BP	1.6664	62,500	104,150	0.02%
Swiss Franc	SF	0.6757	125,000	84,463	0.01%

The CME contract symbols are different from the SWIFT symbols

Source: Financial Times

Exhibit 4-25 JPY Futures, Yen 12.5m, $ per Yen 100, 17 March 1998

	Open	Settle price	Price change	High	Low	Est vol	Open int
Jun	0.7807	0.7849	0.0042	0.7860	0.7803	17,578	68,207
Sep	0.7916	0.7949	0.0043	0.7950	0.7916	78	606
Dec	na	0.8050	0.0044	na	na	77	115

Source: Financial Times

one of the exchange members (also known as *futures commission merchants,* or FCMs) cannot honor its obligation to pay the settlement amounts owned to the clearinghouse, its position can be liquidated immediately, without risk of further variations of its replacement value. Credit risk is further reduced by the following arrangements.

Clearinghouse. After a contract between two exchange members (FCMs) is finalized, the clearinghouse is interposed between the buyer and the seller; it will therefore collect and disburse all the daily settlement amounts. The clearinghouse does not assume any market risk; its books are always balanced because it has a short position toward the buying FCM and a long position toward the selling FCM.

Margin. To enter into a futures transaction, the exchange member has to deposit a *margin,* which provides a buffer against credit risk. If a member becomes insolvent while owing a daily settlement amount, the potential loss is reduced by the amount of the margin on deposit. In turn, the clearinghouse's members will apply daily settlements and margin requirements to their customers. In the United States, the clearinghouses implement a margin system based on an initial margin (when the contract is finalized) and a maintenance margin (lower than the initial margin) that must be kept at all times. Outside the United States, most exchanges use only one margin, which is more rational.

Not surprisingly, margin levels are set in such a way as to take into account the volatility of the underlying instrument (see Exhibit 4-26). A detailed discussion of margin arrangements falls outside the scope of this book. The rules and regulations are rather complex. Higher margins are often required from speculators that take a "naked" long or short position, while lower margins are required from hedgers that use the futures to hedge positions in the underlying instrument. Clearinghouses also allow margin rebates for cross margining, that is, when a member has open positions that behave as partial hedges—for example, a long 100-contract position in the JPY for December delivery is hedged, albeit not perfectly, by a short position in 100 JPY contracts for delivery in March. Once a long or a short position is established, it can be closed in one of the following ways:

• *Offsetting transaction.* A quick glance at the ratio of daily volumes to open positions shows clearly that most open positions are not held to maturity. Closing positions are made a lot easier by the operations of the clearinghouse. When a member wants to close a position, it can simply enter into an offsetting contract, and the clearinghouse will net the two positions.

Exhibit 4-26 Initial and Maintenance Margins on the CME: Q3, 1998

Contract	Initial margin-$	Maint. margin-$	Contract value-$	% maint margin
$/ ¥	3,510	2,600	112,500	2.31%
3-month Euro$	675	500	1,000,000	0.05%

The $ value of the JPY contract is calculated at the $/JPY rate of 0.009

Source: Chicago Mercantile Exchange

• *Delivery of the underlying asset* (known as *physical delivery*). In some cases the deliverable assets are totally straightforward (think of currency contracts where ¥12.5 million can be only a JPY deposit). In other cases, as we shall see in later chapters, delivery terms are more complex and are defined in the contract's specifications.

• *Cash settlement*, which means that the contract held to maturity is closed out by the settlement price on its last trading day. Cash settlement has been instrumental in the development of contracts where a physical delivery would be next to impossible (think of a future on a stock exchange index, such as the S&P 500). When we have cash settlement, we must also have a reliable mechanism to determine in a fair and reasonable way the last settlement price.

• *Exchange for physical* (EFP). When this settlement option is allowed, physical delivery may take place before delivery date provided that there is an agreement reached between the two parties (with the short delivering to the long). In other terms, an EFP involves the sale of an asset outside the exchange by the short to the long, at a contracted price and at a contracted date. Both the short and the long will then notify the clearinghouse, which will offset their two positions.

4-6 FUTURES ON SHORT-TERM INTEREST RATES

Futures on short-term interest rates are widely used by banks and investment banks to price and hedge their open trading positions and their custom-made OTC derivatives (such as FRAs, interest-rate swaps, etc.). Their use is beginning to spread among asset managers due to the growth size and sophistication of this industry. For global asset managers, one of the attractions of interest rate futures is the possibility of taking a view on the relative value of foreign markets while avoiding foreign currency exposure. The FX risk is obviously limited to the gain (loss) on the futures position.

Futures on short interest rates are simple to use, and their success is due to the liquidity and transparency of the markets and to the practical absence of credit risk. Transacting in futures is very inexpensive, and this makes it ideal for short-lived *round-turns*, to hedge for a few days, sometimes for a few hours, a trading position. A round-turn for a US$1 million contract can cost $12.5 (i.e., 0.00125%) or less for a wholesale customer trading in volume. From a technical point of view, interest rate futures can be divided into two categories.

• *Futures on deposit rates*, widely adopted for liquid and transparent markets such as the 3-month contracts for Eurodollars at the IMM, Euro-DM and £ at the LIFFE, and Euro¥ at the TIFFE. These contracts are for cash settlement because physical delivery would be extremely impractical. Daily mark-to-market and settlement are computed with reference to a benchmark rate, such as BBA-LIBOR for LIFFE and the 3-month Eurodollar rate calculated by the IMM clearinghouse.

• *Futures on fixed-income securities* and therefore indirectly on interest rates. These contracts are mostly for medium and long-term treasury securities (U.S. T-bonds and T-notes at the CBOT, German Bunds at the EUREX). These contracts are for physical delivery. Most of the contracts, however, are closed out with a reverse transaction before maturity.

The Quotation Mechanism of Interest Rate Futures

The buyer of an interest rate future (long the future) locks in a future investment rate and not a borrowing rate as in interest rate swaps and FRAs. If interest rates decrease, the seller pays the buyer an amount that will compensate for the lower future investment rate. Conversely, if interest rates increase, the buyer pays the seller an amount equal to the advantage he will reap by investing at a higher rate.

Buying a future is like buying a security for forward delivery; selling a future is like short selling a security. This quotation mechanism finds its historical origin in the fact that the first futures introduced by the Chicago exchanges were futures on deliverable securities. This in turn was in line with the Chicago tradition of trading futures on deliverable commodities, such as soybeans or timber. Futures quotation needs to be consistent with the time-honored tradition of the long making a profit when the futures price increases. With interest rate futures, however, the long gets paid when interest rates decline. The Chicago-IMM exchange therefore developed an ingenious system whereby the futures price is quoted as an index. This presents the advantage of an immediate perception of the implied interest or discount rate (rate = 100 − price index).

Interest Rate Futures Price Index

Price index = 100 − interest rate (for interest rate futures)
Price index = 100 − discount rate (for T-bill futures)

The minimum settlement price movement (tick) is usually 1 bp (0.01%). The settlement amount corresponding to one tick will depend on both the notional value of the contract and the interest elasticity of the security price.

The 3-Month Eurodollar Future (IMM)

In December 1981, the IMM was authorized to begin trading a futures contract on 3-month Eurodollar deposit, which is now the most widely used short-term interest rate future. This contract is based on a $1 million, 90-day deposit. The tick equals 1 bp (0.01%), which corresponds to a settlement amount of $25, given the 90-day maturity.

$$\$25 = \$1,000,000 \times (90 \div 360) \times 0.01\%$$

The last trading date is the second business day before the third Wednesday of the delivery month. The $T + 2$ Eurodeposits settlement entails that the future is synchronized with a 90-day deposit settling on Wednesday. The final settlement price is not based on the BBA-LIBOR (which is fixed at 11:00 A.M. London time, well before Chicago's closing hour). The offered rate is instead determined by the IMM clearinghouse, which randomly polls 12 banks actively participating in the Eurodollar market. This random polling is done twice in the last day of trading—once at a randomly selected time during the last 90 minutes of trading, and once at the close of trading. In each sample, the 2 highest and 2 lowest quotes are deleted before the overall average of 16 bank quotes is calculated.

As you can see from Exhibit 4-27, the futures contract spans a 10yr horizon, with trading volumes and open interest concentrated in the first 5 years. From a series of strips, you can easily compute the equivalent compounded yields and therefore a spot and forward yield curve projected several years into the future. The compounded yields shown in the exhibit are computed in a simplified way, assuming that all quarters have the same length of 91.25 days.

$$Y = (1 + \text{rate} \times 91.25/360)^4$$

4-7   U.S. T-bill Futures and Cash-Futures Arbitrage

The 3M T-bill future was introduced by the IMM in January 1976 and was the first future on short-term interest rates. After the introduction of the 90-day Eurodollar contract, it gradually lost importance, as you can see at a glance by comparing Exhibit 4-28 to Exhibit 4-27. There are two good reasons to discuss this contract in spite of its limited practical relevance.

1. It provides a good example of how the IMM tried to implement a good contract design to maximize liquidity and transparency. Contract design is crucial for the successful introduction of a new future.

Exhibit 4-27 3M Eurodollar Futures, 7 April 1998

Last trading day	High	Low	Settle	Rate	Y	Open int.
Mon-13-Apr-98	94.35	94.33	94.33	5.67%	5.87%	29,402
Mon-18-May-98	94.36	94.34	94.35	5.65%	5.85%	9,312
Mon-15-Jun-98	94.36	94.35	94.36	5.64%	5.84%	485,425
Mon-14-Sep-98	94.40	94.37	94.38	5.62%	5.82%	409,131
Mon-14-Dec-98	94.33	94.31	94.32	5.68%	5.88%	322,680
Mon-15-Mar-99	94.35	94.33	94.33	5.67%	5.87%	273,140
Mon-14-Jun-99	94.31	94.28	94.29	5.71%	5.92%	207,921
Mon-13-Sep-99	94.28	94.25	94.26	5.74%	5.95%	158,151
Mon-13-Dec-99	94.17	94.13	94.14	5.86%	6.08%	152,654
Mon-13-Mar-00	94.22	94.19	94.20	5.80%	6.01%	113,330
Mon-19-Jun-00	94.20	94.16	94.17	5.83%	6.04%	112,692
Mon-18-Sep-00	94.18	94.15	94.15	5.85%	6.06%	71,052
Mon-18-Dec-00	94.11	94.08	94.08	5.92%	6.14%	61,870
Mon-19-Mar-01	94.13	94.10	94.11	5.89%	6.11%	44,775
Mon-18-Jun-01	94.11	94.08	94.09	5.91%	6.13%	53,367
Mon-17-Sep-01	94.10	94.07	94.07	5.93%	6.15%	39,878
Mon-17-Dec-01	94.03	94.00	94.00	6.00%	6.22%	40,693
Mon-18-Mar-02	94.06	94.03	94.03	5.97%	6.19%	43,492
Mon-17-Jun-02	94.03	94.00	94.00	6.00%	6.22%	38,534
Mon-16-Sep-02	94.01	93.98	93.98	6.02%	6.24%	34,313
Mon-16-Dec-02	93.94	93.90	93.91	6.09%	6.32%	28,206
Mon-17-Sep-07			93.53	6.47%	6.72%	2,591
Mon-17-Dec-07			93.46	6.54%	6.80%	2,027
Mon-17-Mar-08			93.48	6.52%	6.78%	1,615

Source: The *Wall Street Journal*

Exhibit 4-28 3M T-bill Future, 14 November 1996 at 11:00 AM, Chicago time

Last trading day	Last	Y	High	Low	Open Int.	Total Vol.	Prev Close
Wed-04-Dec-96	95.00	5.23%	95.00	94.99%	2,877	570	95.00
Wed-26-Mar-97	94.97	5.27%	94.97	94.95%	2,732	253	94.95
Wed-18-Jun-97			94.88 b		1,530	20	94.86
Wed-10-Sep-97							
Wed-03-Dec-97							

At the time of download, several maturities had not been traded.
The symbol (b) indicates an outstanding bid.
Y is computed assuming the delivery of a 91 days bill

Source: Bloomberg

2. It provides a straightforward and easy example of cash-futures arbitrage, which is an important tool in analyzing futures on long-term notes and bonds. Cash-futures arbitrage is much easier to understand with reference to the T-bill contract, which has only one deliverable security (we shall see in Chapter 11 that most bond futures offer the seller a choice among different *deliverable bonds*, which somewhat complicates the analysis).

Contract Design: Supply of Deliverable Bill

There are 4 delivery months in the year (March, June, September, and December). To increase the supply of the deliverable bill, the first delivery date of each contract is always a date on which an original-maturity 1 yr bill has 13 weeks left to maturity (1 yr bills are issued every 4 weeks, on Thursdays, in order to synchronize with the weekly issues of 3M and 6M bills). The last trading day falls on a Wednesday and the first delivery day is the following Thursday.

Synchronizing delivery with the 4-week issuing cycle of 1 yr bills has the disadvantage of producing irregular time intervals between delivery dates (we have three 12-week and one 16-week interval). The U.S. Treasuries market is one of the most liquid and transparent in the world. In spite of this, the supply of 13-week bills on one particular settlement date is not huge and cannot support the physical delivery of too large a number of contracts. This has sometimes allowed some dealers to put a bear squeeze on T-bill futures. M. Stigum (1990) gives the following account: "It is tempting for a dealer . . . to buy a lot of contracts plus a lot of . . . the supply of the deliverable bills. The game is this: when the contract settles, shorts will be unable to get their hands on the deliverable bills; fails to deliver will occur; and as long as these fails last, the squeezer, who is long unsettled . . . bills, will earn the bill rate on bills he hasn't yet to pay for."

Exhibit 4-29 Flowchart of Relevant T-bill Dates

Thu 27-Jun-96	Thu 26-Sep-96	Thu 26-Dec-96	Thu 27-Mar-97	Thu 26-Jun-97
1-year Deliverable bill issued		3M Term repos available	1st delivery delivery date	Maturity of deliverable bill
Q1	Q2	Q3	Q4	Q5
Future strarts trading	Issue of 6M bill maturing on 1st delivery date	6M deliverable issued	3M deliverable issued	

Contract Design: Pricing and Delivery Options

The index = 100 − discount rate. One tick (0.01% of the price index) corresponds to $25 for mark-to-market and daily settlement purposes. The price value of one basis point of discount rate for a $1 million, 90-day bill equals

$$\$25 \ = \ \$1m \ \times \ 0.01\% \ \frac{90}{360}.$$

Example: If the March contract settlement price moves, in any one day, from 94.95 to 95.02, the sellers (short the contract) will pay the buyers $7 \times \$25 = \$175$ per contract. The contract's discount rate has in fact moved from 5.05% to 4.98%, and the 7 basis points of difference correspond to a $175 price decline for a $1 million, 90-day bill.

For the relatively few contracts that are held to maturity, delivery can take place, at the option of the seller, on any of the 3 business days following the last trading day (Thursday, Friday, or Monday). The deliverable bill will be sold with 91, 90, or 87 days to maturity. The invoice price of the bill will be determined by applying the discount rate implied by the final settlement value of the index for the appropriate number of days. The delivery option entails that the seller will have a small incentive to shift forward the delivery, say, to Monday, when the yield curve is positive. In this way the seller would get the 3M rate for an investment of a few days. However, unless the yield curve is extremely steep, this translates to less than one bp advantage.

Cash-Futures Arbitrage

Cash-futures arbitrage is often explained within the context of a frictionless financial system (no transaction costs and identical borrowing and lending rates). This is a very helpful way of proceeding for a number of purposes, but in this section we shall try to examine arbitrage within a more realistic setting (where T-bill yields are, in fact, lower than borrowing and lending rates). For some of the contracts, the deliverable bill is already available (its supply will of course be increased, on the delivery date,

Exhibit 4-30 Summary of Spot and Forward Yields, 14 November 1996
Path Arbitrage–A, Cash and Carry, Long Bill Short Future

	Y		Disc Rate	Price	Mty	Term
Y(0, 132)	5.24%	6M orig. Mty bill	4.99%	98.1703	Thu-27-Mar	132
Y(0, 223)	5.34%	12M orig. Mty bill	5.05%	96.8718	Thu-26-Jun	223
Y(41, 132)	5.27%	Future	5.03%	98.7285	Thu-26-Jun	91
Y(0, 132)	5.39%	Synthetic bill		98.1194	Thu-27-Mar	132

94.97 = *Quotation of 3M T-bill future, delivery 27 March*

Source: Bloomberg

by the issue of the new 13-week bill). The availability of the deliverable bill allows the theoretical possibility of cash-and-carry arbitrage (see Exhibits 4-29 and 4-30).

Path Arbitrage A. Let us assume to be in Q3, and precisely on 14 November. The deliverable bill is already available and so is the 6M bill maturing on the first delivery date. The availability of the two bills and of the future defines two spot yields Y(0, 132) for the time horizon ending on the delivery date. The first yield can be obtained by investing in the 132-day bill. The second possibility consists of buying the longer-dated deliverable bill and selling a future to lock in the sale price (cash-and-carry), thereby producing a *synthetic bill* maturing in 132 days and yielding the implied repo rate.

We can see that the cash-and-carry strategy is marginally more profitable than the outright purchase of the 6M bill maturing on the delivery date (5.39% vs. 5.24%). The 15 bp yield spread, corresponding to just over 5 bp over 132 days, is justified, however, by the fact that the cash-and-carry synthetic bill is less liquid than the equivalent bill.

However, if the yield spread between the cash-and-carry synthetic bill and the maturing bill becomes too high, this will induce path arbitrage, thereby setting an upper bound (albeit not a precisely quantifiable one) on the value of the possible yield spread.

Path Arbitrage B. If the implied repo rate is lower than the yield on the 132-day bill, then you can create a synthetic bill maturing on 26 June 1997 by buying both the 132-day bill and the future (long bill + long future). Liquidity considerations imply that the synthetic bill will probably need a yield spread over the corresponding bill to trigger path arbitrage. This arbitrage is quantified in Exhibit 4-31, where the future index is assumed to be 94.40 and the locked-in rate on the synthetic bill is 5.50%, which is higher than that on the 223-day bill.

Full arbitrage will be profitable if the cash-and-carry yield is higher than the relevant term repo rate. In the case of full arbitrage, liquidity considerations play a much smaller role than in path arbitrage. You could buy the deliverable bill, repo-finance the purchase, short the future, and forget about your arbitrage structure until maturity. The only snag with this neat little arbitrage is that it is rarely if ever available for simple products such as bills.

Exhibit 4-31 Summary of Spot and Forward Yields, 14 November 1996
Path Arbitrage-B, Long Bill and Long Future

	Y		Disc Rate	Price	Mty	Term
Y(0, 132)	5.24%	6M orig. Mty bill	4.99%	98.1703	Thu-27-Mar	132
Y(0, 223)	5.34%	12M orig. Mty bill	5.05%	96.8718	Thu-26-Jun	223
Y(41, 132)	5.89%	Future	5.60%	98.5844	Thu-26-Jun	91
Y(0, 223)	5.50%	Synthetic bill		96.7807	Thu-26-Jun	223

94.40 = *Quotation of 3M T-bill future, delivery 27 March*

Source: Bloomberg

Full Reverse Cash-and-Carry Arbitrage. When the repo rate (the bid rate, 5.30% as of 14 November 1996, if you are not a dealer) is higher than the implied repo rate, you could

- Do a reverse repo (lend money) on the deliverable bill, thereby earning the repo rate (you should do a term repo maturing on the first delivery date of the future)
- Sell the deliverable bill (short sale) and use the proceeds to finance the reverse repo
- Buy the future to lock in the forward repurchase price of the deliverable bill (so that you do not run price risk when you have to cover your short sale to close the reverse repo)

Again, this sounds like a neat arbitrage. The problem is that it would be difficult to find a counterparty ready to pay a term repo rate that would make it profitable (if they wanted to finance the deliverable bill until the first delivery rate, they could sell it and buy the future themselves).

4-8 MATHEMATICAL APPENDIX

Bootstrap Method with Exponential Yields

$C(1)$ = interest payment (coupon) on the 1-yr deposit

$C(2)$ = yearly interest payments (coupons) on the 2-yr deposit

$R(0, 1)$ = 1 yr spot compounded yield

$R(0, 2)$ = 2 yr spot compounded yield (to be computed)

$\$1$ = amount of deposit

$R(0, 1) = \ln[1 + C(1)]$

$1 = C \cdot \exp[- R(0, 1)] + (1 + C) \cdot \exp[- 2 \cdot R(0, 2)]$

$$\exp[-2 \cdot R(0, 2)] = \frac{1 - C \cdot \exp[-R(0, 1)]}{(1 + C)}.$$

Take the logs of both sides of the equation to get:

Exhibit 4-32 Spot and Forward Exponential Yields for 2-yr Deposits

	USD	JPY	DEM	GBP	CHF
CPN (1)	0.058615	0.006970	0.032951	0.065269	0.020278
CPN (2)	0.062101	0.010139	0.041189	0.070339	0.030417
R (0, 1)	5.6961%	0.6946%	3.2420%	6.3227%	2.0075%
R (0, 2)	6.0351%	1.0104%	4.0528%	6.8142%	3.0114%
R (1, 2)	6.3741%	1.3261%	4.8636%	7.3057%	4.0154%

$$R(0, 2) = -\frac{1}{2} \cdot \ln\left[\frac{1 - C \cdot \exp[-R(0, 1)]}{(1 + C)}\right].$$

Having determined $R(0, 2)$ you can extend the process with forward induction to compute $R(0, 3)$, and so on (see Exhibit 4.32).

The Linear Equations Approach to the Boostrap Method

Spot rates can also be computed using a system of linear equations, which is a lot more practical when we need to compute several spot rates. To use a linear system we can use the variable $B(0, T)$ to indicate the present value of $1 discounted for T years at the relevant spot rate.

$$B(0, T) = [1 + Y(0, T)]^T = \exp[-T \cdot R(0, T)]$$

We can now write our linear system in terms of the new variable. With reference to the $ rates we have the following linear system (the rows of the left matrix represent the cash flows for the 1,2, . . . ,5-year deposits).

105.86	0	0	0	0		$B(0, 1)$		100
6.21	106.21	0	0	0		$B(0, 2)$		100
6.40	6.40	106.40	0	0	*	$B(0, 3)$	=	100
6.53	6.53	6.53	106.53	0		$B(0, 4)$		100
6.65	6.65	6.65	6.65	106.65		$B(0, 5)$		100

The cash-flow matrix is nonsingular (the determinant is nonzero). We can therefore compute the inverse and solve the system.

								$B(0, T)$
0.0094	0	0	0	0		100		0.945
-0.0006	0.0094	0	0	0		100		0.886
-0.0005	-0.0006	0.0094	0	0	*	100	=	0.830
-0.0005	-0.0005	-0.0006	0.0094	0		100		0.776
-0.0005	-0.0005	-0.0006	-0.0006	0.0094		100		0.723

Once you have determined the values of $B(0, T)$, it is easy to compute the corresponding values of Y and R.

T	B(0, T)	Y(0, T)	R(0, T)
1	0.945	5.86%	5.70%
2	0.886	6.22%	6.04%
3	0.830	6.42%	6.22%
4	0.776	6.56%	6.35%
5	0.723	6.69%	6.48%

Foreign Exchange Transactions

Let us briefly recall that the FX market is by far the world's largest financial market in terms of $ volume of transactions. It is a mature market; there seems, however, to be room for innovation and rapid growth. In the last decade it has received a new boost by the international diversification of managed portfolios (pensions, mutual funds, corporations, etc.), which brought to the forefront the whole new area of optimal hedging of foreign currency–denominated assets, see Solnik (2000).

With the exception of exchange-traded futures and options, FX is an over-the-counter (OTC) market, dominated by large international banks and investment banks that act as market makers, quoting bid-ask prices. The time difference between Tokyo, London, and New York means that the market is open 24 hours a day. As in most OTC markets, interdealer brokers (IDBs) are quite active and account for a significant amount of total transactions. The IDBs avail themselves of extensive telecommunications networks to keep in real-time contact with the dealers. Given the potentially large credit exposure for foreign exchange products, IDBs must act on a name give-up basis.

The services of IDBs are now finding some level of competition from data-feed providers such as Reuters (with its Dealing 2000-2 automatic trading service). This competition is made easier by the fact that IDBs have to act on a name give-up basis and therefore cannot provide the anonymity that is one of their strong competitive advantages in the securities markets.

In the wholesale FX market, payments and delivery are made by shifting sight deposits with banks. Settlement among banks operating in different countries relies heavily on the worldwide SWIFT network (Society for Worldwide Interbank Financial Telecommunications). The absence of a centralized depository institution guaranteeing payment against delivery implies a certain credit risk in the settlement of FX transactions, the so-called *Herstatt risk,* that we shall briefly examine in Section 5-6.

5-1 SPOT TRANSACTIONS, CROSS RATES, AND ARBITRAGE-FREE PARITIES

In the wholesale FX market, spot transactions usually settle $T + 2$, in sync with the settlement of Eurodeposits. Bid-ask prices quoted by market makers and quotations that appear in the financial press all refer to the regular ($T + 2$) settlement. Spot transactions can, exceptionally, settle after more than 2 business days (up to $T + 7$). However, for nonregular settlement, rates are determined in the same way as for outright forwards.

When the $ is one of the two currencies (spot quotations against the $), market convention dictates that the bid be the price at which the dealer will buy $, while the ask is the price at which he is prepared to sell. The exceptions to this convention, as we saw in Chapter 1, is the £. Quotations can be expressed in two ways:

1. Units of foreign currency per unit of domestic currency, known as *European* or *inverse quotation*
2. Units of domestic currency per unit of foreign currency, known as *American* or *direct quotation* (this is the standard quotation for FX futures and options against the $).

$$\frac{DEM}{\$} = 1.8138 \Rightarrow \frac{DEM1.8138}{\$1} \quad \text{European or inverse quotation (midpoint)}$$

$$\frac{\$}{DEM} = 0.5513 \Rightarrow \frac{\$0.5513}{DEM1} \quad \text{American or direct quotation (midpoint)}$$

FX market practitioners assume a good familiarity with the current levels of FX rates. This implies that they can be rather casual about the way quotations are presented.

Example: If you sell $1 for DEM 1.8135 to a dealer (1.8135 = bid, the price at which the dealer is prepared to buy dollars), it is clear that the quotation should be indicated as DEM/$ = 1.8135. Just compute how many DEM you would get by selling $1 million:

$$\frac{DEM1.8135}{\$1} \cdot \$1,000,000 = DEM1,813,500$$

In spite of this, it is not uncommon to see the above quotation indicated as $/DEM = 1.8135, assuming that the professionals know how to interpret it.

Bid-ask spreads reflect both the liquidity of the market for any given currency and the volatility of its FX spot rates against the $ and therefore the risk that the market maker is taking when quoting firm two-way prices. The bid-ask spreads shown in Exhibit 5-1 represent the cost of a roundturn, as can be easily verified with the following example:

$$DEM\ 1,000,000 \times \underbrace{\frac{1}{1.8140}}_{\text{OFFER}} \Rightarrow \$551,267.9 \times \underbrace{1.8135}_{\text{BID}} \Rightarrow DEM\ 999,724.4$$

Cost of roundturn = $DEM\ 275.6 = 0.0276\%$

Exhibit 5-1 Spot Rates Against the $

	Mid-Point	Bid	Offer	Spread	Pips bid	Pips ask
CND	1.4349	1.4346	1.4351	0.0348%	346	351
FRF	6.0805	6.0790	6.0820	0.0493%	790	820
DEM	1.8138	1.8135	1.8140	0.0276%	135	140
ITL	1,792.1500	1,792.0000	1,792.3000	0.0167%	200	230
JPY	124.3450	124.3000	124.3900	0.0724%	300	390
CHF	1.4627	1.4622	1.4632	0.0684%	622	632
GBP	1.6333	1.6328	1.6338	0.0612%	328	338

Source: Financial Times, Tuesday, 10 February 1998

- We have already seen that the £ (GBP) is always quoted in terms of units of foreign currency per £. The preceding quotations mean that the dealer sells £1 for $1.6338 and buys £1 for $1.6328.
- *Pips,* that is, basis points in FX market parlance, are another example of market conventions that are way past their useful shelf life. Bid and ask are expressed in pips, assuming that market participants know how they apply. A quotation of 135–140 pips for the DEM assumes that you know the current level of quotations, such as 1.8000, to which you add the bid or ask pips. This endearing old tradition is complicated by the fact that one pip equals 10 basis points for the JPY and 100 basis points for the ITL.

  Foreign exchange is an OTC market where there are no fixed commissions or fixed bid-ask spreads. The spreads shown in Exhibit 5-1 (a few basis points) are for sizable commercial transactions with bank customers (normally in the $1–$10 million range).
- Small occasional transactions can cost a lot more in terms of percentage spreads.
- Very sizable transactions (which expose the market maker to a higher risk, given the time it could take to unwind the position, possibly with a series of trades) may take place at negotiated prices that can differ slightly from the broadcasted bid-ask quotations.

Cross Rates and Arbitrage-free Parities

Arbitrage-free pricing implies that the FX rates between two currencies must be tightly linked to their respective rates against the $ (see Exhibit 5-2). In fact, rates quoted by

Exhibit 5-2 Triangular Arbitrage and Spot Cross Rates (Mid-Rates)

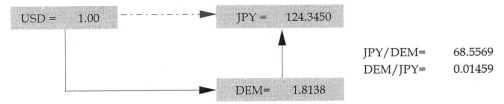

Exhibit 5-3 Cross-Rate Full Arbitrage without Transaction Costs

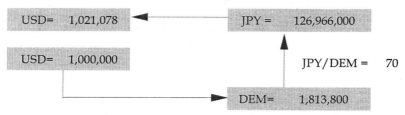

FX dealers are mostly determined with reference to $ rates, and a number of FX transactions take place using the $ as a *vehicle currency* (that is, the transaction takes place in two simultaneous steps: ccy A → $ → ccy B). In a frictionless world (bid = ask; transaction costs = 0), even a small cross-rate misalignment would allow dealers to set up a full arbitrage (see Exhibit 5-3). In real life, such arbitrage opportunities are rare and usually exploited by the large FX dealers. Path arbitrage opportunities are more frequent (in our example, buying JPY via the DEM, if this allows a better price). FX rates are often shown in a matrix format where

- The columns represent the European or inverse quotations against the $, ¥, DEM, £ and so on (to improve the readability we use 100 JPY and 1,000 ITL).
- The rows represent the American or direct quotations against the $, JPY, DEM, GBP, and so on.

You will notice that all the rates in the matrix can be derived, via arbitrage-free cross rates, using either the first column or the first row (see Exhibit 5-4). For example,

$$\frac{DEM}{FRF} = \frac{DEM}{\$} \cdot \frac{\$}{FRF} \Rightarrow 0.2983 = 1.8138 \times \frac{1}{6.0805}.$$

Vehicle Currency and Direct Quotations

When an FX transaction takes place via a *vehicle currency* (usually the dollar), total transaction costs are obviously higher, as you can see in the JPY → $ → DEM roundturn

Exhibit 5-4 Spot Cross-Midrates

	USD	100 JPY	DEM	GBP	CHF	FRF	1000 ITL	CND
USD		0.8042	0.5513	1.6333	0.6837	0.1645	0.5580	0.6969
JPY	124.3450		68.5550	203.0927	85.0106	20.4498	69.3831	86.6576
DEM	1.8138	1.4587		2.9625	1.2400	0.2983	1.0121	1.2641
GBP	0.6123	0.4924	0.3376		0.4186	0.1007	0.3416	0.4267
CHF	1.4627	1.1763	0.8064	2.3890		0.2406	0.8162	1.0194
FRF	6.0805	4.8900	3.3524	9.9313	4.1570		3.3929	4.2376
ITL	1,792.15	1,441.27	988.06	2,927.12	1,225.23	294.74		1,248.97
CND	1.4349	1.1540	0.7911	2.3436	0.9810	0.2360	0.8007	

Source: Financial Times, Tuesday, 10 February 1998

Exhibit 5-5 Bid-Ask Prices on ¥-DEM Transaction Via $

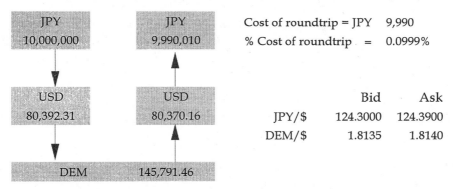

	Bid	Ask
JPY/$	124.3000	124.3900
DEM/$	1.8135	1.8140

shown in Exhibit 5-5. The transit via $ (vehicle currency), with double transaction costs, can be avoided for many pairs of actively traded currencies. When there is a strong customer demand for a currency pair, such as the JPY/DEM, market makers will compete for business by quoting more favorable direct bid-ask prices.

5-2 FORWARD TRANSACTIONS, COVERED INTEREST PARITY, AND BASIS RISK

A forward FX transaction (also known as an *outright forward*) is a commitment to buy or sell a precisely determined amount of currency

- At a predetermined future value date (settlement date). The term of the transaction (say, 3 months) is the time span between the $T + 2$ settlement date of a spot transaction and the settlement date of the forward.
- At a specified *contract rate* fixed at trade date.

Forward transactions were developed in response to the obvious need to cover FX risk in international trade. Locking in future exchange rates by means of forward purchases or sales of foreign currency has long been used by nonfinancial corporations. Like any other hedging instrument, a forward FX transaction can be used to create a speculative position. To understand whether the forward is being used as a hedge or as a speculative device, one must analyze the entire currency balance of the firm (see Section 5-5).

Forward prices usually differ from spot prices (see Exhibit 5-6). If the forward value of a currency is higher than the spot value, then the currency is said to be trading at a forward premium. If the forward is lower than the spot, then the currency is trading at a forward discount. The spot-forward differential is a function of term and of the differential in Euromarket interest rates for the two currencies (see *Covered interest parity*).

Bid-Ask Forward Prices

Market makers quote regularly outright forward rates for periods of up to 1 year. The most common maturities are 1, 3, and 6 months. Broken dates (maturities that contain

Exhibit 5-6 Specularity of FX Transactions, 12 December 1996

	Spot rate	3-month fwrd	% Change	Quotation
JPY at a premium	0.8871	0.8989	1.33%	$ / 100 JPY
USD at a discount	112.7250	111.245	-1.31%	JPY/USD
ITL at a discount	0.65983953	0.65526	-0.69%	$ / 1,000 ITL
USD at a premium	1,515.52	1,526.12	0.70%	ITL/USD

Forward sale of ¥ against $	=	Fwrd purchase of $ against ¥
¥ at a premium against the $	=	$ at a discount against the ¥

a fraction of a month, such as 46 days) are also available. For the most actively traded currencies, outright forwards are quoted for up to 5 years. Exhibit 5-7 is based on the DEM/$, which is the most actively traded currency pair reported in the BIS (Bank for International Settlements) survey. For terms of over 1 year, the market becomes less liquid and the bid-ask spread increases very rapidly.

Forward prices are usually quoted as adjustment values (again, the ubiquitous pips) to the spot bid-ask prices. Pips are negative when the currency trades at a forward premium and positive when the currency trades at a forward discount. This way of quoting was developed before the widespread availability of computing power, because it allowed a series of quotes not to change when only the spot rate changed. Two differentials are needed because the bid-ask spread on forwards is higher than that for spot trades. The ask adjustment is therefore always greater than the bid adjustment (in the case of negative adjustments, this means that the absolute value of the ask adjustment is smaller).

Closeout and Mark to Market of an FX Forward

A forward transaction represents a firm commitment and cannot be canceled. On the other hand, it can be closed out at any time by an inverse transaction with the same value date. When a transaction is closed out, its gain or loss becomes fixed. It can happen that the inverse transaction is done with a bank different from the one that handled the initial forward. In this case the position is fully covered (with a profit or loss lock-in) but is not closed out (there will in fact be two offsetting forwards with two different banks).

Example: In February 1996 a U.S. corporation entered into a 6M forward purchase of ¥ 1 billion at $ 0.99601 for 100 ¥. In August it closes the position by selling ¥ 1 billion (for the same value date of the first forward). The fortunate transaction will lock in the following profit:

$10,869,500	to be received against the sale of ¥ 1 billion
$9,960,100	to be paid for the purchase of ¥ 1 billion
$909,400	locked-in profit

Covered Interest Parity

In the open market there is an arbitrage-free pricing relationship (known as *covered interest parity*) between the level of interest rates (usually Eurodeposits rates) and that

Exhibit 5-7 DEM/$ Spot and Forward European Quotations, 12 December 1996

	Bid pips	Ask pips	Bid	Ask	Spread	Mid point
SPOT	...	...	1.5539	1.5546	0.0450%	1.5543
SN	-0.96	-0.93	1.5538	1.5545	0.0452%	1.5542
1W	-8.60	-8.50	1.5530	1.5538	0.0457%	1.5534
2W	-14.40	-14.20	1.5525	1.5532	0.0464%	1.5528
3W	-20.10	-19.90	1.5519	1.5526	0.0464%	1.5523
1M	-32.60	-32.45	1.5506	1.5514	0.0461%	1.5510
2M	-59.50	-59.30	1.5480	1.5487	0.0465%	1.5483
3M	-87.00	-86.90	1.5452	1.5459	0.0459%	1.5456
4M	117.00	-118.00	1.5656	1.5428	-1.4563%	1.5542
5M	-146.70	-147.00	1.5392	1.5399	0.0435%	1.5396
6M	-180.00	-179.00	1.5359	1.5367	0.0521%	1.5363
7M	-211.10	-210.10	1.5328	1.5336	0.0522%	1.5332
8M	-243.80	-242.00	1.5295	1.5304	0.0575%	1.5300
9M	-276.50	-275.00	1.5263	1.5271	0.0557%	1.5267
10M	-309.00	-307.00	1.5230	1.5239	0.0591%	1.5235
11M	-339.20	-337.20	1.5200	1.5209	0.0592%	1.5204
1Y	-369.00	-367.00	1.5170	1.5179	0.0593%	1.5175
2Y	-685.00	-665.00	1.4854	1.4881	0.1818%	1.4868
3Y	-875.00	-835.00	1.4664	1.4711	0.3205%	1.4688
4Y	-890.00	-850.00	1.4649	1.4696	0.3208%	1.4673
5Y	-920.00	-820.00	1.4619	1.4726	0.7319%	1.4673

SN = spot next, a transaction that settles one day later than a spot transaction (therefore on T+3), in other words this is a 1-day forward.

Source: REUTERS

of forward FX rates. Let us take a close look at Exhibit 5-8, which is built assuming a frictionless economy (no transaction costs; bid = ask for both foreign exchange and interest rates).

To rule out the possibility of arbitrage, it is clear that the 90-day forward rate must be such that the following two strategies lead to the same payoff:

- Change $ into DEM and invest at iDEM for 90 days.
- Invest $ at i$ for 90 days and buy DEM 90 days forward.

When forward rates mispricing exceeds transaction costs, the disequilibrium is very short-lived because market makers will exploit it to lock in a riskless arbitrage profit. This means that published quotations are always transaction-costs close. In real life, however, relatively small mispricing can lead to path arbitrage (e.g., a U.S. firm that needs DEM 3 months forward will choose the strategy that will guarantee the lowest cost). We should remember that the feasibility of path arbitrage depends also on the situation of the firm that wants to implement it. Path arbitrage would quite likely be

Exhibit 5-8 Covered Interest Parity Flowchart, $T = 0.25$

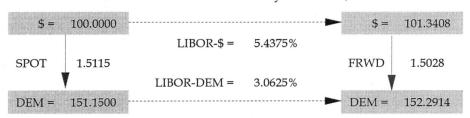

unprofitable if the U.S. firm had to borrow the $ (at the ask rate + spread) and invest the DEM at the bid rate. The very same path arbitrage would be a lot more likely if the U.S. firm owned $ deposits (at the bid rate) and had DEM liabilities (at the ask rate + spread). Some financial publications (such as the *Financial Times*) compute annualized rates of change of FX rates. These annualized rates of change are nearly equal to the difference in the relevant Eurodeposits rates. The effect of a given difference in annualized interest rates will obviously increase as a function of term to maturity.

Box 5-1   Arbitrage-free DEM/$ Forward FX Rate

$$100\$ \cdot s \cdot (1 + iDEM \cdot T) = 100\$ \cdot (1 + i\$ \cdot T) \cdot f$$

$$f = s \cdot \frac{1 + iDEM \cdot T}{1 + i\$ \cdot T}$$

s = spot $(DEM/\$)$, f = forward $(DEM/\$)$.

The rate of change of forward with reference to spot, expressed as simple interest is

$$\frac{f - s}{s} = \frac{1 + iDEM \cdot T}{1 + i\$ \cdot T} - 1 = \frac{T \cdot (iDEM - i\$)}{1 + i\$ \cdot T}$$

For short maturities and relatively low rates, $(1 + i\$ \cdot T) \cong 1$, and therefore we can use the approximation

$$(f - s)/s = T \cdot (iDEM - i\$).$$

If we annualize the rate of change of forward with relative to spot, we therefore obtain

$$(f - s)/s = (iDEM - i\$)$$

Covered interest parity can be neatly expressed using log yields.

$$s \cdot \exp(T \cdot R_{DEM}) = f \cdot \exp(T \cdot R_\$)$$

$$f = s \cdot \exp[T \cdot (R_{DEM} - R_\$)]$$

Therefore, the annualized log rate of change of the forward relative to the spot is simply the difference of Euromarket rates, expressed as log yields.

$$R_{DEM} - R_\$$$

Exhibit 5-9 Forward FX Cross Rates, 1-year Forward

	USD	100 JPY	DEM	GBP	CHF	FRF	1000 ITL	CND
USD		0.8871	0.6546	1.6727	0.7729	0.1929	0.6598	0.7448
JPY	112.73		73.79	188.56	87.13	21.75	74.38	83.95
DEM	1.5276	1.3552		2.5552	1.1807	0.2947	1.0080	1.1377
GBP	0.5978	0.5303	0.3914		0.4621	0.1153	0.3945	0.4452
CHF	1.2938	1.1477	0.8469	2.1641		0.2496	0.8537	0.9636
FRF	5.1828	4.5977	3.3928	8.6693	4.0059		3.4198	3.8600
ITL	1516	1344	992	2535	1171	292		1129
CND	1.3427	1.1911	0.8790	2.2459	1.0378	0.2591	0.8860	

Exhibit 5-10 Covered Interest Pricing over Several Forward FX Rates

Term	i$	iDEM	DEM forward	iJPY	JPY forward
SPOT	...	...	1.55425	...	113.8000
3M	5.4375%	3.0625%	1.54505	0.5156%	112.4034
6M	5.5313%	3.0625%	1.53538	0.5781%	111.0278
9M	5.6250%	3.1250%	1.52599	0.6094%	109.6487
1Y	5.7500%	3.1875%	1.51609	0.6719%	108.2636

The cross-rate parities that we have examined in Section 5-1 must obviously hold for forward FX rates, which therefore can be represented in the same matrix format that we use for spot quotations; see Exhibit 5-9. Covered interest parities hold, transaction-costs close, over all the possible maturities, as shown in Exhibit 5-10. To sum up, you can think of FX forwards as a series of matrices of cross-rates, at different points in the future, where each matrix is derived from the spot matrix via the relevant array (vector) of spot interest rates; see Exhibit 5-11.

Basis Risk in FX Forwards

In a forward FX contract, the basis (that is, the difference between spot and forward price) is a function of the interest differential between the two currencies involved ($ and DEM in our example). This entails that when you use a forward or a future to hedge a foreign currency position, you must try to align the maturity of the hedge to the maturity of the asset or liability that you are hedging. If the two maturities are not

Exhibit 5-11 Forward FX Rates

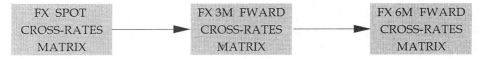

Exhibit 5-12 Basis Risk for a DEM 10 million Liability, Mty = 1-yr

		Time-0 (spot = 0.66)	1M later (spot = 0.70)	Δ
Case A	Liability	-$6,706,449	-$7,103,423	-$396,974
	1M Forward	$0	$391,194	$391,194
	Hedged position			*-$5,780*
Case B	Liability	-$6,706,449	-$7,168,837	-$462,388
	1M Forward	$0	$391,194	$391,194
	Hedged position			*-$71,194*

DEM due in 1 year =	10,000,000	10,000,000
$/DEM spot =	0.66	0.7
$R =	5.60%	5.60%
DEMR =	4.00%	3.00%
$/DEM, 1yr fwrd =	0.670645	...
$/DEM, 1M fwrd =	0.660881	...

In case B, the yield on the DEM decreases from 4% to 3% (exponential yield)

aligned, you run a basis risk that could result in a gain or a loss when the interest rate differential between the two currencies widens or contracts.

Example. US.CORP has borrowed DEM 10,000,000 for 1 year and decides to hedge this FX liability with a 1M forward, with the intention of rolling over the forward from month to month. To simplify the notation, we shall use log yields and assume that the log yields are the same for 1M and for 1 yr. We shall also keep things simple by disregarding the effect of discounting on the value of forwards. This lack of discounting accounts for the $5,780 mis-hedge (see Exhibit 5-12).

FX Forwards and Currency Speculation

If a corporation or an asset manager wants to speculate (take a view) on the FX market, a forward transaction can offer a practical alternative to the cash market. If a U.S. investor wants to bet on the ¥ appreciating against the $, she can buy the ¥ forward and

- Keep the forward to maturity and then sell the ¥ at a gain (if the ¥ appreciates) or at a loss if the currency bet goes bad
- Alternatively, close the forward with an opposite transaction (selling forward the ¥ with the same maturity of the forward purchase), locking in the profit or gain to that point. The lock-in is usually enacted when (a) the market bet has proven successful and the speculator wants to take the profit, or (b) when the market moves against the speculator, who implements a stop-loss transaction.

The cash market alternatives to implement the same strategy (betting on the appreciation of the ¥) could prove to be more complex and costly, especially for a nonbank:

- Borrow $ or disinvest $-denominated assets
- Buy the ¥ spot, using the $
- Invest the ¥ in some liquid asset to allow a prompt disinvestment
- Sell the ¥-denominated asset
- Buy the $ spot against the ¥.

To implement the preceding sequence, a nonbank has to have an efficient treasury department and a good credit rating to obtain a favorable borrowing rate.

5-3 FOREIGN EXCHANGE (FX) SWAPS

An FX swap is the simultaneous spot purchase and forward sale of foreign currency. The largest share of FX swaps is by far represented by interbank transactions. The structure of an FX swap is quite similar to that of a repo. The spot purchase and forward sale of foreign currency is in fact a spot sale and a forward repurchase of your domestic currency. To get a good understanding of FX swaps analytics, consider the case of a U.S. Corporation that needs to borrow DEM, over a defined time horizon, and wants to avoid the FX risk associated with an open short position. The risk problem is easily solved with an FX forward, for the borrowed amount plus interest.

Example: Borrowing DEM and hedging FX risk (12 December 1996). US.CORP borrows DEM 10 million, for 6M, at DEM-LIBOR + 25 bp, and covers its foreign exchange risk by buying forward DEM 10,170,944. As a result, the DEM current liability is matched by a forward asset.

$$DEM = 10,176,944 = 10,000,000 \times \left(1 + \frac{182}{360} \times 3.5\%\right)$$

$ 6M LIBOR = 5.5625%   DEM/$ spot bid = 1.5539
DEM 6M LIBOR = 3.25%   DEM/$ fwrd bid = 1.5367

The DEM bid rate defines the $ value of the borrowed currency, that is, what US.CORP would have paid to buy the DEM spot. The 6M forward bid rate tells you the $ amount that you will need to repay the DEM-denominated loan.

$$DEM\ 10,000,000 \cdot \frac{1}{1.5539} = \$6,435,421$$

$$DEM\ 10,176,944 \cdot \frac{1}{1.5367} = \$6,622,596$$

$$\left(\frac{\$6,622,596}{\$6,435,421} - 1\right) \times \frac{360}{182} = 5.753\%$$

Not surprisingly, the USD rate is nearly equal to $ LIBOR + 25 bp. DEM LIBOR is substantially lower than the corresponding $ rate, but this difference is reflected in the forward premium of the DEM against the dollar.

There are many possible reasons for a financial or nonfinancial corporation to borrow foreign currency while hedging the FX risk. A few instances are:

- An industrial corporation that must pay foreign purchases and knows that within a certain time it will receive foreign currency against foreign sales
- A bank that is extending a foreign currency term loan to a customer (e.g., a DEM 10 million, 6M loan)

- An asset manager or a securities dealer that wants to buy foreign securities without running the associated foreign-exchange risk

FX Swaps as an Alternative to Borrowing and Hedging

Exactly like a repo, a swap is a form of secured borrowing (of currency). If you are a U.S. corporation and you swap into 6M DEM, you gain the use of the DEM for the 6 months, while the FX dealer runs a credit risk (on the second, forward leg of the swap), which is much lower than the credit exposure it would have incurred had it lent you the DEM as a straight 6M loan.

Whether you choose to borrow or to do an FX swap will of course depend on which is the less expensive alternative (some institutional investors are also constrained in their ability to borrow and therefore must go the swap route).

This possibility of decoupling the availability of a given currency from the necessity of borrowing in the same currency is the main attraction of swaps. The cost advantage of this decoupling (that will be further examined in Part 2) bears a strong resemblance to the theory of comparative advantage in international trade (first proposed in 1817 by Davide Ricardo, a pro–free trade British economist and one of the universally recognized founding fathers of economics. Old ideas can take surprisingly new shapes).

The comparison of FX swaps and borrowing is, in essence, quite simple. To keep it that way, Exhibit 5-13 has been constructed doing away with bid/ask spreads and assuming that the DEM/$ forward rate is exactly equal to that implied by the covered interest-parity equation. Furthermore, interest rates have been rounded to realistic but easy to visualize numbers. To determine whether the swap (synthetic borrowing) compares favorably with outright borrowing, we must go through the following steps.

Exhibit 5-13 Flow Chart of a FX Swap Transaction, T = 6M

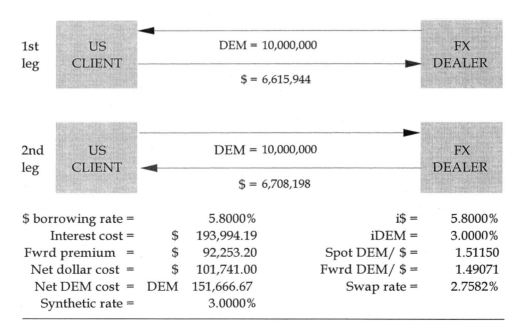

| 1st leg | US CLIENT | DEM = 10,000,000 $ = 6,615,944 | FX DEALER |

| 2nd leg | US CLIENT | DEM = 10,000,000 $ = 6,708,198 | FX DEALER |

$ borrowing rate =		5.8000%	i$ =	5.8000%
Interest cost =	$	193,994.19	iDEM =	3.0000%
Fwrd premium =	$	92,253.20	Spot DEM/ $ =	1.51150
Net dollar cost =	$	101,741.00	Fwrd DEM/ $ =	1.49071
Net DEM cost =	DEM	151,666.67	Swap rate =	2.7582%
Synthetic rate =		3.0000%		

Exhibit 5-14 FX Swap Rate, Portability of Spreads

$ LIBOR =		5.8000%	Synthetic rate =	3.4931%
$ spread=		0.5000%	iDEM =	3.0000%
$ borrowing rate =		6.3000%	Spot DEM/ $ =	1.51150
Interest cost =	$	210,717.83	Fwrd DEM/ $ =	1.49071
Fwrd premium =	$	92,253.20	Swap rate =	2.7582%
Net dollar cost =	$	118,464.63		
Net DEM cost =	DEM	176,596.82		

- Determine the cost of borrowing the amount of $ that you need to buy the DEM 10 million (the exhibit assumes that you pay no spread over the dollar rate). If you do not need to borrow the dollars, you should consider the cost represented by forgone interest on, say, a term bank deposit.
- Subtract from the preceding dollar cost the forward premium that you will get when you sell back the DEM and close the swap. The net cost can be translated in an annualized $ rate, which is equal to the borrowing rate minus the swap rate (the forward premium, expressed as an annualized money market yield, is commonly indicated as the FX swap rate).
- Translate the net dollar cost into DEM by using the forward DEM/$ rate, thereby determining the rate of interest on the synthetic DEM borrowing.
- Compare the synthetic DEM borrowing rate to the outright borrowing rate on DEM. Not surprisingly, the synthetic DEM rate is perfectly identical to the DEM rate on outright borrowing. The higher $ cost is in fact reduced by the forward premium that, in our example, reflects exactly the rates differential.

The interesting thing about FX swaps is that if your $ borrowing costs are above or below the asked rate, this would reflect in a nearly equivalent spread with reference to the synthetic DEM borrowing rate (see Exhibit 5-14, where a 50-bp USD borrowing spread translates in a 49.31-bp borrowing spread in the synthetic DEM borrowing via FX swap). This means that if you have a comparative advantage (lower borrowing spread) in USD you can translate (*port*) this advantage in DEM. This *portability* of spreads via swaps is one of the most interesting developments in modern finance, and we shall examine it again in Part 2. Deciding whether to borrow foreign currency or to do an FX swap depends also on some other factors, such as:

- Bid/ask FX spreads, which are a cost of the swap strategy
- How close forward FX rates are to the theoretical covered interest parity; if the swap rate is a few basis points higher than the theoretical level, this makes the swap more attractive.

5-4 FX FUTURES

FX futures are an interesting product, but in $ terms they are not very important. They represent only a small fraction of the foreign exchange forward market, which is dominated by OTC trading. The $ volume of daily trading and open interest are overshadowed by those of other money-market futures, such as the 90-day IMM Eurodollar that we examined in Chapter 4. FX futures are a very straightforward product. There are no complications in specifying the assets to be delivered (a ¥ is a ¥). The quotation is direct (the future FX rate, not an index). The last trading day is the Monday before the third Wednesday of the delivery month (March, June, September and December). Delivery for outstanding contracts takes place in line with regular FX settlement ($T + 2$).

Hedging and Speculating with FX Futures

Futures can represent an inexpensive way to speculate on currencies, especially for firms or individuals that would find it difficult and expensive to get credit approvals for the borrowing and the FX trading lines that are necessary to set up other kinds of speculative positions. The story goes that in 1971 some Chicago banks refused to enter into a forward contract with Professor Milton Friedman, who wanted to short the £ against the $. As a reaction, Professor Friedman (who had not yet won the Nobel Prize but was already an extremely influential economist) encouraged the officials of the Chicago exchanges to consider trading currency futures; see Levich (1998).

On the other hand, the relatively small dimension of the market makes it unsuitable for large-scale speculative transactions. When George Soros reportedly made $1 billion shorting the £ (before the United Kingdom devalued and abandoned the European Rate Mechanism [ERM] in October 1992), his short position on the £ was in the range of $10 billion; that is, much larger than the open interest in the relevant £ contract; see Soros (1995).

Currency futures, like most futures, are characterized by low transaction costs, due to the high level of standardization and the fixed delivery dates. This makes them ideally suited to set up short-term hedges. As a result, the volume of trading is high when compared to the outstanding amounts, and futures have an average life of a few days. Basis risk is of course present in currency futures as in currency forwards, but it is not very relevant because most of the action takes place in the near future, which obviously does not have much basis risk. However, if you use a short-term future to hedge a long-term position you incur a substantial basis risk.

FX Forwards and Futures, Cash-Flow Comparison

Because of the volatility of the exchange rates (think of the ¥/$), FX futures provide a good example of the possible cash flows difference between a forward contract (settlement at maturity) and a futures contract (daily settlement); see Exhibit 5-15. However, there is no reliable relationship between the price of the future and short-term rate movements; therefore, a number of empirical works have found no significant discrepancy between forward and futures prices for FX contracts; see Levich 1998. Exhibit 5-16 shows the cumulative daily settlement variations for the JPY future. Remember that the contract is for JPY 12.5 million and that the minimum price fluctuation (tick) is 0.0001 points per 100 JPY, equivalent to $12.5 per contract.

5-5 HEDGING FX RISK AND CROSS-CURRENCY HEDGING

Activities in the FX markets are dominated by the issue of risk. A number of transactions are aimed at reducing (hedging) risk, whereas others are of a speculative nature (they increase risk to "bet" on market movements). A company can have a large number of currency positions open at any one time. Furthermore, currency exposure and

Exhibit 5-15 JPY March 1998 Futures Contract, $/100¥

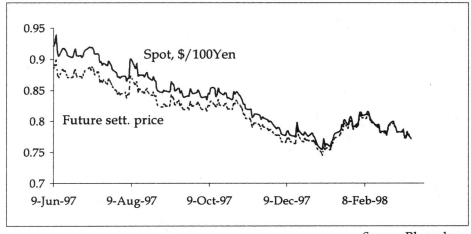

Spot, $/100Yen

Future sett. price

Source: Bloomberg

Exhibit 5-16 JPY March 1998 Futures Contract

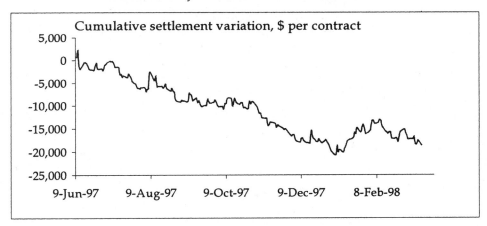

Cumulative settlement variation, $ per contract

hedging can be implemented with a variety of financial derivatives. It is therefore necessary to prepare a currency balance for each foreign currency; see Exhibit 5-17.

FX Risk Profiles

Foreign exchange risk (and the related issue of FX forecasting) have attracted a massive amount of high-level econometric research, which lies outside the scope of this book. It is interesting, however, to examine a few stylized facts that can give a basic understanding of the risks associated with FX positions.

A first relevant point is that currency crises can happen very suddenly, without much of a warning. Exhibit 5-18 shows the case of the South Korean won. Notice that, before the end of 1997 crisis, the won was very stable and displayed a low level of volatility (annualized volatility is computed, over a 21-day rolling window, using the

Exhibit 5-17 Yen Currency Balance for a U.S. Company

Long	Short
Yen bank deposit or any other asset denominated in Yen.	Yen-denominated liabilities
Outstanding forward purchases of Yen against Dollars	Outstanding forward sales of Yen against Dollars
Long Yen futures	Short Yen futures
Long Call options on the Yen (bought the options)	Short call options on the Yen (written the options)
Short put options on the Yen (sold puts on Yen)	Long put options on the Yen (bought puts on Yen)

Exhibit 5-18 The Korean Won Crisis

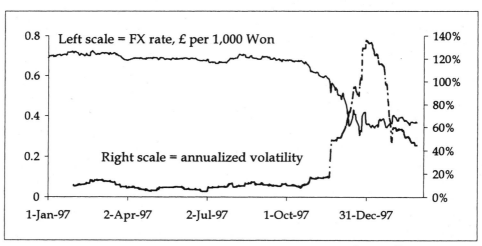

Source: Datastream

logs of price relatives; see Chapter 14). A second relevant point is that forward rates can turn out to be very bad predictors of future spot rates. This entails that LIBOR-based investing in one given currency can turn out to be materially more (less) profitable than in another currency. Exhibit 5-19 shows the recent example of the £ which, in the period under consideration, traded consistently at a discount against the DEM but in fact appreciated against the German currency. As a result, LIBOR-based investment in £ turned out to be a lot more profitable than that in DEM. A third point is that reasonably high levels of volatility can be associated with relatively stable

Exhibit 5-19 Comparative Return of 3-month LIBOR: £ and DEM

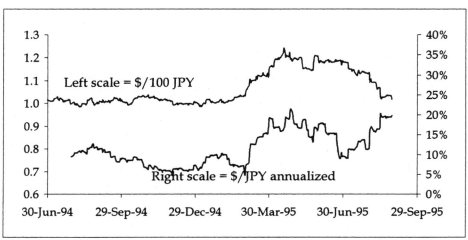

Source: Datastream

foreign exchange rates while huge fluctuations in FX rates can take place with relatively subdued volatility. If you consider the $/¥ FX wave of 1995 (see Exhibit 5-20), you will notice that it happened with an average level of annualized volatility of just 15%.

Cross-Currency Hedging

Say that the FX rate of ccy A and ccy B is both very stable and exhibits a low volatility. It could be tempting to implement a cross-hedge by hedging a long (short) position in ccy A, setting up your hedge in ccy B. This kind of hedge can turn out to be quite

Exhibit 5-20 Volatility and FX Fluctuations, $/100 Yen

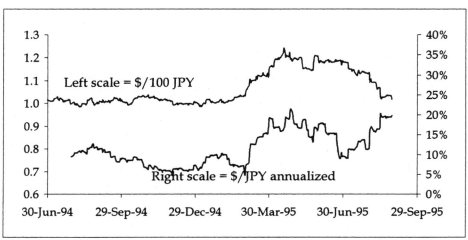

Source: Datastream

Exhibit 5-21 3-month Euromarket Rates on ITL and DEM

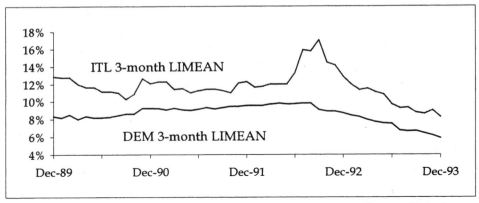

Source: Datastream

Exhibit 5-22 DEM/ITL, September 1992 Crisis

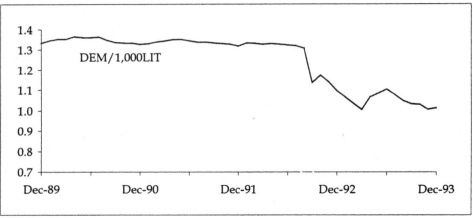

Source: Datastream

dangerous because there is no guarantee that the stability of the FX rate will continue into the future. An interesting example of cross-hedge gone bad is the ITL in the early 1990s. In this period the ITL-LIMEAN was consistently higher than the DEM-LIMEAN (see Exhibit 5-21). This notwithstanding, the ITL/DEM rate was extremely stable and displayed a remarkably low level of volatility (see Exhibit 5-22). A number of speculators went long the ITL and short the DEM and for a while did reap an interesting spread. This attracted the attention of $-based investors, who had to deal, however, with the problem of the relatively high level of volatility of the $ vis-a-vis the European currencies. The obvious answer was to invest in ITL while cross-hedging with the DEM to eliminate the risk of an appreciation of the $. This approach allowed to lock in the ITL-DEM spread. The flaw of this approach was that the past stability of the ITL/DEM rate was no guarantee of future stability. In September 1992 the European Rate Mechanism collapsed, with the ITL and the £ suffering a sudden depreciation (much to the profit of George Soros).

5-6   SETTLEMENT RISK (HERSTATT RISK)

This section is largely based on a report entitled "Settlement Risk in Foreign Exchange Transactions" prepared by the Committee on Payment and Settlement Systems of the Central Banks of the Group of Ten countries and published by the Bank for International Settlements (March 1996).

We have already seen that most securities settle via some clearing structure that allows the practical implementation of delivery versus payment (DVP). When it comes to FX transactions, the absence of an effective DVP mechanism entails that current settlement practices expose FX dealers to the risk of paying the funds they owe on a trade without receiving the funds they are due to receive from its counterparty.

Settlement risk is therefore quite different from the replacement risk we have already examined for spot and forward transactions. The Committee on Payment and Settlement Systems of the central banks of the Group of Ten countries has adopted the following definition of FX settlement exposure:

> A bank's actual exposure—the amount at risk—when settling a foreign exchange trade equals the full amount of the currency purchased and lasts from the time a payment instruction for the currency sold can no longer be canceled unilaterally until the time the currency purchased is received with finality.

The preceding definition includes the replacement cost into the overall settlement risk. When the bought currency has appreciated, a dealer would, however, be exposed to replacement risk quite independently from settlement risk.

The definition also identifies the beginning of the exposure with the moment at which the dealer's payment instruction for the sold currency can no longer be canceled unilaterally either because it has been finally processed by the relevant payment system or because some other factor (internal procedures, correspondent banking arrangements, laws, etc.) makes cancellation dependent on the consent of the counterparty. The end of the exposure coincides with the moment at which the bought currency has been received with finality.

The Herstatt Case

Settlement risk in FX transactions is commonly known as *Herstatt risk*, from the case that forced bankers to focus on this possibility. Bankhaus Herstatt was a small German bank, quite active in the FX market. On 26 June 1974, in the afternoon, Frankfurt time, it was ordered into liquidation by the banking supervisory authority of the Federal Republic of Germany (the *Bundesaufsitchamt für das Kredietwesen*).

Prior to the liquidation order, in the morning of 26 June, a number of FX counterparties had irrevocably paid DEM to Herstatt, through the German payment system, against anticipated payments of $ that were supposed to take place later in the day through Herstatt's New York correspondent bank. In fact, Herstatt had transmitted the payment instructions to New York before 26 June.

At 10:30 A.M. in New York (4:30 P.M. Frankfurt time), on being advised of the liquidation procedure, Herstatt's correspondent bank suspended $ payments from Herstatt's account. This entailed that Herstatt's counterparties found themselves creditors of the failed German bank for the entire amount of the $ payments they did not receive.

The Committee on Payment and Settlement Systems report also relates a few other instances of FX settlement risk, the latest being Barings, the venerable British merchant bank that collapsed as a result of losses of £ 800 million resulting from the inadequately supervised proprietory trading in derivatives by a relatively junior trader in their Singapore office.

Part 2

Long-Term Securities, Futures, and Swaps

Chapter 6

Zero-Coupon Bonds

Zero-coupon bonds (*zeros*, for short) have gained a prominent position, especially in the more innovative dollar market (both U.S. domestic and Euromarket). They are widely used, not only as investment vehicles but also as the instrument of choice for hedging bonds and swaps. Zeros are also quite important in the French treasury bonds market, which is similar to the U.S. market in terms of sophistication and liquidity. It would be desirable for zeros to be more widely adopted in other government bond markets, where moves in this direction have been proceeding at a glacial pace. In the United Kingdom, home to the world's largest international financial market, the Treasury allowed the stripping of Treasury securities issue strips only at the beginning of 1997. The Euro should foster the development of a wide and liquid zero coupon bonds market in the new European currency.

Zeros have brought to the forefront of fixed-income analysis some important issues relative to the meaning of spot yield and implied structure of forward yields. In this chapter we shall take advantage of the simplicity of zeros to lay the basis for a thorough understanding of a number of concepts.

- Duration and convexity
- *Zero yield curve* (ZYC).
- Implied term structure of forward yields

Extending the analytical results to coupon bonds and sinking fund bonds (amortizing bonds) will follow naturally. Coupon bonds can, in fact, be viewed as consisting of a set of zeroes with different maturities, corresponding to the different coupon payments and to the reimbursement of principal (the *corpus*).

6-1 THE DEVELOPMENT OF ZERO-COUPON BONDS

Short-term zero-coupon securities have been around for many years in the form of bills, commercial paper, and the like. The long-term zero-coupon bond is, however, a product of the high interest rates and interest-rate volatility prevalent in the late 1970s and early 1980s. The story of how the zero-coupon market developed in the United States in the early 1980s represents an interesting case study in the emergence and progressive refinement of an important financial innovation.

The first issues of zeros, in the form of private placements, took place in 1980. The following year, private placements were followed by public issues (the first, for J. C. Penney, a U.S. corporation, took place in April 1981). In 1982 the U.S. municipal market followed with an issue of tax-exempt zeros by the Massachusetts Bay Transportation Authority.

Synthetic Zero-Coupon Bonds

In 1982 a number of investment houses (notably Salomon Brothers and Merrill Lynch) pioneered the concept of creating zeros based on U.S. Treasury bonds. These investment banks made substantial profits by supplying the market with a much-in-demand product that also benefited from the perceived zero credit risk usually associated with U.S. Treasury securities.

The mechanics worked as follows: a certain quantity of T-bonds or T-notes was bought by the investment house and deposited in a fiduciary account with a bank. The investment house would then issue a set of zeros, with maturities corresponding to the maturity of all the coupons and principal of the T-bond or T-note. The payments to the holders of the zeros was fully collateralized by the payments that the depository bank would receive on the T-bonds; these payments would flow through to the holders of the zeros. If a set of zeros was created by depositing $20 million of 8% T-notes with a 10-yr maturity, each semiannual coupon payment would total $800,000 (see Exhibit 6-1). Neither the custodian bank nor the investment bank guaranteed the payments to the holders of zeros (such a guarantee would have added next to nothing to the perceived absence of credit risk of the instrument). These receipts were not directly guaranteed by the full faith and credit of the U.S. government. There was always the possibility, albeit minimal, that the custodian bank would go bankrupt after having improperly utilized the treasuries it held in custody. Synthetic zeros had names designed to catch the attention of the prospective clients. The best-known of such names are:

- TIGRs (Treasury Investment Growth Receipts—Merrill Lynch)
- CATS (Certificates of Accrual on Treasury Securities—Salomon Brothers)

Exhibit 6-1 Zeros Based on $20 million of 10yr, 8% T-notes

T	Face value	
0.5	800,000	Zero based on first coupon
1.0	800,000	
1.5	800,000	
....	....	
9.0	800,000	
9.5	800,000	
10.0	800,000	Zero based on last coupon
10.0	20,000,000	Zero based on principal (corpus)

• LIONS (Lehman Investment Opportunity Notes—Lehman Brothers)

The product was an instant hit. By the end of 1982, $14 billion of Treasury securities had been utilized to issue zero coupon bonds. On the other hand, such instruments were proprietary to the issuing firms, that branded them. Therefore, other firms were somehow unwilling to make markets in them. This did limit liquidity, and only CATS—given their large volumes and the clout of Salomon Brothers in fixed-income trading—really became available in the general market. To overcome this liquidity problem, in 1984 a group of primary dealers began issuing a "generic" product known as Treasury receipts (TR).

The Callable Tail Problem

In finance, things are seldom as simple as we would like them to be. Distilling synthetic zeros out of 30yr T-bonds created a problem because such bonds were, as a rule, callable at par on any coupon date in the last 5 years to maturity. This problem, known as the *callable tail*, was solved in an ingenious way by issuing

• A series of zeros corresponding to the coupons payable before the possible call (for a maximum of 50 zeros corresponding to the 50 semiannual coupons in the first 25 years of noncallable life of the bond; see Exhibit 6-2, based on a CATS issue)
• A certificate representing both the corpus and the coupons that would be paid after the possible call date. This certificate could turn out to be either a zero-coupon bond (payable on the first possible call date), or a coupon bond paying interest from the first possible call date to the repayment date (either call or final maturity).

It is intuitively evident that, after 25 years, the value of the callable tail can be

Exhibit 6-2 Salomon Brothers Inc., CATS for 12½% U.S. T-bonds, Mty = 15 August 2014

$5,312.5 million coupon CATS, $1,700.0 m callable CATS

* This CATS offering is based on $1,700 million of 30yr T-bonds, held by Morgan Guarantee Trust as custodian. There are 50 coupon CATS, each for a value of $106.25 million

* The callable CATS are based on the corpus of the bonds. If the bonds are never called, the callable CATS will pay 10 coupons of $106.25m each.

Coupon CAT	Mty	$ million
1	15-Feb-85	106.25
2	15-Aug-85	106.25
....	....	....
49	15-Feb-09	106.25
50	15-Aug-09	106.25

- $100 if the call is exercised at par 5 years prior to maturity
- Less than $100 if the call is not exercised at the first call date; the Treasury will not exercise the call if the bonds trade below par

Treasury Strips

In February 1985 the zero-coupon market received an important boost by the U.S. Treasury, which introduced STRIPS (Separate Trading of Registered Interest and Principal of Securities). This system, based on the fact that Treasury securities are held in book-entry form accessible through Fed Wire, allows a holder of treasuries to ask them to be converted into a series of zeros. Strips based on coupons are identified with the code ci, while zeros based on principal are identified as bp (bond principal) or np (note principal).

When it introduced STRIPS, the treasury began issuing noncallable 30yr bonds. The absence of a call option allowed the origination of 30yr STRIPS and avoided the complication of dealing with the callable tail. STRIPS were also made easier to trade in August 1985, when the Treasury decided to assign a generic CUSIP (Committee on Uniform Securities Identifying Procedures) code to all interest-based STRIPS with the same maturity.

A step that further enhanced the STRIPS market liquidity was taken by the U.S. Treasury in May 1987 when it decided to allow coupon and principal STRIPS to be pooled and recombined into the original T-note or T-bond in a process known as *reconstitution*. When reassembling a bond or note, only ci's can be used for coupons and only bp's or np's for principal. This constraint avoids recompositions that could create synthetic coupon bonds that were never issued by the U.S. Treasury.

6-2 PRICE-YIELD RELATIONSHIP, DURATION, AND CONVEXITY

The yield equations for zeros are those that we have already examined in Chapter 2 for short-term discount securities. (This is not surprising; zeros are long T-bills.) For zeros with a term of 6 months or more, we always use compounded yield (U.S. bond basis or International Securities Market Association (ISMA) method). There is no interest accrual; therefore the *PV* of a zero is always identical to its clean price. In a number of applications, especially in the field of derivatives pricing, exponential yield is commonly used.

$$PV = FV \cdot (1 + Y)^{-T}; \; PV = FV \cdot \left(1 + \frac{1}{2} Y_{us}\right)^{-2T}; \; PV = FV \cdot \exp(-R \cdot T)$$

In the Euromarkets, term to maturity was computed in years and a fraction of a year, according to the 30/360 daycount rule (the fraction of a year equals $DSC/360$, where DSC = days between settlement, included, and nearest virtual coupon date, excluded). In the United States, prices for T-strips are often quoted using the same convention that is used for treasury coupons, expressing fractions of dollars in 32nds; therefore, 84-22 = 84.6875.

Always in the United States, the term to maturity of zero-coupon bonds or STRIPS is computed as a whole number of semiannual periods plus an initial fraction of a semester. If we follow the Securities Industry Association (SIA) convention, the fraction of a semester will equal DSC/DCP (DSC = days from settlement to coupon; DCP

Exhibit 6-3 Daycount Effect on PV, $Y = 6.50\%$, U.S. Bond Basis

Term		$A = PV$	$B = PV$		
Years	Days	93/181	93/184	$A - B$	$(A-B)/A$
1	93	92.275	92.300	-0.025	-0.03%
2	93	86.557	86.580	-0.023	-0.03%
3	93	81.194	81.216	-0.022	-0.03%
5	93	71.443	71.463	-0.019	-0.03%
10	93	51.887	51.901	-0.014	-0.03%
20	93	27.369	27.376	-0.007	-0.03%
29	93	15.390	15.394	-0.004	-0.03%

= number of days in the current virtual coupon period). This SIA convention means that an initial period of, say, 93 days will give the following:

- 0.5138 semesters when the virtual coupon period is 181 days (e.g., January $\rightarrow$ June)
- 0.5054 semesters when the virtual coupon period is 184 days (e.g., March $\rightarrow$ August)

Exhibit 6-3 shows the effect of the SIA day-count convention for a 93-day initial stub, at a yield level of 6.50%. To avoid this sort of discrepancy, a number of securities dealers consider a standard semester to be 182.5 days. Quotations for T-strips are published in the financial press (the *Wall Street Journal*) and are available, as live data, on the screens of information providers. The quotations shown in Exhibit 6-4 will serve

Exhibit 6-4 Treasury STRIPS, Trade = 14 November 1996,
Settlement 15 November 1996

	T	Mty	Bid Y	Ask Y	Ask Price	PVbp	D	YV32nd
ci	1	15-Nov-97	5.45%	5.43%	94.783	0.00923	0.97	0.03%
ci	2	15-Nov-98	5.69%	5.67%	89.421	0.01739	1.94	0.02%
ci	3	15-Nov-99	5.84%	5.82%	84.189	0.02454	2.92	0.01%
ci	4	15-Nov-00	5.93%	5.91%	79.218	0.03077	3.89	0.01%
ci	5	15-Nov-01	5.98%	5.96%	74.554	0.03619	4.86	0.01%
ci	25	15-Nov-21	6.79%	6.75%	19.022	0.04594	24.18	0.01%
ci	26	15-Nov-22	6.73%	6.69%	18.071	0.04540	25.16	0.01%
ci	27	15-Nov-23	6.70%	6.66%	17.053	0.04450	26.13	0.01%
ci	28	15-Nov-24	6.66%	6.62%	16.146	0.04370	27.10	0.01%
ci	29	15-Nov-25	6.60%	6.60%	15.213	0.04264	28.07	0.01%
ci	30	15-Nov-26	6.54%	6.54%	14.507	0.04208	29.05	0.01%

Source: Bloomberg

as a basis for a number of examples. There are a lot more T-strips outstanding (all with maturity on the 15th of the month); those shown in the exhibit have been chosen to provide an uninterrupted series of whole-year maturities, reaching to the maximum of 30 years. The data refer only to coupon-based strips. A number of principal-based strips mature on the selected dates, but they do not cover all the maturities.

Price and Term to Maturity

PV will decrease with the increase in maturity; for any given level of yield, the zero has to be discounted for a longer time. For any given maturity, the higher the yield, the lower the *PV*. With the passing of time, *PV* will converge to face value ($100). Market yields, however, are bound to change in time, and *PV* will converge to $100, moving among different functions $PV(T \mid Y)$ with changes in *Y* (see Exhibit 6-5). If we examine a set of *PVs* at any point in time, the different present values will reflect differences in both time to maturity and spot yields for different maturities.

   Note that some authors now refer to the rate of change of *PV* due to the passing of time as the theta of the bond (theta, Θ, is the Greek letter for T).

$$\Theta = \frac{\partial}{\partial T} PV(Y, T)$$

Price-Yield Function: Macaulay's Duration

The function $PV(Y \mid T)$ displays a visible convexity. However, for small changes in yield around a given value Y_0, the price-yield function is rather flat, and it can be accurately approximated by a straight line (tangent computed at Y_0). Note that the tangent approximation of the convex function produces a result that errs on the side of pessimism, since it underestimates the gain in case *Y* decreases and overestimates the loss when *Y* increases (see Exhibit 6-6). The slope of the tangent is, of course, measured by the derivative of *PV* with respect to *Y*. The change in present value ΔPV due to a small change in yield ΔY is clearly proportional to the slope of $PV(Y \mid T)$.

Box 6-1   Tangent Approximation to the Price-Yield Function

$\Delta PV = \dfrac{\partial PV}{\partial Y} \cdot \Delta Y$, and:

$\dfrac{\partial PV}{\partial Y} = -T \dfrac{FV}{(1 + Y)^{T+1}}$ = derivative when using annual yield

$\dfrac{\partial PV}{\partial Y} = -T \cdot \dfrac{FV}{(1 + 0.5 \cdot Y_{US})^{2T+1}}$ = derivative when using U.S. bond yield

$\dfrac{\partial PV}{\partial R} = -T \cdot FV \cdot \exp(-R \cdot T)$ = derivative when using log yield

---

Yield changes happen in time, and *PV* will change due to variations of both *Y* and *T*. The preceding equation can be interpreted as the change in *PV* due to a ΔY that takes place in a short time interval, thereby making the effect of changes in *T* immaterial,

Exhibit 6-5 *PV* as a Function of *T*, *PV (T | Y)*

T	5%	8%
2	90.60	85.48
4	82.07	73.07
6	74.36	62.46
8	67.36	53.39
10	61.03	45.64
12	55.29	39.01
14	50.09	33.35
16	45.38	28.51
18	41.11	24.37
…	…	……

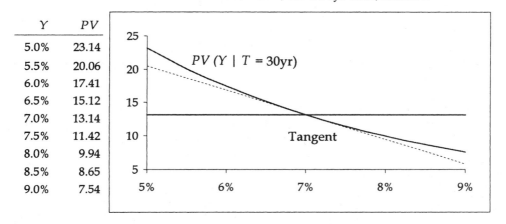

Exhibit 6-6 *PV* as a Function of *Y*, for a 30yr zero, ISMA-*Y*

Y	PV
5.0%	23.14
5.5%	20.06
6.0%	17.41
6.5%	15.12
7.0%	13.14
7.5%	11.42
8.0%	9.94
8.5%	8.65
9.0%	7.54

such as yield changes that take place in one trading day. *PV* changes that can take place within 1 or 2 trading days are obviously extremely relevant for risk management in a securities trading operation (market making and/or proprietary trading).

The equations for the derivative of the price-yield function are clearly dependent on term to maturity, expressed in years. This fact was first evidenced by Macaulay (1938), who coined the bond-speak word *duration*. For zero coupon bonds, time to maturity in years is known as *Macaulay's duration* (D_M, so as not to confuse it with *duration*, interpreted as the proportional change in PV due to a small absolute change in yield, referred to as *modified duration*).

Macaulay introduced the term duration for a very good reason. With coupon bonds, the slope of the price-yield function is dependent on the weighted average of the terms to maturity of all the coupons and of the principal (see Exhibit 6-7). This average cash flow maturity was therefore named duration to distinguish it from the average life of a sinking-fund bond, which is calculated only on the repayments of

Exhibit 6-7 Slope of $PV = f(Y)$ as a Function of T, for $FV = 100$

T	Y =6%	Y =9%
1	89.00	84.17
5	352.48	298.13
10	526.79	387.53
15	590.47	377.80
20	588.31	327.40
25	549.53	265.98
30	492.76	207.44

principal. Zeros have only one payment at maturity, and therefore Macaulay's duration = term to maturity of principal ($D_M = T$).

• The slope of $PV = f(Y)$ is, of course, negative. The value of the derivative has been converted to positive because of the way interest elasticity is usually quoted by market participants.

• The slope of the curve first increases (longer zeros are more sensitive to yield changes) and then declines, due to the PV compression (PV compression also explains why the slope of the 6% curve is higher than that of the 9% one).

• The values of the slope may appear to be huge when compared to the apparent flatness of the graphs in Exhibit 6-6. This apparent flatness depends, however, on the choice of scale for the PV and the Y axes. To make the graph clearly legible, the same distance that corresponds to 1% on the Y axis corresponds to 10 on the PV axis; therefore the curve appears to be 1,000 times flatter than it is in reality. The derivative has such a high value because we measure PV with reference to the conventional face value of $100. If PV were computed using a face value of $1, more in line with the fact that Y is measured in percentage terms, the slope would be 100 times smaller.

Measuring Price Risk: Duration

In volatile financial markets, price sensitivity to gyrations in yield (also known as *price risk*) is a crucially important issue that has attracted a large volume of first-class research. One widely used measure of price risk is *duration* (D), also called *modified duration*, which is defined as the *proportional* change in PV due to a small, *absolute* change in Y. Duration is clearly related to Macaulay's duration, as shown in the following equation box. Take the duration column in Exhibit 6-4, which is plotted in Exhibit 6-8: we can immediately see that D increases quasi-linearly with the number of years to maturity. The longer the zero, the larger the swings in value due to a given change in prevailing market yield. We also see that the level of Y does not have much effect (it increases from 5.43% to 6.74% and then declines to 6.54% without visibly changing the linearity of the plot).

Exhibit 6-8 Duration, Plotted from Exhibit 6-4

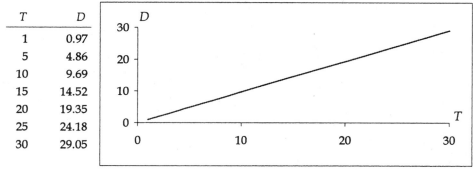

T	D
1	0.97
5	4.86
10	9.69
15	14.52
20	19.35
25	24.18
30	29.05

Source: Bloomberg

Box 6-2   Duration and Macaulay's Duration

$$D = \frac{\dfrac{\partial PV}{\partial Y}}{PV} = \frac{T}{(1 + Y)} = \frac{D_M}{(1 + Y)}$$

and, for a small variation ΔY

$$\frac{\Delta PV}{PV} = D \cdot \Delta Y$$

With semiannual compounding, we have

$$\frac{T}{1 + 0.5 \cdot Y_{us}} = D_{us}.$$

If we measure the change in yield in bp, a duration of, say, 3.5 ($D = 3.5$) implies $\{D = 3.5 | \ \Delta Y = 0.01\%\}$.

$$\frac{\Delta PV}{PV} = D \cdot \Delta Y = 0.035\%$$

Example. Take the 14yr STRIP, maturity 15 November 2010 (ask $Y = 6.57\%$; ask price = 40.45; term to maturity = 14yr).

$$D = \frac{14}{1 + \dfrac{6.57\%}{2}} = 13.55$$

If $\Delta Y = \pm 10$ bp, we compute the variation in PV as follows:

$$\left|\frac{\Delta PV}{PV}\right| \cong D \cdot \Delta Y = 13.55 \times 0.10\% = 1.355\%$$

$$|\Delta PV| \cong 40.454 \cdot 1.355\% = 0.54835$$

If you compute the PV of the zero you obtain the following values that are close enough to the linear approximation implied by the duration method.

Exhibit 6-9 *PVbp*, Plotted from Exhibit 6-4

T	Ask Y	Ask price	PVbp
1	5.43%	94.783	0.0092
2	5.67%	89.420	0.0174
3	5.82%	84.189	0.0245
4	5.91%	79.217	0.0308
5	5.96%	74.554	0.0362
10	6.36%	53.467	0.0518
15	6.60%	37.756	0.0548
20	6.74%	26.559	0.0513

$$\Delta Y = +0.10\% \Rightarrow \Delta PV \cong -\$0.5445$$

$$\Delta Y = -0.10\% \Rightarrow \Delta PV \cong +\$0.5522$$

Further Comments on Duration: Dollar Duration

Note that duration is used as a simple and intuitive way of gauging the price risk of bonds. Duration is now commonly used in the securities industry as a synonym of proportional price variation as a reaction to a small change in yield. This means that duration is routinely used for fixed-income instruments for which D is clearly not equal to Macaulay's duration divided by $1 + Y$. A typical example, which we shall examine in Chapter 8, are inverse floaters, which have a duration higher than term to maturity.

The securities industry has developed somewhat of an obsession with the word duration. The tangent approximation to the price-yield function is routinely called dollar duration because it measures the change in PV in $ (per face value of 100) and not as a proportional change $\Delta PV/PV$.

Price Value of One Basis Point of Yield (*PVbp*)

One traditional measure of price sensitivity is the price value of one basis point, *PVbp*, that measures the price change, due to a 0.01% change in yield, of a zero with face value = 100. When we graph *PVbp* as a function of term, we notice that it first increases (price sensitivity increases with maturity) and then decreases, due to the *PV* compression of the zero. *PVbp* is always quoted as a positive number (see Exhibit 6-9). The values of *PVbp* are calculated by computing PV at two different levels of yield, separated by 0.01%. *PVbp* clearly depends on the slope of $PV = f(Y)$, which, as we have seen, is nearly linear for small values of ΔY. If we use this linear approximation, *PVbp* can be very accurately calculated by multiplying the slope of $PV = f(Y)$ by 0.01%.

Example. Take the 14yr STRIP, maturity 15 November 2010 (ask $Y = 6.57\%$; ask price = 40.45). The computed *PVbp* is 0.0548, the derivative is −$548, and therefore

Exhibit 6-10 *PV for 5yr and 10yr Zeroes, ISMA-Y*

Y	5yr	10yr
6.5%	104.78	109.80
7.0%	102.36	104.77
7.5%	100.00	100.00
8.0%	97.71	95.47
8.5%	95.48	91.16

5yr	FV =	143.56
10yr	FV =	206.10

$$\frac{\partial PV}{\partial Y} = -548 \Rightarrow PVbp \cong \frac{\partial PV}{\partial Y} \cdot 0.01\% = \$0.0548.$$

The preceding equation (that gives a dollar duration) produces a result nearly identical to that obtained using duration.

Comparing Bonds with Different Duration

In Exhibit 6-10 we graph the $PV = f(Y)$ function for 5 and 10yr maturities. Over a 200 bp interval (from 6.5% to 8.5%), their curvature (convexity) is so small that the two functions look like straight lines. It is visually evident that, at the 7.5% yield level, the 10yr zero has a slope twice as steep as that of the 5yr; therefore, its price sensitivity to changes in yield will be twice as large as that of the shorter-term zero.

Note that the exhibit shows $PV = f(Y)$ for two zeros that have the same $100 present value at the 7.5% yield level. (Due to PV compression it would be impossible to visually compare the slopes of zeros with the same face value).

Duration and *PVbp* of a Portfolio of Zeros

Duration and duration-linked measures are simple to use for a portfolio consisting of a number of zeros. The $PVbp$ of the portfolio equals the sum of the $PVbp$ of the different zero holdings. The duration of the portfolio equals the weighted arithmetic average (weighted mean) of the duration of the different zeros, using their PVs as weights.

Example. Using the STRIPS in Exhibit 6-4, take the portfolio of Exhibit 6-11; for a 10 bp movement in both the 14 and the 23yr spot rates (parallel yield curve shift); the two duration-based measures of price risk yield approximatively the same result.

$$\text{Duration} \Rightarrow 18.30 \times \$178{,}009.84 \times 0.1\% = \$3{,}256.8$$

$$PVbp \Rightarrow 10 \times \$325.35 = \$3{,}253.50$$

Yield Value of 1/32d

Another measure of price sensitivity is the yield value of a 1/32 change in price (YV32nd). This measure is used in the United States, where Treasury bonds and notes

Exhibit 6-11 Duration of a Portfolio of Strips—U.S. Bond Y

T	Price	Y	FV	Value	D	PVbp
14	40.4545	6.57%	$200,000	$80,907.15	13.55	$0.0548
23	21.5780	6.78%	$450,000	$97,095.68	22.25	$0.0479
	Portfolio		$650,000	$178,002.82	18.30	$0.0501

The Pvbp for the whole portfolio is $325.34

are quoted in 32nds. The near-linearity of $PV = f(Y)$ over a small interval of Y makes it possible to determine, with a simple proportion, the YV32nd, given *PVbp*.

$$\frac{YV32nd}{(1/32)} = \frac{0.01\%}{PVbp} \Rightarrow YV32nd = \frac{0.01\%}{PVbp} \, (1/32)$$

Again, this measure refers to a zero with $100 face value, irrespective of price compression. Because of this, YV32nd is not a very useful indicator for zeros (as you can easily see from Exhibit 6-4, where it has a value of 0.01% for all maturities equal to or greater than 3yr).

Convexity

We have seen that $PV = f(Y)$ is convex. Convexity is measured by the second derivative of PV with respect to Y and defines the speed at which the slope changes. The well-known physics equivalent of the second derivative is acceleration, while the first derivative is speed. From a financial point of view, the importance of convexity lies in the asymmetry between the effect on present value of an increase and a decrease in yield.

We have already seen that the tangent underestimates the gain due to a decrease in market yields and overestimates the loss due to an increase in Y. When you take convexity into account, the result will always be somewhat better than that predicted by the duration method, irrespective of yields increasing or decreasing. This is usually referred to in the securities industry as *gain from convexity*. It can be proved (see Section 6-6, Mathematical Appendix) that the gain from convexity

- Increases very rapidly with duration (in fact, convexity is proportional to the square of duration)
- Increases with the magnitude of the change in yield
- Is not very sensitive to the starting level of Y

The mathematical measure of convexity cannot be used in the same straightforward way as duration. Therefore, the most intuitive way of looking at it is to consider a numerical example. In Exhibit 6-12 we therefore plot the difference between $PV = f(Y)$ and the present value we would have obtained using a tangent-based linear approximation (using the 7% yield level as the starting point).

In a number of books you will find equations that use convexity (measured by the second derivative of PV with respect to Y) to improve the tangent approximation of $PV = f(Y)$. This is a straightforward application of Taylor series expansion but is

Exhibit 6-12 Gains from Convexity, Tangent at $Y = 7\%$, ISMA-Y

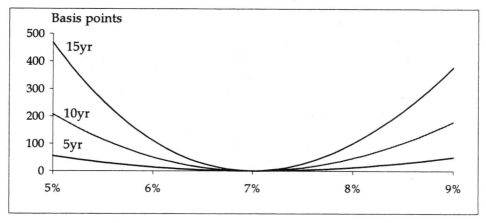

seldom, if ever, used in the securities industry, where the price-yield function is computed with more accurate numerical methods.

Box 6-3   Duration and Duration + Convexity Approximations

$$\Delta PV = \frac{\partial PV}{\partial Y} \cdot \Delta Y = \text{(first-order Taylor approximation)}$$

$$\Delta PV = \frac{\partial PV}{\partial Y} \cdot \Delta Y + \frac{1}{2} \cdot \frac{\partial^2 PV}{\partial PV^2} (\Delta Y)^2 \text{ (second-order Taylor approximation)}$$

$$\frac{1}{PV} \cdot \frac{\partial^2 PV}{\partial PV^2} = \text{convexity}$$

$$\frac{1}{2} \cdot convexity \cdot \Delta Y^2 = \text{proportional price variation due to convexity}$$

6-3   SPOT AND FORWARD YIELDS

In the U.S. bond market, T-STRIPS quotations provide a straightforward way to compute a meaningful spot yield curve. The Treasuries market is very liquid, and arbitrage-free pricing is assured by the possibility of stripping coupon bonds and of reconstituting coupons out of the appropriate set of STRIPS. In less homogeneous and liquid markets, computing a spot yield curve out of zero-coupon bonds may be less meaningful and require a number of adjustments to account for differences in rating and liquidity.

When you can use a set of reliable zero-coupon yields, the next step consists in interpolating the entire set of spot yields to obtain a smooth yield curve. This is useful for a number of reasons.

- The small irregularities in the raw data can imply noticeable jumps in forward rates.

Exhibit 6-13 Interpolating T-STRIP Yields, 14 November 1996

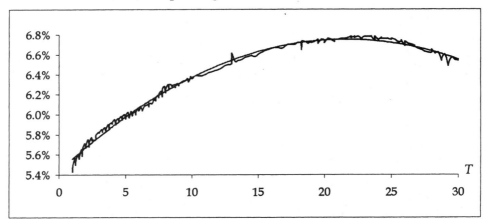

- An interpolated curve allows you to have a better view of which zeros are over-priced and which are relatively cheap.
- Some on-line prices could be less recent or less meaningful (small transactions, less-liquid maturities, etc.).
- Pricing applications of the ZYC are a lot easier to implement if the yield curve is summarized by an analytical formula that can be plugged into other applications (working with hundreds of data is certainly not computationally efficient).

Note that there is a budding literature on yield-curve fitting. Some of the methods that have been proposed utilize nonlinear fitting procedures, which are available only in specialized econometric software packages. For illustrative purposes we have fitted the more than over 220 T-STRIPS outstanding as of 14 November 1996 with a simple quadratic equation, which in this particular case gives a quite acceptable approximation and is very easy to use.

$$\hat{Y} = a_0 + a_1 \cdot T + a_2 \cdot (T)^2$$

For the ZYC as of 14 November 1996, the parameters are

$$\hat{Y} = 5.439\% + 0.1216\% \cdot (T) + -0.00282\% \cdot (T)^2.$$

Note that the preceding equation implies that $\hat{Y} = 5.439\%$ when $T = 0$. This value is not a good estimate of the rate on short T-bills; therefore the fitted curve should be used only for zeros with maturities equal to or greater than 1 year (see Exhibit 6-13).

Forward Yields

Given the spot-yield curve, we can determine the implied structure of forward yields, utilizing the bootstrap method (see Chapter 3). When we examine medium and long-term spot rates, we must always utilize compounded yields.

Example: Compute the 1yr forward yield (from year 9 to year 10) when the ISMA yields are 6.373% for 10 years and 6.305% for 9 years.

Exhibit 6-14 Spot and 1yr Forward Y on U.S. Treasury STRIPS

T	Y(T-1)	Y(T)	FWRD
5	5.88%	5.98%	6.36%
10	6.31%	6.37%	6.99%
15	6.59%	6.63%	7.19%
20	6.73%	6.74%	6.97%
25	6.74%	6.72%	6.33%
30	6.60%	6.55%	5.27%

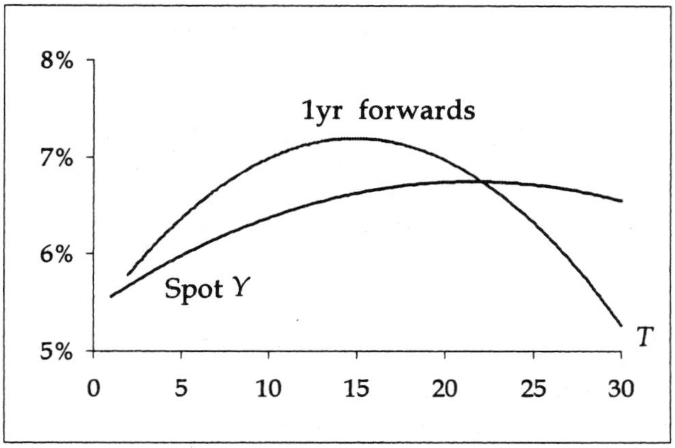

- Investing $1 in the shorter zero will yield $FV(0, 9)$ = $1.73375 after 9 years.
- The same $1 amount invested in the 10yr zero will yield $FV(0, 10)$ = $1.85491.

The forward rate will be:

$$6.988\% = \frac{(1 + 6.373\%)^{10}}{(1 + 6.305\%)^9} - 1 = \frac{1.85491}{1.73375} - 1$$

Box 6-4   Computing Forward Yields for Annual Periods

$$Y(T-1, T) = \frac{(1 + Y_T)^T}{(1 + Y_{T-1})^{T-1}} - 1$$

If you use the exponential yield notation you get

$$R(T-1, T) = T \cdot R(0, T) - (T-1) \cdot R(0, T-1)$$

You can see in Exhibit 6-14 that forward yields follow a pattern that is a lot more irregular than that of spot yields. This is intuitive enough. Let us indicate with ΔY the change in spot yield between two consecutive years. The forward yield must absorb in one year the effect of ΔY, which affects $FV(0, T)$ for T years.

$$Y(T - 1, T) = \frac{[1 + Y(T - 1) + \Delta Y]^T}{[1 + Y(T - 1)]^{T-1}} - 1, \text{ where } \Delta Y = Y(0, T) - Y(0, T - 1)$$

When two consecutive spot yields are equal:

$$Y(0, T - 1) = Y(0, T) \Rightarrow f Y(T - 1, T) = Y(0, T - 1).$$

When $\Delta Y \neq 0$, the forward rate will be equal to $Y(T - 1)$ plus an adjustment factor:

$$Y(T - 1, T) \cong Y(T - 1) + T \cdot \Delta Y.$$

Using the exponential notation we can interpret the spot yield curve as the arithmetic average of the forward yields.

Exhibit 6-15 Spot and 1yr Forward Y on U.S. Treasury STRIPS, Raw Data

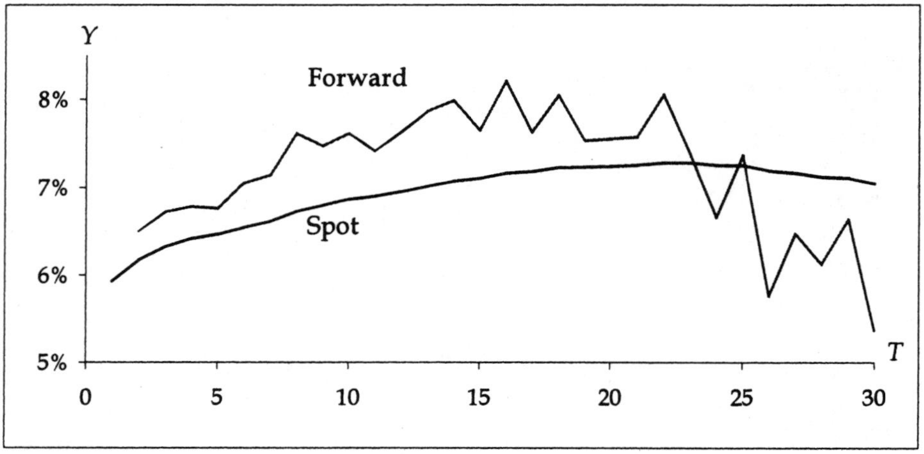

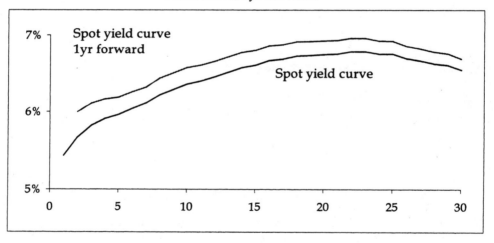

Exhibit 6-16 U.S. T-STRIPS: Spot Yield Curve, and Implied Spot
Yield Curve, 1yr Forward

$$\exp[R(0, T) \cdot T] = \exp[R(0, 1)] \cdot \exp[R(1, 2)] \cdot \ldots \cdot \exp[R(T - 1, T)]$$

$$= \exp\left[T \cdot \frac{R(0, 1) + \ldots + R(T - 1, T)}{T}\right]$$

Forward Spot-Yield Curve

Given the spot yield curve (ZYC in our case), we can project the implied forward structure of the spot yield curve at some future date.

Example: Compute the 9yr spot yield, 1 year forward (U.S. bond basis).

• Investing \$1 in the 10yr STRIPS will yield $FV(0, 10) = \$1.87269$.

- Investing \$1 in the 1yr STRIPS will yield $FV(0, 1) = \$1.0554$.

$$2 \cdot \left[\left(\frac{1.87269}{1.0558} \right)^{\frac{1}{18}} - 1 \right] = 6.29\%$$

(see Exhibit 6-16).

6-4   HEDGING, BARBELL TRADES, AND SPREAD OVER BENCHMARK

In this section we shall often refer to shifts in the spot yield curve (= zero-coupon yield curve). To visualize the concept, Exhibit 6-17 shows

- A bottom yield curve, based on a simple quadratic interpolation of the asked yield curve for U.S. Treasury STRIPS prevailing on 15 November 1995
- A top yield curve *A*, identical to the bottom curve shifted upward by 1%. This is known as a *parallel yield curve shift*.
- Two intermediate curves that represent a steepening and a flattening of the yield curve (note that the exhibit is constructed in such a way that if you add the two nonparallel shifts, you obtain a 1% parallel shift).

There are, of course, many other possible shifts of the spot yield curve, but graphing them would result in a cluttered exhibit without adding much to what we need to proceed with our analysis.

Duration and Hedging

Duration has several advantages that explain its widespread popularity in the securities industry. It is a compact indicator, expressed with one single number, and can be used in a straightforward way to calculate, with sufficient accuracy, the percentage change in *PV* that would follow from a given, relatively small, absolute change in yield. Duration is also used to compare the price sensitivity of different bonds (zeros in this chapter). Let us now concentrate on this use of duration, which is related to the twin issues of hedging and risk management.

Exhibit 6-17 Yield Curve Shifts

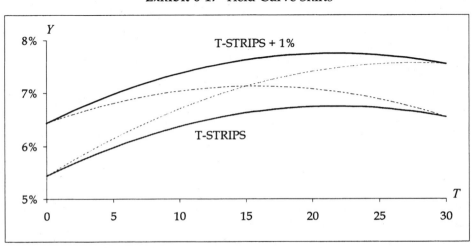

It is intuitively evident that the duration of a portfolio of two or more zeros is the average of their durations (each duration weighted by the *PV* of the relevant zero). In other words, each of the zeros contributes to the overall portfolio duration in proportion to its value and to its duration (see Mathematical Appendix). Indicating with $D(W)$ the duration of a portfolio W, we can write the following equation:

$$D(W) = PV_1 \cdot D_1 + \ldots + PV_N \cdot D_N$$

Once the average duration is determined, it is tempting to use it to express the price sensitivity of the portfolio in terms of some benchmark bond (thereby extending the ease of use of a single-digit indicator to a whole portfolio). The next step is to use duration in what is known as duration-weighted hedging, whereby a portfolio is hedged by combining long and short positions in such a way as to obtain a zero overall duration.

$$PV_1 \cdot D_1 + \ldots + PV_N \cdot D_N \cong 0$$

This simple approach however, is, fraught with the problem of nonparallel ZYC shifts. Let us consider hedging a $10 million long position in 5yr zeros with a short position in 20yr zeros (the yields in Exhibit 6-18 are those on the 5yr and the 20yr U.S. T-STRIPS as of 14 November 1996).

Using the portfolio duration concept, we could therefore be tempted to say that the $10 million long position could be hedged by a short of $2.5 million.

In fact, this duration-weighted hedge works well for parallel shifts of the ZYC (+0.10% in the example). The difference in convexity between the 5yr and the 20yr zeros accounts for an irrelevant hedging discrepancy of $300. However, the hedge will not work for nonparallel shifts of the spot yield curve, and the "hedged" portfolio will experience a gain or a loss as exemplified in Exhibit 6-18.

Constant-Duration Barbell Trades

Another crude application of duration analysis are *constant-duration barbells*. Take three zeros $(Z_S : Z_M : Z_L)$, with maturities $T_S < T_M < T_L$, where the subscripts stand for short, intermediate, and long. It is always possible to construct a portfolio $Z_S + Z_L$ that will have the same duration of Z_M. This kind of portfolio is usually known as a barbell (the name comes from the fact that the portfolio is distributed over two balanced maturities, like weights on a barbell). The quantities of the two bonds can be easily determined by solving the following equations.

Exhibit 6-18 Duration Hedging with Parallel and Nonparallel Spot Yield Curve Shifts ($000)

	T	PV	FV	Y	D	Spot yield curve shift		
						Parallel	Steeper	Flatter
Long	5	10,000	13,413	5.96%	4.86	-48.4	0.0	-48.4
Hedge	20	-2,509	-9,449	6.74%	19.35	48.1	48.1	0.0
Portfolio		*7,491*	*3,965*		*0.00*	*-0.3*	*48.1*	*-48.4*

Exhibit 6-19 Barbell Portfolio Implemented with T-STRIPS

	T	Y	D	FV	PV
A	12	6.45%	11.63	9,553.5	4,459.9
B	30	6.54%	29.05	38,191.6	5,540.1
Barbell			21.28	47,745.1	10,000.0
C	22	6.78%	21.28	43,356.6	10,000.0

Box 6-5   Constant-Duration Barbell Trade

First, the barbell must have a PV that equals that of the intermediate bond.

$$PV(Z_S) + PV(Z_L) = PV(Z_M)$$

$$PV(Z_S) = PV(Z_M) - PV(Z_L)$$

Second, the duration of the barbell must equal that of the intermediate bond

$$[PV(Z_M) - PV(Z_L)] \cdot D_S + PV(Z_L) \cdot D_L = PV(Z_M) \cdot D_M$$

$$PV(Z_L) = PV(Z_M) \frac{D(Z_S) - D(Z_M)}{D(Z_S) - D(Z_L)}$$

If we conveniently forget the problem of nonparallel yield curve shifts, we can say that the barbell portfolio is as risky as Z_M. The natural consequence would be

- Sell Z_M and buy the portfolio (barbell trade) if the barbell has a better yield than Z_M.
- Buy Z_M and sell the barbell if Z_M offers a better yield (reverse barbell trade) (see Exhibit 6-19).

The portfolio composed by $Z_S + Z_L$ has the same duration of Z_M but a lower yield; we are therefore in a situation that would allow a reverse barbell. The simple fact that this could be possible in a liquid market such as that for T-STRIPS suggests that a reverse barbell is not a riskless arbitrage.

Convexity Arbitrage: Barbell Trades

One strategy that you are likely to come across is that of trying to construct a portfolio $W\alpha$ with the same yield and duration of another portfolio Wz, but with a higher convexity. The $W\alpha$ portfolio would outperform Wz whenever there is a change in yield, irrespective of the direction of the change.

One could even think of a strategy consisting of being long $W\alpha$ while shorting Wz. This would lock in a riskless profit (convexity arbitrage) whenever rates move, thereby implementing a market-neutral probabilistic arbitrage. The serious limitation of this strategy is that it will expose the investor to losses when there are nonparallel yield curve shifts. The unpleasant corollary of this is that a number of so-called market-neutral strategies are in fact market-directional and can expose the investor to mis-understood risks, as confirmed by the debacle of a number of hedge funds in 1998.

Exhibit 6-20 Convexity Arbitrage with Barbell Trade, ISMA-Y

Y	PV Interm	PV Barbell
5.0%	132.71	137.74
5.5%	123.59	126.19
6.0%	115.12	116.20
6.5%	107.28	107.53
7.0%	100.00	100.00
7.5%	93.25	93.46
8.0%	86.98	87.77
8.5%	81.15	82.80
9.0%	75.75	78.47
9.5%	70.72	74.69
10.0%	66.05	71.37

If we compare two STRIPS, the longer zero will have a higher convexity but also a higher duration than the shorter zero. Therefore, being long the 10yr while shorting the 5yr would also result in a clear market-directional bet for parallel ZYC shifts.

An ingenious solution is again to set up a barbell portfolio, which can be constructed in such a way as to have the same duration but a higher convexity than an intermediate bond. As shown in Exhibit 6-20, the barbell would outperform the intermediate zero for parallel shifts in the yield curve.

Example. The intermediate zero has a 15yr maturity, $D = 14.02$, and PV at 7% $= 100$. The barbell is constructed for $Y = 7\%$ as a starting point and is composed of the following two zeros:

1yr zero, PV at 7% $= 51.72$; $D = 0.93$; $FV = 55.34$
30yr zero, PV at 7% $= 48.28$; $D = 28.04$; $FV = 367.49$

6-5 HORIZON YIELD, EXPECTATIONS, AND RISK PREMIUM

In most cases, both portfolio managers and traders are interested in trying to assess the return of a bond over a period of time that is much shorter than the term to maturity of the bond (a noticeable exception is represented by insurance companies or pension funds, which want to invest to cover long-term liabilities). The horizon yield HY will depend on two factors:

1. The spot yield over the time horizon; this in turn will be equal to the spot yield for the time horizon and therefore will be independent from the term of the zero.
2. The change in price (PV) due to a change in market yields; this will depend heavily on the duration of the zero.

Example: We have invested $100 in the 10yr zero (face value of the zero $= 182.86$, $Y = 6.22\%$). Given the 1yr spot rate (5.58%), the $100 investment yields 105.58 at the end of the first year if the ZYC will coincide with that implied at the T_0. (the 9-year spot rate, 1yr

Exhibit 6-21 Horizon Yield on a 5yr and a 15yr zero

Y shift	5yr zero	15yr zero
-1.0%	9.66%	20.47%
-0.8%	8.83%	17.32%
-0.6%	8.00%	14.26%
-0.4%	7.19%	11.28%
-0.2%	6.38%	8.39%
0.0%	5.6%	5.6%
0.2%	4.78%	2.84%
0.4%	4.00%	0.18%
0.6%	3.22%	-2.40%
0.8%	2.44%	-4.91%
1.0%	1.68%	-7.36%

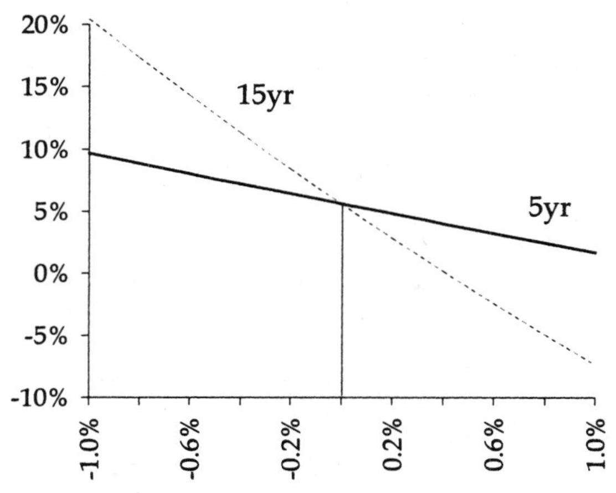

forward, will be = 6.29% and the price of the 9yr zero at 6.29% is in fact 105.58) (see Exhibit 6-21).

6-6 MATHEMATICAL APPENDIX

Evaluating the derivative of *PV* with respect to yield requires a rather straightforward application of the *chain rule* for differentiating a *function of a function*, taking the derivative of *PV* with respect to *T* and multiplying it for the derivative of $(1 + Y)$ with respect to *Y*.

$$\frac{\partial}{\partial Y} PV = \frac{\partial}{\partial Y} FV \cdot (1 + Y)^{-T} = -T \cdot (1 + Y)^{-(T+1)} \cdot FV \cdot \frac{d}{dY}(1 + Y)$$

$$\frac{d}{dY}(1 + Y) = 1 \Rightarrow \frac{\partial}{\partial Y} PV = \frac{-T \cdot FV}{(1 + Y)^{T+1}}$$

The second derivative is therefore proportional to T^2, and therefore becomes a rather large number for long-dated zeros (see Exhibit 6-22).

$$\frac{d^2}{dY^2} PV = \frac{d}{dY}\left[\frac{-T \cdot FV}{(1 + Y)^{(T+1)}}\right] = \frac{T \cdot (T + 1) \cdot FV}{(1 + Y)^{(T+2)}}$$

U.S. Bond Yield Basis

The derivative is marginally higher with U.S. bond basis than with annual *Y*. This result is intuitively evident because a marginal increment in Y_{us} is compounded twice a year and therefore results in a slightly higher annual compounded yield.

Exhibit 6-22 First and Second Derivatives of $PV = f(Y)$

Y	$T = 1$	$T = 5$	$T = 10$	$T = 20$	$T = 30$
First derivative: $f'(Y)$					
6%	-89.00	-352.48	-526.79	-588.31	-492.76
7%	-87.34	-333.17	-475.09	-483.03	-368.32
8%	-85.73	-315.08	-428.88	-397.31	-276.05
Second derivative: $f''(Y)$					
6%	167.92	1,995.17	5,466.66	11,655.21	14,411.04
7%	163.26	1,868.25	4,884.13	9,479.95	10,670.92
8%	158.77	1,750.47	4,368.25	7,725.50	7,923.60

$$\frac{\partial}{\partial Y_{us}} PV = \frac{\partial}{\partial Y_{us}} FV \cdot \left(1 + \frac{Y_{us}}{2}\right)^{-2T} = -2 \cdot T \cdot \left(1 + \frac{Y_{us}}{2}\right)^{-(2 \cdot T + 1)}$$

$$\cdot FV \cdot \frac{d}{dY_{us}}\left(1 + \frac{Y_{us}}{2}\right) = \frac{-2T}{\left(1 + \frac{Y_{us}}{2}\right)^{2T+1}} \cdot \frac{1}{2} = \frac{-T}{\left(1 + \frac{Y_{us}}{2}\right)^{2T+1}}$$

Differentiating the exp($R \cdot T$) function

If we use the exponential format, the mathematics are much simplified.

$$PV = FV \cdot \exp(-R \cdot T)$$

$$\frac{d}{dR} PV = -T \cdot FV \cdot e^{-R \cdot T}$$

$$\frac{d^2}{dR^2} PV = T^2 \cdot FV \cdot e^{-R \cdot T}$$

Convexity

The mathematics behind convexity are really very simple. It is in fact well known that you get a better approximation to a function by using a second-order Taylor series.

$$\Delta PV \cong \left[\frac{d}{dY} PV\right] \cdot \Delta Y + \left[\frac{d^2}{dY^2} PV\right] \cdot \frac{(\Delta Y)^2}{2}$$

$$\cong \left[\frac{-T \cdot FV}{(1 + Y)^{(T+1)}}\right] \cdot \Delta Y + \left[\frac{T \cdot (T + 1) \cdot FV}{(1 + Y)^{(T+2)}}\right] \cdot \frac{(\Delta Y)^2}{2}$$

We can now divide by PV to obtain the proportional variation:

$$\frac{\Delta PV}{PV} \cong \frac{1}{PV} \cdot \left[\frac{-T \cdot FV}{(1 + Y)^{(T+1)}}\right] \cdot \Delta Y + \frac{1}{PV} \cdot \left[\frac{T \cdot (T + 1) \cdot FV}{(1 + Y)^{(T+2)}}\right] \cdot \frac{(\Delta Y)^2}{2}$$

The convexity of a function is measured by its second derivative; therefore the adjustment based on $f''(Y)$ is known as convexity, which we shall indicate as CXY.

$$CXY = \frac{1}{PV} \cdot \left[\frac{d^2}{dY^2}\right] = \frac{1}{PV} \cdot \left[\frac{T \cdot (T + 1) \cdot FV}{(1 + Y)^{(T+2)}}\right]$$

$$\frac{\Delta PV}{PV} \cong D \cdot \Delta Y + CXY \cdot \frac{(\Delta Y)^2}{2}$$

Chapter **7**

Fixed-Interest Coupon Bonds

7-1 INTRODUCTION

A coupon bond can be considered as a bundle of zeros, one for each forthcoming coupon payment and one for the principal (corpus). Yield analysis will therefore be carried out in the light of modern spot yield curve–based developments. Yield to maturity (*YTM*) is now considered an oversimplified index for most applications. It is widely utilized, however, because it can be concisely expressed with one number whereas more accurate bond-pricing formulae require a set of data to describe the spot yield curve. The use of *YTM* is not limited to traditional bonds but extends to the quotation mechanism of swaps and bond futures.

Most medium- and long-term fixed-income securities are issued in the form of fixed-interest bonds or notes, which pay interest at regular intervals at a rate that is predetermined at the time of issue. With floating rate securities, changes in market conditions are reflected in the level of the coupon rate, which changes in sync with some meaningful market index (usually LIBOR). In the case of fixed-interest coupon bonds, it is the market price that changes to adjust yields to reflect current market conditions (exactly as for zero coupon bonds).

Bonds that represent a general obligation of the issuer and do not have any collateral to guarantee their payment are usually called *debentures* and are backed only by the full faith and credit of the borrower. Most government, corporate, and international bonds and notes are unsecured debentures.

Unless stated otherwise, unsecured debentures are considered to be senior unsecured debt, ranking pari passu (i.e., equally) with all unsecured debts of the issuer. A common feature of unsecured issues is the *negative pledge* clause, whereby the issuer covenants that it will not secure any other indebtedness, liabilities, or guarantees without securing equally and ratably the issue to which the negative pledge covenant applies.

The same issuer can issue debentures that have different degrees of seniority when it comes to repayment of capital and interest. A senior debenture will have the right to be paid before a junior one. An important class of debentures is represented by *subordinated debentures*, which rank junior to all other liabilities and senior only to equity in case of liquidation or bankruptcy. Subordinated debentures are important in the capital structure of banks and investment houses because, within certain limits, they can count as regulatory capital.

Many bonds are not general debentures but have preferential claim on a designated stream of revenues. *Revenue bonds* are quite common in the U.S. municipal bond market, where they can be used to finance toll roads, airports, water systems, hospital buildings, and the like. Sources of revenue include fees and tolls.

Another important class of bonds is represented by bonds that are guaranteed by certain well-defined revenue-producing assets (*asset-backed securities*), that may not represent a liability of the issuer. The most important class of asset-backed securities is, without doubt, represented by *mortgage-backed* bonds, which are based on pools of real estate mortgage loans (see Chapter 13). The issuance of bonds backed by pools of credits (but not by the full faith and credit of the issuer) is commonly indicated as *securitization*. It allows banks to extend credit without having to keep it on their books, thereby avoiding the absorption of regulatory capital.

Depending on their repayment conditions (which are described in the *indenture* of the bond), coupon bonds can be classified as follows.

- Bonds entirely redeemable at maturity (also called *bullet bonds* or *bullets*).
- Bonds that must be redeemed with a number of installments, starting before final maturity (*sinking-fund bonds*). This redemption feature has fallen out of grace in the corporate and government bond sectors. It remains, however, the standard method for asset-backed bonds, where the bonds' sinking fund reflects the progressive repayments by the end borrowers (e.g., mortgage borrowers).
- *Callable bonds*, which give the issuer the right, but not the obligation (*call option*), to repay the bonds before maturity. Call options are still in use. Until 1985 all U.S. T-bonds were callable, at par, on any semiannual coupon date, in the last 5 years before maturity (the call feature was discontinued to allow the creation of treasury STRIPS).
- *Puttable bonds*, that give the owner the right, but not the obligation, to be reimbursed before maturity. This feature is very rare; it would in fact expose the borrower to the risk of having to refinance in unfavorable market conditions.

Another subdivision that you will often find is that between notes and bonds and involves the original maturity (maturity at issue) of the instrument, with notes having a shorter maturity than bonds. In the case of the U.S. Treasury market, the following classification is currently and consistently used.

- T-bills: up to 52 weeks
- T-notes: from 2 years to 10 years
- T-bonds: from 10 years to 30 years (long bond)

This distinction between bonds and notes has no practical importance. First, it refers to maturities at issue, and therefore you can easily find recently issued notes with maturities exceeding those of seasoned bonds. Second, outside of the U.S. treasury market, the distinction between bonds and notes is not always used in a consistent way. For example, Exhibit 7-1 describes the well-known Walt Disney 100yr issue, which is called a note.

Exhibit 7-1 Walt Disney CO 7.55% 100yr note

Issue 21 Jul 1993	Amount Issued $300 m
1st settlement 28 Jul 1993	Coupon = semiannual
1st Accrual 15 Jul 1993	Day count = 30/360
Maturity 15 Jul 2093	Market = US domestic

The note is callable, with 30 days' notice, as of 15 Jul 2023, according to the following schedule

After	At	After	At	After	At
15-Jul-23	103.02	15-Jul-30	101.96	15-Jul-37	100.91
15-Jul-24	102.87	15-Jul-31	101.81	15-Jul-38	100.76
15-Jul-25	102.72	15-Jul-32	101.66	15-Jul-39	100.60
15-Jul-26	102.57	15-Jul-33	101.51	15-Jul-40	100.45
15-Jul-27	102.42	15-Jul-34	101.36	15-Jul-41	100.30
15-Jul-28	102.27	15-Jul-35	101.21	15-Jul-42	100.15
15-Jul-29	102.11	15-Jul-36	101.06	15-Jul-43	100.00

Source: Bloomberg

- The first settlement date was $T + 5$ after issue. The $T + 3$ rule was implemented in 1995; before that it was $T + 5$.
- The first accrual date (also known as dated date) preceded the first settlement date.

7-2   YIELD ANALYSIS

A number of simple bond-yield indexes were developed prior to the widespread acceptance of the compounded *YTM* approach. We shall briefly examine two of them (current yield and simple yield) before getting on with the analysis of *YTM*. There are some good reasons for this apparent diversion:

- You can find reference to current and/or to simple yield in other publications.
- Current yield has an accounting relevance and is used in other sectors of the fixed-income markets such as perpetual floating rate notes.
- Some markets, such as Japan, quote yields according to the simple yield formula.

Current Yield and Simple Yield

Current yield (*CY*) adjusts the coupon rate (*cr*) to take into account the price of the bond. This adjustment is quite rudimentary, however, because it does not take into account the capital gain (loss) deriving from being reimbursed at face value having bought the bond at a discount (premium). A better adjustment is achieved by the simple yield (*SY*) formula, used in the Japanese bond market. The capital gain or loss (par value—price) is divided by the number of years to maturity and added to the coupon. You can see from Exhibit 7-2 that when prices are close to par, all yield indexes

Exhibit 7-2 Current Yld, Simple Yld and *YTM* for U.S. Treasuries

	Maturity	Coupon	Price	Current yield	Simple yield	YTM
T-note	Jan-2001	5.250%	95.5625	5.49%	6.53%	6.39%
T-note	Jan-2000	6.375%	100.0625	6.37%	6.35%	6.35%
T-bond	Nov-2011	14.000%	152.4688	9.18%	6.93%	6.83%

Source: The *Wall Street Journal*, Friday, 19-Jul-1996

give similar readings. When prices diverge from par, *SY* gives a much better approximation to *YTM* than *CY*.

A number of ingenious mathematical equations have been proposed to analyze the interrelationship among current yield, simple yield, and *YTM*. We shall dispense with them because they have become somewhat irrelevant in the context of modern fixed-income analysis.

Box 7-1 Current Yield and Simple Yield

$$CY = \frac{C}{cP} \text{ current yield}$$

$$SY = \frac{C + (Par - cP)/T}{cP} \text{ simple yield (Japanese bond market)}$$

C = coupon; cP = clean price; Par = par value

Compounded Yield to Maturity

The compounded *YTM* concept was developed well before the analysis of the zero-coupon yield curve and represented a noticeable step forward when compared to more rudimentary return indicators such as current and simple yield. Yield to maturity used to be related to the yield over the entire life of a bond, under the assumption that all the coupons could be reinvested at the *YTM*. This implies not only a flat yield curve but also a yield curve that does not change over the life of the bond (or, more accurately, until the reinvestment date of the last coupon before maturity).

The developers of the *YTM* approach were, of course, fully aware that this coupon-reinvestment assumption was completely unrealistic. A number of authors (see the classic Homer and Leibowitz, 1972), took great care to decompose the overall dollar return of a bond in the following three components:

1. The return attributable to the coupon stream
2. The capital gain (loss) at maturity when the bond is bought at a discount (premium)
3. The interest due to the reinvestment of the coupon stream (the interest-on-interest component).

This apparently clumsy approach turned out to be quite fruitful because it clarified the advantages of zero coupon bonds that do not expose the long-term holder to

coupon reinvestment risk. This certainly contributed to the important financial innovation represented by zeros. It also focused attention on finding ways and means to
lock in a certain rate of return over a defined long-term time horizon (a very relevant
issue for those institutional investors who must fund fixed future liabilities, such as
defined-benefit pension plans). This led to the so-called immunization approach, which
in turn laid the groundwork for a careful analysis of the price elasticity of coupon
bonds and the development of duration and convexity analysis.

The coupon reinvestment interpretation is still referred to in a number of well-
known books; see Fabozzi 1995. It hinges on interpreting *YTM* as the yield on the
whole amount invested over the entire life of the bond (for a simple proof of the
reinvestment condition, see Section 7-6). Yield to maturity also has a less literal but
more meaningful interpretation that derives from the zero-coupon approach. If we
discount all the zeros that compose a coupon bond, using a single rate instead of the
different spot rates, we obtain the *YTM* pricing formula.

Box 7-2   YTM Bond Pricing, Annual Coupon, Annual Compounding

$$PV = \frac{C}{(1 + YTM)} + \frac{C}{(1 + YTM)^2} + \cdots + \frac{100 + C}{(1 + YTM)^T}$$

Par value $= 100$

$C =$ coupon, relative to par value

$T =$ number of years to maturity

The equation assumes that the price is computed at the beginning of a coupon
period.

When *PV* is given, the equation can be solved to determine the value of *YTM*. The
solution requires numerical methods, however, that are preprogrammed on both financial calculators and all commonly used spreadsheets. Looking at things this way
does not require assumptions about the future level of interest rates. It also means that
YTM is that single yield at which you can invest $C/(1 + Y)$ for 1 year; $C/(1 + Y)^2$ for

Exhibit 7-3 Discounting a 5yr, 6% Annual Coupon Bond

Cash flow	YTM 4%	YTM 5%	YTM 6%	YTM 7%	YTM 8%	YTM 9%
6	5.77	5.71	5.66	5.61	5.56	5.50
6	5.55	5.44	5.34	5.24	5.14	5.05
6	5.33	5.18	5.04	4.90	4.76	4.63
6	5.13	4.94	4.75	4.58	4.41	4.25
106	87.12	83.05	79.21	75.58	72.14	68.89
	108.90	104.33	100.00	95.90	92.01	88.33

Exhibit 7-4 Price of 5yr Bonds, Annual Coupons: 6% and 8%

YTM	cr = 6	cr = 8
5%	104.33	112.99
6%	100.00	108.42
7%	95.90	104.10
8%	92.01	100.00
9%	88.33	96.11
10%	84.84	92.42

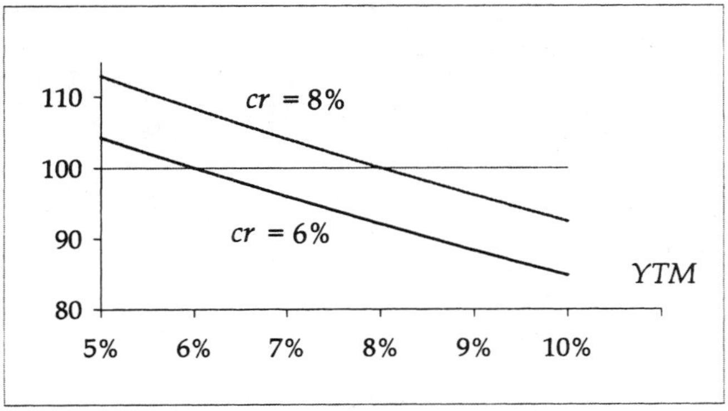

Exhibit 7-5 Price as a Function of YTM for two 8% Bonds

YTM	5yr	10yr
5%	112.99	123.17
6%	108.42	114.72
7%	104.10	107.02
8%	100.00	100.00
9%	96.11	93.58
10%	92.42	87.71

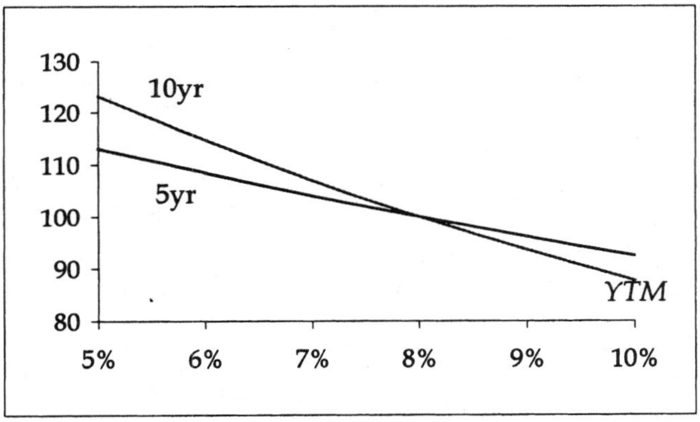

2 years; ...; $(C + 100)/(1 + Y)^T$ for T years (see Exhibit 7-3). Present value as a function of YTM has a downward sloping and convex shape (see Exhibit 7-4) quite similar to that of the *PV* function for a zero coupon bond. This is hardly surprising when we consider that the coupon bond is a set of zeros. When two bonds have the same maturity, the higher coupon obviously translates into a higher price, given any level of YTM. When YTM = *coupon rate*, the bond is priced at par. This is intuitively evident; a simple proof is found in the Mathematical Appendix.

When we compare two bonds with the same coupon but with different maturities, we see that the longer bond is more interest elastic. Again, this is a quite straightforward result when we remember that the interest elasticity of zeros is proportional to their modified duration (see Exhibit 7-5).

A bond will trade at a premium when YTM < cr, and at a discount when YTM > cr. This divergence between *PV* and par value decreases as maturity decreases, which is intuitively evident when we consider that the bond will be reimbursed at par. This *reversion to par* implies that the price fluctuations of a bond due to changes in market rates tend to happen within a narrowing range (i.e., the bullet shape in Exhibit 7-6).

Exhibit 7-6 *PV* as a Function of *T* for an 8% Annual Coupon

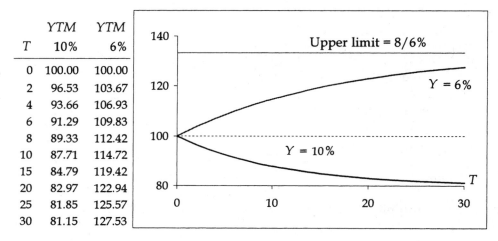

T	YTM 10%	YTM 6%
0	100.00	100.00
2	96.53	103.67
4	93.66	106.93
6	91.29	109.83
8	89.33	112.42
10	87.71	114.72
15	84.79	119.42
20	82.97	122.94
25	81.85	125.57
30	81.15	127.53

Exhibit 7-7 Bond Pricing: 10yr, 8% Coupon

	8.00% ISMA-YTM	8.00% USYTM
annual coupon	100.0000	98.9341
semiannual coupon	101.0399	100.0000

- When $YTM > cr$, PV will decline with the increase in maturity, having the value C/YTM as its lower limit.
- When $YTM < cr$, PV will increase with the increase in maturity, having the value C/YTM as its upper limit.

7-3 YIELD TO MATURITY: OPERATIONAL DETAILS

The analysis can be extended in a very straightforward way to semiannual coupon bonds and/or to semiannual compounding. The relevant equations are summarized in Box 7-3. There are a few properties to remember (see Exhibit 7-7); they all relate to the case in which $cr = YTM$.

- With annual compounding, a semiannual coupon bond will be priced above par.
- With U.S. bond yield basis, a semiannual coupon bond will be quoted at par. In fact, semiannual yield compounding was adopted because of this property; in the U.S. market the majority of bonds pay interest semiannually.
- With semiannual compounding, an annual coupon bond will quote below par.

$8.16\% = (1 + 4\%)^2 - 1 =$ annual yield corresponding to 8% U.S. bond yield

$7.8461\% = 2 \cdot [\sqrt{(1 + 8\%)} - 1] =$ U.S. bond yield corresponding to 8% annual yield

---

Box 7-3   Yield to Maturity

semiannual coupon, annual compounding

$$PV = \frac{C/2}{(1 + YTM)^{0.5}} + \frac{C/2}{(1 + YTM)} + \cdots + \frac{100 + C/2}{(1 + YTM)^T}$$

semiannual coupon, semiannual compounding (TS = term, semesters to maturity)

$$PV = \frac{C/2}{(1 + YTM_{US}/2)} + \frac{C/2}{(1 + YTM_{US}/2)^2} + \cdots + \frac{100 + C/2}{(1 + YTM_{US}/2)^{TS}}$$

annual coupon, semiannual compounding

$$PV = \frac{C}{(1 + YTM_{US}/2)^2} + \cdots + \frac{100 + C}{(1 + YTM_{US}/2)^{TS}}$$

Coupon Accrual and Bond Pricing

When you price a bond within a coupon period, you must remember that the discounted value of the bond equals the dirty price, which includes the accrued coupon. In the case of annual coupon and annual compounding, you can use the following pricing equation.

$$PV = (1 + Y)^h \cdot \left(\frac{C}{(1 + Y)} + \cdots + \frac{100 + C}{(1 + Y)^T} \right)$$

PV = dirty price, also called invoice price
h = elapsed fraction of the current coupon period $h < 1$
T = number of coupons carried by the bond

We can now subtract accrued interest to obtain the clean price.

$$cP = PV - h \cdot cr \cdot 100 = \text{clean price}$$

Some bonds are issued with an initial settlement date that comes a few days after the beginning of the coupon period (also known as the *dated date*); therefore the first settlement price is a dirty price (an interesting example is the Walt Disney note; see exhibit 7-1. The first coupon period started on 15 July 1993 while the first settlement date was 28 July).

We shall now examine some of the analytics relating to the determination of PV. We shall refer to straightforward computations, using the 30/360 rule, to keep things simple and avoid irrelevant details. Note, however, that banks and investment houses carry out precise calculations to determine the *true yield*, utilizing the exact number of days that separate the pricing day from the payments of all the coupons. This will capture the price effect (usually minimal) of leap years and of coupon payment dates that get shifted because they fall on non–business days (an example is the World Bank 6⅜ bond, which pays interest on 21 January and 21 July; it happened that 21 July 1996 was a Sunday, and the coupon was paid on the following Monday).

Exhibit 7-8 Clean Price Within the Annual Coupon Period for a 6% Bond Priced to Yield 6%, and a 10% Bond Priced to Yield 10%

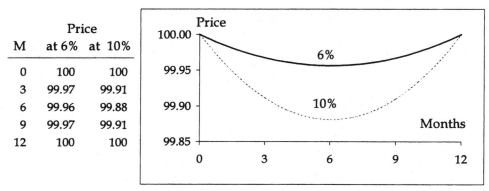

	Price	
M	at 6%	at 10%
0	100	100
3	99.97	99.91
6	99.96	99.88
9	99.97	99.91
12	100	100

Exhibit 7-9 Clean Price Within the Semiannual Coupon Period for a 6% Bond Priced to Yield 6% and a 10% Bond Priced to Yield 10%

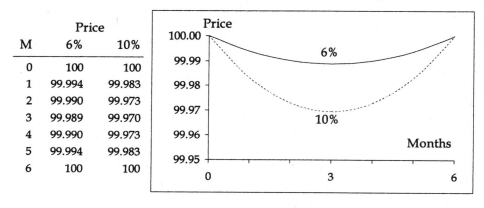

	Price	
M	6%	10%
0	100	100
1	99.994	99.983
2	99.990	99.973
3	99.989	99.970
4	99.990	99.973
5	99.994	99.983
6	100	100

When you buy a bond within a coupon period, you pay immediately for the accrued coupon, and therefore you lose interest on this accrued amount (you will be paid the coupon at maturity). The effect of this loss of interest is that the price must adjust downward by a few basis points to compensate. A neat way to visualize this effect is to consider a bond that is priced at $YTM = cr$. Such a bond will quote at par ($= 100$) when bought at the beginning of a coupon period and will quote marginally below par within the time interval between two consecutive coupon dates. Exhibit 7-8 shows that

- The price adjustment is more than proportional to cr; this is intuitively evident when you consider that a higher coupon means both a higher accrued value and the loss of interest on such accrued value at a higher YTM.
- The price adjustment reaches a maximum at the midpoint of the coupon period.

Note that Exhibits 7-8 and 7-9 (which reflect standard securities industry calculations) assume that the loss of interest on the accrued coupon is calculated at YTM. This could be somewhat inaccurate when the short-term rate is materially different from the bond rate.

Exhibit 7-10 Downward *PV* Adjustment to Compensate Coupon-Accrual Jump

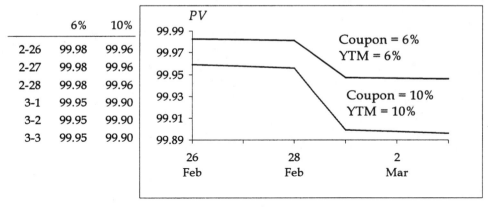

	6%	10%
2-26	99.98	99.96
2-27	99.98	99.96
2-28	99.98	99.96
3-1	99.95	99.90
3-2	99.95	99.90
3-3	99.95	99.90

Exhibit 7-11 *YTM* calculations

	U.S.-Treasury note	World Bank global Bond	World Bank global Bond
Amount issued $m	$15,003	$1,500	DEM3000
Coupon rate	6.50%	6.375%	5.875%
Coupon frequency	semi ann.	semi ann.	annual
Coupon date 1	15-Feb	21-Jan	10-Nov
Coupon date 2	15-Aug	21-Jul	*not-app.*
Day-count	ACT/ACT	30/360	30/360
Maturity	15-Aug-05	21-Jul-05	10-Nov-03
Call date	non-call.	non-call.	non-call.
Asked price	97.75	96.00	99.50
Trade date	24-Jul-96	24-Jul-96	24-Jul-96
Settlement date	25-Jul-96	29-Jul-96	29-Jul-96
USYTM	6.84%	6.98%	5.87%
YTM-ISMA	6.95%	7.10%	5.96%

Source: The *Wall Street Journal* and *Financial Times*

When the coupon accrues semiannually, the price adjustment is much lower, at the coupon period midpoint, only 3 months of interest have accrued and you lose interest for only 3 months.

When interest accrues according to the 30/360 rule, you must add 3 days between 28 February and 1 March. Again, this means that the price must adjust downward to take into account the discontinuity in coupon accrual. When a month has 31 days, you miss a day's accrual at month's end. Therefore price will adjust upward by a few basis points (see Exhibits 7-10 and 7-11).

You find a summary of *YTM* calculations in Exhibit 7-11. Remember that:

Exhibit 7-12 Example

T	USY(T)	Y(T)	Spread	Y(T) + s	B(0, T)	Cash flow	PV
1	5.43%	5.50%	0.945%	6.45%	0.9394	7	6.5759
2	5.67%	5.75%	0.945%	6.70%	0.8784	7	6.1490
3	5.82%	5.90%	0.945%	6.85%	0.8197	7	5.7382
4	5.91%	6.00%	0.945%	6.94%	0.7645	7	5.3517
5	5.96%	6.05%	0.945%	6.99%	0.7132	7	4.9922
6	6.04%	6.13%	0.945%	7.08%	0.6635	107	70.9930
							99.8000

- The Treasury note settles regular way ($T + 1$) on Thursday, 25 July, while the two World Bank bonds settle $T + 3$, via Euroclear and/or Cedel, on Monday, 29 July.
- The World Bank $ global bond, which can be sold like a local bond in the United States, carries semiannual coupon, U.S. bond style.
- The World Bank $ bond is quoted in both the *Wall Street Journal* (WSJ) and the *Financial Times* (FT). Note that WSJ quotes *YTM* according to the U.S. bond yield basis (6.98%), while FT relies on annual compounding (7.10%).

7-4   YIELD CURVE PRICING, YIELD SPREADS, AND PAR YIELD CURVE

Let us take a brief look at the relationships between pricing coupon bonds with *YTM* and with the zero-coupon yield curve (ZYC). This will allow us to better understand the limitations of *YTM* and of some commonly used indicators, such as the *YTM* spread between two bonds. Pricing a coupon bond using the ZYC means discounting the "virtual" zeros represented by the coupons and principal payments using the spot rates for the relevant maturities. The following equation is for annual coupon, annual compounding, and integer number of years to maturity. The equation can be easily modified for U.S. bond basis compounding and/or for noninteger number of coupon periods to maturity.

The ZYC is usually the T-STRIPS yield curve, and bonds will, as a rule, trade at a spread above Treasuries. If we assume that the spread is constant over all the maturities we can compute it by solving numerically the following equation (see also Exhibit 7-12):

$$PV = \frac{C}{[1 + Y(0,1) + s]} + \cdots + \frac{C + 100}{[1 + Y(0,T) + s]^T}, \ (s = \text{spread})$$

If you want to use exponential rates you get:

$$PV = C \cdot \exp[-(R(0,1) - s] + \cdots + (C + 100) \cdot \exp[-T \cdot (R(0,T) + s)]$$

Example: Take a 6yr, 7% annual coupon Eurobond priced at 99.80, *YTM* = 7.04%, and determine its spread relative to the Treasuries STRIPS ZYC (taking the data from Exhibit 6-4 and expressing the ZYC in terms of International Securities Market Association (ISMA)

Exhibit 7-13 Pricing a 5yr, 7.5% U.S. T-note, *YTM* = 5.99%, Price = 106.47

T	ZYC	PV
0.5	5.20%	3.65
1.0	5.43%	3.55
1.5	5.56%	3.45
2.0	5.67%	3.35
2.5	5.74%	3.26
3.0	5.82%	3.16
3.5	5.84%	3.07
4.0	5.91%	2.97
4.5	5.93%	2.88
5.0	5.96%	77.35
		106.70

Source: Bloomberg

yield). The 0.95% spread is over the ISMA yield derived from the U.S. Treasury STRIPs. If we compute the spread over U.S. bond yield basis, we obtain a marginally lower spread of 0.92%

Finding a numerical solution to the preceding spread equation is very similar to determining *YTM*. Increasing the spread will increase all the discount factors, thereby decreasing *PV*, and the solution to the equation is that spread that equates *PV* to invoice price. In sophisticated and liquid markets, such as that for U.S. Treasury coupon bonds and STRIPS, the pricing of bonds using the ZYC produces results quite in line with current market prices for coupons. For U.S. Treasuries, this is especially true because of the possibility of stripping coupon bonds and notes and of reconstituting coupon securities out of the appropriate set of T-STRIPS. This straightforward and inexpensive arbitrage possibility implies that ZYC pricing and market prices are always quite close (see Exhibit 7-13).

Example: The limited 23 (bp) price discrepancy between the market price and the *PV* computed with the ZYC does not allow a full arbitrage (buy the note, sell the STRIPS) when we consider the transaction costs and marginal price adjustments of trading.

In other less-liquid and well-organized markets, arbitraging a discrepancy between ZYC pricing and market prices can imply substantial transaction costs and, sometimes, the setting up of complex structures, such as asset swaps. In this case, the discrepancy between ZYC pricing and market prices can in fact be quite large. Transaction costs can also be greatly influenced by tax considerations.

Zero Coupon Yield Curve and *YTM*

When we utilize the same ZYC to price two bonds with the same maturity but with different coupons, we notice that the resulting *YTMs* can be different; see Exhibit 7-14. For an upward sloping ZYC, this is intuitively evident. The higher coupon bonds will have more of their price represented by the *PV* of the coupons, which in turn are zeros with a lower yield; this will produce a lower *YTM*.

Exhibit 7-14 *YTM* for 20yr Bonds, Annual Coupons = 5.5% and 9%

T	ZYC
1	6.00%
2	6.20%
3	6.40%
4	6.60%
5	6.80%
10	7.80%
15	8.80%
20	9.80%

YTM [c = 5.5%] = 8.85%

YTM [c = 9%] = 8.65%

ZYC

It would be wrong to say that the 5.5% bond (which yields 20 bp more than the 9% coupon) is a better buy. The two bonds are, in fact, priced off the same spot yield curve. The 9% bond is simply a shorter-duration bond, and its lower *YTM* reflects the upward slope of the ZYC. If the yield curve were to flatten, the differences in *YTM* would vanish. If the yield curve became inverted, the 9% bond would display a higher *YTM* than the 5.5% one.

Exhibit 7-14 is constructed in such a way as to obtain a noticeable 20-bp discrepancy between the *YTM* of the two bonds. The ZYC is quite steep (it increases by 20 bp per year), and the two bonds have very different coupons. Quite often, however, the differences in *YTM* are minimal and can be disregarded. With the ZYC prevailing at 14 November 1996, the *YTM* on 10yr, 6% and 8% bonds would diverge by only 2 bp. In any case, when we compare two coupon bonds with similar redemption dates but with different coupons, we cannot take their *YTM*s at face value, but we should check as to whether we need to introduce an adjustment.

Yield Spread

When comparing bonds, one standard tool of analysis is their *YTM* spread over some reference (benchmark) bond, usually an actively traded treasury security with comparable maturity. The *YTM* spread will reflect a number of factors, such as the following:

- *Credit rating*—a riskier bond trades at a larger spread over the benchmark to compensate for credit risk.
- *Liquidity*—large and actively traded issues command a premium, which translates into a smaller spread over the benchmark.
- *Differences in tax treatment*—a noticeable example comes from the United States, where Treasury securities are exempt from state and city taxes and where municipal securities are exempt from federal tax (and often from state and city taxes as well).

When the ZYC is steep and coupon rates differ in a significant way, yield spreads should be recalculated utilizing the spot yield curve. The necessity of an adjustment

Exhibit 7-15 Zero Yield Curve and Par Yield Curve

T	ZYC	YTM
2	6.10%	6.10%
3	6.20%	6.19%
4	6.30%	6.28%
5	6.40%	6.38%
10	6.90%	6.79%
15	7.40%	7.14%
20	7.90%	7.42%
25	8.40%	7.64%
30	8.90%	7.79%

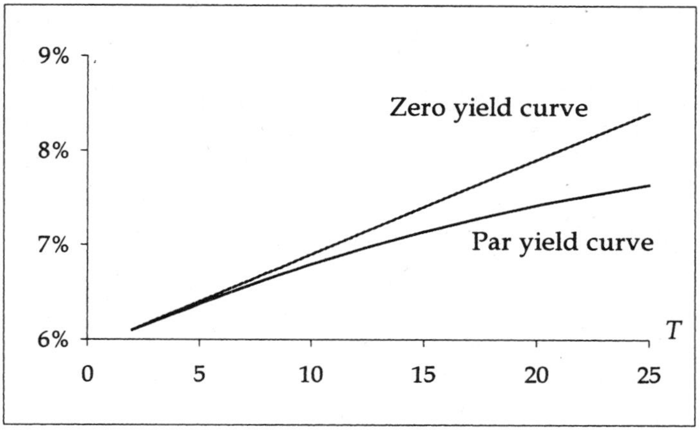

can also reflect the fact that a risky bond may have to pay increasing spreads for more distant maturities, further contributing to the steepness of the ZYC.

Par Yield Curve

Yield curves, showing yield as a function of time to maturity, were produced and analyzed well before the zero coupon approach. Such curves, based on the *YTM* of coupon bonds, are still widely utilized and published in financial papers and on market-data screens (the U.S. Treasuries yield curve published daily by the *Wall Street Journal* is a typical example).

To mitigate some of the problems arising from different coupons, these yield curves are usually constructed utilizing coupon bonds that trade at par or near to par, therefore carrying a coupon rate close to the *YTM* rate.

Government bonds are usually issued at coupon rates that will allow them to be traded close to par at the then-prevailing market rates. Therefore, *on the run* issues are important in building a par yield curve. A 6.50% value for the 5yr maturity would therefore reflect the *YTM* of a 6.50% coupon bond, whereas on the same par yield curve, a 7.20% value for 20yr bonds reflects the *YTM* of a 7.20% coupon bond. In spite of this precaution, the shape of the par yield curve reflects only to a point that of the ZYC, especially when the spot yield curve has a significant slope (see Exhibit 7-15). You should remember, however, that the *YTM* curve allows you to calculate the ZYC, applying a straightforward adaptation of the bootstrap method; see Mathematical Appendix.

7-5   DURATION, CONVEXITY, AND HORIZON YIELD

We can think of the duration of a coupon bond as a weighted average of the duration of its component zeros, the weights being the present values of the zeros; see the Mathematical Appendix. Note that duration is related to *YTM* and therefore measures the proportional change in *PV* due to a small change in *YTM*. We are therefore assuming that all the spot yields underlying the price of the bond will move in the same direction and for the same amount (also known as *parallel yield curve shift*). This parallel yield curve shift assumption represents the weak point of traditional duration analysis. On the other hand, duration is still widely used, albeit as a first approximation. Duration, like *YTM*, has the advantage of being expressed with one number, and this makes it practical to use. A more useful but more complex measure is the so-called *key rate duration*, proposed by T. Ho; see Section 8-2.

Example. Take the 10yr, 7% annual coupon bond priced at 100 to yield 7%. The duration is 7.024, which implies that a 0.10% parallel shift in *YTM* should affect *PV* by

$$\$100 \times 7.024 \times 0.10\% = \$0.7024$$

If you compute the *PV* of the bond, you obtain

$$\begin{cases} PV(7.00\%) = 100.00 \\ PV(7.1\%) = 99.301 \Rightarrow \mathit{\Delta}PV = 0.699 \end{cases}$$

The approximation is quite adequate for gauging price risk. The discrepancy between duration-based values and computed values is of course due to the convexity of the *PV* function.

Box 7-4   Duration of Coupon Bonds

In Macaulay's duration the number of years $(1, 2, 3, \ldots, T)$ after which the coupons and the principal will be paid are weighted by the present values of the payments.

$$D = \frac{\dfrac{C}{(1 + YTM)} + 2 \cdot \dfrac{C}{(1 + YTM)^2} + \ldots + T \cdot \dfrac{(C + 100)}{(1 + YTM)^T}}{PV} \cdot \frac{1}{(1 + Y)} = \frac{D_M}{(1 + Y)}$$

The preceding equation assumes annual coupons and annually compounded yield. It can be easily adapted to fit semiannual coupons and U.S. bond-yield basis.

$$D_{us} = \frac{1}{2} \cdot \frac{\dfrac{0.5 \cdot C}{(1 + 0.5 \cdot YTM_{us})} + \ldots + TS \dfrac{0.5 \cdot C + 100}{(1 + 0.5 \cdot YTM_{us})^{TS}}}{PV} \cdot \frac{1}{(1 + 0.5 \cdot YTM_{us})}$$

TS = the number of semesters to maturity. Dividing by 2 is therefore necessary to express duration in yearly terms.

- Duration is always shorter than term to maturity because of the weight of the coupons that are paid before maturity. Given both maturity and *YTM*, the higher the coupon, the shorter the duration.
- Zeros' duration does not change much with changes in yield. For coupon bonds, the yield elasticity of duration is much higher due to the fact that an increase in yield will increase the proportional weight of the coupons (see Exhibits 7-16 and 7-17).
- For zeros, the increase in duration is a linear function of the increase in term to maturity. The duration of a coupon bond tends to flatten out, as shown in Exhibit 7-18, and has a well-defined limit (and precisely 1/*YTM*). A simple proof of this property is found in the Mathematical Appendix.
- When a bond trades at deep discount (coupon rate much lower than *YTM*), duration can overshoot the preceding limit before converging back again; see Exhibit 7-19. Deep-discount bonds were common in the early 1980s when yields soared and long-term bonds issued at lower rates dropped in value.

Exhibit 7-16 Duration as a Function of Coupon for 10yr Bonds Priced to Yield 7%. Annual Coupon, ISMA Yield

Cpn	PV	D
6%	92.98	7.20
7%	100.00	7.02
8%	107.02	6.87
9%	114.05	6.73
10%	121.07	6.61
11%	128.09	6.50
12%	135.12	6.40
13%	142.14	6.31

Exhibit 7-17 Duration of a 7%, 10yr Bond and of a 7yr Zero, ISMA-Y

Yld	D 7% cpn	D zero
6%	7.180	6.604
7%	7.023	6.542
8%	6.868	6.481
9%	6.714	6.422
10%	6.562	6.363
11%	6.412	6.306
12%	6.263	6.250
13%	6.116	6.194

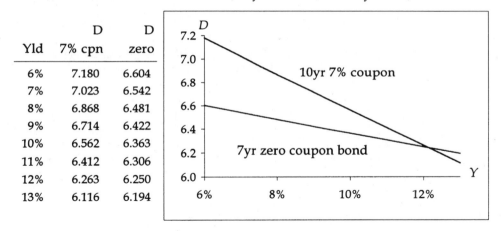

Avoiding Pitfalls when Using Duration

Duration is widely quoted and used, but some precautions are necessary to avoid potentially costly mistakes. Being based on one single rate, duration implies parallel shifts of the spot yield curve. This assumption can be very inaccurate. An example will be useful to clarify the concept. Assume that we have a long position in 3yr notes (see Exhibit 7-20). Based on duration analysis, we could well hedge this position with a short position in 10yr notes. The short position would have to be smaller than the long position to take into account the fact that a 10yr note is more interest elastic than the 3yr one. In fact, the positions should be inversely proportional to the ratio between the durations. Using a smaller position to set up the hedge has the advantage of a lower hedge cost.

If we examine the exhibit, we see that the hedge works quite well under the assumption that the *YTM* for both notes changes by the same amount ($\Delta = 0.5\%$). The loss on the 3yr note is compensated fairly accurately by the gain on the 10yr note, the small difference being due to the difference in convexity.

Exhibit 7-18 Duration of a 7% Coupon Priced to Yield 6% and 8%

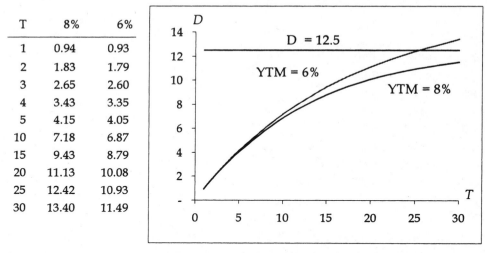

T	8%	6%
1	0.94	0.93
2	1.83	1.79
3	2.65	2.60
4	3.43	3.35
5	4.15	4.05
10	7.18	6.87
15	9.43	8.79
20	11.13	10.08
25	12.42	10.93
30	13.40	11.49

D = 12.5 is the duration limit evaluated at YTM = 8% (12.5 = 1/0.08)

Exhibit 7-19 Duration for a 6% Deep-Discount Bond Priced to Yield
12% Annual coupon, ISMA-Y

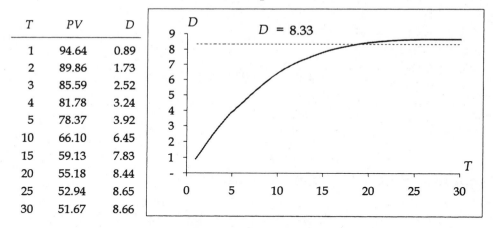

T	PV	D
1	94.64	0.89
2	89.86	1.73
3	85.59	2.52
4	81.78	3.24
5	78.37	3.92
10	66.10	6.45
15	59.13	7.83
20	55.18	8.44
25	52.94	8.65
30	51.67	8.66

This approach to hedging and risk measurement over a diversified portfolio is deceptively simple: duration allows us to convert all positions into a single equivalent duration position in some representative bond (such as 10yr or 30yr). At this point we can consider the algebraic total of all duration-adjusted positions.

An interesting statement of this oversimplified approach is found in Soros (1995, page 6): "For instance, when we deal with interest rate exposure, we reduce everything to the equivalence of a 30-year bond. So we convert even a T-bill to a 30-year bond equivalent." The problem with this approach is that it breaks down when we have nonparallel shifts of the yield curve (see cases 2 and 3 in Exhibit 7-20). Such nonparallel shift are the rule more than the exception in present-day financial markets (see Exhibit 7-21).

Exhibit 7-20 Hedging a $10 million Long Position in a 3yr note with a Short of $3,777,680 on a 10yr note, Annual Coupon

T	Coupon	Price	YTM	D	YTM shift	Price	Gain (loss)
Case 1 = Parallel YTM shifts							
3	6.375%	100.00	6.375%	2.65	0.50%	98.68	($131,516)
10	7.000%	101.00	6.859%	7.05	0.50%	97.52	$131,348
							($168)
Case 2 = Adverse non-parallel YTM shifts							
3	6.375%	100.00	6.375%	2.65	1.00%	97.39	($260,644)
10	7.000%	101.00	6.859%	7.05	0.35%	98.55	$92,699
							($167,945)
Case 3 = Favourable non-parallel YTM shifts							
3	6.375%	100.00	6.375%	2.65	0.35%	99.08	($92,315)
10	7.000%	101.00	6.859%	7.05	1.00%	94.20	$256,912
							$164,598

Exhibit 7-21 Yields on 3yr and 10yr U.S. Treasury Coupons

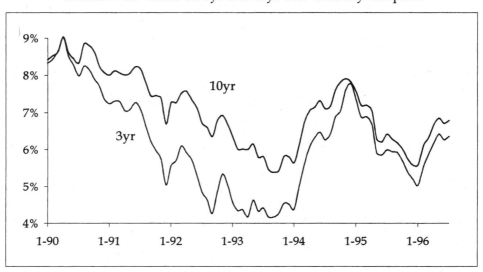

Exhibit 7-22 *PVbp* for Two Coupon Bonds and One Zero, Yld = 7%

T	6%	8%	Zero
1	0.009	0.009	0.009
2	0.018	0.018	0.016
3	0.026	0.027	0.023
4	0.033	0.035	0.029
5	0.040	0.042	0.033
10	0.067	0.073	0.047
15	0.085	0.097	0.051
20	0.098	0.114	0.048
25	0.106	0.127	0.043
30	0.112	0.136	0.037

Price Value of One Basis Point and Yield Value of One 32nd of Price

These indicators have already been examined in Chapter 6, and therefore we do not need to belabor the point. Note, however, that *PVbp* measures the absolute change in *PV* and therefore,

- Coupon bonds do not display the typical price compression of *PVbp* that we find in zeros (see Exhibit 7-22).
- *PVbp* is higher the higher the coupon (for the same maturity and *YTM*), while we know that duration decreases with the increase of the coupon.

Convexity

Again, there is not much to add to the analysis of convexity developed in Chapter 6. We shall therefore focus on a few issues that somehow differentiate convexity for coupon bonds from convexity in a zero-coupon context.

Pure Barbell Trades

The convexity gain obtainable with a pure barbell (same *YTM* and same duration) is lower than that which can be obtained with zeros. This is intuitively evident; while the duration of zeros grows linearly with time to maturity, the duration of coupons converges to an upper limit (1/*YTM*).

This smaller gain from convexity is quite visible if you compare the barbell shown in Exhibit 7-23 with the zero-coupon barbell. Also be well aware of a couple of important points:

• Pure barbell opportunities are difficult to find given the constant quest for arbitrage possibilities by sophisticated investment houses and quantitatively oriented asset managers. These players face very low transaction costs and therefore can exploit relatively small price discrepancies.

• The success of pure barbell trades, exactly as for zeros, is predicated on parallel shifts of the yield curve. Assuming it is feasible to construct a barbell similar to that

Exhibit 7-23 Barbell Trade, all Bonds with 7% Coupons

YTM	10yr	2yr	30yr	Barbell	Gain
5%	115.44	53.93	62.76	116.69	124.79
6%	107.36	52.95	54.61	107.56	20.04
7%	100.00	52.00	48.00	100.00	0.00
8%	93.29	51.07	42.60	93.67	37.90
9%	87.16	50.17	38.14	88.31	114.31

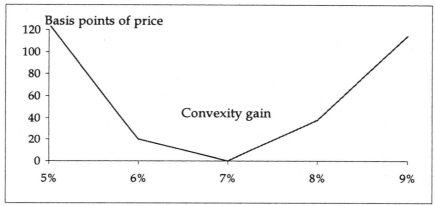

depicted in Exhibit 7-23, there is no doubt that a nonparallel shift of the yield curve could result in the barbell being seriously outperformed by the 10yr bond.

Relative Convexity of Two Coupon Bonds

In the zero coupon world, a longer dated STRIP has both higher duration and higher convexity than a shorter STRIP. This means that a longer zero will outperform the shorter one if rates decrease but will be outperformed if rates increase (we are assuming, as usual, a flat yield curve and parallel shifts).

It is possible, however, to have two coupon bonds with the same duration and different convexities (remember that each of the two bonds is a basket of zeros). The longer bond must have a much higher coupon than the shorter bond in order to have matching duration at the same level of YTM (see Exhibit 7-24).

Beware of Size Distortions

When looking for convexity opportunities, it is necessary to make sure that pricing data relate to the same invested amounts and not to the face values of the different bonds. An example will clarify the issue. If we look at the chart on the left-hand side of Exhibit 7-25, we see that the price difference (PVA − PVB) decreases when YTM moves away from the 6.8% level. If you are not careful, you could draw the wrong conclusion that bond B has a convexity advantage over bond A.

If you compare the two bonds on the basis of the same invested amount at 6.8%, you get the right-hand side chart, which displays no gain from convexity. These mistakes are easy to make. Exhibit 7-25 is adapted from a well-known fixed-income book,

Exhibit 7-24 Relative Convexity of Two Coupon Bonds

YTM	20yr 6%	26yr 10%
4%	127.181	129.444
6%	100.000	100.447
8%	80.364	80.364
10%	65.946	66.078
12%	55.183	55.643

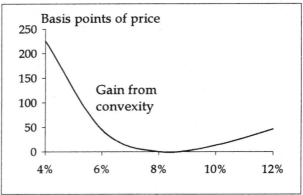

Exhibit 7-25 Price Spreads: Bond-A (18yr, 14%), Bond-B (30yr, 9%)

	Unadjusted		18yr	Adjusted		18yr
	18yr	30yr	minus	18yr	30yr	minus
YTM	14%	9%	30yr	14%	9%	30yr
5.0%	206.00	161.82	44.19	118.32	126.42	-8.10
6.0%	187.33	141.51	45.82	107.59	110.56	-2.96
6.8%	174.11	128.00	46.11	100.00	100.00	0.00
7.0%	171.02	124.94	46.07	98.22	97.61	0.61
8.0%	156.72	111.31	45.41	90.02	86.96	3.05
9.0%	144.17	100.00	44.17	82.80	78.12	4.68
10.0%	133.09	90.54	42.56	76.44	70.73	5.71
12.0%	114.62	75.76	38.86	65.83	59.19	6.65
14.0%	100.00	64.90	35.10	57.44	50.70	6.73

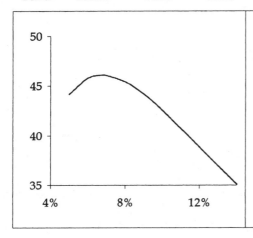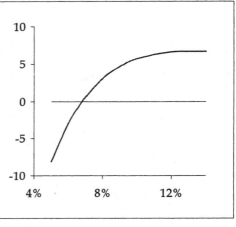

where it is used as an example of convexity gain that portfolio managers should be looking for. Not a good idea, really.

7-6 MATHEMATICAL APPENDIX

Value of the Unit Annuity

A coupon bond can be viewed as both a collection of zeros and an annuity (= the stream of coupon payments) plus a zero represented by the reimbursement of the principal. As we shall see, this decomposition is useful in some mathematical manipulations.

$PVca$ = present value of the coupon annuity
cr = annual coupon rate

$$PVca = 100 \cdot \left[\frac{cr}{(1 + Y)} + \frac{cr}{(1 + Y)^2} + \ldots + \frac{cr}{(1 + Y)^T} \right]$$

$$= 100 \cdot cr \cdot [(1 + Y)^{-1} + \ldots + (1 + Y)^{-T}]$$

The term in square brackets is the sum of a geometric progression; therefore

$$PVca = 100 \cdot cr \cdot [(1 + Y)^{-1} + \ldots + (1 + Y)^{-T}] \cdot \frac{1 - (1 + Y)^{-1}}{1 - (1 + Y)^{-1}}$$

$$= 100 \cdot cr \cdot \frac{(1 + Y)^{-1} - (1 + Y)^{-T-1}}{\dfrac{1 + Y - 1}{1 + Y}} = 100 \cdot cr \cdot \frac{(1 + Y)^{-1} - (1 + Y)^{-T-1}}{Y \cdot (1 + Y)^{-1}}$$

$$= 100 \cdot cr \cdot \frac{1 - (1 + Y)^{-T}}{Y}.$$

The preceding result is quite well known (it was also used by Keynes in *The General Theory*) and implies that the present value of a unit annuity tends to $1/Y$ when $T \rightarrow \infty$ (see Exhibit 7-26).

Reinvesting All the Coupons at Y is a Sufficient Condition for Investing PV at Y, over the Whole Life of the Bond

$$PV = \frac{c}{(1 + Y)} + \frac{c}{(1 + Y)^2} + \ldots + \frac{c + 100}{(1 + Y)^T}$$

Investing PV at Y for T years means obtaining a future value $FV = PV(1 + Y)^T$. We can therefore multiply the two sides of the preceding equation by $(1 + Y)^T$.

$$PV(1 + Y)^T = \frac{c(1 + Y)^T}{1 + Y} + \ldots + \frac{(c + 100)*(1 + Y)^T}{(1 + Y)^T}$$

$$PV(1 + Y)^T = c(1 + Y)^{T-1} + c(1 + Y)^{T-2} + \ldots + c + 100$$

Exhibit 7-26 Value of the Ordinary Annuity of $1/yr

T	6%	8%
1	0.94	0.93
2	1.83	1.78
3	2.67	2.58
4	3.47	3.31
5	4.21	3.99
10	7.36	6.71
15	9.71	8.56
20	11.47	9.82
25	12.78	10.67
30	13.76	11.26
40	15.05	11.92
60	16.16	12.38

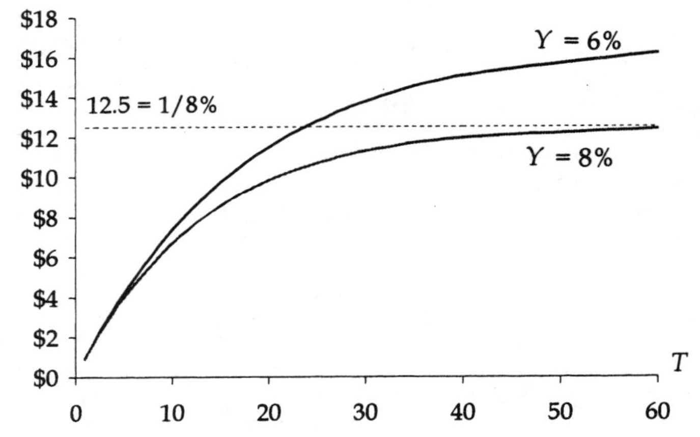

When we examine the right-hand side of the preceding equation, we immediately notice that the first term is the *FV* of the first coupon, the second term equals the FV of the second coupon, etc.

When $Y = cr$ the Present Value of a Bond Will Equal Par = 100

$$PV = PVca + \frac{100}{(1 + Y)^T} = 100\left[cr\,\frac{1 - (1 + Y)^{-T}}{Y} + (1 + Y)^{-T}\right]$$

$$= 100\left[\frac{cr}{Y} - \frac{cr}{Y} \cdot (1 + Y)^{-T} + (1 + Y)^{-T}\right]$$

$$= 100[1 - (1 + Y)^{-T} + (1 + Y)^{-T}] = 100$$

Modified Duration (Annual Coupon, Annual Compounding)

Macaulay's duration is defined as the average maturity of all payments weighted by their present values:

$$D_M \equiv \frac{c \cdot (1 + Y)^{-1} + 2c \cdot (1 + Y)^{-2} + \ldots + T \cdot (c + 100) \cdot (1 + Y)^{-T}}{PV}$$

We now want to prove that, for coupon bonds

$$D = \frac{D_M}{(1 + Y)}$$

The derivative of a sum of functions equals the sum of the derivatives; therefore

$$D = \frac{dPV}{dY} \cdot \frac{1}{PV}$$

$$= \frac{d}{dY}[c \cdot (1 + Y)^{-1} + c \cdot (1 + Y)^{-2} + \dots + (c + 100) \cdot (1 + Y)^{-T}] \cdot \frac{1}{PV}$$

$$D = [-c \cdot (1 + Y)^{-2} - 2 \cdot c \cdot (1 + Y)^{-3} - \dots - T \cdot (c + 100) \cdot (1 + Y)^{-T-1}] \cdot \frac{1}{PV}.$$

Multiply and divide the right-hand side of the equation by $(1 + Y)$ to obtain:

$$D = \left[\frac{-c \cdot (1 + Y)^{-1} - 2 \cdot c \cdot (1 + Y)^{-2} - \dots - T \cdot (c + 100) \cdot (1 + Y)^{-T}}{PV} \right]$$

$$\cdot \frac{1}{(1 + Y)} = \frac{D_M}{(1 + Y)}$$

Note that duration is always expressed as a positive number; this is why we change the sign of the derivative of PV as a function of Y.

Modified Duration for Coupon Bonds when $T \to \infty$

For zeros, duration increases linearly with term to maturity, whereas for coupon bonds it converges to the value $(1/Y)$. This is easy to prove using the limit of PV.

$$\lim(PV \,|\, T \to \infty) = \frac{100 \cdot cr}{Y}$$

$$D = \frac{d}{dY}\left[\frac{100 \cdot cr}{Y} \right] \cdot \frac{1}{PV}$$

$$D = -100 \cdot cr \cdot Y^{-2} \frac{Y}{100 \cdot cr} = \frac{1}{Y}$$

Modified Duration (U.S. Bond Yield Basis)

$$D_{us} = \frac{d}{dY_{us}}\left[\frac{c}{2} \cdot \left(1 + \frac{Y_{us}}{2}\right)^{-1} + \frac{c}{2} \cdot \left(1 + \frac{Y_{us}}{2}\right)^{-2} + \dots + \left(\frac{c}{2} + 100\right) \cdot \left(1 + \frac{Y_{us}}{2}\right)^{-2T} \right]$$

$$\cdot \frac{1}{PV_{us}}$$

$$D_{us} = \left[-\frac{c}{2} \cdot \left(1 + \frac{Y_{us}}{2}\right)^{-2} - 2 \cdot \frac{c}{2} \cdot \left(1 + \frac{Y_{us}}{2}\right)^{-3} - \dots - 2T \cdot \left(\frac{c}{2} + 100\right) \right.$$

$$\left. \cdot \left(1 + \frac{Y_{us}}{2}\right)^{-2T-1} \right] \cdot \frac{1}{PV_{us}}$$

First, divide by 2 the right-hand side of the equation to measure Macaulay's duration in years and not in semesters (this is market practice). Second, multiply and divide the right-hand side of the equation by $(1 + \tfrac{1}{2}Y_{us})$ to obtain

$$D_{us} = \frac{D_M}{1 + 0.5 \times Y_{us}}.$$

Chapter **8**

Coupon Bonds: Advanced Topics

8-1 SIMPLE DURATION PITFALLS: THE ORANGE COUNTY CASE

On 1 December 1994 the board of supervisors of the $7.4 billion Orange County Investment Pool (OCIP) officially announced a staggering $1.5 billion loss. A few days later, the county filed for protection under the provisions of U.S. bankruptcy legislation (the reason for this bankruptcy filing will soon be evident). The loss was later adjusted upward to $1.7 billion—that is, to nearly 23% of the assets under management. (For a detailed and highly readable account of the Orange County fiasco, see Jorion [1995]). The news of the loss was all the more shocking because Orange County's treasurer, Robert Citron, had directly managed the fund for many years with consistently good results. Due to his track record, Citron was a minor celebrity in the world of public treasurers.

The county subsequently sued a number of securities houses that had acted as brokers to OCIP. The main broker, Merrill Lynch, settled out of court for more than $400 million in mid 1998. In August 1998, although denying any wrongdoing, Merrill Lynch agreed to pay a $2 million penalty imposed by the Securities and Exchange Commission.

The Orange County fiasco attracted a lot of publicity and press coverage. The main reason for this was that some of the strategies and products Robert Citron used had a distinctive derivatives-like flavor. In 1994–1995, derivatives made good news after a series of well-publicized fiascoes (Procter and Gamble, Metallgesellschaft, Barings, etc.). A number of financial commentators used the D-word as if derivatives were inherently evil.

The evil-derivatives interpretation provided good headlines for newspaper and magazine articles. It also suited very well Orange County, which could claim that it had been misled by greedy Wall Street types. The same line of defense was adopted by Robert Citron, who claimed that the investment strategies he implemented were suggested by the OCIP broker/dealers and were too complex for him to understand. The exceedingly favorable settlements that Orange County has collected owe a lot to this populist line of defense.

Exhibit 8-1 Stylized Financial Scenario in the U.S., end 1993

	Rate/YTM	D	$PVbp$
Short term borrowing	3.20%		
3yr notes	4.40%	2.78	$0.028
10yr notes	5.50%	7.62	$0.076
Ratio of durations		2.74	

Exhibit 8-2 Extra Return on Leveraged Portfolio

Return on $274 million 3yr notes	$6,028,000
Repo cost on $174 million	-$2,784,000
Return on leveraged portfolio	$3,244,000
Return on $ 100 million 10yr notes	$2,750,000

In fact, the Orange County fiasco had very little to do with complex derivatives; rather, it involved using duration in a naive way, that is, assuming that the parallel yield shift paradigm holds well enough to be adopted in investment strategies. Let us consider the following stylized fixed-income environment, that gives a simplified but true picture of the U.S. fixed-income market conditions at the end of 1993, after several years of decline in market yields (see Exhibit 8-1).

If you assume parallel term-structure shifts, then $274 million of 3yr notes appear to carry the same market risk as $100 million of 10yr notes. Let us further assume that you are relatively optimistic about the bond market, that is, you don't believe that the increase in future yields implied by the positively sloped yield curve will in fact materialize. Let us say that you believe that the yield curve will remain roughly unchanged, and therefore you expect your horizon yield on the 3yr and 10yr notes to be in line with their yield to maturity (YTM). Under this scenario you can enhance your return by (1) holding $274 million of 3yr notes instead of $100 million of the 10yr, and (2) financing the $174 million of extra investment through repos (see Exhibit 8-2).

Under the parallel-shift assumption, this repo-leveraged strategy entails a "free lunch." It yields more than investing in straightforward 10yr notes and has the same duration risk. The problem is, of course, the possibility that 3yr yields can very well go up by more than the 10yr yields. This is precisely what happened in 1994, as shown by Exhibit 8-3.

The fact that 3yr YTM increased 30% more than the par yield on 10yr notes certainly contributed to the losses suffered by OCIP. In fact, the OCIP had a 2.7 leverage, and its losses were very similar to those on a pure 3yr notes portfolio leveraged 2.7 times through repos. The situation of Orange County was in fact more complex than its stylized representation. Part of the portfolio was invested in instruments such as inverse floaters, which display a surprisingly high duration, see Chapter 9. The repo-financed nature of the OCIP also explains why the county sought protection under the bankruptcy code. All the county officials were trying to achieve—unsuccessfully—was to get the court to order a stay, which would prevent its repo counterparties from selling the repo collateral (see Section 4-4).

Exhibit 8-3 Market Yields Changes in 1994

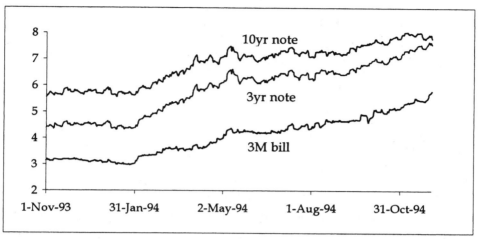

Source: Bloomberg

8-2   KEY RATE DURATION

We have seen that duration is heavily dependent on unrealistic assumptions about near-parallel yield curve shifts. An interesting (and very easy to implement) way to overcome the limitations of traditional duration has been proposed by Ho (1992). This approach consists of starting with the spot yield curve and defining a certain number of key maturities, also called *factors*. Ho proposed using a key maturity for each of the on-the-run Treasuries, but we shall simplify our description by using only four key rates:

$R(0,t)$: some very-short-term-rate T-bills, Fed Funds. etc.

$R(0,2)$: 2yr T-note

$R(0,10)$: 10yr T-note

$R(0,30)$: 30yr T-bond

The next step is based on the simplifying assumption that a change in any key rate will not, by itself, change the adjacent key rates but will change the intermediate rates in a linearly declining fashion. This sounds like a mouthful but is easily visualized in Exhibit 8-4, which shows the effect of a 100–basis point increase of the 10yr key rate. If you assume that there is more than one key rate change, the effect will be simply that of adding together the linear changes. Exhibit 8-5 shows the changes due to short rate = +80 bp, 2yr = +130 bp, 10yr = +100 bp, and 30yr = +80 bp. Given this construction, you can define the duration (or the *PVbp*) of a fixed-income instrument with respect to each key rate. A 7yr note will clearly have a duration relative to the short-term, 2yr, and 10yr key rates. And its total duration will be the sum of the relevant key rate durations (see Exhibit 8-6).

Exhibit 8-4 Effect of a 100 Basis Points Change in the 10yr Key Rate

R(0, 1)	0
R(0, 2)	0.0
R(0, 3)	12.5
R(0, 9)	87.5
R(0, 10)	100.0
R(0, 11)	95.0
R(0, 29)	5.0
R(0, 30)	0

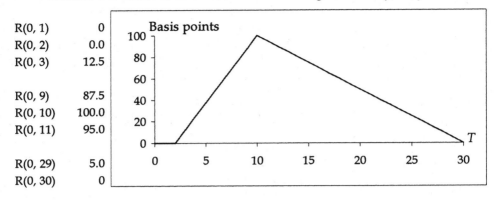

Exhibit 8-5 Changes in Four Key Rates, in Basis Points

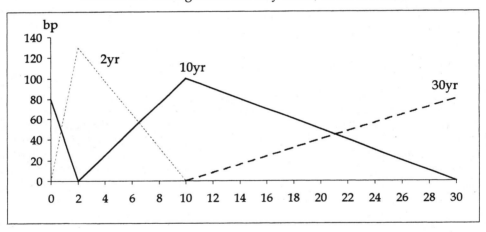

8-3 CALLABLE BONDS, SINKING FUND BONDS, AND OPTION-ADJUSTED SPREAD

Callable bonds embed a call option in favor of the issuer, which has the right—but not the obligation—to redeem the bond prior to maturity at a stated price(s). The clauses that define the right to call are described in the indenture of the bond. The bond can be called at par or at a premium. Some bonds have several dates on which they can be called and premiums that decrease as the call gets nearer to maturity. The 100-year Walt Disney note is an interesting example of multiple call dates.

The call feature is in favor of the issuer and allows it to take advantage of both a general decline in interest rates and an improvement of its credit rating, which will allow it to raise funds at a lower rate. When the coupon rate of a callable bond is higher than the coupon that would be paid on new debt, the issuer will profit from calling the bond and refunding it at the going rate.

If the issuer limits itself to a pure refunding of a callable bond, it can also take advantage of a positively shaped yield curve. If a bond with an original term of 20 years could be called in July 1996, 5 years prior to maturity, the issuer could refund

Exhibit 8-6 Computing Key Rate Duration on a 7yr Note, Cpn = 5.25%

T	Cash flow	Baseline spot Y	Short Y + 10 bp	2yr Y + 10 bp	10yr Y + 10 bp
1	5.25	4.95%	5.00%	5.0500%	4.95%
2	5.25	5.00%	5.00%	5.1500%	5.00%
3	5.25	5.05%	5.05%	5.1375%	5.06%
4	5.25	5.10%	5.10%	5.1750%	5.13%
5	5.25	5.15%	5.15%	5.2125%	5.19%
6	5.25	5.20%	5.20%	5.2500%	5.25%
7	105.25	5.25%	5.25%	5.2875%	5.31%
Price		100.1175	100.1151	99.8692	99.7884
$PVbp$			0.0002	0.0248	0.0329
D			0.0238	2.4858	3.2977

Exhibit 8-7 Yield to Call (*YTC*) for a U.S. T-bond

Cpn	Mty	1st call	Bid	Ask	Y	YTC
14%	6-Nov-11	6-Nov-06	151 :00	151 :04	8.11%	6.97%

Source: The *Wall Street Journal*, 24 July 1996

by issuing 5yr bonds at a rate that is about 50 bp lower than the 20yr rate. The exercise of the call option must, however, take into account some additional factors.

- The transaction costs connected to the exercise of the call
- The transaction costs related to the new issue to refund the call
- Certain public-relations considerations; this means that issuer could well decide not to exercise a call to keep the goodwill of investors.

Some bonds are noncallable (such as U.S. T-bonds issued after 1985). Other issues are protected only against refunding, that is, against a call that requires the issuer to refund itself through a new bond issue. Protection against refunding is therefore weaker and also less clearly defined than outright protection against call.

Yield to Call: The Simple, One-Call-at-Par Case

Yield to call (*YTC*) is nothing more than *YTM* calculated by substituting the call date for the maturity date and the call price for the reimbursement price. This is a commonly used indicator, widely quoted both on market-data screens and in the financial press, when *YTM* is lower than the coupon rate and the bond is priced above par.

Exhibit 8-7 shows the *Wall Street Journal* quotation for the 14% U.S. T-bond, maturity 15 November 2011, callable at par on any coupon date starting 15 November

Exhibit 8-8 Price of the 10% May 2010 U.S. T-bond, Callable at Par

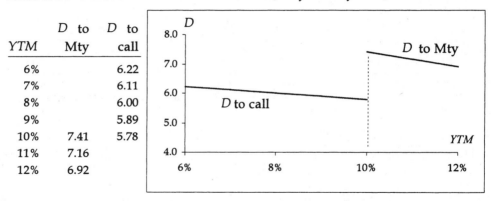

Y	Price to Mty	Price to call
5%	149.48	135.34
6%	137.22	127.10
7%	126.29	119.50
8%	116.53	112.47
9%	107.80	105.98
10%	99.97	99.97
11%	92.95	94.41
12%	86.63	89.25
13%	80.93	84.47

Exhibit 8-9 Duration of the 10% U.S. T-bond, Mty = May 2010, Callable at Par

YTM	D to Mty	D to call
6%		6.22
7%		6.11
8%		6.00
9%		5.89
10%	7.41	5.78
11%	7.16	
12%	6.92	

2006. Ask YTM is referred only to the first call date and therefore is a YTC (or, more accurately, a yield to first call). The relationship between price and yield for callable bonds is often defined in terms of two separate functions (see Exhibit 8-8):

- The first is YTM and is used when $YTM >$ coupon rate and $PV < 100$
- The second is YTC and is used when $YTM <$ coupon rate and $PV > 100$

The overall P function displays a negative convexity at the intersection of $P = f(YTM)$ and $P = f(YTC)$. It is also intuitively evident that a callable bond displays a discontinuity in duration when we shift from YTM to YTC (see Exhibit 8-9).

YTM and YTC are widely used and quoted indicators but must be interpreted as only a first approximation. To simplify our discussion of this issue, let us consider a bond callable at par at one fixed date only ($T_c < T$). If the market price is higher than par and you use YTM (T), you are clearly inflating the yield measure because you are implicitly assuming that the call will not be exercised. A better way of looking at this is to remember that the bond comes with an embedded call option in favor of the issuer. The value of this contingent liability should be detracted from the market price to obtain an option-adjusted price. Having done that, you can compute an option-adjusted yield (OAY). On the basis of the OAY you can easily compute the option-adjusted spread with reference to some benchmark bond, usually a Treasury coupon.

$$P^* = P - C(P, Par, T_C) = \text{call-adjusted price;}$$

$$C(P, Par, T_C) = \text{Value of a call at par}$$

YTC is an inflated yield measure. Using YTC entails that you are considering a bond that will reimbursed at par at $T_C < T$. Compare this callable bond with a similar straight bond with term T_C. If market yields continue to be lower than the coupon rate, both bonds will be redeemed at par on the same date. However, market yields could well soar; in this case the straight bond will be redeemed at par while the callable bond will not be called, and the bondholders will be stuck with a bond trading below par. The correct way to deal with this problem is to adjust the price for the value of a put in favor of the issuer. When a callable bond is priced above par, you can therefore consider it in two different ways:

1. As a bond with maturity T with an embedded call option in favor of the issuer
2. As a bond with maturity $T_C < T$ with an embedded put option, always in favor of the issuer.

When the bond is priced below par, most quotation services will give you only its YTM. Once more, this is an inflated yield measure. The call option may be worth less than when the bond is priced above par, but it still has a value that should be detracted from the market price of the bond.

Yield to Call: Several Call Dates and Declining Call Premiums

When we have several call dates and declining call premiums (think of the Walt Disney bonds), we can determine YTC for each of the call dates. The lowest among these YTC is usually indicated as yield to worst-call. It is useless to spend time on this issue, which is rather easy from a computational point of view.

Sinking Fund Bonds

Some corporate and municipal bonds are issued with a sinking fund provision that obliges the issuer to reimburse the bonds with a series of installments, starting well before the final maturity. The origin of the sinking fund provision is related to the idea of bonds being used to finance specific long-term investments, which in turn were supposed to produce a cash flow sufficient both to pay interest and to reimburse the bonds. The concept underlying the sinking fund bond was therefore to utilize the cash flow (based on some educated guess) to gradually repay the bond instead of accumulating a cash pool to finance redemption at maturity. There are a number of sinking fund patterns, such as:

- *Constant capital amortization,* which implies that total payments to bondholders will decline in time because interest is computed on a decreasing outstanding debt

Exhibit 8-10 Level Payment Amortization: Cpn = 6%, T = 30

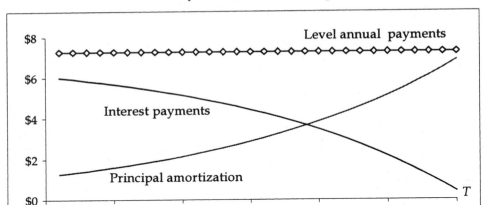

- *Level total payment*, which entails increasing principal reimbursements to compensate for declining interest payments; see Exhibit 8-10. The total annual payment, relative to a $100 face value, is given by the equation for the ordinary annuity, which we examined in Section 7-6.

$$CF = 100 \left/ \frac{1 - (1 + YTM)^{-T}}{YTM} \right.$$

using the exponential notation we obtain

$$CF = 100 \left/ \frac{1 - (\exp(-T \cdot R))}{\exp(R) - 1} \right.$$

When the bond trades below par, some sinking fund provisions allow the issuer to buy the bonds on the open market, thereby paying less than par for redemption. This will usually have a positive effect on the price of the bond, that will benefit from the knowledge that the issuer will have to come to the market and buy in size.

Other sinking fund provisions stipulate that the issuer will have to repay at par, selecting the bonds either on the basis of "fair and reasonable" pro rata rules or by lottery. The lottery system was more widespread when bonds were represented by physical certificates because it allowed the issuer to determine in a fair way what certificates would be redeemed.

Now that bonds are represented by book entries with some depository trustee (Federal Reserve, Depository Trust Co., Euroclear, Cedel), it is more feasible to reimburse on a pro rata basis (which eliminates unnecessary uncertainty about cash flows and yields). When bonds are repaid on a pro rata basis (such as in the case of pass-through mortgage-backed securities), the bonds will have both an original face value and an amortized value, expressing how much has already been repaid.

When the bond is trading above par, the issuer has a right to partial calls for the quantities of bonds that will be, from time to time, needed to comply with the sinking fund provision. Again, the dematerialization of bonds allow pro rata repayments.

When pro rata provisions apply, it is possible to calculate the *YTM*, for each single bond, utilizing the following equation:

Box 8-1   *YTM* with Fixed-Amortization Plan

$$PV = \frac{cr \cdot 100 + k_1}{1 + YTM} + \frac{cr \cdot (100 - k_1) + k_2}{(1 + YTM)^2} + \ldots + \frac{cr \cdot \left(100 - \sum_1^{T-1} k_j\right) + k_T}{(1 + YTM)^T}$$

k_j = amount repayable at time j

cr = coupon rate

8-4   EXTRACTING THE SPOT YIELD CURVE FROM COUPON BONDS

It is often necessary to derive the spot yield curve from a set of coupon bonds, and this poses certain complications with regard to both of the following:

- The scrubbing of data (e.g., eliminating bonds that are known not to be representative either for their lack of liquidity or because the quotations are influenced by shorts that must cover their positions)
- The statistical methods that must be employed

We already noted in Chapter 5 that yield-curve fitting and stochastic modeling have become budding applications of financial econometrics. Although financial econometrics lies outside the scope of this book, it is interesting to examine, albeit briefly, the simple technique of fitting a cubic polynomial. This requires only elementary mathematics but will give you a good feel for the sort of manipulations used in curve building. Note that things become somewhat more complicated when the yield curve has a shape that requires the use of more than one cubic polynomial.

Using a Cubic Polynomial to Derive Spot Yields from Coupon Bonds

The method consists of approximating the discount factors using a cubic function of time. Discount factors (the present value of $1 payable at time T) can be expressed in several ways, depending on which yield basis we use:

$$d(T) = \frac{1}{(1 + Y)^T} = \text{ISMA yield}$$

$$d(T) = \frac{1}{\left(1 + \dfrac{Y_{US}}{2}\right)^{2T}} = \text{U.S. bond basis}$$

$$d(T) = \exp(-R \cdot T) = \text{continuous compounding}$$

Irrespective of the way we define discount factors, the method tries to approximate them with a cubic function

$$\hat{d}(T) = a_0 + a_1 \cdot (T) + a_2 \cdot (T)^2 + a_3 \cdot (T)^3.$$

The discount factor for $T = 0$ ($1 immediately available) must necessarily be one; therefore $a_0 = 1$, and the preceding equation can be rewritten as:

$$\hat{d}(T) - 1 = a_1 \cdot (T) + a_2 \cdot (T)^2 + a_3 \cdot (T)^3.$$

The invoice price of a coupon bond can now be written in terms of discount factors (in the following equation all coupons are assumed to be equal and the principal amount, $100, is paid at maturity):

$$PV = CPN \cdot (dT_1) + CPN \cdot d(T_2) + \ldots + (CPN + 100) \cdot d(T_N)$$

Using the cubic polynomial the preceding equation becomes

$$PV = CPN \cdot [1 + a_1 \cdot (T_1) + a_2 \cdot (T_1)^2 + a_3(T_1)^3]$$
$$+ \ldots + (CPN + 100) \cdot [1 + a_1 \cdot (T_N) + a_2 \cdot (T_N)^2 + a_3(T_N)^3].$$

We can now easily rearrange the equation to express it in terms of the coefficients of the cubic function

$$PV = 100 + \Sigma(CPN)$$
$$+ a_1 \cdot [CPN \cdot T_1 + \ldots + (CPN + 100) \cdot T_N]$$
$$+ a_2 \cdot [CPN \cdot (T_1)^2 + \ldots + (CPN + 100) \cdot (T_N)^2]$$
$$+ a_3 \cdot [CPN \cdot (T_1)^3 + \ldots + (CPN + 100) \cdot (T_N)^3].$$

We can now write

$$PV - (100 + \Sigma CPN) = a_1 X_1 + a_2 X_2 + a_3 X_3.$$

Example: Compute the relevant values for a 5yr bond, coupon rate $= 6\%$, semiannual interest payments, priced at 99-16.

$$100 + \Sigma CPN = 100 + 10 \times 3 = 130$$
$$PV - (100 + \Sigma CPN) = 99.50 - 130.0 = -31.50$$
$$X_1 = (3 \times 0.5) + (3) + (3 \times 1.5) + \ldots + (103 \times 5) = 582.5$$
$$X_2 = [3 \times (0.5)^2] + (3) + [3 \times (1.5)^2] + \ldots + [103 \times (5)^2] = 2{,}789$$
$$X_3 = [3 \times (0.5)^3] + (3) + [3 \times (1.5)^3] + \ldots + [103 \times (5)^3] = 13{,}634$$

If we take a set of coupon bonds and we compute the preceding values for each of them, we can then use a linear regression to find the best-fit values of the coefficients of the cubic equation. Exhibit 8-11 shows the discount factors and the yield curve obtained from a set of 34 T-coupons. To simplify the numerical computations, the bonds have been chosen to have a whole number of semiannual periods to maturity (and consequently, zero accrued coupons). The exhibit also shows the relevant values for some of the bonds.

Why not the Bootstrap Method?

In Chapter 3 we examined the bootstrap method, solved either recursively or by using a system of linear equations. In theory the bootstrap method is applicable to coupon bonds, but in practice this method runs into the constraint of having to use a number

Exhibit 8-11 Discount Factors Derived from a Set of U.S. T-coupons

Cpn	Mty	PV	T	CF	PV - CF	X1	X2	X3
6.5000	May-97	100.58	0.5	103.25	-2.67	52	26	13
8.5000	May-97	101.55	0.5	104.25	-2.70	52	26	13
7.3750	Nov-97	101.78	1	107.38	-5.60	106	105	104
8.8750	Nov-97	103.25	1	108.88	-5.63	107	106	105
6.1250	May-98	100.73	1.5	109.19	-8.46	159	236	351
9.0000	May-98	104.88	1.5	113.50	-8.62	164	241	358
5.5000	Nov-98	99.64	2	111.00	-11.36	214	421	834
8.8750	Nov-98	105.95	2	117.75	-11.80	222	433	855
6.3750	May-99	101.42	2.5	115.94	-14.52	274	669	1,652
9.1250	May-99	107.78	2.5	122.81	-15.03	284	688	1,691
5.8750	Nov-99	100.14	3	117.63	-17.49	331	967	2,862
7.8750	Nov-99	105.58	3	123.63	-18.05	341	990	2,917
8.8750	May-00	109.45	3.5	131.06	-21.61	412	1,380	4,722
8.5000	Nov-00	109.09	4	134.00	-24.91	477	1,817	7,089
8.0000	May-01	108.03	4.5	136.00	-27.97	540	2,310	10,125
13.1250	May-01	128.08	4.5	159.06	-30.98	598	2,493	10,774
7.5000	Nov-01	106.47	5	137.50	-31.03	603	2,861	13,918
15.7500	Nov-01	141.98	5	178.75	-36.77	717	3,258	15,478
7.5000	May-02	106.97	5.5	141.25	-34.28	674	3,499	18,679
11.6250	Nov-02	128.05	6	169.75	-41.70	827	4,545	26,020
10.7500	May-03	124.78	6.5	169.88	-45.10	895	5,326	33,026
11.8750	Nov-03	132.39	7	183.13	-50.74	1,012	6,407	42,483
7.2500	May-04	106.72	7.5	154.38	-47.66	968	6,749	48,713
12.3750	May-04	137.09	7.5	192.81	-55.72	1,121	7,543	53,325
7.8750	Nov-04	110.72	8	163.00	-52.28	1,068	7,873	60,304
11.6250	Nov-04	134.09	8	193.00	-58.91	1,195	8,574	64,639
6.5000	May-05	102.16	8.5	155.25	-53.09	1,099	8,675	70,922
8.2500	May-05	106.44	8.5	170.13	-63.69	1,166	9,066	73,483
12.0000	May-05	137.97	8.5	202.00	-64.03	1,309	9,903	78,969
5.8750	Nov-05	97.86	9	152.88	-55.02	1,151	9,649	83,637
6.8750	May-06	104.73	9.5	165.31	-60.58	1,277	11,148	101,249

Source: Bloomberg, 14 November 1996

of equations—one equation per bond—that are identical to the number of time intervals for which we want to define the forward rates. In Exhibit 8-11 we used 34 bonds with only 19 different maturities ($T = 0.5, 1, \ldots, 9.5$). To use the bootstrap method, we would have to drop a number of bonds, thereby losing some information, to obtain a cash-flow matrix similar to that in Exhibit 8-12.

Exhibit 8-12 Cash Flows for U.S. T-coupons

Cpn	Mty	PV	T	0.50	1.00	1.50	2.00	2.50	3.00
6.500	15-May-97	100.58	0.5	103.25	0	0	0	0	0
7.375	15-Nov-97	101.78	1	3.6875	103.688	0	0	0	0
6.125	15-May-98	100.73	1.5	3.0625	3.0625	103.063	0	0	0
5.500	15-Nov-98	99.64	2	2.75	2.75	2.75	102.75	0	0
6.375	15-May-99	101.42	2.5	3.1875	3.1875	3.1875	3.1875	103.188	0
5.875	15-Nov-99	100.14	3	2.938	2.938	2.938	2.938	2.938	102.938

Exhibit 8-13 Computed and Estimated Values of $B(0, T)$

T	Y (0, T)	B (0, T) Comp.	B (0, T) Est
0	5.50%	100.00	100.00
1	5.60%	94.70	94.69
2	5.70%	89.51	89.50
3	5.80%	84.44	84.44
4	5.90%	79.51	79.51
5	6.00%	74.73	74.73
6	6.10%	70.10	70.10
7	6.20%	65.63	65.63
8	6.30%	61.34	61.33
9	6.40%	57.22	57.21
10	6.50%	53.27	53.28

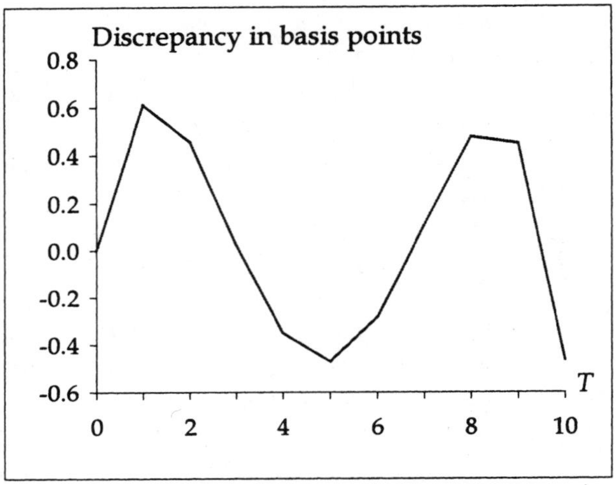

Chapter **9**

Floating-Rate Securities

This chapter is only 9 pages long. This conciseness is mostly due to the fact that the necessary analytical tool kit has already been covered in Chapters 6 to 8.

Floating-rate notes (floaters, FRNs) are medium- to long-term coupon bonds characterized by the fact that the rate for each coupon period is determined at the beginning of the coupon period itself, based on some relevant contractual short-term money-market *reference rate* (mostly LIBOR, T-bill rate, etc.). Coupons are usually paid semiannually or quarterly.

Floaters are less important than coupon bonds, representing less than 10% of the $20 trillion outstanding in the global bond market (U.S. domestic market plus Euromarkets). The price-yield analysis of FRNs is very straightforward and is based entirely on the tools covered in the preceding chapters. In turn, the yield analysis of floaters is related to the pricing of interest-rate swaps, which now represent a multitrillion-dollar market.

Floating-rate loans and notes are one of the products developed in the early 1970s in response to the dramatic increase in interest-rate volatility (see Exhibit 9-1). In a volatile interest-rate scenario, the price of FRNs is relatively insensitive to fluctuations in market yields because the periodic coupon repricing synchronizes the FRN with current market conditions. Floaters have a very limited duration; see Section 9-2.

9-1 THE DEVELOPMENT OF FLOATING-RATE SECURITIES

The coupon rate of a floater will usually be equal to the contractual *reference rate* plus a spread to compensate for:

- The credit risk of the issuer relative to the credit risk implied by the reference rate. Therefore, for the same issuer and maturity, spreads above treasuries (e.g., 90-day T-bills) will be higher than spreads above LIBOR.
- The credit risk associated with a long-term loan compared to the credit risk implicit in a short-term rate. A highly rated borrower (AA or higher) that could buy 3M deposits at LIBOR will have to pay a spread on a 5yr FRN (e.g., LIBOR + 15 basis points [bp]).
- Differences in liquidity and taxation (e.g., U.S. T-bills are extremely liquid and, for U.S. taxpayers, have the advantage of not being subject to state and city taxes).

Exhibit 9-1 3M $ LIBOR

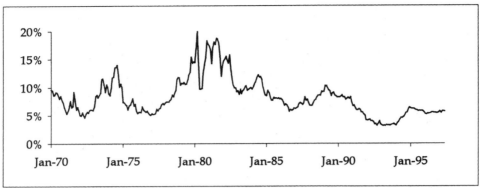

Source: Datastream

- Differences in regulatory status. Banks and investment banks hold inventories of FRNs; therefore the way such notes are treated from a capital adequacy point of view is obviously relevant to determine the required spread (see also Section 9-3).

Floating-rate loans and FRNs were propelled into the mainstream of financial markets instruments due to the growth of Euromarkets. The international banks that dominated the Euromarket and often acted as the end buyers of loans and bonds relied for their funding on short-term deposits. The volatile interest-rate scenario made it imperative to develop a floating-rate market that could allow banks to provide medium- and long-term funds to customers (corporations, sovereign borrowers, and public-sector entities) without running unacceptable interest-rate risks. FRNs were also used by banks to fund their books of floating-rate loans.

As it happens, floating-rate instruments turned out to be essential for the development of the Euromarkets, that survived relatively unscathed the drastic rate increases of the 1970s and 1980s. If Eurobanks had extended fixed-rate long-term credit while funding themselves in the money market, they would have met a debacle similar to that of the savings and loans in the United States, which had to be bailed out by the Savings and Loans Insurance Corporation (SLIC). According to some authors (see Grabbe [1996]), when interest rates peaked in 1980–1981, the U.S. savings and loan sector faced a shortfall of more than $100 billion in assets compared to liabilities. Additionally, in the early 1980s, international banks had to cope with the insolvency of a number of sovereign borrowers (Brazil, Mexico, etc.) and were in no position to deal with large-scale interest-rate mismatch losses.

On an historical note, the first sizable syndicated floating-rate loan was arranged in 1969 by Minos Zombanakis, CEO of the London investment-banking subsidiary of Manufacturers Hanover Trust Corporation, a U.S. bank. ManTrust was taken over in 1993 by Chemical Bank, another New York City–based bank, which in 1995 merged with Chase Manhattan Corporation. The first FRN issue is credited to Warburg, a London merchant bank, which in 1995 was acquired by the Swiss Banking Corporation (and now operates in London under the name SBC-Warburg).

In the U.S. domestic market, floating-rate bonds are mainly a mortgage-backed market product (see Chapter 13) based on adjustable-rate mortgages (ARMs), which are financed through the issuance of pass-through floating-rate bonds. ARMs tend to

Exhibit 9-2 Current Margin as a Function of LIBOR and P

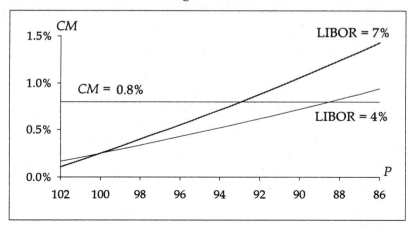

be issued in moments of interest-rate volatility and are often bought as an investment by banks, who fund themselves through short-term customer deposits and on the money market.

9-2 PRICE, YIELD, AND SPREAD

Take an FRN on the day the coupon has been repriced. At this point, the reference rate is by definition aligned to current market conditions, and therefore the price of the floater does not have to compensate for a discrepancy between contractual rate and market yield level. A quotation below or above par therefore implies that the contractual spread on the floater is out of kilter with market requirements for that particular issue (quite likely the credit rating of the FRN issuer has changed).

When the FRN is not priced at par, we can calculate its effective margin, that is, the spread that would be required by the market to price the floater at par. A first approximation to the effective margin is a simple *current margin* measure, computed with the following equation:

P = price, at coupon repricing date, relative to face value = 100
L = reference rate, say, 6-month LIBOR, at repricing date
M = contractual margin, say, 20 bp above 6-month LIBOR
CM = current margin, inclusive of contractual margin

$$CM = (L + M) \cdot \frac{100}{P} - L$$

The preceding measure, which is very similar to the current yield in fixed-rate bonds, is somewhat inaccurate because it does not take into account the capital gain (loss) entailed by reimbursement at par when the FRN is quoted at a discount (premium). In the case of perpetual floating-rate notes, however, the simple margin is the most appropriate measure because there is no defined maturity date; see Section 9-3.

The contractual margin is usually constant; therefore the current margin will change in time due to changes in LIBOR and P. To keep CM constant when LIBOR decreases, P must also decrease, as shown in Exhibit 9-2, which is computed assuming a contractual margin of 25 bp. A more accurate measure can be easily obtained by solving, with numerical methods, the following self-explanatory equation, where $PV(\cdot)$ stands for the present value operator based on the spot yield curve:

$$100 - P = PV[100 \cdot (EM - M)]$$

where EM = discounted cash flow measure of effective margin

Note that you should discount $EM - M$, which is an annuity, using the spot yield curve (SYC), and not a YTM measure such as the swap rate. Moreover, you should use a SYC that reflects the credit rating of the floating-rate note for which you are computing the effective margin. A straight spot LIBOR curve would be appropriate only for highly rated issues. It is therefore possible to compute both the duration and the $PVbp$ of a floater with respect to the market-required margin. Defining a SYC that accurately reflects the credit rating of the issue you are pricing often requires accepting a certain level of approximation because there may well be no readily available SYC. An acceptable approach is to take the LIBOR-SYC and add to it the contractual margin on the FRN. This will allow you to compute a first approximation to the effective margin by solving

$$100 - P = PV[100 \cdot (EM_A - M)]$$

EM_A = first approximation to EM, $L + M$ = SYC
L = LIBOR-based SYC

At this point you can add the first approximation to the effective margin to the reference spot yield curve and solve the equation again, using the modified spot yield curve, to obtain an accurate value.

$$100 - P = PV[100 \cdot (EM_B - CM)]$$

EM_B = second approximation to EM, $L + EM_A$ = SYC

This method allows you to capture the slope of the spot yield curve for the reference rate but has the disadvantage of attributing the same spread to all the maturities, which we know is not fully accurate. If you need a better pricing, you will have to use available market data to get some estimate of how the margin changes with time to maturity (e.g., the margin for a 5yr maturity is approximately twice the value of the spread for 1yr). At this point you will be able to solve for EM while respecting the slope of the relevant spot yield curve (see Exhibit 9-3). Exhibit 9-3 is somewhat of a hybrid. The floater is real and its price, as of the March 1998 coupon repricing date, was 97,50; this entails that $(100 - P = \$2.5)$. The LIBOR curve is steeper, however, than that of 26 March to show how the iterative procedure can capture the slope of the reference rate.

- Term is expressed in years, assuming, as usual, equal-length quarters.
- The second column is the PV of a \$1 quarterly margin, computed using $L + M$ as the SYC. Dividing ($\$2.5 = 100 - P$) by \$14.69 yields the quarterly basis points for $PV = \$2.50$.
- The third column is the PV of a \$1 quarterly margin, computed using $L + M_A$ as the SYC.

Exhibit 9-3 United States of Mexico, $1 billion Floater, Mty = 27 June 2002.
Q-coupon = (3M LIBOR + 1.25%). Price as of 27 March 1998 = 97.50

| T | PV of $1 per quarter | | L | L + M | L + EMA |
	L + M	L + EMA			
0.25	$0.985	$0.983	5.07%	6.34%	7.02%
0.50	$0.970	$0.966	5.12%	6.39%	7.07%
0.75	$0.954	$0.950	5.17%	6.44%	7.12%
1.00	$0.939	$0.933	5.22%	6.49%	7.17%
1.25	$0.924	$0.917	5.27%	6.54%	7.22%
1.50	$0.909	$0.900	5.32%	6.59%	7.27%
1.75	$0.894	$0.884	5.37%	6.64%	7.32%
2.00	$0.879	$0.867	5.42%	6.69%	7.37%
2.25	$0.864	$0.851	5.47%	6.74%	7.42%
2.50	$0.849	$0.835	5.52%	6.79%	7.47%
2.75	$0.834	$0.819	5.57%	6.84%	7.52%
3.00	$0.819	$0.803	5.62%	6.89%	7.57%
3.25	$0.804	$0.788	5.67%	6.94%	7.62%
3.50	$0.789	$0.772	5.72%	6.99%	7.67%
3.75	$0.775	$0.757	5.77%	7.04%	7.72%
4.00	$0.760	$0.741	5.82%	7.09%	7.77%
4.25	$0.746	$0.726	5.87%	7.14%	7.82%
SUM	$14.692	$14.494			
bp/Q	17.0157	17.2487			
bp/ yr	68.06	68.99			

All rates adjusted for 365/360 daycount

Source: Bloomberg

The Mexico floater provides a good example of how sensitive the price of a floater can be to an increase in the required spread. The crisis of confidence in developing countries that took place in summer 1998 entailed in fact a drop in price of well over 10 points (see Exhibit 9-4).

Fixed-Rate Equivalent

Consider the case of a corporation that can issue 5yr fixed-interest bonds at a coupon rate *CR* and 5yr FRNs at a spread *CM* over 6-month LIBOR. The obvious question is whether the floater is fairly priced when compared to the fixed-rate coupon.

A number of different approaches have been proposed to tackle this problem. The development of a huge and liquid market for interest-rate swaps has, however, allowed an answer to the preceding question based on the law of one price. We can say that the two bonds are fairly priced if by issuing the fixed-rate bond and swapping it into floating rate, the corporation achieves a spread that is transaction-costs-close to the contractual margin it would have to offer if it chose to issue the floater.

Exhibit 9-4 Price Fluctuations of the Mexico, $1 billion Floater

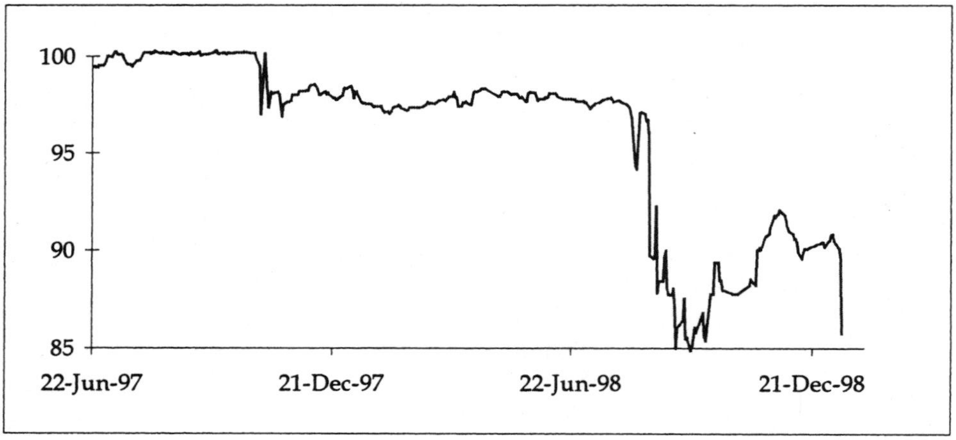

Source: Bloomberg

Price and Yield between Coupon Repricing Dates

Floaters do exhibit a duration, but this is limited to the effect of reference rate changes between two coupon-repricing periods. If the current level of reference rate changes after the coupon has been fixed, the price of the floater will change to compensate for this discrepancy. It is clear, however, that this duration is quite limited—less than 0.5 for a semiannual coupon and less than 0.25 for quarterly coupons.

9-3   INVERSE FLOATERS AND FLOATING RATE PERPETUITIES

Inverse floaters, as implied by their name, are FRNs where the contract rate moves inversely to the reference rate (if LIBOR increases, the coupon rate decreases, and if LIBOR decreases, the coupon rate goes up). Inverse floaters are not widely used. It is interesting to examine them, though because they provide a very interesting example of how it is possible to create a highly leveraged financial product by combining two plain-vanilla securities, that is, a fixed-rate bond and a floater. In Chapter 8 we saw that the Orange County portfolio contained some inverse floaters.

In spite of their being a floating-rate product, inverse FRNs have a duration that in fact exceeds by far their term to maturity. This apparently absurd result caught several market professionals off-guard when inverses were introduced as a member of the collateralized mortgage obligations (CMOs) family of securities (see Section 13-3). Inverse floaters are also characterized by embedded options.

There are several ways to structure an inverse floater. In order not to get bogged down by a morass of detail, let us concentrate only on the most straightforward issuing mechanism. This consists in taking a plain-vanilla fixed-coupon bond issued at par, known as *collateral* (and often kept in trust with a bank), and to issue a floating-rate note and an inverse FRN for a total par amount equal to that of the fixed-rate bond. The most usual proportion between the par values of the FRN and the inverse FRN is 50-50.

The fixed interest paid by the collateral is then used to pay interest on the FRN and on the inverse floater, which gets all of the interest that is not paid out to the FRN. A number of investment banks market their own label inverse floaters. Those created by Lehman Brothers, using fixed-rate municipal bonds as collateral, were called residual interest bonds (RIBs), a name that clearly defines the interest-allocation process to inverse floaters.

$PARFIX$ = par value of the fixed rate collateral, say, $100 million
$PARFRN$ = $Q \cdot PARFIX$ = par value of the floater, say, $50 million

where $0 < Q < 1$, usually 0.5

$PARINV$ = $(1 - Q) \cdot PARFIX$ = par amount of the inverse floater

As negative interest is not feasible, the coupon rate on the inverse floater has a floor (usually 0%) and the rate on the FRN must therefore be capped (the cap and the floor are both interest-rate options, see Chapter 13).

$$\frac{C_{FIX}}{Q} = \text{cap on the coupon rate payable on the FRN}$$

C_{FIX} = coupon rate on the collateral

Let us now come to the duration issue. Because of the law of one price, the market value of the collateral must equal the sum of the market values of the FRN and the inverse FRN. In turn, the price of the collateral must be aligned with that of comparable fixed-rate bonds. Translating this into prices, we obtain

$$P[FIX] = Q \cdot P[FRN] + (1 - Q) \cdot P[INV].$$

As the floating-rate note has a very short duration, we can write the following equations:

$$P[FIX] = Q \cdot 100 + (1 - Q) \cdot P[INV]$$

$$P[INV] = \frac{P[FIX] - Q \cdot 100}{(1 - Q)}$$

$$\frac{dP[INV]}{dY} = \frac{dP[FIX]}{dY} \cdot \frac{1}{(1 - Q)}$$

The preceding equations entail that the price of the inverse floater is very sensitive to YTM on the collateral. All the value changes of the collateral map into value changes of the inverse floater. The price value of one basis point for the inverse will therefore be:

$$PVbp[INV] = \frac{PVbp[FIX]}{1 - Q}.$$

Computing duration is also relatively straightforward:

Exhibit 9-5 Price of the Collateral and of the Inverse Floater
$T = 10$, Cpn of Collateral = 7%, $Q = 50\%$

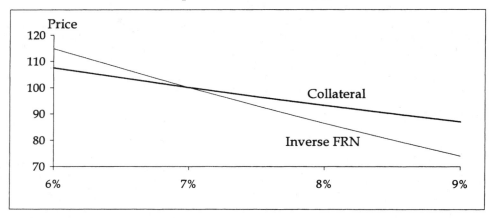

	Price		PVbp		Duration	
USYTM	Collateral	Inverse	Collateral	Inverse	Collateral	Inverse
6.00%	107.44	114.88	0.0778	0.1556	7.24	13.54
7.00%	100.00	100.00	0.0710	0.1421	7.10	14.21
8.00%	93.20	86.41	0.0649	0.1298	6.96	15.02
9.00%	86.99	73.98	0.0594	0.1188	6.83	16.05

$$D[INV] = \frac{\partial P[INV]}{\partial Y} \cdot \frac{1}{P[INV]}$$

$$D[INV] = \frac{\partial P[FIX]}{\partial Y} \cdot \frac{1}{(1 - Q)} \cdot \frac{1}{P[INV]}$$

Recalling that

$$\frac{\partial P[FIX]}{\partial Y} = D[FIX] \cdot P[FIX]$$

we can write

$$D[INV] = \frac{D[FIX]}{1 - Q} \cdot \frac{P[FIX]}{P[INV]}.$$

Not only is the duration of the inverse floater much higher than that of the collateral, but it also increases with an increase in *YTM* of the collateral, while the duration of regular bonds decreases (see Exhibit 9-5).

Perpetual Floating-Rate Notes

Perpetual floaters are FRNs that do not have a defined repayment date. They are not very common. A number of them were issued in the 1980s when banking supervisory

Exhibit 9-6 Price Fluctuation of the Subordinated Perpetual FRN Issued by
NatWest Bank in 1985. Coupon = 6M LIMEAN + 25bp

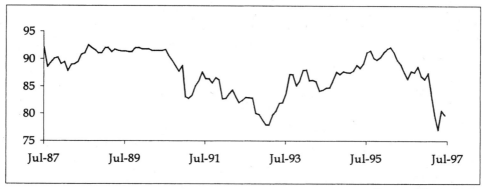

Source: Bloomberg

authorities imposed an improvement of bank capital adequacy ratios. One of the components of bank capital is the so-called Tier 2 capital, which includes, among other liabilities, subordinated debentures with residual maturities exceeding certain well-defined thresholds. Subordinated perpetuals therefore appeared to be an interesting way to boost bank capital without having to worry about residual maturity. Subordinated floaters paying LIBOR plus were also easily sold to other banks that funded themselves on the money market. These instruments also appealed to banks because the Basle Concordat established that the capital reserve against bank liabilities is 20% of the usual 8% reserve.

A change in market sentiment and in regulation meant that the market-required spread on subordinated perpetuals increased, and this in turn implied a sharp downward adjustment in the price of these instruments, as shown in Exhibit 9-6.

Chapter **10**

Interest-Rate and Currency Swaps

10-1 INTRODUCTION

This chapter is relatively compact and equation-free. In fact, the analytical tool kit has been covered in Chapters 4 and 6 through 9.

Swaps are certainly the most important over-the-counter (OTC) derivative, due mainly to their great flexibility, which allows swap dealers to tailor them to fit the diverse needs of clients. A swap is basically a very simple product; it is also referred to as a *generic* or *plain-vanilla swap*. It is often used as a building block for complex transactions, comprising a number of swaps (also called *cocktail swaps*). These complex packages often include financing or lending and are sometimes spruced up with a touch of options.

Swaps came to the forefront of innovative financial products in 1981 with the IBM–World Bank *currency swap* transaction, arranged by Salomon Brothers, which involved $, DEM, and SFR. The simpler *interest-rate swap* (IRS), limited to only one currency, was developed soon after the currency swap but experienced a much faster grow in aggregate *notional amounts*.

In January 1998 the International Swaps and Derivatives Association (ISDA) released the swap market data relative to the first half of 1997. The notional amount outstanding exceeded $22,000 billion for IRS, while currency swaps totaled $1,585 billion. The contracts arranged in the first 6 months of 1997 totaled $10,792 billion and $436 billion, respectively.

The word swap now has three different meanings in finance.

1. The most recent meaning of swaps, which we shall cover in this chapter, is a contract whereby two parties agree to exchange the cash flows deriving from two notional assets. They come in two basic flavors: interest rate swaps and currency swaps.
2. In foreign exchange (FX) markets (see Section 5-3), a swap is the purchase and simultaneous forward sale of foreign currency. The FX swap has many points in common with the currency swap but is a quite distinct financial product.

3. In Wall Street–speak, a *bond swap* (also called a *bond switch*) is a transaction whereby an asset manager or a trader sells one bond to buy another that better fits his investment or trading objectives.

Banks and investment banks that were early movers in this market have raked in above-market returns. The growth of swaps on the books of banks prompted the regulators of the G-10 to include them, together with other off-balance-sheet derivatives, in the determination of minimum capital adequacy ratios (first Basel Concordat, 1988).

In this chapter we will focus on the basics of swap transaction. Once you develop a clear understanding of these building blocks, examining complex structures becomes relatively straightforward. Running a complex swap book requires paying a lot of attention to fitting the different pieces together and carefully monitoring positions. This entails voluminous legal documentation and adequate processing systems. The importance of systems in monitoring complex multicurrency swap books is clearly evidenced in the following excerpt from Salomon Brothers' annual report for fiscal 1994: "The combination of rapidly increasing volume, addition of new products, and accounting systems ill-adapted to Salomon Brothers' increasingly complex multicurrency, multi-entity operating environment, caused mistakes to accumulate. With regard to swaps, Salomon Brothers' activities outpaced the capabilities of its accounting system, both in volume and sophistication, thereby increasing the possibility for errors in recording and accounting for swap transactions."

The growth of swaps prompted the establishment of the ISDA (which originally stood for the International Swap Dealers Association). In turn, the ISDA exerted an important role in rationalizing and standardizing swap agreements and documentation. The first big step was taken in June 1985, when the ISDA published its "Code of Standard Wording, Assumptions and Provisions for Swaps," also known as the ISDA Swap Code. The ISDA master agreement has of course been modified several times since 1985 to reflect both market developments and best-practice improvements.

10-2 INTEREST-RATE SWAPS: PRICING, VALUATION, AND ASSET SWAPS

In its simplest form (i.e. *fixed-for-floating swap*), an interest-rate swap is a contract by which two parties agree to exchange, on designated future dates, two streams of interest payments, one fixed-rate and one floating-rate, computed according to well-defined formulas, on a given notional principal.

When floating and fixed-rate payments are due on the same date, which is generally the case, only the netted amount changes hands. For example, if the semiannual fixed-rate payment is $255,000 and the floating-rate payment is $240,000, then the fixed payer will pay $15,000 to the fixed receiver. These interest payments are also known as fixed and floating coupons, in analogy with the terminology used for bonds. There is obviously no need for an exchange of principal in an interest-rate swap (exchanging, say, $10 million for $10 million, on the same value date, serves no financial purpose), and in fact we speak of notional principal.

When the notional principal remains constant throughout the life of the contract, we have a *nonamortizing swap*, and the interest flows that are exchanged can be interpreted as the interest payments on two bullet bonds: a regular fixed-rate bond and a floating-rate note, both issued at par. This in turn means that we will be able to use the analytical results that we have covered in Chapters 6, 7, and 8.

Exhibit 10-1 IRS Cash Flow at each Interest Payment Date, Before Netting

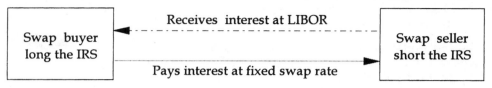

The bond analogy must be interpreted with some level of caution, however. The swap structure allows a dramatic reduction in credit risk and the fixed rate is paid against a specified floating rate coupon (usually LIBOR flat). This means that the swap rate may be very different from the fixed par coupon that a corporation would have to pay if it issued a fixed-rate bond.

To standardize and simplify the quotation mechanism, the floating rate is conventionally set at LIBOR flat, and only the fixed contract rate is quoted. It is easy to see that this simplifying convention does not imply any loss of generality. A 6.20% swap rate, paid semiannually, against 6M LIBOR is perfectly equivalent to, say, a 6.50% swap rate against LIBOR + 0.30%, where the 0.30% is already adjusted for the ACT/360 LIBOR day count.

Determining the fixed swap rate is also known as *pricing the swap*. The swap rate is usually fixed in such a way that the swap value at time-0 is zero, that is, we have an at-the-market *par swap*. T-notes have a lower yield than LIBOR; therefore the swap rate is higher than T-notes yield. A rather common convention is that of quoting swap rates as a spread over on-the-run treasuries of comparable maturity. The swap rate is therefore a yield to maturity. Swap rates for different maturities determine a par yield curve.

The buyer of a swap, long the IRS, will pay fixed-income interest to the seller and receive interest at LIBOR (see Exhibit 10-1). The buyer therefore stands to gain if LIBOR increases above the level of the contract rate. Most swaps take place through a swap dealer, which we shall indicate as SwapCo (usually a large bank, investment bank, or insurance company).

Swaps and Back-to-Back Loans

A swap replicates the financial effects of a pair of back-to-back loans. Buying a swap (*pay fix*) is equivalent to borrowing fixed-rate and on-lending the proceeds at floating rate, thereby hedging a floating-rate liability. Selling a swap (*receive fix*) is equivalent to borrowing floating-rate and on-lending fixed-rate, thereby hedging a fixed-rate liability (see Exhibit 10-2). The big advantage of the swap contract consists of a drastic decrease in the level of credit risk when compared to the back-to-back loan. The notional principal cannot be defaulted, and the netting of coupon payments substantially mitigates the risk associated with the interest streams. Swaps and forward rate agreements (FRAs) are both driven by credit risk. This has an important effect on the determination of the swap midrate quoted by dealers, which is rather insensitive to credit risk considerations.

Swaps, FRAs, and Futures

You will often find the statement that a swap is somewhat equivalent to a series of back-to-back forwards or futures (*strip of FRAs, strip of futures*). This is clearly true

Exhibit 10-2 IRS Swaps and Liability Hedging

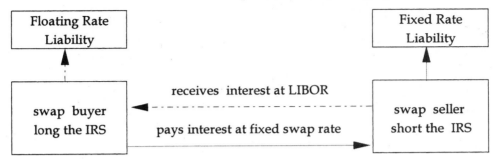

when we consider that with an IRS or with a future you buy, at a predetermined price, future values of LIBOR-based payments.

• The buyer of an FRA strip buys a series of future LIBOR interest payments, each at a predetermined rate, based on the forward values of LIBOR. These rates will most likely differ from one another. All the FRAs have zero replacement value at time-0.

• The buyer of an IRS buys a series of future LIBOR interest payments at a single predetermined fixed swap rate. Therefore, the IRS as a whole has zero replacement value at time-0, while the individual forwards that compose it do not. Thus a par swap is a series of off-market FRAs plus a first exchange of interest at the fixed swap rate against interest at LIBOR.

Pricing of Interest-Rate Swaps

The procedure to determine the fixed-interest rate, also known as the *fixed coupon leg*, in a par IRS is in fact very simple. First, determine the series of future LIBOR payments on the notional principal, based on hedgeable forward yields (such as a series of FRAs or of futures). Second, find the level of fixed-interest payments that will have the same present value of the series of hedgeable future LIBOR payments, when discounted with the same spot market yield curve. Using the present value operator PV(•), based on the term structure of spot yields, we have

$$PV(FIX) \ = \ PV(FLT) \ \Rightarrow \ PV(SWAP) \ = \ 0.$$

FIX = stream of fixed-rate payments (fixed-rate coupons)
FLT = stream of hedgeable floating-rate payments (FRA or futures based)

Because of the law of one price, the swap rate and the FRA rates cannot diverge materially from the result of the above fair-pricing equation. Exhibit 10-3 details the computation of the fixed-income leg of a 2yr $10 million IRS with semiannual payments. Note that with the FRA strip you cover only the last three interest payments, whereas with the IRS all four LIBOR payments are substituted with fixed-income payments. Solving the preceding equation numerically gives a swap rate of 6.09% (U.S. bond yield equivalent). If you want your swap to be nonpar, it is sufficient to modify the fixed coupon to obtain the required positive or negative present value of the swap.

Exhibit 10-3 Determining the Fixed Income Leg of an IRS,
Notional Principal = $10 million

Days	Spot Y	Disc factors	Fwrd Y	FRA Rates	FRA $ interest	IRS $ interest	Fix less float
182	5.72%	0.9727	5.72%	5.56%	281,089	304,262	23,173
183	5.89%	0.9443	6.07%	5.90%	299,917	304,262	4,346
182	6.06%	0.9156	6.39%	6.20%	313,444	304,262	(9,182)
183	6.19%	0.8868	6.58%	6.39%	324,825	304,262	(20,563)
				PVs =	1,131,693	1,131,693	(0)

The first rate in the FRA column (5.56%) is the 6-month spot LIBOR
The rates are as of Mon 28 Oct 1996

$$PV(FIX) - PV(FLT) = PV(SWAP)^* \neq 0$$

Valuation of Interest-Rate Swaps

Most swaps are born as at-the-market swaps—that is, they have a zero value (like forwards and futures). After the contract is signed, the yield curve will of course change and the swap will become an off-the-market. The value of a swap is very easy to compute.

• First, compare the fixed-rate leg with the fixed-rate payments that would be generated by a new at-the-market swap. The difference between the two fixed-rate streams should then be discounted with the current structure of swap rates.

• Second, the floating-rate leg has par value at every repricing date, like a constant-spread floating-rate note (see chapter 8). If you are pricing the swap between two repricing dates, you must adjust its value to take into account the difference between the current and the locked-in LIBOR (for, say, the next 3 months if you are pricing the swap in the middle of a 6M repricing interval).

Like all forward contracts, the off-market swap has an absolute value. Whether this absolute value translates into an asset or into a liability depends on what your position is in the swap transaction.

Hedging a Floating-Rate Liability with a Swap

In Section 4-2 we examined the case of a corporation that locked in its quarterly $ borrowing rate over a 1yr time horizon starting January 1994 by means of a strip of three FRAs. With the wisdom of hindsight, that FRA hedge proved successful because of the Fed tightening of 1994. Let us now examine the case of a corporation that locked in its semiannual $ borrowing cost starting 28 October 1996 by means of a 2yr interest-rate swap. In this case the hedging strategy worked against the corporation, which missed the opportunity of taking advantage of a flattening of the yield curve (see Exhibit 10-4).

Asset Swaps

An *asset swap* is just a regular swap. Its name derives from the fact that it is implemented to hedge the income stream generated by a financial asset (e.g., bond, loan,

Exhibit 10-4 Financial Result of an IRS

LIBOR fixing	Payment date	Days	FRA rates	Spot LIBOR	Float cpn	Fixed cpn	Net
Mon-28-Oct-96	30-Apr-97	182	5.56%	5.56%	281089	304262	23,173
Mon-28-Apr-97	30-Oct-97	183	5.90%	6.06%	308050	304262	(3,788)
Tue-28-Oct-97	30-Apr-98	182	6.20%	5.78%	292211	304262	12,051
Tue-28-Apr-98	30-Oct-98	183	6.39%	5.74%	291783	304262	12,479
Contract date	28-Oct-96		Swap rate	6.09%			
Settlement date	30-Oct-96						

Exhibit 10-5 Asset Swap Flowchart

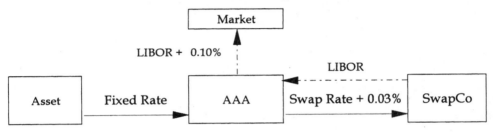

etc.). You can easily understand the structure of an asset swap transaction by looking at the flowchart in Exhibit 10-5. The underlying financial reason for implementing such a strategy could be the desire to receive the fixed-rate interest on your asset, avoiding the interest-rate risk associated with a possible change in the yield curve. You are therefore decomposing the risk on the asset into (1) a credit-risk component you are willing to accept and (2) an interest-rate risk you want to hedge away.

10-3   SWAPS AND COMPARATIVE ADVANTAGE IN FUNDING

One of the reasons that propelled swaps to the forefront of financial innovation is that they can be used to exploit comparative advantage in funding. These comparative advantages, which were quite material in the early and mid 1980s, have been significantly eroded by the widespread diffusion of swaps, which allowed to arbitrage away intermarket price discrepancies.

Let us use a simple example to demonstrate how this works. Take two borrowers (corporations, banks, public-sector entities), which we shall indicate with AAA and BBB. The rates at which the two borrowers could raise a 5yr, $100 million financing are summarized in Exhibit 10-6. We are considering $ financing; therefore the fixed rate is assumed to be paid in two equal semiannual installments of 3% and 3.5%, respectively, for AAA and BBB.

You can see that AAA can borrow at more favorable terms in both the fixed-rate and the floating-rate markets. AAA is a better credit risk than BBB and has an *absolute*

Exhibit 10-6 Comparative Advantage (quality spread differential)

	BBB	AAA	BBB - AAA
Fixed-rate borrowing	7.00%	6.00%	1.00%
LIBOR-based borrowing	0.60%	0.10%	0.50%
Comparative advantage			0.50%
5-year T-note		5.50%	
Swap rate		5.65%	
6-month LIBOR		5.64%	

advantage in raising financing. You will also notice that AAA has a *comparative advantage*, sometimes referred to as *quality spread differential*, when it comes to borrowing fixed-rate, where its costs are lower than BBB's by a full 100 bp as compared with a 50-bp advantage for LIBOR-based borrowing (see Exhibit 10-6).

In a perfectly frictionless market, this discrepancy of comparative advantages would not exist. In real life it does exist and is due mainly to the fact that fixed-rate funds are usually available through the issuance of bonds that in turn are bought by institutions that are constrained in their investments (e.g., they buy only investment-grade bonds) or by private investors who want to buy only "safe" bonds because they do not have the capability of carefully analyzing the creditworthiness of issuers and of diversifying their portfolios to diminish portfolio risk. Floating-rate monies, on the other hand, are also available through banks that enjoy economies of scale in both credit-risk assessment and portfolio diversification.

In the case of currency swaps, which for many years have been an interesting source of quality spread differentials, the comparative advantage is usually attributable to the desire of institutional investors to diversify credit risk while investing in a designated currency. Say you were an Australian asset manager and you wanted to invest in AU$ bonds; you would certainly welcome the diversification offered by AU$ bonds issued by, say, the World Bank, IBM, Deutsche Bank, and so on.

If AAA is willing to fund itself at floating rate and if BBB wants fixed-rate funds, the two can swap financing, thereby decreasing their aggregate payments to the market, as shown in Exhibit 10-7. Also note that the amount of aggregate saving equals the comparative advantage spread (quality spread differential). This is an interesting financial reincarnation of the comparative advantage theorem in international trade, which is attributed to Davide Ricardo (1772–1823), a pro–free trade British economist and one of the fathers of economic science. According to Ricardo's theorem, two countries, say, East and West, will gain in trading two goods also when one of the two countries is more efficient than the other in the production of both goods. What makes trading profitable is that one of the two countries has a comparative advantage in the production of one of the two commodities. (For an interesting and very readable exposition of comparative advantage in international trade, see Krugman 1994.)

The swap rate is determined by supply and demand within the limits of arbitrage-free pricing. Therefore, the swap rate between the contracting parties is largely an exogenous variable (even more so considering the dealer nature of the swap market; see the next subsection). In turn this entails that the way the aggregate saving of 50 bp is divvied up between AAA and BBB is determined in a quasi-automatic way by the level of the swap rate. Let us examine this issue more closely.

Exhibit 10-7 Comparative Advantage Flowchart

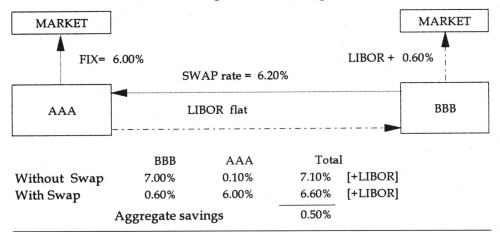

	BBB	AAA	Total	
Without Swap	7.00%	0.10%	7.10%	[+LIBOR]
With Swap	0.60%	6.00%	6.60%	[+LIBOR]
Aggregate savings			0.50%	

• AAA will gain the difference between the 6% market rate it pays on its 5yr borrowing and the swap rate it receives (20 bp). To this we must add the difference between LIBOR flats it pays to BBB and the 10 bp it would have to pay on LIBOR-based borrowing.

• BBB has a 0.6% cost on the floating leg of the swap and saves 0.8% on the fixed-rate leg, yielding a gain of 20 bp.

Rolling Over Short-Term Borrowing

BBB could enhance its gain by borrowing short-term and rolling over the financing every six months, thereby paying a lower margin over LIBOR. This strategy will be successful if BBB's credit rating remains stable or improves in time. It can backfire, however, if BBB gets downgraded and has to pay a higher spread. Reliable data are not available, but many borrowers enhance the attractiveness of *swap-linked funding* by borrowing short-term.

10-4 SWAP DEALERS AND SWAP WAREHOUSING

In the early days, swaps took place between the interested parties. Banks and investment banks acted as brokers and arrangers and were usually compensated with an up-front flat fee (we have already seen that the groundbreaking World Bank–IBM swap was arranged by Salomon Brothers). With the growth of the market, banks and investment banks began to act as dealers, quoting swap rates to their clients and putting the swaps on their books (known as *swap warehousing*). This development met a number of market needs.

• Swap dealers can deal immediately with their clients without having to scramble to find another client with matching needs.

Exhibit 10-8 Dealer Swap Flow Chart

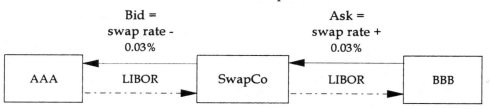

- Dealers can also arrange swaps when they know that there is only a remote chance of finding two parties that want to take the opposite sides of the same transaction. In turn, this allows banks to customize swaps, that are inherently flexible, to better fit their clients' needs.
- Dealers become the counterparty of all swaps, thereby contributing to mitigation of the credit-risk problem (a dealer is obviously in a better position than its clients to assess creditworthiness and diversify credit risk. It also has a much better chance of taking advantage of netting agreements).

In the early days of swap dealing, the bid/ask spreads were much larger than now, and this resulted in above-average returns on invested capital for the early movers in the new market (e.g., Salomon Brothers, Bankers Trust, J. P. Morgan, CS Financial Products, etc.).

The swap market is now an established dealer market; however, there are a few active inter–dealer brokers who disseminate quotations on telecommunications networks and contribute to a smoother and faster turnover. Inter–dealer brokers are usually compensated with an up-front flat fee. The presence of inter–dealer brokers is, for the time being, a characteristic of many OTC markets, such as the FX market, the U.S. bond markets, the Euromarket, and others.

The quotation mechanism universally adopted by dealers is based on keeping the floating rate at LIBOR-flat and charging a bid/ask spread on the fixed swap rate or *dealer midrate*. The already examined swap between AAA and BBB would, in real life, have the structure depicted in Exhibit 10-8.

Quite often the swap rate is quoted with reference to the *on-the-run* Treasuries yield for bonds and notes with the same maturity of the swap. This is a practical way of quoting because spreads over Treasuries are usually more stable than the underlying yields that are subject to continuous change, often several times in one single trading day.

This quotation mechanism has produced the term *swap spread*, which is the spread of the swap rate over and above the Treasury of equal maturity. Remember, however, that the swap rate is correlated more to LIBOR spot rates than to Treasuries yields (see Exhibit 10-9). Dealing in swaps is in some respects quite different from dealing in fixed-income securities.

- A bond dealer will trade existing bonds, mostly issued by third parties. A swap dealer acts more like a futures clearinghouse, taking one side in all the swaps it writes.
- A dealer will usually keep a swap on its books until maturity (or closeout date if the swap is terminated before maturity, either by mutual agreement of the counterparties or because a default clause is triggered). This in turn entails that successful

Exhibit 10-9 Swap Spread over 5yr U.S. T-notes

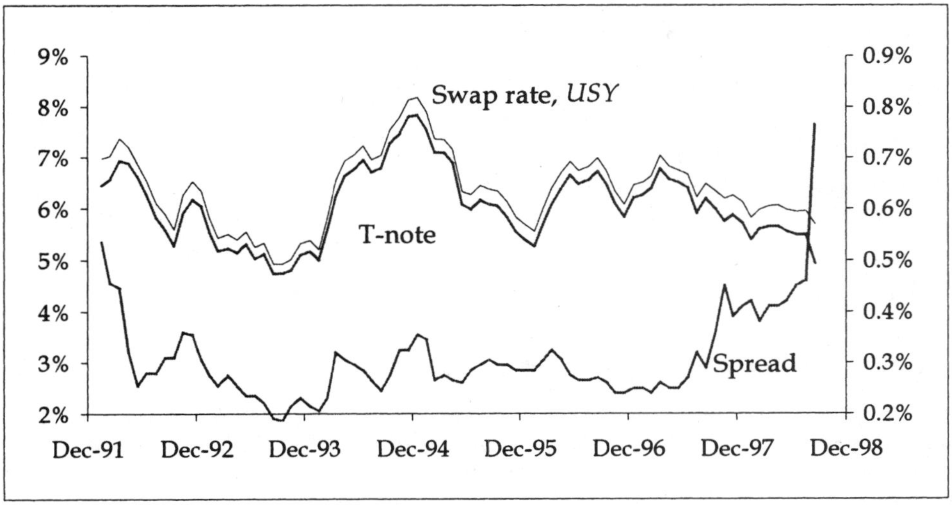

Source: Datastream

swap dealers run impressively large swap books. Contrast this with a well-run bond dealing operation, where the average turnover of the inventory is quite high.

• The client of a bond dealer is not subject to much credit risk (payment against delivery clauses and short settlement times are quite effective in mitigating counterparty risk). The long-term nature of swaps means that there is a credit-risk problem. Therefore, the big players in the swap market are large, creditworthy institutions.

Matched Swap Book

From a dealer point of view, it is not necessary that the swaps on its books exactly match each other. What is relevant is that their aggregate value is insensitive to a wide range of changes in the yield curve. When the dealer wants to mismatch its swap book to speculate on interest-rate movements, it must be able to know accurately what the financial risk will be.

Matched swap books therefore include not only swaps but also other instruments, typically Treasuries and bond futures and options, that are necessary to achieve and optimize the desired level of hedge against yield curve shifts.

10-4 CURRENCY SWAPS

Currency swaps involve the exchange of interest payments and principals in two different currencies. The two interest streams can be both fixed-rate (the World Bank–IBM transaction was fix-fix) or else can replicate the fixed-for-floating structure of interest-rate swaps.

As two currencies are involved, we must necessarily have two notional principals, which usually are exchanged on the value date of the swap. To have an at-the-market swap, the two notional principals must have the same value at time-0, usually 2 business days before value date. For example,

$$NP_{USD} = 50,000,000; \ NP_{JPY} = 6,400,000,000; \ JPY/\$ = 128.$$

If we are dealing with a fixed-for-floating currency swap, there is only one swap rate, determined in the relevant currency, exactly as in the case of a plain-vanilla interest-rate swap. If we are dealing with a fix/fix swap, we must necessarily have two swap rates, each determined with reference to the yield curve of its own currency. At maturity the principals are again exchanged. This means that currency swap replicates, borrowing foreign currency:

- First, you get the foreign currency principal on the effective date.
- Second, you pay the fixed-for-floating interest stream in the foreign currency.
- Finally, you reimburse the foreign currency principal.

Currency Swaps and FX Swaps

A currency swap is often likened to a series of FX swaps. This is a perfectly legitimate comparison because a currency swap is an up-front exchange of principals followed by a stream of future exchanges of payments expressed in different currencies (remember that a FX swap is an up-front exchange of principals followed by a forward offsetting exchange).

There is an important difference, however. In the FX swap, the forward exchange is done at a predetermined contract rate that in turn is determined on the basis of the forward exchange rate and implicitly incorporates the effect of the difference in LIBOR rates in the two currencies. In the currency swap, all future exchanges of currency payments take place at the current exchange rate and the interest rates are explicitly different. Furthermore, FX swaps are usually available only for relatively short maturities whereas currency swaps can be negotiated for multiyear terms that include several interest payments before final maturity.

Currency Swaps as FX Risk Hedges

It is clear that the currency swap is a medium- and long-term hedging instrument that is suitable if you need to hedge FX exposure on an asset that you intend to keep for a reasonably long time. For short-term currency hedging, the FX swap is the instrument of choice. By choosing the fix/float terms of a currency swap, you can hedge the relevant interest-rate risk originating from the both the asset you want to hedge and the terms of the borrowing with which you have financed its purchase. Exhibits 10-10 and 10-11 illustrate two typical cases. You could, of course, use a swap to hedge a liability instead of an asset. Assume you are a bank and you have borrowed by issuing AU$ bonds, a market on which you had a comparative advantage in buying long-term funds. The problem is that you lend in $, mostly floating-rate. The swap structure depicted in Exhibit 10-12 would solve the problem. A word of caution: In spite of their straightforward range of applications, currency swaps are sometimes explained in a less-than-satisfactory way. Take the following excerpt from a well-known book on derivatives: "SwissCo is a well-known borrower in Switzerland that can easily issue bonds at favorable interest rates. It plans a bond issue of SFR 20 million, but actually needs the equivalent amount in $ for some purchases of American raw materials. AmericanCo is a well-known borrower in the U.S. bond market but needs Swiss francs for some purchases of Swiss components. . . . Both firms go to a swap dealer."

Exhibit 10-10 Fix/Flt Currency Swap

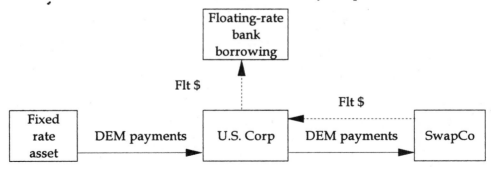

Exhibit 10-11 Fix/Fix Currency Swap

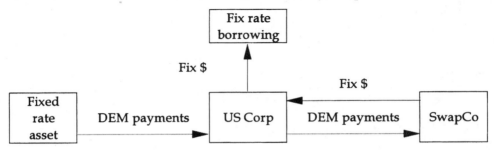

Exhibit 10-12 Using a Currency Swap to Hedge Borrowing in AU$

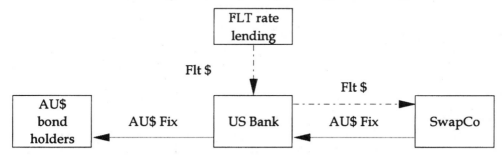

In the aforementioned situation, the corporations have a number of alternatives, none of which happens to be a currency swap. Let us look at things from the point of view of AmericanCo. Its best strategy is clearly to buy SFR forward (maturity equal to the payment date agreed on with SwissCo). If AmericanCo knows that it will sell part of its finished products on the Swiss market, with payment in SFR, it can hedge the estimated future receipts with a forward sale of SFR. If its purchases are for SFR 5 million and its expected sales for SFR 2 million, AmericanCo could buy forward SFR 3 million and get the remaining 2 million with an FX swap that it will close with the revenue from its sales in Switzerland.

Exhibit 10-13 Using a Currency Swap to Hedge Floating-Rate DEM Lending

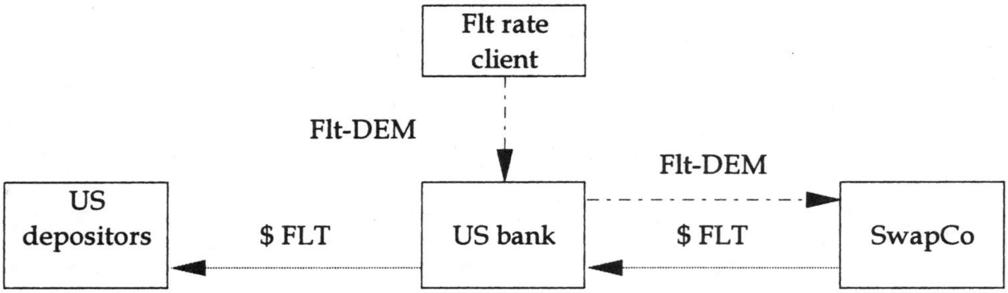

```
                          ┌─────────┐
                          │ Flt rate│
                          │ client  │
                          └────┬────┘
          Flt-DEM              ┆
                               │          Flt-DEM
                               ▼
┌──────────┐            ┌──────────┐            ┌──────────┐
│   US     │  $ FLT     │          │  $ FLT     │          │
│depositors│ ◄───────── │ US bank  │ ◄───────── │ SwapCo   │
└──────────┘            └──────────┘            └──────────┘
```

Pricing and Valuation of Currency Swaps

Pricing currency swaps is a mostly straightforward procedure. A good way to grasp the logic is to start with a float/float swap. Think of a bank or a finance company that extends a medium-term floating-rate loan to a customer in foreign currency, such as DEM. The bank could well borrow floating-rate on the Euromarket, but for the purpose of this construction let us assume it prefers to enter into a currency swap and finance the loan out of its $-denominated deposit base (see Exhibit 10-13).

It is clear that apart from the spread demanded from SwapCo, the float/float currency swap rates will be LIBOR against LIBOR; any other pair of rates would immediately offer arbitrage opportunities, such as hedging the FX exposure through a series of back-to-back forwards that in turn, are linked to LIBOR levels via the covered interest parity. At this point you just determine the float/fix swap rate in the foreign currency with the same straightforward method you would employ for a single-currency interest-rate swap. The same argument leads to a fix/fix pricing based on the current swap rates in the two relevant currencies.

Currency-swap valuation is exactly the same as IRS valuation, with the addition of the necessary adjustment for the change in interest rate that may have occurred from trade date to mark-to-market date. Each leg of the swap is therefore priced in its own currency, and the relevant leg is converted to the foreign currency.

10-5 CREDIT RISK IN SWAPS

Swap pricing has clear implications for credit risk. If your counterparty defaulted on its obligations under the swap contract, your contingent loss would equal the replacement cost of the swap, which in turn is nothing else but its value.

If your counterparty pays fixed-rate at 6.20% on $50 million and the swap rate has meanwhile dropped to 5.75%, you would have to pay an up-front premium to enter into a new swap, paying fix at 6.20%. This premium to *buy up* equals exactly the value of the swap (assuming that the repricing of LIBOR does not play a material role).

If you turn back to the section on repos in Chapter 3, you will see that in the early days, when a term repo was terminated before maturity (usually because some default clause was triggered), the terminating party was allowed to keep the overage of the repo. Something analogous happened in the swap market. If the swap had a positive value for the terminated party, the terminating party was not obliged to indemnify for such loss in value, and this resulted in an extra profit for the terminating party, usually a swap dealer (a very well-known case took place between Bankers Trust and

General Motors; this obviously resulted in a souring of the relationship between the two companies).

The 1992 ISDA swap master agreement included the *full two-way payment clause,* which states that in the case of an insolvency and consequent termination, the party whose swap position has a negative value has a contractual obligation to pay such value to the counterparty.

Chapter **11**

Futures on Bonds and Notes

Futures on bonds and notes are a widely used derivative product, available for all the major currencies and traded on several futures exchanges. They are more complex than foreign-exchange (FX) and short-term interest-rate futures; their pricing and use for hedging and asset management requires an accurate understanding of their functioning.

Bond futures analytics will be introduced with reference to the U.S. T-bond future, which is the most widely traded future on long-term interest rates due to the predominant role of the USD in global finance and to the importance of the T-bond as a benchmark for domestic and international dollar bonds.

The T-bond future contract is also interesting because its design features make it somewhat complex to price and to use for hedging purposes. It therefore represents an interesting case study on how to deal with complex structured financial products. The T-bond contract was listed in 1977 by the Chicago Board of Trade (CBOT) and later was followed by contracts on 10yr, 5yr, and 2yr T-notes. The CBOT had already introduced, without much success, the first bond future in 1975, in the shape of a contract on *pass-through certificates* issued by the Government National Mortgage Association (GNMA). The GNMA contract, due to its unsatisfactory design, was eventually discontinued. For an interesting analysis of this design flaw see Duffie (1989).

This chapter will also succinctly survey two other important contracts: U.S. T-notes and German government bonds (*bunds*). Now that the Euro has been successfully implemented, futures on Euro-denominated bonds will necessarily replace the contracts on bonds denominated in the local currencies of the 11 countries that joined the single currency.

Bond futures are used mainly for short-term, low-transaction-cost hedging purposes, and only a small percentage of contracts give rise to physical delivery. Brokerage fees, usually quoted in terms of roundturn, can be as low as $8.5 for a $100,000-value T-note future contract for institutional clients who deal in volume.

A glance at the data published in the financial press shows that trading volume on T-bond futures is quite impressive but that the outstanding amounts are not all that large when compared to those of interest-rate swaps, floating rate agreements (FRAs), repos, and futures on short-term interest rates such as the IMM 3M Eurodollar.

Exhibit 11-1 U.S. T-bond Future: Trading Volume and Open
Interest on 3 March 1998

	Volume, $ m	Open Int, $ m
US T-bonds (face value)	70,000	74,490
US T-bonds (sett. value)	85,050	90,505
3M Eurodollar	586,725	2,850,289

Source: The *Wall Street Journal*

Furthermore, the dollar value of the trading volume in the U.S. T-bond future is much
lower that that on the 3M Eurodollar contract (see Exhibit 11-1).

11-1   U.S. T-BOND FUTURES ANALYTICS AND THE CHEAPEST-TO-DELIVER BOND

For short-term interest-rate futures such as the 3M Eurodollar, the quotation mechanism translates immediately into a forward yield (percentage yield = 100 − futures
price) for a well-defined future time interval. The futures price is therefore easy to
determine on the basis of the relevant spot yield curve. With the T-bond future, things
are somewhat more complex, and the delivery mechanism gives the short a number
of embedded delivery options.

Conversion Factors and Cheapest-to-Deliver

To better understand the T-bond contract design, recall that futures on commodities
(grain, oil, etc.) are quoted in terms of a well-specified *standard grade*, delivered in well-defined locations. To get broadly-based contracts, however, the delivery mechanisms
identify a range of acceptable deliverable grades. This entails that it is necessary to
predetermine a set of price adjustments to put the different delivery alternatives on a
level playing field. Which of the acceptable grades will eventually be delivered is at the
option of the shorts.

The same logic applies to the T-bond future. The quotation does not represent a
yield index but refers to the future price of the *standard-grade deliverable bond*, which is
an 8% T-bond with at least 15 years to maturity (*YTM*); that is, 15 years to maturity
or to the first call date. The first-call-date clause has now lost its relevance due to the
fact that since 1985, the U.S. Treasury has been issuing-noncallable bonds to facilitate
coupon stripping (see chapter 6). The quotations in Exhibit 11-2 therefore refer to the
standard-grade 8% T-bond with no price adjustment.

If you check the list of deliverable bonds in Exhibit 11-6 you will notice that the
quotation of the only available 8% bond, maturity November 2021, is clearly out of
sync with futures' settlement prices in Exhibit 11-2. This noticeable discrepancy between the futures settlement and the forward prices of the standard-grade deliverable
bond is due to the *cheapest-to-deliver* problem, also referred to as the *quality delivery
option*.

A straightforward way to approach the cheapest-to-deliver issue is to assume that
there are two available 8% bonds, with maturities in the required 15 to 30yr range.
There is no grade adjustment associated with maturity; therefore both 8% bonds would
command the same (settlement) price if delivered by the short. This would be fine

Exhibit 11-2 U.S. T-bond Futures, CBOT, Trade Date 20 February 1998

	Sett price	Volume	Open int.
March 1998	121-20	387,212	563,407
June	121-11	35,493	117,698
September	121-00	1,358	36,490
December	120-20	n.a.	10,523

The contract is for $ 100,000 face value (par) of deliverable T-bonds.
The quotation is identical to that of T-bonds, e.g. 121-20 = 121+20/32.
One tick is therefore worth $ 31.25 in settlement variation.
SHORTS have the option to deliver on any business day of the
delivery month (aka spot month).

Source: Financial Times and The *Wall Street Journal*

with a flat 8% yield curve, because the two bonds would sell for the same price. In real life, the market prices of the two bonds are almost guaranteed to be different whereas their invoice price for delivery by the short would be identical. This entails that one of the two bonds will be cheapest-to-deliver and therefore the market will price the future taking into account that only the cheapest bond is likely to be delivered. The price-*YTM* function will therefore display a negative convexity at the 8% *YTM* level, as shown by Exhibit 11-3.

To have a broadly based contract, the T-bond future allows delivery of any bond with a residual life of at least 15 years, as of the first day of the delivery month (known as the *spot month*). To adjust for the different coupons the contract prescribes that the futures price be multiplied by a *conversion factor* (V), which equals the price rounded to four decimal places, that is necessary to obtain a *YTM* of 8% relative to a $1 face value bond. The conversion factor is often known as the *price factor*.

To streamline the process, conversion factors are computed rounding down the term to maturity of each bond to the nearest quarter, as of the first day of the delivery month (the 7½% bond maturing in November 2016 would therefore be considered as having 18½ years to maturity for the March 1998 spot month). It is possible to compute

Exhibit 11-3 Price-Yield Function for 8% U.S. T-bonds, Negative Convexity

YTM	15yr	30yr
7.6%	103.54	104.70
7.7%	102.64	103.49
7.8%	101.75	102.31
7.9%	100.87	101.14
8.0%	100.00	100.00
8.1%	99.14	98.88
8.2%	98.29	97.78
8.3%	97.45	96.70
8.4%	96.62	95.64

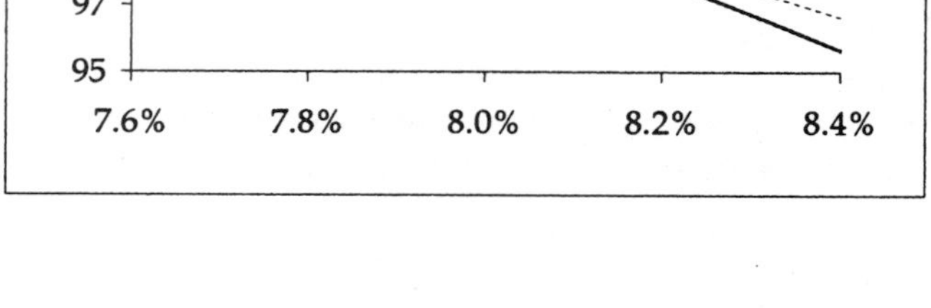

Exhibit 11-4 Conversion Factors as a Function of Term and Coupon

T	6.50%	7.00%	7.50%	8.50%	9.00%	9.50%
18.00	0.8582	0.9055	0.9527	1.0473	1.0945	1.1418
18.25	0.8571	0.9047	0.9522	1.0474	1.0949	1.1425
18.50	0.8564	0.9043	0.9521	1.0479	1.0957	1.1436
18.75	0.8554	0.9035	0.9517	1.0479	1.0961	1.1442
19.00	0.8547	0.9032	0.9516	1.0484	1.0968	1.1453
19.25	0.8538	0.9024	0.9511	1.0485	1.0972	1.1458
19.50	0.8531	0.9021	0.9510	1.0490	1.0979	1.1469
19.75	0.8522	0.9014	0.9506	1.0490	1.0982	1.1474

conversion value tables similar to that shown in Exhibit 11-4. The invoice price received by the short will be

$F_D \cdot V_j + C_j$ = delivery invoice price
F_D = delivery settlement price
V_j = conversion factor for the jth bond
C_j = accrued coupon on the jth bond as of delivery day

This brings to the forefront the cheapest-to-deliver issue in a multicoupon, multimaturity context. The short will, in fact, maximize its net return by delivering the cheapest-to-deliver bond, that is, the bond characterized by the largest net revenue. Arbitrage-free pricing entails that such net revenue will be close to zero.

$(F_D \cdot V_j + C_j) - (P_j + C_j) = F_D \cdot V_j - P_j$ = net revenue for the short
P_j = market price of the jth bond
$F_D \cdot V_j^* - P_j^* \cong 0 \Rightarrow F_D \cong P_j^*/V_j^*$ for the cheapest-to-deliver bond

The conversion-factor method therefore implies that term to maturity plays a role for bonds with a coupon that is different from the 8% standard. On the other hand, given that the market yield curve is unlikely to be a flat 8%, the ratio between conversion factor and market price (known as the *conversion factor bias*) can change very significantly across the range of different deliverable bonds. Arbitrage-free pricing entails that the conversion factor bias (Vb) will be about equal to the settlement price for the cheapest-to-deliver bond. The higher the Vb, the more expensive it is to deliver the bond.

$$Vb = \frac{P_j^*}{V_j^*} \cong F_D$$

The deliverable bond for the U.S. T-bond futures spans a wide range of maturities (15–30 years) and coupon rates (from 6%, up to 11¼%, for the 1998 and 1999 spot months). In this case, the functioning of the conversion factor is bound to play an important role, especially when the fixed 8% conversion rate is widely different from the prevailing market yields. Exhibit 11-5 shows the values of the 15 lowest values of the conversion factor bias, sorted in ascending order, for the March 1998 spot month.

Pricing a Bond Future

If we had only one deliverable bond and one fixed delivery date, pricing the bond future would be a straightforward process. First, you would determine the fair-value

Exhibit 11-5 Conversion Factor Bias, March 1998 Spot Month Quotations as of 20 February 1998

Cpn	Mty	T	Ask	V	V-bias
11.250	Feb-15	16.75	158.1250	1.2968	121.9361
10.625	Aug-15	17.25	151.6250	1.2431	121.9766
9.875	Nov-15	17.50	143.5625	1.1750	122.1829
9.250	Feb-16	17.75	136.9375	1.1172	122.5725
6.750	Aug-26	28.25	111.3750	0.8606	129.4120
6.500	Nov-26	28.50	108.0313	0.8325	129.7596
6.625	Feb-27	28.75	109.8125	0.8460	129.8044
6.000	Feb-26	27.75	101.0313	0.7782	129.8260
6.375	Aug-27	29.25	106.7188	0.8172	130.5911
6.125	Nov-27	29.50	103.7188	0.7888	131.4900

Source: The *Wall Street Journal*

forward price with the usual cost-of-carry equation. Second, you could refine the analysis by introducing some adjustments to take into account the fact that the *YTM* of the bond is correlated to the short-term rates, which are relevant in evaluating possible discrepancies between future and forward prices. Disregarding the futures-forward adjustment, we can write

$P(0,T) \cong P_0 + Carry$
$P(0,T) \cong P_0 + (P_0 + C_0) \cdot rr \cdot T - CI(0,T)$
$P(0,T) =$ fair-value forward price
$P_0 =$ clean price of the bond at time-T
$C_0 =$ accrued coupon at time-0
$rr =$ repo rate, at time 0, for a term T
$CI(0,T) =$ coupon income over the term of the future.

Carry is treated as a cost; therefore, when *carry* $< 0 \Rightarrow F(0,T) < P_0$, we speak of *positive carry* (which means negative cost and therefore net revenue). Note that in some texts, you will find statements such as, "When the yield curve is inverted (downward sloping), the carry is negative; when the yield curve is normal, the carry is positive." This is not necessarily true. You could well have a regular cost of carry with an upward-sloping yield curve and a positive carry with an inverted yield curve.

$F(0,T) \cong P(0,T)/V =$ future's price

The future's price is therefore linked to the forward price of the cheapest-to-deliver bond via the conversion factor. A change (ΔP) in the forward price entails a proportional change ($\Delta P/V$) in the future's price.

The T-bond future can be delivered in any day of the spot month, whereas the conversion factor is fixed throughout the month. This generates the so-called *accrued-interest option*. For *any given settlement price,* the short will find it profitable to deliver at the following times:

• At the end of the spot month when *carry* < 0

Exhibit 11-6 Deliverable Bonds, Conversion Factors, and Cheapest-to-Deliver Quotations as of 20 February 1998

Cpn	Mty	T	Ask	*Ytm*	Fwrd	V	V * Sett	Gain
11.250	Feb-15	16.75	158.1250	5.82	157.89	1.2968	157.72	-0.16
10.625	Aug-15	17.25	151.6250	5.87	151.41	1.2431	151.19	-0.22
9.875	Nov-15	17.50	143.5625	5.88	143.38	1.1750	142.91	-0.47
9.250	Feb-16	17.75	136.9375	5.89	136.78	1.1172	135.88	-0.90
7.250	May-16	18.00	115.0000	5.89	114.92	0.9291	113.00	-1.92
7.500	Nov-16	18.50	117.8125	5.91	117.72	0.9521	115.80	-1.92
8.750	May-17	19.00	132.3750	5.91	132.24	1.0726	130.46	-1.78
8.875	Aug-17	19.25	133.9688	5.92	133.83	1.0850	131.96	-1.87
9.125	May-18	20.00	137.5313	5.92	137.39	1.1113	135.17	-2.22
9.000	Nov-18	20.50	136.4375	5.92	136.30	1.1000	133.78	-2.52
8.875	Feb-19	20.75	135.1875	5.92	135.06	1.0877	132.29	-2.77
8.125	Aug-19	21.25	126.4688	5.93	126.36	1.0125	123.14	-3.22
8.500	Feb-20	21.75	131.3750	5.93	131.26	1.0509	127.82	-3.44
8.750	May-20	22.00	134.6250	5.93	134.50	1.0771	131.00	-3.51
8.750	Aug-20	22.25	134.7500	5.93	134.63	1.0772	131.01	-3.62
7.875	Feb-21	22.75	124.1563	5.94	124.06	0.9868	120.02	-4.04
8.125	May-21	23.00	127.3438	5.94	127.24	1.0131	123.21	-4.03
8.125	Aug-21	23.25	127.5000	5.94	127.40	1.0129	123.19	-4.21
8.000	Nov-21	23.50	126.0625	5.94	125.97	1.0000	121.63	-4.34
7.250	Aug-22	24.25	116.8125	5.94	116.74	0.9201	111.90	-4.84
7.625	Nov-22	24.50	121.7500	5.94	121.67	0.9600	116.76	-4.91
7.125	Feb-23	24.75	115.4063	5.94	115.34	0.9061	110.21	-5.13
6.250	Aug-23	25.25	104.2188	5.93	104.18	0.8113	98.67	-5.50
7.500	Nov-24	26.50	121.0000	5.92	120.93	0.9453	114.97	-5.95
7.625	Feb-25	26.75	122.7813	5.92	122.70	0.9587	116.60	-6.10
6.875	Aug-25	27.25	112.7813	5.93	112.72	0.8758	106.52	-6.21
6.000	Feb-26	27.75	101.0313	5.92	101.00	0.7782	94.65	-6.35
6.750	Aug-26	28.25	111.3750	5.92	111.32	0.8606	104.67	-6.65
6.500	Nov-26	28.50	108.0313	5.91	107.98	0.8325	101.26	-6.73
6.625	Feb-27	28.75	109.8125	5.91	109.76	0.8460	102.89	-6.87
6.375	Aug-27	29.25	106.7188	5.89	106.68	0.8172	99.39	-7.29
6.125	Nov-27	29.50	103.7188	5.86	103.69	0.7888	95.94	-7.75

FWRD = forward price as of the end of the delivery month, computed with the current repo rate of 5.50%.

CtD computation for the March spot month, futures price of 121-20 = 121.625.

The cheapest-to-deliver bond and the 8% standard-grade bond are highlighted.

Quotations: The *Wall Street Journal*

- At the beginning of the delivery month when *carry* > 0, provided that the existence of the *wild-card* and *end-of-month* options does not suggest delaying the delivery

A number of empirical studies have shown that deliveries of the future in fact follow the expected pattern. The March 1998 delivery month is characterized by a positive carry for the deliverable bond; therefore the forward price computed in Exhibit 11-5 is referred to the end of the spot month.

The U.S. T-bond Future

In the case of the U.S. T-bond future, pricing is not so simple. Yield movements could imply a change in the cheapest-to-deliver bond, which in turn would change the price of the forward, the conversion factor, and the price of the future; see Section 11-2 for a numerical example of the quality delivery option.

This option, together with the wild-card and the end-of-month options, is priced into the futures settlement value, which therefore should be lower than the fair-value forward price after taking into account the conversion coefficient. If you examine the $11\frac{1}{4}\%$ cheapest-to-deliver in Exhibit 11-5, you will see that the settlement price multiplied by V is in fact a few basis points lower than the forward fair value. The delivery option of the short is not very relevant for near futures, but can play a bigger role for long-dated contracts, when the shape and volatility of the yield curve make the cheapest-to-deliver switch a real possibility.

The complexities of the T-bond future do not end here, as we shall see in the next subsection.

Operational Details: The Wild-Card and the End-of-Month Options

The futures price is also influenced, to a limited amount, by some aspects of the delivery rules, over a $T + 2$ settlement cycle. Let us see how this works.

- Trading of the T-bond future stops at 2:00 P.M. Chicago time; this is the reference time at which the settlement price (and therefore the invoice price) is fixed, and it does not change until the next day of trading. The cash Treasuries market, however, is open for longer hours (in fact, it has no official closing time, being an over-the-counter (OTC) market).
- The short can choose to deliver in any business day of the spot month. Notice of the intention to deliver must be submitted to the CBOT clearinghouse in the form of a *delivery notice* and a *delivery tender card* by 8:00 P.M. 2 business days before delivery. This is known as *position day*. The first admissible position day is 2 business days before the first business day of the spot month.
- Early the next business day, known as *intention day*, the clearinghouse matches short to oldest long and notifies both parties. By 2:00 P.M. the short invoices the long, sending that party a delivery notice. At this point the short must select irrevocably which bonds it is going to deliver.
- The following day ($T + 2$) is *delivery day*, and by 1:00 P.M. the transaction must be settled via Federal Reserve book-entry wire-transfer system (Fed wire).

The process outlined here generates the so-called wild-card option, that is, a series of about 15 short-lived put options, one for each trading day (except the last) in the delivery month, to take advantage of a fall in the bond price that occurs after the futures price has been fixed. Note that to take full advantage of the wild-card option, you should be a short who has written a naked speculative contract.

T-bond futures cease to trade at noon of the eighth business day before the end of the delivery month. A trader who is short futures at that time must proceed to physical delivery within the last business day of the month. The invoice will be based on the futures price of the last trading day (because there is no mark to market of the contract after that point in time). Again, this leaves an option to the short, the so-called end-of-month option.

11-2 HEDGING AND PRICING

We have seen that the T-bond future is widely used for setting up short-lived hedges without incurring heavy transaction costs. The conversion-factor mechanism and the wide range of deliverable grades, however, entail that this kind of hedge may behave quite unpredictably, especially if you want to use the T-bond future to implement a long-term *hedge-and-forget* strategy.

Say you want to use the future to hedge a 16yr at-the-market interest-rate swap with notional principal of $40 million and swap rate of 6.30% (0.40% above the Treasuries yield). To implement the hedge, you cannot just buy one futures contract for each $100,000 of notional principal. You must examine the situation of the deliverable grades and calibrate your hedge to take into account that the cheapest-to-deliver bond is the 11¼ with a term of 16yr. Given the deliverable bond, you must hedge, taking into account the *PVbp* for the swap, the cheapest-to-deliver bond, and the futures contract (see Exhibit 11-7).

$$PVbp(F) = \frac{PVbp(Bond)}{V}$$

The hedge ratio will therefore be 0.9199 (= 0.0998/0.1085) futures contracts for every $100,000 of notional principal of the swap, that is, 368 contracts to hedge the $40 million swap. This figure does not take into account any adjustment for the difference in convexity between the swap and the deliverable bond or for the possible effect of the wild-card and end-of-month options. This hedge would perform rather well vis-a-vis a parallel shift of the *YTM* curve (see Exhibit 11-8).

Let us now consider the case of the *YTM* curve steepening. This will entail a switch in the cheapest-to-deliver bond (which now becomes the 7½% with a term of 26yr) and a swing in the settlement variation that now equals $1,543 per contract. Note that if the only deliverable grade had been the 16yr 11¼% bond, there would have been

Exhibit 11-7 Hedging a Swap with an Interest Rate Future

	T.	Cpn	Ytm	Price	PVbp	V
Par swap	16	6.30%	6.30%	100.00	0.0998	
CtD bond	16	11.25%	5.90%	154.91	0.1400	129.0445
T-Bond future				1.20	0.0011	
			hedge ratio		91.9884	

Exhibit 11-8 Hedging a Swap, Parallel *Ytm* Shift

	Ytm	$ values
Par swap	6.30%	40,000,000
Swap mark-to-market	6.80%	38,067,760
Gain on swap		1,932,240
Sett variation on 368 futures		-1,936,066
Gain (loss) on hedged portfolio		-3,826

Exhibit 11-9 Hedging a Swap, Steepening *Ytm* Curve

	Ytm	$ values
Par swap	6.30%	40,000,000
Swap mark-to-market	6.30%	40,000,000
Gain on swap		0
Sett variation on 368 futures		-567,883
Gain (loss) on hedged portfolio		-567,883

no settlement variation because the 16yr *YTM* is unchanged with reference to the baseline case (see Exhibit 11-9).

The lesson from this simplified example is that you cannot really hedge and forget when you want to use the T-bond future. If you use the contract as a cheap hedge for a few days, or maybe a few hours, you are relatively safe. For longer periods you are better off with products such as interest-rate swaps. In asset management you cannot really use the T-bond future as a substitute for cash-market Treasuries unless you avail yourself of a fully fledged stochastic model of the yield term structure (see Chapter 19).

11-3   OTHER IMPORTANT BOND FUTURES

We have seen that the wide range of maturities that are deliverable grades for the T-bond contract (15–30 years) results in the possibility of a wide range of coupons. Some deliverable bonds were issued nearly 15 years ago, when market yields (and therefore coupons) were much higher than they were as of the beginning of 1998.

The other bond and note futures that we shall concisely survey in this section are characterized by a much shorter range of maturities and consequently by a smaller range of deliverable coupons. This entails that the cheapest-to-deliver switching is a lot less relevant, thereby making these futures easier to use for hedging and for portfolio-management purposes.

The U.S. T-notes Futures

The U.S. T-bond futures are complemented by three contracts on T-notes, always listed on the CBOT. These futures are very similar to the bond contract, but their identification of deliverable grades implies a more contained set of maturities and coupons.

Exhibit 11-10 Yield curve shifts

	T	Cpn	V	Inv	Yld	Price	Gain	Sett
	16	11.250%	1.2904	154.91	5.90%	154.91	0.000	120.05
	18	7.250%	0.9291	111.53	5.90%	114.85	-3.313	
	20	9.125%	1.1113	133.41	5.90%	137.58	-4.164	
Baseline	22	8.750%	1.0771	129.30	5.90%	134.86	-5.567	
case	24	7.250%	0.9205	110.50	5.90%	117.21	-6.709	
	26	7.500%	0.9456	113.52	5.90%	121.14	-7.619	
	28	6.750%	0.8611	103.37	5.90%	111.58	-8.204	
	30	6.125%	0.7879	94.58	5.90%	103.15	-8.562	
	16	11.250%	1.2904	148.12	6.40%	148.12	0.000	114.79
	18	7.250%	0.9291	106.65	6.40%	109.01	-2.363	
	20	9.125%	1.1113	127.56	6.40%	130.50	-2.939	
Parallel	22	8.750%	1.0771	123.63	6.40%	127.54	-3.912	
shift	24	7.250%	0.9205	105.66	6.40%	110.36	-4.702	
	26	7.500%	0.9456	108.54	6.40%	113.86	-5.319	
	28	6.750%	0.8611	98.84	6.40%	104.55	-5.710	
	30	6.125%	0.7879	90.44	6.40%	96.38	-5.942	
	16	11.250%	1.2904	152.92	5.90%	154.91	-1.991	
	18	7.250%	0.9291	110.10	6.10%	112.48	-2.384	
	20	9.125%	1.1113	131.70	6.26%	132.43	-0.731	
Ytm	22	8.750%	1.0771	127.63	6.39%	127.73	-0.098	
steepening	24	7.250%	0.9205	109.08	6.48%	109.36	-0.279	
	26	7.500%	0.9456	112.06	6.53%	112.06	0.000	118.50
	28	6.750%	0.8611	102.05	6.55%	102.58	-0.531	
	30	6.125%	0.7879	93.37	6.53%	94.70	-1.331	

• *10yr T-note futures* ($100,000 face value). Deliverable grades are U.S. T-notes with a residual term to maturity between 6½ and 10 years as of the first day of the delivery month. The conversion factor is the price of the delivered note ($1 par value) to yield 8%. The tick size is 1/32nd of a point ($31.25) as for the T-bond contract.

• *5yr T-note futures* ($100,000 face value). Deliverable grades are T-notes with an original maturity of not more than 5¼ years and a remaining maturity of not less 4¼ years. The conversion factor is the price of the delivered note ($1 par value) to yield 8%. The limitation on the original maturity is to exclude 7yr and 10yr original-maturity notes, which could have been issued at a coupon level that has in the meantime become widely different from market yields. The tick size is one half of 1/32nd of a point ($15.625), that is, 109-025 = 109 + 2.5/32.

• *2yr T-note futures* ($200,000 face value). Deliverable grades are U.S. T-notes that have an original maturity of not more than 5¼ years and a remaining maturity of not more than 1 year and 9 months from the first day of the delivery month, but not more

Exhibit 11-11 U.S. T-notes Futures, Trade Date 27 February 1998

		Sett	Volume	Open int
10yr	March-98	112-22	266,662	254,879
	June	112-20	n.a.	249,335
	September	112-22	n.a.	6,268
5yr	March-98	109-025	155,545	133,150
	June	109-02	n.a.	155,102
2yr	March-98	104-01	14,000	21,691
	June	104-005	n.a.	26,779

The volume figures are the totals for all the delivery months: The Wall Street Journal does not split the volume figure by spot month.

Source: The *Wall Street Journal*

Exhibit 11-12 T-note future (10 year) 27 February 1998

Cpn	Mty	T	Ask	Fwrd	V	V-Bias	V * Sett	Gain
7.875	Nov-04	6.50	112.2500	112.08	0.9938	112.95	111.98	-0.10
7.500	Feb-05	6.75	110.4375	110.30	0.9741	113.37	109.77	-0.53
6.500	May-05	7.00	104.8438	104.77	0.9208	113.86	103.76	-1.01
6.500	Aug-05	7.25	104.9375	104.87	0.9185	114.25	103.51	-1.36
5.875	Nov-05	7.50	101.1563	101.13	0.8819	114.71	99.38	-1.75
5.625	Feb-06	7.75	99.5938	99.58	0.8646	115.19	97.43	-2.15
6.875	May-06	8.00	107.5938	107.50	0.9345	115.14	105.30	-2.20
7.000	Jul-06	8.25	108.5000	108.40	0.9403	115.39	105.96	-2.44
6.500	Oct-06	8.50	105.3438	105.28	0.9088	115.92	102.41	-2.87
6.250	Feb-07	8.75	103.9063	103.86	0.8912	116.59	100.43	-3.43
6.625	May-07	9.00	106.6250	106.55	0.9130	116.79	102.88	-3.67
6.125	Aug-07	9.25	103.2188	103.18	0.8789	117.44	99.04	-4.13
5.500	Feb-08	9.75	99.1563	99.15	0.8328	119.06	93.85	-5.31

The cheapest-to-deliver computation is for March spot month, future = 112:22

Quotations: The *Wall Street Journal*

than 2 years from the last day of the delivery month. The conversion factor is the price of the delivered note ($1 par value) to yield 8%. The tick size is one quarter of 1/32nd of a point ($15.625), that is, 104-005 = 104 + 0.5/32 (see Exhibits 11-11 and 11-12).

The German Treasury Bond (*Bund*) Contract

The *bund* future was traded first on the LIFFE, and only a few years later by the Deutsche Termine Borse, which is now the main exchange for *bund* futures. If the

European monetary union is successfully implemented, the *bund* contract stands a good chance of becoming the basis for the future on Euro-denominated bonds. The *bund* contract is more modern than the U.S. T-bond, and its design avoids a number of the implicit options that add to the complexity of the T-bond contract.

- Contract size: DEM 250,000 par value of 6% bonds (notional bond) issued by the Treasury or by the *Treuhandanstalt*
- Deliverable grade: Maturities between 8½ and 10½ years as of the delivery day (the range of deliverable maturities is therefore narrower than that of the CBOT contract, which greatly reduces the impact of the quality option)
- Decimalized minimum price movement (tick): 0.01%
- Last day of trading: 2 business days before the delivery day (there is no end-of-month option)
- Delivery day: Tenth calendar day of the delivery month (there is no wild-card option)
- Invoice price: Based on the official delivery settlement price on the last trading day of a contract
- Conversion value (price factor): The price of the delivered bond (DEM 1 par value) to yield 6%, ISMA rules. The term to maturity is rounded down to the nearest month to compute the price factor (see Section 11-4).

11-4 APPENDIX

Computing the conversion coefficients (also known as price factors) requires a straightforward application of the equations we covered in Chapter 7. For the U.S. T-bond future, term to maturity is *rounded down* to the nearest quarter, and all the quarters are assumed to be exactly one-half of a half-year period, without the actual day count, which is the rule in the U.S. Treasuries market. If the term is an integer number of half-years (H), we have the following equation:

$$V = \frac{c}{2} \cdot \frac{1}{1.04} \cdot \left(1 - \frac{1}{1.04^H}\right) + \frac{1}{1.04^H}$$

If the term to maturity is H half-years plus one quarter, we have

$$V = \frac{1}{\sqrt{1.04}} \cdot \left[\frac{c}{2} \cdot \frac{1}{1.04} \cdot \left(1 - \frac{1}{1.04^H}\right) + \frac{1}{1.04^H} + \frac{c}{2}\right] - \frac{c}{4}.$$

For the German *bund* future the pricing equation follows ISMA rules, and maturity is rounded down to the nearest full month. We therefore obtain the following equation:

$$V = \frac{1}{1.06^F} \cdot \left[\frac{c}{6} \cdot \left(1 - \frac{1}{1.06^N}\right) + \frac{c}{100} + \frac{1}{1.06^N}\right] - \frac{c \cdot (1 - F)}{100}$$

N = integer number of years to maturity
F = *months*/12

Bond futures analysis is often expressed in terms of basis, defined as the difference between the bond price in the spot cash market and the delivery price in the futures market.

Exhibit 11-13 Cheapest to Deliver Bond and Implied Repo Rate

Cpn	Mty	T	Ask	Fwrd	V	V * Sett	Net basis	Implied repo rate
11.250	Feb-15	16.75	158.1250	157.877	1.2968	157.72	0.16	4.47%
10.625	Aug-15	17.25	151.6250	151.403	1.2431	151.19	0.22	4.03%
9.875	Nov-15	17.50	143.5625	143.384	1.1750	142.91	0.48	2.22%

$$P_0 - F(0,T) \cdot V = \text{basis}$$
$$\frac{\text{basis}}{P_0} \cdot \frac{360}{\text{days}} = \text{implied repo rate}$$

We can now introduce the concept of *basis after carry* (also called *net basis*), which is the forward bond price minus the delivery price of the bond.

$$P_0 + \text{carry} - F(0,T) \cdot V = \text{basis after carry}$$

The cheapest-to-deliver is clearly the bond with the highest implied repo rate (= the bond with the lowest basis after carry; see Exhibit 11-13).

Part 3

Options

Chapter 12

An Introduction to Options

12-1 INTRODUCTION

An option gives the *owner* (*buyer* of the option = *long the option*) the right, but not the obligation, to buy (*call option*) or to sell (*put option*) a defined asset, at a specified price (*exercise price* or *strike price*), at a future date or within a future date. The buyer will *exercise the option* only when the price of the *underlying asset* moves in such a way as to make the exercise profitable. Once the option's price is paid, the buyer has no further obligations. Option buyers are sometimes referred to as having *limited liability*.

Options are radically different from forwards and futures, where both buyer and seller enter into a commitment. Due to the reciprocal contractual obligation, a forward usually has a zero price at time-0. In the case of an option, the buyer's limited liability implies that the option must have a nonnegative price (known as *premium*, due to the insurancelike character of options). The absence of a future commitment of the option buyer entails that the *writer* (*seller*) of the option runs no credit risk. Only the buyer runs the risk of the writer defaulting on his future commitment.

Not all options are self-standing and clearly identified (*pure option*); rather, they are often embedded in some more complex contract or structured financial product. To restrict ourselves to the fixed-income area, convertible bonds, callable and puttable bonds, and dual-currency bonds are all examples of financial instruments with optionlike features. Pure options on shares of stock are more straightforward and easier to understand than options on currencies and interest rates. We shall therefore introduce most of the basic concepts with reference to stock options and then extend them to fixed-income and currency products.

In one form or another, options have been around for a long time. The first recorded use of what we would now call an option is attributed to Thales of Miletus, a Greek scientist and philosopher who lived in the early sixth century B.C. The story goes that Thales once predicted a plentiful olive crop. To take advantage of his agricultural forecast, he bought the right to use all the olive presses in Miletus and in the nearby town of Chios at a fixed rental price. The crop happened to be extremely abundant, and Thales made a small fortune by renting out at a high price the olive presses that he had an option to use.

Those who consider options inherently dangerous and somewhat evil will be happy to know that they did play an important role in the tulip bulb speculative craze that swept the traditionally sound and surefooted Dutch in the 1630s. That this episode took place while most of central Europe was torn apart by the terrifying Thirty Years War is a sad testimony to the power of irrational greed. The tulip-bulb "bubble" has been described by more than one author; I would recommend the highly readable and informative account by Malkiel (1995).

In more recent times, options were traded in the United States in the nineteenth century. A well-known financier, Russel Sage, clearly understood the mechanism of the put-call parity and used it to create synthetic loans with which he could circumvent the existing statutory limitations on interest rates. For a more detailed account, see Chance (1998).

At the beginning of this century, a number of firms (which identified themselves as members of the Put and Call Brokers and Dealers Association) attempted to create an embryonic options market. This early attempt failed, however, due to the lack of adequate measures to prevent fraudulent practices and to cope with credit risk.

Exchange-Traded Options (Listed Options)

Exchange-traded financial options are a relatively new product. The first modern market, the Chicago Board Options Exchange (CBOE), was established in 1973 by the Chicago Board of Trade (CBOT). The first options to be traded at the CBOE were calls on shares of stock; puts followed only in 1977.

The Chicago Mercantile Exchange (CME) followed suit and established itself as a prominent options-trading exchange (the widely used options on the S&P 500 futures trades at the CME). Chicago is still the number-one spot for options trading. In the wake of the success of Chicago, other options' exchanges were established both in the United States (e.g., Philadelphia) and abroad (LIFFE, MATIF, OSAKA, etc.).

Listed options have registered an impressive growth. The volume of trading in options on stocks and stock market indexes is often larger than the volumes registered on the stock markets themselves. Exchange-traded options have also received a considerable boost from the introduction of options on futures, known as *futures options*. All the important financial futures (Eurodollars, U.S. T-bonds, German *bunds*, etc.) have associated options contracts, and most of the large derivatives exchanges trade both futures and options.

Exchange-traded options clear through centralized clearinghouses such as the Options Clearing Corporation in the United States (which is jointly owned by the U.S. options exchanges, with the exception of the exchanges dealing only in options on futures), thereby avoiding the credit-risk problem associated with a possible insolvency of the *writer of the option*. The clearinghouse mechanism entails that when you want to sell an existing option that you own, you do not sell it to a buyer but extinguish it with an *offsetting trade* with the clearinghouse, in the same way as with a futures contract.

Exhibit 12-1 Stock Option Quotations, 8 July 1998

Stock	Strike	Expiration	Call	Put
AMD	22.5	OCT	1: 1/4	...
18 : 3/16	25.0	OCT	7/8	7 : 1/4
Disney	115.0	OCT	15/16	7 : 3/4
108 : 1/8	120.0	OCT	7/16	...
Yahoo	210.0	OCT	7: 3/8	21: 1/8
186 : 6/32	220.0	OCT	5: 1/4	29 : 1/4

The quotation under the stock symbol is the relevant stock price

Clearinghouses enforce a system of margins to deal with credit risk. There is, however, no need for daily settlement (which is one of the defining characteristics of futures) to standardize option contracts. Two options contracts are identical when they have the same exercise price and the same maturity, irrespective of when and at what price they were initiated. Therefore, option exchanges determine well-defined monthly or quarterly maturities and standard exercise prices. For example, the CBOE range of exercise prices on stock options generally follows the rule that the strike prices are at $2.5 or $5.0 intervals, depending on the underlying stock price. A $10 strike price interval may also be adopted for stock prices well above $100 (see Exhibit 12-1). Modern option markets are carefully organized and regulated. In the United States, there was for some years a conflict in asserted jurisdiction over who should regulate options on futures given that options were under the autority of the Securities and Exchange Commission (SEC), whereas futures were regulated by the Commodities and Futures Trading Commission (CFTC). A compromise agreement (known as the Shad-Johnson accord, from the names of the chairmen of the SEC and the CFTC) was finally reached and ratified by legislation in 1982. This agreement established that jurisdiction over options follows jurisdiction over the underlying asset. Thus the SEC oversees options on securities and the CFTC has jurisdiction over options on futures. This opened the way for active trading of options on futures, that started in 1982 on an experimental basis and was institutionalized in 1987. For a more detailed coverage of this topic, see Edwards and Ma (1992).

Over-the-Counter Options

We have also witnessed the emergence of a flourishing market in over-the-counter (OTC) tailor-made options. Many OTC options can be resold by the owner; therefore, the seller of an option does not necessarily coincide with the writer.

Due to credit-risk concerns, the OTC options market is dominated by large banks and investment banks, as clearly shown by the ranking in Exhibit 12-2 compiled by *Institutional Investor*. The involvement of banks has raised regulatory worries, and the Basle Capital Accord has been amended to impose minimum capital-adequacy requirements as a function of market risks.

Complexity of Options

Options are certainly more complex than cash instruments or derivatives such as forwards, swaps, and futures. Option pricing cannot escape the use of concepts borrowed

Exhibit 12-2 Ranking of Derivatives Dealers

1	Citicorp	11	Hong Kong Banking Corporation
2	Goldman, Sachs & Co.	12	Credit Suisse First Boston - CSFB
3	J. P. Morgan	13	BancAmerica Robertson Stephens
4	Chase Manhattan Bank	14	Societe Generale
5	Deutsche Morgan Grenfell	15	Barclays De Zoete Wedds -BZW
6	Morgan Stanley Dean Witter	16	National Westminster Markets
7	Swiss Bank Corporation	17	Dresdner Kleinworth Benson
8	Union Bank of Switzerland	18	Banque Paribas
9	Merrill Lynch & Co.	19	Salomon Brothers Smith Barney
10	Bankers Trust Alex Brown	20	Lehman Brothers

Source: Institutional Investor, February 1998

from probability and statistics. While non-optionlike interest-rate derivatives can be priced off the yield curve, options need estimates of future volatility and assumptions about the random behavior of prices and rates of return. One of the most important results of the option-pricing models described in the following chapters is to show that, *under certain conditions*, it is possible to:

- Write an option, setting up a dynamic hedge in such a way as to lock in a profit irrespective of the appreciation or depreciation of the underlying asset. This may well appear to be counterintuitive, but it is nevertheless relatively easy to implement.
- Structure a portfolio in such a way that it behaves as if it comprised a *protective put*, thereby implementing what is known as portfolio insurance. This technique is also widely used in creating hedges against foreign exchange (FX) risk in internationally diversified portfolios (*currency overlays*).

It is important, however, to stress that the dynamic hedge is only as good as the assessment of the random process of future price movements on which it is based. The preceding hedging strategies are far from fail-safe and must be implemented with the appropriate risk-management procedures firmly in place. There is no simple hedge-and-forget alternative.

The analysis of options value has also cast a new light on a number of products and strategies that have optionlike characteristics (think of collateralized mortgage obligations [CMOs]; see Chapter 13). Many areas of corporate finance now incorporate concepts and techniques deriving from options theory, see Brealey and Myers (1996) and Bodie and Merton (1998). The relationship between option pricing and corporate finance issues, such as the pricing of corporate liabilities, was clearly recognized in the breakthrough articles by Black and Scholes (1973) and Merton (1973). Merton and Scholes shared the 1997 Nobel Prize in economics. This recognition of their pathbreaking work came too late for Fisher Black, who died in 1996.

12-2 STANDARD TERMINOLOGY

Options are so different from other financial instruments that they have prompted the development of an extensive ad hoc terminology. This short section presents only that limited subset of options-speak that you need to get started. More terms will follow in other sections and chapters. Gastineau and Kritzman (1996) provide a detailed coverage of options terminology.

Call Option.   The buyer of a call acquires the right to purchase the *underlying asset* at a specified price from the *writer of the option* (writer = short the option).

Put Option.   The buyer acquires the right to sell the underlying asset, at a specified price, to the writer of the option.

Underlying Asset.   Financial options are written on shares of stock, bonds, stock exchange indexes such as the S&P 500, FX, interest-rate futures, and so on. FX options reflect the already examined ambiguity of all FX transactions: a call on DEM can be interpreted as a put on the $. The underlying asset of an option can be another financial derivative, such as a future or a swap.

Futures Options.   This is a somewhat abbreviated name for options on futures. These options are also known as *commodity options*. *Swaptions* are options that have a swap as an underlying asset.

Premium.   The price paid by the buyer to the seller (writer). The seller commits to sell the asset (when he writes a call) or to buy the asset (when she writes a put).

Exercise Price or Strike Price.   The price, usually set at contract date, at which the buyer of a call can buy and the buyer of a put can sell the underlying asset. We indicate the exercise price with X.

Maturity Date or Expiration Date.   The last day of life of the option.

European Options.   These give the right to buy (European call) or to sell (European put) at the maturity date. Note that there are European options traded in the United States, such as the option on the Standard & Poor 100, traded on the CBOE.

American Options.   These give the right to buy (American calls) or to sell (American puts) on any day up to the expiration date (maturity date). Note that several American-style options are traded on European option exchanges.

In-the-Money.   An option is in-the-money when it would have a nonzero value if it were exercised immediately. This means that the asset price must exceed the strike price for a call (asset price > X) and must be lower than the strike price for a put (X < asset price). A self-explanatory piece of jargon is *deep-in-the-money*.

Out-of-the-Money.   For a call this means that the exercise price is higher than the current market price (X > asset price). A put is out-of-the-money when the exercise price is lower than the asset price (X < asset price). Another self-explanatory term is *far-out-of-the-money*.

At-the-Money.   When the asset price equals or is very close to the exercise price (X = asset price, for both puts and calls).

Intrinsic Value or Tangible Value.   For in-the-money options it is the gain that could be made from their immediate exercise (exercise the in-the-money call and sell the asset; buy the asset and exercise an in-the-money put). Strictly speaking, one should apply the term only to American options that can be exercised before maturity. In practice, the term intrinsic value is also commonly used also for European options.

Time-Value.   The amount by which the price of an option exceeds its intrinsic value. The name time-value derives from the fact that an option's price can exceed its intrinsic value only if the option has time left before it expires. For out-of-the-money options, market price = time value.

Time-Value Decay.   The loss of time-value as maturity approaches. Call options always display time-value decay (puts are more complicated, as we shall see in Section 12-4).

Covered Call.   Written by someone who owns the underlying asset (or is long a forward or future on the same asset). If the price of the asset increases above the strike price, the writer of the call will not incur a loss but will forgo the profit, being contractually obliged to sell at X. On the other hand, the writer will lose if the asset declines in price.

Naked Call.   Written without being long the underlying asset (or forward or future on the same asset). The writer stands to lose a large amount if the price rises well above X. This could affect the solvency of the writer and therefore creates a credit risk for the buyer. Exchanges have implemented strict margin requirements for writers of naked calls.

Covered Put.   Written by someone who is short the asset (or forward or future on the same asset). In case of declining prices, the put will be exercised and the writer will therefore cover his short by acquiring the underlying asset (forgoing the extra profit he could have realized buying at market price to cover the short).

Naked Put.   Written by someone who is not short the underlying asset. This could generate a large loss and is consequently a credit risk for the buyer. As with naked calls, exchanges have implemented strict margin requirements.

Class.   The set of all listed options of a certain type (puts or calls) on a given stock. For example, all existing listed calls on IBM, irrespective of maturity and strike price, are a class (and all listed puts on IBM shares are another class).

Series.   The set of all options of the same class that have identical expiration dates and exercise prices (series ⊆ class).

Dividend Protection.   Listed options are not protected against cash dividends that are deemed to be the property of the investor who owns the stock on the *holder-of-record date.* A cash dividend will therefore decrease the value of a call and increase the value of a put. Listed options are protected, however, against stock splits and stock dividends.

Exotic Options. A generic term used to indicate all options that are not straightforward puts and calls. A well-known example are *Asian options,* where the strike price is determined on the basis of the average price of the underlying asset over a period of time preceding the expiration date (therefore the exercise price is not known when the option is written).

Mid-Atlantic Options. (also called *Bermudan options,* from the geographic position of the Bermuda islands). These are somehow in between American and European options; they can be exercised before maturity but only on certain predetermined dates. U.S. Treasury bonds, which could be called on coupon dates in the last 5 years of their life, are an example of fixed-income instrument with embedded Bermudan calls.

Lookback Options. Give the holder the right to buy (calls) or to sell (puts) the underlying asset at the most favorable price achieved during the lookback period, which often coincides with the entire life of the option.

Cash-or-Nothing Call. This has a fixed payoff if the price of the underlying asset ends up at or above the strike price. Cash-or-nothing options are *binary options* (also called *digital options*), that is, options that have a discontinuous payoff.

12-3 PAYOFF AT MATURITY OF PUTS AND CALLS

The payoff at maturity of options and options strategies is traditionally presented by means of a set of graphs that provide a self-evident and easy-to-memorize visualization. This graphical analysis is quite helpful and therefore we shall adopt it, albeit with some adjustments and integration. Some of the Exhibits are straightforward linear functions; we can therefore dispense with showing the numerical values on which they are based.

The put and call values in the exhibits are computed with the standard Black-Scholes option-pricing equation (see Chapter 18), setting stock price at \$100 ($S = 100$), volatility at 30% ($\sigma = 0.3$), riskless yield at 5% ($R = 0.05$), and maturity at three months ($T = 0.25$). We shall adopt a few simplifying assumptions.

- We consider only European stock options; therefore we don't need to deal with the early exercise problem.
- The underlying stock does not pay dividends over the life of the option.
- Frictionless markets—no transaction costs or taxes, no restrictions on short selling; no stock-borrowing costs; and identical borrowing and lending rates. Such conditions may well appear unrealistic but in fact are a good approximation of the operating environment of large dealers.

We compute interest on the cost (revenue) relative to the purchase (sale) of options and on the purchase (or short sale) of stock for those option strategies that involve holding or short selling the underlying stock as well as options. The net gain (loss) at maturity on a long or short stock position equals:

$S_T - S \cdot \exp(R \cdot T) =$ gain (loss) on long stock position
$-S_T + S \cdot \exp(R \cdot T) =$ gain (loss) on short-sale
$S_T =$ stock price at the option's expiration date
$S =$ stock price at time-0.

Payoff of Puts and Calls

In general, it will pay to exercise a European option when it expires in-the-money. This is not true, however, if the option is in-the-money by an amount insufficient to cover the transaction costs associated with the exercise. Disregarding transaction costs, that in most cases are quite low, the value at maturity and the net payoffs of European puts and calls can be concisely expressed as follows.

$C_T = \max(0, S_T - X) =$ value at maturity of call
$P_T = \max(0, -S_T + X) =$ value at maturity of put
$X =$ exercise price (strike price)
$C_T - C \cdot \exp(R \cdot T) =$ net payoff of call
$P_T - P \cdot \exp(R \cdot T) =$ net payoff of put

We shall from time to time need more symbols to avoid ambiguity. This will be accomplished by using suffixes:

- L and S indicate long or short positions when a strategy includes both (e.g., X_L will stand for the strike price of a long option and C_S will indicate the premium for a short call).
- P and C indicate put and call, when we must distinguish between different strike prices, such as X_C and X_P.
- W, M, and H refer to loW, interMediate, and High and indicate the ranking of exercise prices.

The net gain on a long call cannot be defined with any degree of certainty; it is a random variable that depends on the stock price at expiration (known as the *realization* of the stock price). Therefore the *maximum potential loss* on a naked call is undefined, being the mirror image of the gain on the call. You are likely to come across option diagrams where the potential payoff of the call is indicated as *infinite*. This is clearly nonsensical because it implies that the price of the underlying stock could become infinitely large. It is true, however, that naked calls can expose the writer to significant losses when the stock price rallies. Exhibit 12-3 shows the payoff of a call, with $X = 100$. It also shows the payoff of a long position in the underlying stock, bought at $S = X = 100$. Both strategies are *bullish* and will yield a profit only when the stock price goes up. The payoff of the call is as follows:

- Marginally lower than the stock when the stock price goes up. The outright stock purchase implies an interest cost whereas the exercise price is paid at maturity. The cost of the call, however, is higher than this interest cost.
- A lot better than the stock when the stock price declines below the strike price. The stock could lose all of its value whereas the maximum loss on the option is $C \cdot \exp(R \cdot T)$.

Exhibit 12-4 compares a put with a short position in the underlying stock. These are clearly *bearish strategies*, that will generate a gain only when the stock price declines. The put outperforms the short stock if the bearish forecast proves to be wrong and the stock price increases: you lose only $P \cdot \exp(R \cdot T)$ when your put expires worthless.

Exhibit 12-3 Net Payoff at Maturity: European Call and Stock

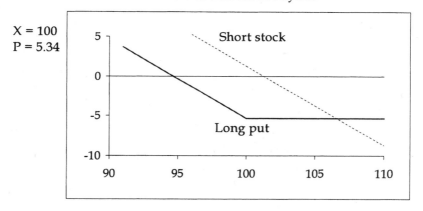

Exhibit 12-4 Put and Stock Payoffs

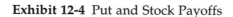

The short stock, however, is worth more than the put when the stock price declines. The short strategy has the advantage of earning interest, contrary to the long-stock strategy that implies an interest cost. It is therefore natural to expect that the put premium should be lower than the call premium when $S = X$.

12-4 TIME VALUE AND EARLY EXERCISE OF AMERICAN OPTIONS

An in-depth analysis of the time value of puts and calls requires the use of a fully fledged option-pricing model. We can, however, explore some interesting aspects of option prices and of the optimal early exercise of American options using the simple tools that we explored in Section 12-3. In this section we shall concentrate only on non-dividend-paying stocks. This is sufficient to explore the underlying logic and allows a noncluttered analysis.

Calls on Non-Dividend-Paying Stock

We can think of the time-value of an in-the-money call as being attributable to the following two elements:

1. The *insurance premium* against the possibility of the stock declining below the exercise price. The longer the term of the option, the higher the value of this insurance against an adverse performance of the stock.
2. An *interest-cost element,* because the option will allow you to defer the payment of the exercise price until the day the call expires in-the-money. This interest-cost element will, in practice, coincide with the time-value of the premium if the stock price is so high, relative to the exercise price, that the insurance element becomes irrelevant.

Take a portfolio composed by one call and by a riskless bill, face value X, and maturity equal to that of the call. The portfolio's payoff at maturity will be better than or equal to the payoff you would obtain by holding the stock. Therefore, to avoid arbitrage, the call price must always exceed the following lower bounds:

$$C + \exp(-R \cdot T) \cdot X \geq S$$

$$C \geq S - \exp(-R \cdot T) \cdot X \Rightarrow C > \underbrace{S - X}_{\text{Intrinsic Value}}$$

It is therefore always suboptimal to exercise an American call on non-dividend-paying stock before maturity. The call is *worth more alive than dead.* Due to the nonoptimality of early exercise, European and American calls must have the same price when the stock is not expected to pay dividends over the life of the option. Assume you bought an at-the-money American call with the stock price at 100. The stock price has climbed to 120 and your personal judgment (right or wrong) is that it no longer has any growth potential, and therefore you want to take your profit. The call will still have a market price exceeding its intrinsic value. You are therefore better off selling the call instead of exercising it.

If the call sold for less than its fair price (e.g., at its intrinsic value, $C = S - X$), there would be an arbitrage opportunity that dealers would be quick to exploit. This works by shorting the stock and using the revenue to buy the (at-the-money call) + (riskless bill) portfolio, thereby generating an up-front cash flow.

$$S - \underbrace{(S - X)}_{\text{cost of call}} - \underbrace{\exp(-R \cdot T) \cdot X}_{\text{cost of bill}} = X \cdot [1 - \exp(-R \cdot T)] = \text{arbitrage profit}$$

At maturity you will buy back the stock you shorted. If the stock price turns out to be higher than the strike price, you will exercise the call and purchase the stock at a cost of X, using the cash flow from the riskless bill. If $S_T < X$, you will be able to buy the stock for less than X, thereby increasing your arbitrage profit.

Consider the case where the option is out-of-the-money. The intrinsic value will be zero, but the call will still command a positive premium (time-value) because there is a chance that it will expire in-the-money and produce a gain. The lower the stock price relative to the strike price, the lower the chance of ending in-the-money and the lower the option premium.

Exhibit 12-5 shows the premium and the intrinsic value for two calls. The lower curve is for a 3-month option while the higher curve is for 6 months. This shows that the time-value is a function of both the time to maturity (there is *time-value decay*) and of the ratio of the stock price to the strike price. Time-value decay is illustrated in Exhibit 12-6 for two levels of stock price {95, 105} relative to a strike price of 100 and for terms from 1 year to zero.

Exhibit 12-5 Call Premium and Intrinsic Value

Stock price	Call premuim 3M	Call premuim 6M
80	0.48	1.76
85	1.14	3.00
90	2.31	4.71
95	4.11	6.93
100	6.58	9.63
105	9.71	12.80
110	13.40	16.37
115	17.53	20.27
120	21.99	24.46
125	26.66	28.86
130	31.47	33.43

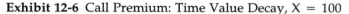

Exhibit 12-6 Call Premium: Time Value Decay, X = 100

T	S = 95	S = 105
1	11.27	14.23
0.917	10.62	13.54
0.833	9.94	12.83
0.75	9.24	12.09
0.667	8.51	11.32
0.583	7.74	10.50
0.5	6.93	9.63
0.417	6.06	8.71
0.333	5.13	7.70
0.25	4.11	6.58
0.17	2.94	5.29
0.08	1.55	3.66
0.0	0.00	0.00

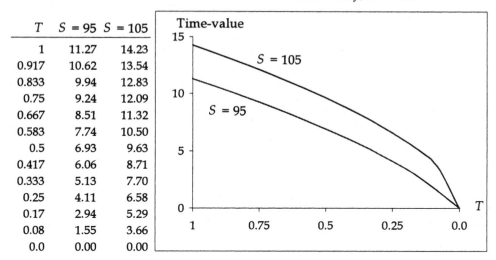

Puts on Non-Dividend-Paying Stock

Compare a put with shorting the underlying stock. The time-value of the put is exclusively attributable to the insurance element against an increase in the underlying stock price. The interest component plays a negative role on the premium; when you short the stock you earn interest on the proceeds of the short sale. This entails that the put can have a negative time-value when there is no chance that it will expire out-of-the-money. It can therefore be optimal to exercise the put before maturity. It follows that an American put should be worth more than its European counterpart. Exhibit 12-7 shows clearly that it is optimal to exercise a six-month put immediately if the stock price declines below $83.

Exhibit 12-7 European PUT Premium and Intrinsic Value, $X = 100$, $T = 0.5$

S	Put	Int Val
60	37.59	40
65	32.71	35
70	27.97	30
75	23.47	25
80	19.29	20
85	15.53	15
90	12.25	10
95	9.46	5
100	7.17	0
105	5.33	
110	3.90	

12-5 PAYOFF AT MATURITY OF OPTIONS STRATEGIES

An extremely relevant feature of options is their great versatility as building blocks for investment and hedging strategies. By combining puts and/or calls (with or without long or short positions in the underlying stock), it is possible to obtain a variety of payout profiles that would otherwise be difficult to attain; options contribute to the completeness of financial markets. We shall also see that quite often, the same payout profile can be engineered in more than one way, such as creating a *synthetic call* out of a long stock position plus a *protective put*. These equivalent strategies highlight a number of arbitrage-free upper and lower bounds to option prices.

In this section we shall examine a number of option strategies, mainly to gain familiarity with arbitrage-free pricing bounds. However, we shall not attempt to cover all the possible strategies used by market participants (some of which have been given colorful and somewhat improbable names such as *seagull, condor, alligator, mambo combo, strip, strap,* and *surf-and-turf*). More expanded coverage can be found in a number of recent manuals such as Chance (1998), Gastineau and Kritzman (1996), and Hull (1997).

Stock plus Options Strategies

Exhibit 12-8 shows the net payoff of holding the stock plus a put, referred to as a protective put because it insures the stock position against a decline in the stock price. In the example, you buy the stock at $100 and insure against a decline below the $95 strike price of the protective put. This is a *bull strategy* because you will make money if the stock price moves up. This strategy is also known as a synthetic call because its payoff is identical to that of a call; this equivalence is the basis of the *put-call parity* that we will examine more closely in the next section.

If you are a market maker in OTC options, it can very well happen that you come across arbitrage opportunities. Selling a call and fully hedging your position by manufacturing a synthetic call is known as a *conversion* (it converts a put into a call).

Exhibit 12-9 shows the net payoff of holding a short stock plus a long call (again, a protective option that insures you against an increase in the stock price). In the

Exhibit 12-8 Synthetic Call = Long Stock + Protective Put

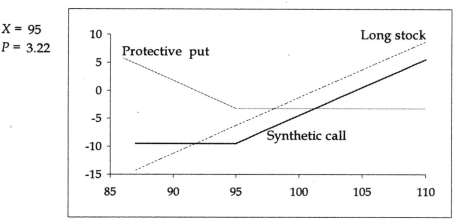

X = 95
P = 3.22

Exhibit 12-9 Synthetic Put = Short Stock + Protective Call

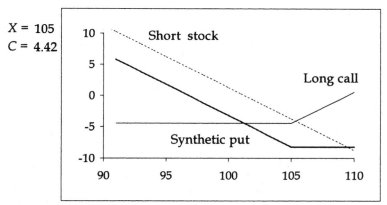

X = 105
C = 4.42

example, you sell short a stock at $100 and insure against a stock price rise by buying a call with an exercise price of $105. This is obviously a *bear strategy*, also called a *synthetic put* because its payoff is identical to that of a put. If there is an arbitrage opportunity in selling a put and fully hedging by manufacturing a synthetic put, this is known as a *reverse conversion* (it converts a put into a call).

Writing a covered call is a bull strategy because you will lose money if the stock price declines (see Exhibit 12-10). You will adopt this strategy if you hold the view that the stock should go up but does not have a great upside potential (you "sell" the possible increase above the exercise price for a fixed premium).

Option Spreads

A *spread* is a strategy in that you short one option and buy another within the same *class* (short + long, calls or puts). The terminology of spreads is easier to visualize with reference to the following matrix format for quotations (quotations of IBM stock

Exhibit 12-10 Writing a Covered Call

X = 110
C = 2.84

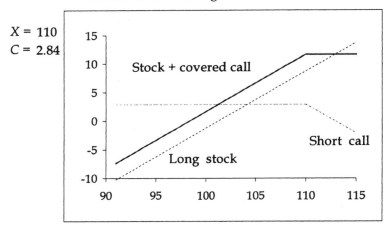

options, Thursday, 11 December 1997, reported in The *Wall Street Journal* [WSJ] of 12 December).

The WSJ quotations are useful approximations, but if you want to plug them into some option-pricing equation, you should remember that the quotations of the stock and of the different options series are not necessarily synchronized; in fact, they reflect the last transaction of the day. Also remember that options quotations are expressed in $/16 and stock quotations are in $/8 (see Exhibit 12-11).

- A *vertical spread* is one where the short-long position refers to the same expiration date, obviously with different strike prices. For example, buy the $100 December call at $4.75 and sell the $105 December call at $1.625, at a total cost of $3.125.
- A *horizontal spread* is characterized by the same strike price and by different maturities for the long and the short positions. For example, buy a $100 December call at $4.75 and sell a $100 January call, generating a net revenue of $2.25.
- A *diagonal spread* is one in which both the strike prices and the expiration dates are different.

Horizontal and diagonal spreads are widely used by market participants because they allow a range of investment strategies, especially in the stock and index options markets. However, we shall restrict our focus to vertical spreads because they are quite

Exhibit 12-11 Quotation Matrix

Stock Price	Strike	Calls Dec	Calls Jan	Strike	Puts Dec	Puts Jan
102.31	90	13.6250	14.7500	90	0.1875	0.9375
	95	9.0000	10.5000	95	0.4375	1.6250
	100	4.7500	7.0000	100	1.1250	2.9375
	105	1.6250	4.1250	105	3.0000	5.1250
	110	0.4375	2.1875	110	6.6250	8.2500
	115	0.1250	1.0000	115	11.3750	13.3750

sufficient for our purpose of exploring payouts at maturity and arbitrage-free relationships. There is additional terminology that relates to spreads.

- You *buy the spread* when the premium that you pay to purchase your long option position is higher than the premium you receive for writing the option that you short (e.g., you buy a call with $X = 100$ and sell a call with $X = 110$). A spread that implies an initial cost is also known as *debit spread,* with reference to the debit entry in your brokerage account. A debit spread with calls is a capped bullish strategy. A debit spread with puts is a capped bearish strategy.
- You *sell the spread* when you have a positive premium cash flow (e.g., you buy a put with $X = 90$ and sell a put with $X = 100$). A spread that provides you with an initial revenue is also known as *credit spread,* with reference to the credit entry in your brokerage account. A credit spread with calls is a capped bearish strategy. A credit spread with puts is a capped bullish strategy.

Compare two calls with different strike prices, for example, $X_W = 100 < X_H = 105$. The call with the lower strike price will generate a higher payoff when it expires in-the-money and should command a higher premium to avoid the obvious arbitrage of selling the X_H call and using the proceeds to buy the X_W call. The following condition must therefore be respected:

$$X_H > X_W \Rightarrow C_H < C_W$$

The difference in payoffs at maturity reaches a maximum of $X_H - X_W$ when both options expire in-the-money.

$$\max(0, S_T - X_W) - \max(0, S_T - X_H) = X_H - X_W \text{ for } S_T \geqslant X_H$$

The increase in premium must therefore be smaller than the difference between exercise prices because there is the possibility that both the calls will expire worthless; therefore the following inequality must hold:

$$C_W - C_H < (X_H - X_W) \cdot \exp(-R \cdot T): \text{ no arbitrage condition}$$

If the preceding condition does not hold, you could exploit an arbitrage opportunity by writing the W call and buying the H call. Assume that

$$C_W - C_H = (X_H - X_W) \cdot \exp(-R \cdot T): \text{ probabilistic arbitrage opportunity.}$$

If both calls end up in-the-money, you will come out even. In every other case you will register a net gain. The up-front net gain will have a maximum value of $C_W - C_H$ when both calls expire out-of-the-money.

A *bull spread* implemented with calls is a debit spread (see Exhibit 12-12). The payoff of a bull spread can be replicated with a *collar,* which consists of holding the underlying stock, buying a protective put, and writing an out-of-the-money call. This is a bull strategy, but it implies that you do not believe that your stock has a great upside potential. In fact, you sell the upside over and above the exercise price of the call. The collar depicted in Exhibit 12-13 has a near-zero cost.

Exhibit 12-12 Bull Spreads with Calls and with Puts

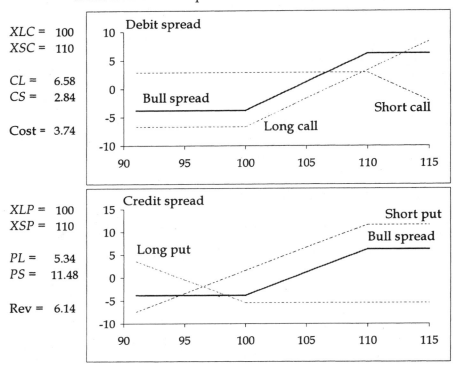

$XLC = 100$
$XSC = 110$

$CL = 6.58$
$CS = 2.84$

$Cost = 3.74$

$XLP = 100$
$XSP = 110$

$PL = 5.34$
$PS = 11.48$

$Rev = 6.14$

Exhibit 12-13 Collar = Long Stock + Long Put + Short Call

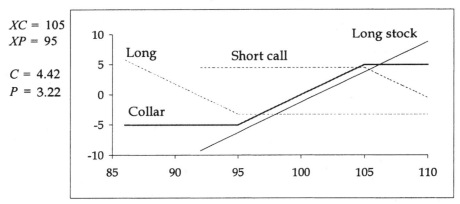

$XC = 105$
$XP = 95$

$C = 4.42$
$P = 3.22$

You can also engineer a bull spread using puts. To do this you must sell the spread by writing a put with a higher strike price and premium than the put you buy to protect your position against a sizable fall in the underlying stock price. If your bullish forecast comes true, both options will expire out-of-the-money and you will keep the upfront cash flow $P_H - P_W > 0$. A *bear spread* (see Exhibit 12-14) can be engineered both with puts (buying the spread) and with calls (selling the spread).

Exhibit 12-14 Bear Spread = Long Put + Short Put (buy the Spread)

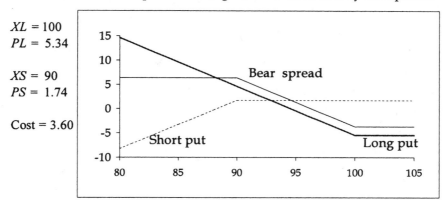

XL = 100
PL = 5.34

XS = 90
PS = 1.74

Cost = 3.60

Combinations

A combination is an option strategy that includes both puts and calls. A collar is a combination plus a position in the underlying stock. As you can imagine, a large number of combinations are possible. We shall examine only two, however, which are sufficient for our purposes.

A *straddle* is set up by buying a put and a call with the same expiration date and the same strike price (see Exhibit 12-15). If you are buying a straddle, you are clearly betting on market volatility, but you do not make a *market-directional* bet. If the stock price does not change (moves sideways, in Wall Street parlance), you lose an amount equal to the two premiums you paid up-front.

If the stock price declines, your gain reaches a maximum if the stock price plummets to zero. If the stock price increases, it is impossible to quantify the maximum gain, which depends on how much the stock rallies. The net outcome at maturity is given by the following equation:

$$\max[\max(0, S_T - X), \max(0, -S_T + X)] - (C + P) \cdot \exp(R \cdot T)$$

Exhibit 12-15 Long Straddle

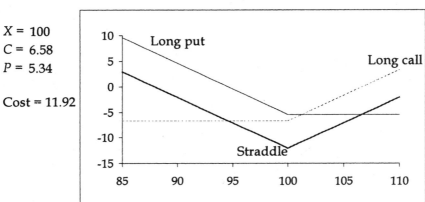

X = 100
C = 6.58
P = 5.34

Cost = 11.92

Exhibit 12-16 Long Strangle (aka Spraddle)

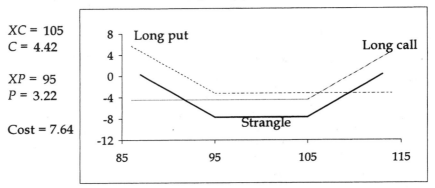

$XC = 105$
$C = 4.42$

$XP = 95$
$P = 3.22$

Cost = 7.64

When the stock price moves away from the strike price, the writer of the straddle is exposed to the same kind of loss as a writer of a naked put or call. A *strangle* (also called a *spraddle*) is a straddle where the call's exercise price is higher than that of the put (see Exhibit 12-16). The strangle is therefore somewhat cheaper to buy but has a lower probability of expiring in-the-money (you lose all the purchase price when $X_P < S_T < X_C$).

Straddles and strangles can be made somewhat market directional by buying more calls that puts (bullish) or more puts than calls (bearish). There is no need, however, to dwell on these strategies. For example, if you buy a *strap*, that is, a straddle with one put and two calls, your payoff is simply that of buying a regular straddle and a plain-vanilla call.

Complex Strategies

Vertical spreads can be a lot more complex than those that we have already examined. A first level of complexity can be attained using *ratio spreads*, in which the number of contracts purchased is different from the number of contracts sold. Complex payoffs can also be engineered by buying and writing puts and calls at more than two strike-price levels; a well-known example of this is the *butterfly spread*, (see Exhibit 12-17), which consists of:

Exhibit 12-17 Butterfly Spread Implemented with Calls

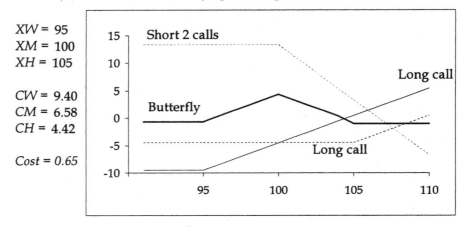

$XW = 95$
$XM = 100$
$XH = 105$

$CW = 9.40$
$CM = 6.58$
$CH = 4.42$

Cost = 0.65

Exhibit 12-18 Convexity of Call Price as a Function of S/X

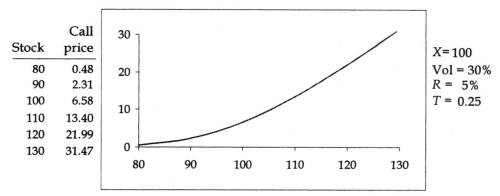

Stock	Call price
80	0.48
90	2.31
100	6.58
110	13.40
120	21.99
130	31.47

$X = 100$
Vol $= 30\%$
$R = 5\%$
$T = 0.25$

Exhibit 12-19 Synthetic Loan "Manufactured" with Options

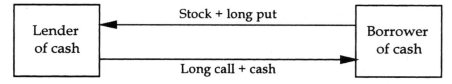

- One long low-strike-price call
- One long high-strike-price call
- Two short calls at a strike the is in between the strike prices of the long calls

If you *buy the butterfly*, you are betting that the stock price will move sideways (like the writer of a straddle), but you are also covering your downside in case the stock rallies or plunges. This is a low-cost, low-risk, low-reward strategy. There is an interesting arbitrage-free condition that we can derive from the butterfly. If the two calls we sell covered the cost of the two calls we buy, we would get a free option; therefore the butterfly must have a cost:

$$C_W + C_H > 2 \cdot C_M$$

where W = low strike, H = high strike, and M = intermediate strike

In turn, this entails that the call price as a function of the strike price must be a convex function. If we examine the European call prices used to calculate Exhibits 12-17 and 12-18 we see that the call price as a function of the strike price is indeed a convex function.

12-6 PUT-CALL PARITY AND THE BOX

The values of European puts and calls on the same stock are linked by a well-known arbitrage-free relationship known as *put-call parity*, provided that they have the same strike price and same maturity date. We shall now examine in some detail the put-call parity, not only because of its widespread application in option pricing but also

Exhibit 12-20 Short Synthetic Put

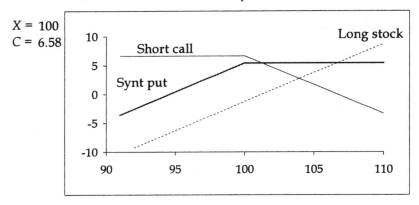

$X = 100$
$C = 6.58$

because it allows us to introduce in a straightforward way the construction of port-folios, comprising both options and T-bills, that replicate the behavior of stocks. A simple way of visualizing the parity is to assume:

- That you purchase the underlying stock
- That you buy a protective put, strike price X
- That you write a covered call, at the same strike price X of the protective put

Irrespective of the price dynamics of the stock, you will get X at the expiration date. Therefore, arbitrage-free pricing implies that, at any moment before expiration:

$$S + P - C = X \cdot \exp(-R \cdot T) = PV(X)$$

$$P = C + PV(X) - S.$$

When the put-call parity is respected, a mispricing of the call entails an identical mispricing of the put. The put-call parity implies that the power of the put and of the call must be equal when the excercise price equals the forward value of the stock.

$$X = S \cdot \exp(R \cdot T) \Rightarrow P = C$$

Arbitrage-Free Pricing

We have already seen, in Section 1-4, that arbitrage-free pricing holds only when there is an available market mechanism that allows you to lock in a riskless profit when a mispricing occurs. We have two possible cases:

First, $S + P - C < PV(X)$. You can set up the arbitrage by borrowing $PV(X)$, that you will repay at maturity when the portfolio will generate a payoff X irrespective of the stock's performance. This entails that you must be able to borrow at the riskless rate R.

$$PV(X) - [S + P - C] = \text{up-front arbitrage profit.}$$

Second, $S + P - C > PV(X)$. You can set up the arbitrage by selling the stock + put-call portfolio (we have seen that in a frictionless economy short selling the stock will give you the full availability of its market price). With the revenue of the portfolio sale, you buy a T-bill with which you will satisfy your future commitment to pay X.

$$(S + P - C) - PV(X) = \text{up-front arbitrage profit}$$

The Brunswick Corporation Case

In real life we come across cases where the second arbitrage is not feasible due to the practical impossibility of selling short the stock, and the put-call parity may be violated. The following case is described by Haugen (1993). In March 1981 a takeover bid was directed at Brunswick Corporation. This resulted in a huge violation of the put-call parity. It was in fact impossible to borrow shares in order to sell them short, because the owners needed to have them available to tender them at $30 to the bidder.

Synthetic Stock, Synthetic Loan (Synthetic Repo)

Another interesting way to look at the put-call parity is to engineer a synthetic stock by:

- Buying a call
- Selling a put with the same exercise price and expiration date of the call
- Investing $PV(X)$ in T-bills with the same term of the put and the call

At maturity this portfolio will make you the owner of one share of stock, without any further cash outlay. Because of the law of one price,

$$S = C - P + PV(X).$$

The put-call arbitrage can therefore be interpreted as

- Buying the synthetic stock and selling the stock when the stock is expensive (this requires being able to borrow the stock to sell it short)
- Selling the synthetic stock and buying the stock when the stock is cheap

This synthetic stock construction can be adapted to create a synthetic loan. If the put-call parity holds, you can sell the synthetic stock and use $PV(X)$ to fund your own operations instead of buying T-bills, thereby borrowing money at the favorable T-bill rate when this is allowed by the regulatory framework. You can also use a put-call combination to replicate a repo and lend or borrow money at any contractually determined rate. (This is exactly what Russel Sage used to do; see the introduction to this chapter).

Put-Call Parity on Dividend-Paying Stock

Exchange-traded options are not *dividend-protected*. The put-call parity must therefore be adjusted to take into account the resulting asymmetry between stock and synthetic

Exhibit 12-21 The Box Spread

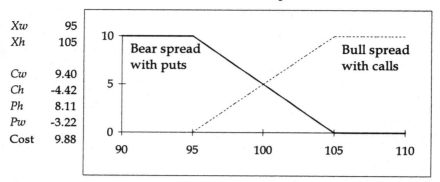

Xw	95
Xh	105
Cw	9.40
Ch	-4.42
Ph	8.11
Pw	-3.22
Cost	9.88

stock whenever a dividend is expected to be paid before the maturity of the put and call options. It is intuitively clear that the present value of the expected dividend must be subtracted from the value of a call and added to the value of a put. We can therefore use the following equations, where D is the dividend expected by the market:

$$P = C + PV(X) + PV(D) - S$$

$$C = P - PV(X) - PV(D) + S$$

If you take the view that the market over- or underestimates the value of a forthcoming dividend, you can bet on your forecast. Indicate with $D^* \neq D$ your estimate of the future dividend.

- $D^* > D$ entails that in your view, the put is underpriced and the call is overpriced. You can therefore buy a put and sell a synthetic put, or else sell a call and buy a synthetic call.
- When $D^* < D$ you can sell a put and hedge with a synthetic put, or else buy a call and write a synthetic call.

The Box Spread

When there are available puts and calls for two strike prices ($X_W < X_H$) and the same expiration date you can *buy the box*, which is the term for buying a *bull spread with calls* and a *bear spread with puts*. It is easy to verify that the payoff at expiration box will always equal the difference between the two strike prices.

$$BOX = X_H - X_W$$

Arbitrage-free pricing requires

$$PV(X_H - X_W) = \underbrace{(C_W - C_H) + (P_H - P_W)}_{\text{Cost of Box}}.$$

If the preceding condition is not satisfied, you can lock in a riskless gain (buying the box when the cost is lower than the fair price or *selling the box* when the cost is higher than the arbitrage-free price) (see Exhibit 12-21). When the put-call parity holds for both strike prices, the arbitrage-free box price must also hold.

$$PV(X_H) - PV(X_W) = (S + P_H - C_H) - (S + P_W - C_W)$$

$$= (C_W - C_H) + (P_H - P_W).$$

Under certain conditions, the box can be used to arbitrage a put-call mispricing that could not be otherwise exploited because of the difficulty of shorting the underlying stock. To see how this works, consider first the case where the put-call parity holds only for X_H and is violated for X_W.

$$S + P_W - C_W - \lambda_W = PV(X_W), \text{ where } [\lambda_W > 0]$$

$$\lambda_W = \text{put-call parity discrepancy for } X_W$$

To arbitrage the preceding put-call violation and lock in a profit of λ_W, you must be able to borrow the stock to short it. An alternative route is provided by the fact that the parity violation produces an underpriced box.

$$PV(X_H) = S + P_H - C_H$$

$$PV(X_W) = S + P_W - C_W - \lambda_W$$

$$PV(X_H - X_W) = \underbrace{[P_H - P_W] + [C_W - C_H]}_{\text{Cost of Box}} + \lambda_W$$

You can therefore lock in an up-front arbitrage profit buying the box. Let us now examine the case when you have a put-call parity violation for both strike prices.

$$PV(X_H) = S + P_H - C_H - \lambda_H$$

$$PV(X_W) = S + P_W - C_W - \lambda_W$$

$$PV(X_H - X_W) = \underbrace{[P_H - P_W] + [C_W - C_H]}_{\text{Cost of Box}} + \lambda_W - \lambda_H$$

You have three possible cases:

$$\lambda_W - \lambda_H = 0: \text{ the put-call mispricing cannot be arbitraged}$$

$$\lambda_W - \lambda_H > 0: \text{ buy the box}$$

$$\lambda_W - \lambda_H > 0: \text{ sell the box}$$

The RJR Nabisco case

Another well known case of put-call parity violation occurred at the beginning of 1989 on the occasion of the famous takeover of RJR Nabisco by the leveraged-buyout firm of Kohlberg, Kravis and Roberts (KKR). RJR Nabisco, a huge, publicly quoted tobacco and food corporation, had been put in play by its chairman, Ross Jonson, who hoped to carry out, to his advantage, a *leveraged-management buyout* (LMBO). This hope soon

Exhibit 12-22 The RJR Nabisco Case

X	C	P	S	S + P- C	PV(X)	Parity violation
80	16.500	4.000	94.875	82.375	79.25	3.12
85	11.875	6.625	94.875	89.625	84.21	5.42
90	7.250	10.250	94.875	97.875	89.16	8.71
95	3.000	13.750	94.875	105.625	94.11	11.51
100	0.625	18.125	94.875	112.375	99.07	13.31

The above data are only a first approximation because they do not take int account the expected dividend of $0.50 a share.

vanished as other players with larger war chests entered the field. In the end, KKR prevailed with an offer claimed to be worth $24 billion. The RJR Nabisco case has been described in a number of articles and books, the best known of which is *Barbarians at the Gate: The Fall of RJR Nabisco* by Burrough and Helyar (1990). The leveraged takeover also required the issuance of several billion dollars' worth of junk bonds by the investment bank Drexel, Burnham, Lambert (which soon afterward collapsed, due also to criminal indictments against the bank and its famous junk-bond supremo, Mike Milken).

The takeover bid produced huge violations of the put-call parity, shown in the Exhibit 12-22. Notice that the range of strike prices would have allowed to lock in an arbitrage profit by selling the box. For example:

$$X_H = \$100; \ X_W = \$80; \ PV(X_H - X_W) = \$19.8135$$

$$[P_H - P_W] + [C_W - C_H] = \$30.00$$

$$[P_H - P_W] + [C_W - C_H] - PV(X_H - X_W) = \$10.187 = |\lambda_H - \lambda_W|$$

12-7   BUTTERFLY SPREAD AND ARROW-DEBREU SECURITIES

Nuclear physics studies the smallest particles of which matter is composed. A particle approach is also used in financial economics and was pioneered by Kenneth Arrow and Gerard Debreu, both Nobel laureates in economics. Their approach (commonly known as the Arrow-Debreu paradigm or *time-state-paradigm*) is based on an abstract security, the *Arrow-Debreu security* (see Exhibit 12-23).

An Arrow-Debreu security is a time-state contingent claim, that is, a security that would have a unit payoff at a well-defined future time and for one specified *state of the world* (see Chapter 14). An Arrow-Debreu security will have zero payoff at all other times and states of the world.

The use of Arrow-Debreu securities to explore the foundations of finance is beyond the scope of this book, but it is interesting to note that this purely theoretical construction can be approximated with a butterfly spread (and also with other option strategies, such as a combination of digital options).

If you set the values of the three strike prices close enough to each other, you obtain a portfolio that will yield a payoff only in a very narrow state of the world, and will have a zero payoff in all other states of the world, thereby approximating an Arrow-Debreu security.

Exhibit 12-23 Butterfly Spread and Arrow-Debreu Securities

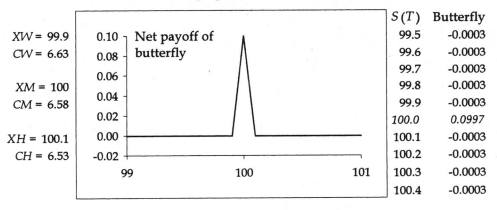

$S(T)$	Butterfly
99.5	-0.0003
99.6	-0.0003
99.7	-0.0003
99.8	-0.0003
99.9	-0.0003
100.0	*0.0997*
100.1	-0.0003
100.2	-0.0003
100.3	-0.0003
100.4	-0.0003

XW = 99.9
CW = 6.63

XM = 100
CM = 6.58

XH = 100.1
CH = 6.53

Chapter **13**

Fixed-Income Options: Bonds with Optionlike Features

13-1 Exchange-Traded Options and Futures Options
13-2 Caps, Floors, Collars, and Swaptions
13-3 Mortgage-Backed Securities and Collateralized Mortgage Obligations

Options on stocks and stock indexes, such as the S&P 500, are widely traded and used to set up complex investing and hedging strategies. The vast majority of stock options are exchange-traded and have relatively short maturities.

In the fixed-income sector, we have a number of traded options (mainly on currencies and interest-rate futures). Most options, however, are issued and traded over the counter moreover, they are often embedded in bonds and other securities and may have expiration dates that extend many years into the future, making them very difficult to price. For example, 30yr U.S. T-bonds were once callable on every coupon date in the last 5 years of their life—that is, they embedded a call option that could be exercised over a 5yr time horizon, 25 years after the issuing date.

In this chapter we shall give a brief overview of the most common fixed-income options you are likely to come across. As usual we will not go into detail and will restrict ourselves to outlining the features that are necessary to gain a clear understanding of the basic concepts.

13-1 EXCHANGE-TRADED OPTIONS AND FUTURES OPTIONS

Exchange-traded options in the fixed-income sector are usually options on some traded future (also known as futures options). The reason underlying this market practice is that traded futures represent a liquid market, with official and transparent prices (settlement prices), where the issues related to delivery and settlement have found a functional solution.

Instead of reinventing the delivery rule book for options on, say, U.S. T-bonds or German *bunds*, it is a lot more efficient to write the options on the *bund* or T-bond futures. Moreover, using the future as the underlying asset for the option makes trading and hedging a lot easier to implement. Hedging an option with futures is clearly easier when the option is written on the future itself. Options on futures also exist for a number of commodities (corn, soybeans, cotton, live cattle, copper, silver, crude oil, gasoline, etc.).

FX Options and Options on Currency Futures

One noticeable exception to the futures options market practice is represented by options on foreign currency which were first introduced by the Philadelphia Stock Exchange in 1982. Not using the future as the underlying asset is justified, however, by the fact that straightforward spot foreign exchange (FX) transactions are very simple to settle and that the market is extremely liquid. You will recall that due to this inherent standardization, the market for FX forwards dwarfs that for FX futures. It is also fair to say that there is a huge over-the-counter (OTC) market in customized FX options, with FX dealers quoting two-way prices for spot, forwards, and options.

The Philadelphia options cover a number of currencies (DEM, GBP, JPY, etc.). Most are American-style but some are European options. The most heavily traded options are against the $ but some are on cross rates, such as the GBP against the DEM. Cross-rate options are quite useful due to the nonlinearity of options payoffs. A call on the GBP priced in DEM is a quite different thing from a call on the DEM and on the GBP, both expressed in $.

FX options are not limited to the direct options traded on the Philadelphia Stock Exchange. Exchanges such as the Chicago Mercantile Exchange (CME), which trade FX futures, also offer options on their futures contracts. Direct options and futures-style options differ somewhat because of the daily mark to market and settlement of the futures contract (daily realization of gains and losses).

Options on Futures (Futures Options)

You will remember that a futures contract value is reset to zero at each daily mark to market and settlement. This entails that the strike price cannot represent the price at which you buy the future. The exercise price mechanism has therefore been adjusted to take into account the mechanics of futures trading. Let us see how this works. Say you bought a call of the U.S. T-bond future at 120, and market yields have declined so that the future is now priced 122. At the moment of exercise you are delivered a future (which in itself is worthless because of daily gain or loss settlement) plus a payment equal to the difference between the strike price and the current futures price.

$$\max(0, F_T - X) = \text{payoff at exercise of a call on futures}$$

This replicates the position you would be in if you had bought the future at a price equal to the call's exercise price (you would have received $F_T - X$ in variation settlements). Having bought a call, however, protected you against an increase in market yields, that would have resulted in a loss had you bought the future. A good way to visualize a call on futures is to consider it like a regular stock option that is settled in cash and not with the delivery, at the exercise price of the underlying asset. Therefore, if the option is exercised in-the-money, you get a cash payment equal to its value, which as we saw in Chapter 12, equals $\max(0, S_T - X)$. A put on futures settles in the same way as a call, and therefore its payoff will be

$$\max(0, -F_T + X) = \text{payoff at exercise of a put on futures.}$$

The settlement mechanism of options on futures also requires an adjustment of the put-call parity equation, which we shall examine in Chapter 17.

13-2   Caps, Floors, Collars, and Swaptions

When we move from exchange-traded options to OTC products, we find a number of regularly traded pure interest-rate options, that is, options not embedded in some security. Most of the following options exist also in an embedded version. A collar is a pure put-call combination, but we also have collared floating-rate notes (FRNs). As we saw in Chapter 9, an inverse floater includes a floor, and the companion FRN embeds a cap.

Caplets and Caps

A logical way to visualize a caplet is to think of it as the option equivalent of a forward rate agreement (FRA). With an FRA you lock in a future rate; with a caplet you lock in a defined maximum level of future rate. The payoff of a caplet is as follows (see also Exhibit 13-1):

$\max[0, NP \cdot (CDY_T - X_C) \cdot H]$ = payoff of a caplet;
NP = notional principal of the caplet, say \$10 million;
CDY_T = money market yield at the option's expiry date;
X_C = cap rate (strike rate);
H = time horizon covered by the option.

Note that when we deal with caplets, terms such as at-the-money, in-the-money, and out-of-the-money should refer to a comparison between the strike rate and the current forward rate. The caplet, like a forward rate agreement (FRA), is seen from the point of view of a borrower. If you buy a caplet and market yield rises, the caplet expires in-the-money. Options on interest-rate futures are seen from the standpoint of an investor; if market yield declines the future expires in-the-money.

A *cap* is a series (strip) of caplets, covering a series of back-to-back forward periods, with which you can hedge a medium- to long term floating rate liability (FRN or floating-rate loan). Say you have issued an FRN, paying interest semiannually at 6M LIBOR + 0.30%, with a residual term to maturity of 5 years and 3 months. You can effectively lock in the maximum level of your future borrowing rate by buying a cap that consists of 10 half-year caplets, starting in 3 months' time (the level of LIBOR for

Exhibit 13-1 Payoff at Maturity of a Caplet

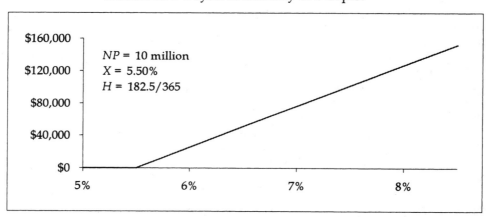

the next 3 months has already been fixed when the coupon was repriced at the beginning of the current semiannual interest period).

Note that a cap is usually expressed as one single rate for all the forward periods you are hedging, irrespective of the fact that the forward yields relative to these periods are not equal to each other, unless the spot yield curve is perfectly flat. A cap is therefore the option equivalent of a swap; instead of locking in a series of future interest costs, you lock in a series of maximum interest costs.

You can also use a cap to hedge your future borrowing costs when you do not have an outstanding FRN or floating-rate loan. For example, you know that on average, you will have outstanding liabilities of $15 million, funded on a revolving basis. A cap will provide an effective hedge against an increase in market yields. Clearly, if you borrow short-term on a revolving basis, the cap will not protect you against an increase of your borrowing costs due to a deterioration of your credit standing, which can result in an increase of the spread over LIBOR you will have to pay to fund your company.

If you buy a stand-alone cap, each maturity will be settled in cash, like a series of caplets. When a cap is embedded in a security (such as a capped FRN or loan), the wording of the FRN prospectus or loan contract will usually state that the rate cannot be higher than the cap strike. In this case there is no separate settlement of the cap.

Floorlets, Floors, and Collars

A floorlet is the opposite of a caplet and therefore can be used by a floating-rate investor to set a minimum level, or *floor*, to her revenue. Buying a floorlet is like buying a put on a pure discount security yielding the strike rate.

$$\max[0, NP \cdot (X_F - CDY_T) \cdot H] = \text{payoff of a floorlet}$$
$$X_F = \text{floor rate (strike rate)}$$

A floor consists of a series of florlets, covering a series of back-to-back forward periods, usually at one single rate. Floors and caps are often combined to produce a collar, which will constrain the future interest cost of floating-rate borrowing between a minimum represented by the floor and a maximum given by the cap. Clearly the cap represents a cost for the borrower while the floor represents a revenue paid by the investor for the downside protection. It is therefore possible to tailor a collar determining the net option cost for the issuer (e.g., of a collared FRN). If the cap and the floor have the same strike rate, the collar will become a synthetic swap (this provides a different version of the put-call parity). If the cap equals the swap rate, the revenue from the floor should equal the cost of the cap.

$$X_F = X_C = \text{swap rate}$$

Swaptions

One last important OTC product is a swaption, which gives the right to buy or sell a swap at a predetermined swap rate, usually set at-the-money, that is to coincide with the swap rate of a forward swap. On the basis of what we have seen in Chapter 10, a call option on a swap is analogous to a put option on a coupon bond with a strike at par (when you exercise a swaption, your fixed-income payments are priced at par exactly as the floating leg rate of the swap).

13-3 MORTGAGE-BACKED SECURITIES AND COLLATERALIZED MORTGAGE OBLIGATIONS

The U.S. mortgage sector is quite complex, with a variety of players and instruments. For an extensive introduction, see the recent books by Fabozzi (1996) and Sundaresan (1997). The mortgage sector is also a rich source of embedded interest-rate options, which is the subject on which we shall concentrate our attention. Mortgage-related securities are extremely important in the U.S. market, where they total well over $3 trillion. This huge size is due to the following factors:

• The generous level of tax deductibility of interest payments on home mortgages (you can deduct from your taxable income mortgage-interest payments on a principal that is capped at more than $1 million)
• The fact that the U.S. banking sector has been quite efficient in seizing the opportunity to sell bonds collateralized by pools of mortgages, thereby avoiding holding mortgage loans on their books.

In the United States, most housing mortgages are fixed rate, with maturities ranging between 15 and 30 years. Repayment is usually through *level monthly payments*, that is, equal monthly installments that include both interest payment and principal repayment, according to a well-defined amortization plan (see Exhibit 13-2).

An important characteristic of mortgage loans in the United States is that the borrower has the right to prepay the loan (the mortgage is characterized by an embedded put option). Prepayment is often due to homeowners selling their property; some mortgages, however, are *assumable* by the buyer of the property and do not necessarily require repayment. Prepayment is also a put option for the mortgage borrower that can be exercised when market yields decline and the borrower seizes an opportunity to refinance at a lower cost. The prepayment option must of course translate into a call option on the pass-through bonds.

The aforementioned call is not the only option associated with pass-through certificates. A lot of trading on these instruments takes place on not fully identified pools of mortgages. These trades, known as *TBAs* (*to be announced*), are somewhat similar to when-issued (wi) trades on Treasuries.

Exhibit 13-2 Amortization Plan for a 30yr, $100,000 Home Mortgage

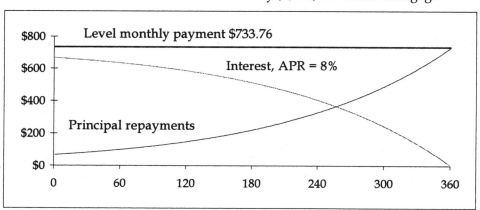

The industry's self-regulatory organization, the Public Securities Association (PSA), has established rules that define what are acceptable pools to deliver (there is some analogy to the concept of deliverable grades in futures contracts). To be applicable in practice, these PSA rules must allow some element of flexibility, which in turn represents a delivery option. Furthermore, PSA rules allow a ±2.5% margin of over- or underallocation (against a $10 million commitment you must deliver an amount between $9,750,000 and $10,250,000). This again represents an option on interest rates because the pool originator will have an incentive to overallocate when market yields have increased and to underallocate when they have decreased.

Let us return briefly to the issue of prepayment. As you can well imagine, investment banks have developed sophisticated econometric models to help them in forecasting the likely early repayment rate as a function of the characteristics of the underlying mortgage pool, including its weighted average maturity (WAM) and its weighted average coupon (WAC), of alternative interest rate scenarios, and the like. Refinancing a mortgage means incurring relatively high transaction costs, and it is certainly not optimal for borrowers to do so as soon as the current market rates drop marginally below the rate of their mortgages.

The PSA has identified a pool-amortization profile that is often used in the mortgage industry in spite of its not being very realistic. The PSA profile in fact used as a synthetic indication of payment speed.

Collateralized Mortgage Obligations (CMOs)

The put option embedded in the mortgage loans created the opportunity to decompose the cash flow deriving from a pool of mortgages into more than one tranche of bonds, each with different repayment characteristics. This fission in several bonds with different options content allows them to better fit the needs of different classes of investors (this breaking up into different tranches to avoid the one-size-fits-all problem is somewhat similar to the stripping of Treasury bonds and notes that we examined in Chapter 6).

The first mortgage-backed obligations (MBOs) were issued in 1983 and consisted of splitting the cash flow from a pool of mortgages in, say, three bond tranches or classes (A, B, and C). These tranches would be repaid sequentially (*sequential-pay tranches*). Class A would get all the principal repayments, both contractual and prepayments, before any repayments to Class B could start. Class A would therefore consist of a shorter-maturity bond with a good level of protection against extension risk and would therefore appeal to investors seeking a relatively low duration.

Class B would have a much longer duration than class A but would get a level of protection against both contraction risk (provided by class A) and extension risk (provided by class C). Finally, class C would have a very good level of protection against contraction and would appeal to investors seeking long duration. Clearly, the coupon rates of the different tranches would be different and based on the underlying spot yield curve, although with a stochastic maturity.

An illustration is provided by Exhibits 13-3 and 13-4, which show the outstanding principal amounts as a function of number of months elapsed for three CMO tranches, with a total principal of $120 million. To simplify calculations, we have assumed all tranches have the same APR (= 8%) and that the underlying mortgage pool is repaid according to a level-payment amortization plan (and not according to the PSA profile). Both assumptions are highly unrealistic, but they are functional for the purpose of showing how the sequential-pay mechanism works in practice. In Exhibit 13-3 we

Exhibit 13-3 CMOs, Outstanding Principals, 3 Sequential-Pay Tranches

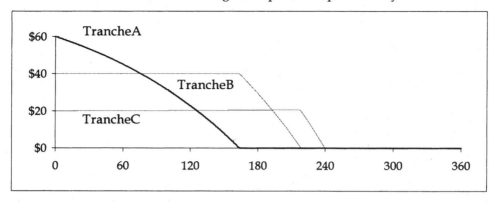

Exhibit 13-4 CMOs, Outstanding Principals, 3 Sequential-Pay Tranches

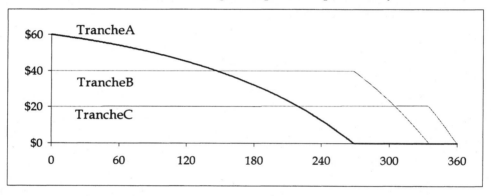

assume that the pool is repaid in 20 years, whereas Exhibit 13-4 illustrates repayment in 30 years. We do not need to compute average maturity values to see that an acceleration of the principal repayment schedule changes in different measure the average maturity of the different classes. With the sequential-pay structure, tranche A does get a fair level of protection against extension and contraction; its cash flow, however, is far from being stable like that of a plain bond. A solution to the problem of improving the stability of the cash flow was implemented with a structure called *planned amortization class* (PAC). Take a simple two-tranche construction where the PAC has a level-payment target-amortization schedule, defined in such a way as to be compatible with a wide range of prepayment scenarios. Tranche B, also called *support bond* or *companion bond*, gets that share of principal payments that is in excess of what is needed to realize the target amortization of the PAC. If prepayments are accelerated, the support bond will be reimbursed quickly and could well end up with an average maturity that is shorter than that of the PAC. On the other hand, with a slow prepayment, the support bond could end up with an amortization schedule similar to that of tranche B in a sequential-pay structure, that is, it begins to be repaid only after the PAC has been fully amortized.

Exhibit 13-5 PAC and Support Bond Outstanding Principals

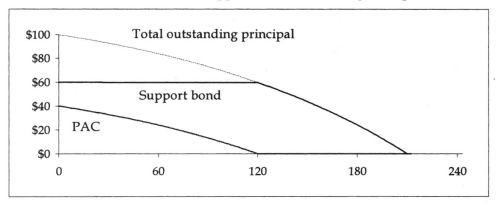

The PAC does not get a fully defined amortization schedule; it gets only a highly probable one. The prepayment of the mortgage pool could turn out to be faster (slower) than the shortest (longest) prepayment scenario on which the PAC was based. Exhibit 13-5 shows the case of a 10yr PAC representing 40% of the face value of the mortgage pool. The target maturity of the PAC can be fully respected with a pool prepayment ranging between 10 years and 210 months. The exhibit is highly unrealistic and is only meant to show how a PAC can function under different scenarios (in real life, we do not have level payments, and the APR on the PAC is clearly lower than that on the support bond). The imagination of investment bankers did not stop here. A number of other CMO structures followed, some characterized by a very high level of duration (one of these CMO is the inverse floater, which we examined in Chapter 9). Due to the fact that these tranches are fission products of the original mortgage pool, they were quickly dubbed nuclear waste when some dealers and investors experienced heavy losses, often due to an inadequate understanding of some of these CMO products. Let us conclude this section by mentioning two more CMOs that can display extreme duration.

The *accrual tranche,* or *Z tranche* (Z stands for zero, because of some similarity with zero coupon bonds). Interest on the Z-tranche is not paid but only accrued until all the other tranches have been fully amortized. Adding a Z tranche to a number of sequential-pay tranches has the effect of speeding up their reimbursement, thereby decreasing their stochastic duration.

The interest-only/principal-only strip consists of paying all the principal of a mortgage pool to the *principal only* (PO) tranche and all the interest to the *interest only* (IO) tranche. At first sight, this could appear like an ordinary coupon stripping, similar to that routinely done on Treasuries. There is a very important difference, however, that translates in an unexpected level of duration for the IO. Let us see why. The PO tranche is clearly issued at a discount to its face value, and the realized return will be a function of how quickly the mortgage pool is amortized (given the price and the redemption value, a zero will yield more if it is repaid quickly). Given that mortgages tend to be reimbursed when interest-rates decline, the PO tranche will reap the double benefit of higher yield when market yields are low. The PO tranche can therefore be interpreted as a basket of zeros with defined face values and stochastic maturities.

At first sight, the IO tranche could appear similar to the POs, that is, a basket of zeros with stochastic maturities. There is a very important difference, however. If a mortgage is repaid, it stops paying interest, which entails that the principal of the IOs will change; not only is their maturity stochastic, but their face value is also.

Chapter **14**

Basic Statistical Tools

This chapter can be skipped without any loss of continuity by readers who have a firm grounding in elementary statistics and probability theory. The purpose of the following sections is to give an intuitive summary, based on several numerical examples and charts, of the basic statistical concepts underlying option pricing. The focus is clearly on how to handle frequently used elementary probability tools.

An easy-to-understand coverage of the same concepts and tools can, of course, be found in a number of modern statistics textbooks. The motivation for including this chapter here is that in most textbooks, these concepts and tools are unlikely to be regrouped with an eye to options pricing and with examples designed to fit financial applications. Moreover, a number of the available texts have steeper mathematical prerequisites than does this book.

Many professionals find it confusing to read sections that shift between elements of statistics and concepts of finance. Condensing the statistical tools into two dedicated chapters allows a more fluid analysis of both the tools themselves and of the financial issues related to options pricing.

Some familiarity with statistics is assumed. Rigor and terse analysis have been willingly sacrificed to gain conciseness and intuitive ease of understanding. To further streamline the analysis, some elementary proofs have been placed in Section 14-7, the Mathematical Appendix.

If you want to get a really good grasp of the material covered in this chapter, you are well advised to keep a personal computer at hand. A large number of elementary statistical functions (arithmetic mean, variance, standard deviation, permutations, combinations, probability distributions, etc.) are readily available in spreadsheet format. Experimenting with them will give you a good feel for the subject.

14-1 VARIANCE, STANDARD DEVIATION, AND EXPECTED VALUE

Before we move on to random variables, it is useful to review some basic concepts in a nonstochastic setting. Let us consider the ex-post returns on a simple portfolio composed of five securities (see Exhibit 14-1). We use two kinds of arithmetic average, or *mean*, usually indicated with the letter μ:

• For *PV* and *FV* we use the simple mean to obtain the average amount invested in each of the 5 securities and the corresponding average FV. A simple average can be considered as a weighted average with weights = 1 for all the elements.

• For returns, we must use weighted average to get a meaningful result (using the invested amounts as weights). In the following equations we measure returns with simple yield y:

$$\mu(FV) = \frac{FV_1 + FV_2 + \ldots + FV_N}{N} = \frac{1}{N} \sum_{J=1}^{N} FV_J = \text{simple mean}$$

$$\mu(y) = \sum_{J=1}^{N} W_J \cdot y_J$$

$$W_J = \frac{PV_J}{PV_1 + \ldots + PV_N} = \text{weight} - J$$

The weighted return equals the return on the total investment. The weighted return column can be immediately interpreted as the contribution of each security to the total return.

$$y = \$33,000 \times (1 + 7.88\%) = \$35,600$$

One of the useful properties of the arithmetic mean is that its value is expressed in the same units of measure as the values from which it is calculated ($ or rates, in our case). Adding a constant, b, to the values on which we are calculating the mean will

Exhibit 14-1 Annual Returns on a Five-Securities Portfolio

	PV	FV	FV/PV	weighted FV/PV	y	weighted y
	4,000	5,200	1.30	0.1576	30.0%	3.6364%
	5,000	6,000	1.20	0.1818	20.0%	3.0303%
	10,000	11,000	1.10	0.3333	10.0%	3.0303%
	8,000	8,000	1.00	0.2424	0.0%	0.0000%
	6000	5400	0.90	0.1636	-10.0%	-1.8182%
mean	6,600	7,102	...	1.0788	...	7.8788%
var	...	...	...	1.56%	...	1.56%
std	...	...	...	12.49%	...	12.4943%
sum	33,000	35,600				

increase the mean by b. If we multiply by a constant a, we multiply the mean by the same constant:

$$\mu(a \cdot X + b) = W_1(a \cdot x_1 + b) + \ldots + W_N(a \cdot x_N + b)$$

$$= a \cdot (W_1 \cdot x_1 + \ldots + W_N \cdot x_N) + b$$

$$= a \cdot \mu(X) + b$$

Variance and Standard Deviation

The deviation about the average is commonly measured by the variance, indicated as var(X) or $\sigma^2(X)$:

$$\sigma^2(X) = W_1 \cdot [x_1 - \mu]^2 + \ldots + W_N \cdot [x_N - \mu]^2 \text{ where } \mu \equiv \mu(X)$$

Adding or subtracting a constant from the values on which we are calculating the variance will leave the variance unchanged; multiplying by a constant will multiply the variance by the constant squared.

$$\sigma^2(a \cdot X + b) = W_1 \cdot [a \cdot x_1 + b - a \cdot \mu - b]^2$$

$$+ \ldots + W_N \cdot [a \cdot x_N + b - a \cdot \mu - b]^2$$

$$= W_1 \cdot [a \cdot (x_1 - \mu)]^2 + \ldots + W_N \cdot [a \cdot (x_N - \mu)]^2$$

$$= a^2 \cdot \sigma^2(X)$$

Variance has a strange property. The units of measurement in which it is expressed are the square of the units of measurement of the values on which it is computed. The expected value of \$ payoffs is expressed in \$; the variance is expressed in \$^{2}.

The standard deviation is defined as the square root of the variance and is therefore expressed in the same units of measurement as the observations (the square root of \$^{2} is plain \$). Adding a constant will leave σ unchanged, whereas multiplying by a constant will multiply σ by the same constant.

$$\sigma(X) = \sqrt{\sigma^2(X)} \Rightarrow \sigma(a \cdot X + b) = a \cdot \sigma(X)$$

Expected Value and Volatility of Returns With Discrete Distributions

Consider the investment in a relatively volatile stock. Let us assume that there is only a discrete number of mutually exclusive possible outcomes, to which we can assign *subjective probabilities*. The result of the investment (measured as either *FV* or yields) is a *random variable*, usually indicated with a capital X. The possible values that can be assumed by the random variable X are usually indicated with a lower case x. Let us further assume that there is a function that associates probabilities with the values of the random variable.

- The probability of each single outcome, given by the *probability mass function*
- The *probability distribution function* associates the values of the random variable with the probability of such value being equal to or less than a given value x

Exhibit 14-2 Expected Annual Returns, $PV = 100$

Pr	R	FV
1.6%	-30%	74.08
9.4%	-20%	81.87
23.4%	-10%	90.48
31.3%	0%	100.00
23.4%	10%	110.52
9.4%	20%	122.14
1.6%	30%	134.99
E (*)	0.0%	100.75
var	1.50%	152.96
std	12.25%	12.37

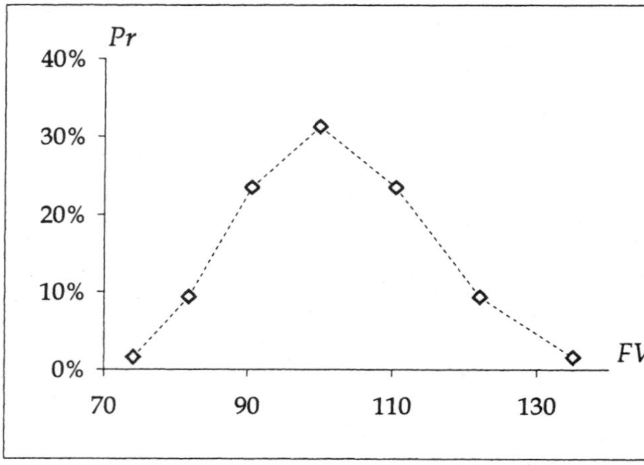

$$\Pr(X \leq x)$$

For a *discrete distribution,* such as that in the Exhibit 14-2, the random variable can take only a well-defined number of values (the line that connects the dots in the graph is there only to facilitate visualization). Always referring to *FV*, the probability distribution function will have value zero for $FV < 74.1$, and value 1 for $FV > 135.0$. The *expected value* (or *mathematical expectation*) of the random variable, often represented by the expected value operator $E(X)$, is a weighted average of the possible outcomes, using mass point probabilities as weights. It is usually assumed that the different values of the random variable x cover all possibilities (all possible *states of nature*), and therefore the sum of the probabilities adds up to one.

$$E(X) = p_1 x_1 + \ldots + p_N x_N = \sum_{J=1}^{N} p_J x_J$$

$$\sum_{J=1}^{N} p_J = 1$$

A linear transformation of the random variable will transform in the same way its expected value (the proof of the following equation is similar to that for the mean, using probabilities as weights):

$$E(a \cdot X + b) = a \cdot E(X) + b$$

The equation for variance is identical to the one we have already met, again using probabilities as weights. Variance can also be expressed as the expected value of the squared outcomes, minus the squared value of the expected outcome. This alternative equation is used quite often because it simplifies algebraic manipulation; see the Mathematical Appendix.

$$\sigma^2(X) = p_1[x_1 - E(X)]^2 + \ldots + p_N[x_N - E(X)]^2$$

$$= E[X^2] - [E(X)]^2$$

Adding a constant to a random variable will leave the variance unchanged; multiplying by a constant will multiply the variance by the constant squared.

$$\sigma^2(a \cdot X + b) = a^2 \cdot \sigma^2(X)$$

$$\sigma(a \cdot X + b) = a \cdot \sigma(X)$$

We can therefore define a new variable that has zero expected value and unit standard deviation.

$$Z = \frac{X - E(X)}{\sigma(X)} \Rightarrow \sigma(Z) = 1, \ E(Z) = 0.$$

Measuring Returns with Logs of Price Relatives

The log of the price relative computed on the expected return is larger than the expected value of the logs of price relatives of the possible outcomes.

$$\ln\left[E\left(\frac{FV}{PV}\right)\right] > E\left[Ln\left(\frac{FV}{PV}\right)\right]$$

For example, using the data from the exhibit we obtain

$$\ln\left(\frac{106.9}{100}\right) = 6.71\% > E\left[Ln\left(\frac{FV}{PV}\right)\right] = 6.0\%.$$

The preceding inequality (known as *Jensen's inequality*) is a direct consequence of the concavity of the logarithmic function that we have already examined in Chapter 3. For a better intuitive understanding of the issue, let us turn to Exhibit 14-3, where we consider only two possible outcomes, respectively the worst ($FV = 74.1$) and the best ($FV = 135.0$) of those used in Exhibit 14-2. Depending on the probability $Pr(u)$ of the favorable outcome, $E(FV)$ can span all the values between 74.1 for $Pr(u) = 0$ and 135.0 for $Pr(u) = 1$.

Exhibit 14-3 Log of Expected Value and Expected Value of Logs

FV/PV	ln (E)	E (ln)
0.741	-30.0%	-30.0%
0.802	-22.1%	-24.0%
0.863	-14.8%	-18.0%
0.924	-8.0%	-12.0%
0.984	-1.6%	-6.0%
1.045	4.4%	0.0%
1.106	10.1%	6.0%
1.167	15.5%	12.0%
1.228	20.5%	18.0%
1.289	25.4%	24.0%
1.350	30.0%	30.0%

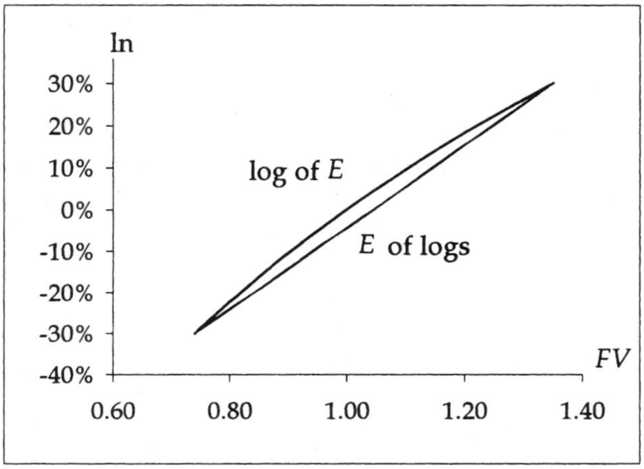

$$E\left(\frac{FV}{PV}\right) = \frac{74.1 + \text{Pr(u)} \cdot 135.0 - 74.1}{100}$$

The expected value of the logs of the price relatives will be a linear function of p, which, as you can see, lies below the log of the expected value.

$$E\left[\ln\left(\frac{FV}{PV}\right)\right] = -30\% + \text{Pr}(u) \cdot 60\%$$

The distance between the two curves in the graph is, visibly, a function of the spread between worst and best outcomes, and this spread is measured by variance. For Pr(u) = 50%, and for levels of standard deviation that are relatively contained, we can use the following equation, that we already examined in Chapter 3.

$$\ln\left[E\left(\frac{FV}{PV}\right)\right] \cong E\left[Ln\left(\frac{FV}{PV}\right)\right] + \frac{\sigma^2}{2}$$

where $[\sigma^2]$ is the variance of the logs

Independent Random Trials

If a given random experiment is performed N times in such a way that the outcome of the experiment neither influences nor is influenced by the outcome of any other trial, we say that the individual realizations $(\mathfrak{R}_j \mid j = 1, \ldots, n)$ are independent trials. Think of tossing a coin. The coin has no memory, and the chance of getting heads is totally independent from the previous heads/tails sequence. In this case we have two important properties:

1. The mean of the sum of N independent random experiments equals the sum of the means. Think of N coin flips, where you gain $10 for heads-up and you lose $10 for heads-down. The expected value is obviously $0, and will go on being $0 no matter how many times you play the game.
2. The variance will equal the sum of variances (the more you play, the larger the possible spread of results). Indicating with $\mathfrak{R}$ the stochastic process consisting of N independent trials, we can write the following equations:

$$E(\mathfrak{R}) = E(\mathfrak{R}_1) + \ldots E(\mathfrak{R}_N)$$

$$\sigma^2(\mathfrak{R}) = \sigma^2(\mathfrak{R}_1) + \ldots + \sigma^2(\mathfrak{R}_N)$$

Numerical examples based on repetitions of independent random trials will be found in the next section, with reference to binomial and normal distributions. If you think of the process as one that is continuously carried out in time, at a regular pace—for example, once a day—then you can measure expected value and variance as yearly rates. The expected value, the variance and the standard deviation for a fraction of a year $h = \Delta T$ will be

$$h \cdot E(X), \ \sigma^2 \cdot (X) \cdot h, \ \sigma(X) \cdot \sqrt{h}.$$

14-2 EXTRACTING VOLATILITIES FROM TIME SERIES

A large number of methods exist for estimating and modeling the volatility of stock prices, foreign exchange (FX) rates, yields, and so on. Some of these techniques are fairly sophisticated and are part of the field of financial econometrics. We should stress that volatility measurements are by no means confined to options pricing. They constitute the foundation for portfolio management (which is carried out in terms of risk return) and of risk management. Although financial econometrics is not covered in this book, a simple measure of past volatility is so common that it deserves mention. In essence this is done by taking, say, daily data; computing the logs of price relatives; and determining their average and their variance. Take a set of $N + 1$ consecutive FX rates, say, daily values provided by Datastream, Bloomberg, and others. The daily value relatives of the FX rates will be

$$R_D(j) = \ln\left[\frac{FX(j)}{FX(j - 1)}\right] \{j = 1, \ldots, N\}$$

$$R_D = \text{daily rate, non annualized}$$

$$\mu(R_D) = \frac{1}{N} \cdot \sum_{j=1}^{N} r_D(j)$$

$$\sigma^2(R_D) = \frac{[R_D(1) - \mu(R_D)]^2 + \ldots + [R_D(N) - \mu(R_D)]^2}{N - 1}$$

$$\sigma(R_D) = \sqrt{\sigma^2(R_D)}.$$

The reason why we determine variance using $N - 1$ as the denominator derives from the fact that we are trying to estimate variance using a sample, and *sample variance* is determined using $N - 1$ to correct for the degree of freedom (see the Mathematical Appendix for a brief discussion). There are some issues you should be aware of.

• First, which day count you should use to annualize the daily variances (business days or calendar days). There is no cut-and-dried answer, but the most common method is to consider only business days; this is based on the fact that a number of statistical studies have shown that most of the volatility occurs over trading days; volatility therefore seems to be concentrated on trading days (e.g., French [1980] and French and Roll [1986]).

$$\sigma^2 = \frac{1}{h} \cdot \sigma^2(r_D)$$

$$\sigma = \sigma(r_D) \cdot \sqrt{\frac{1}{h}}$$

$$\sigma^2(r_D) = \sigma \cdot \sqrt{h}$$

$$\Delta T = h = \frac{1}{260}$$

• Second, and more important, volatility changes over time. This begs the question of how many observations you want to choose for your estimate of volatility. There is no generally accepted rule. It all depends on for which purpose you are estimating volatility. If you need them for short-term *risk management* (trying to determine your *value-at-risk* over a one-day time horizon), you can use a fairly short series of observations. If you are trying to price a long-term option, your volatility measure should, as a rule of thumb, cover a long enough period of time to make it meaningful. Exhibit 14-5 shows the JPY/$ rate volatility over the FX wave of 1995. It is measured over rolling 20- and 40-trading-day periods, and you can see that the length of the observation period changes the volatility values.

14-3   THE BINOMIAL DISTRIBUTION

The binomial distribution has been used for more than two centuries and has important applications in the pricing of options because it underpins the widely used technique of binomial trees (also known as *binomial random walks*). If a given random experiment is performed N times in such a way that the outcome of each experiment neither influences nor is influenced by the outcome of any other trial, the individual performances are independent trials. When the individual performances can have only two possible results $\{u, d\}$, such as in tossing a coin, we have a binomial distribution:

$ES = \{u,d\}$ = event set for $(\Re_j \mid j = 1, \ldots, N)$
u = the random variable takes the value *head up*
d = the random variable takes the value *head down*

A binomial process is obtained precisely by repeating N independent trials of the preceding experiment. The binomial distribution can also accommodate the case in which the probabilities of the two outcomes are not the same. The physical model you can think of is that of drawing a ball at random from an urn containing Mu balls marked *up* and Md balls marked *down*. Referring to up-down balls instead of the usual black-red color-coding allows us to use immediately the up-down terminology that is

Exhibit 14-4 JPY/$, Frequency Distribution of Daily Variations

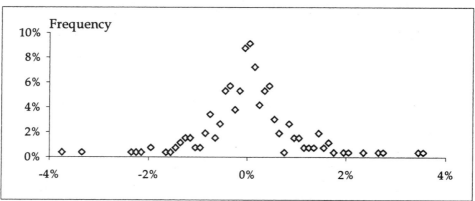

The frequency of daily variations is measured on 10 bp intervals, for example the highest frequency, 9.13%, is in the { -0.05%: +0.05% } interval.
In order to make the scatter diagram more readable, zero frequencies are not shown

Exhibit 14-5 Annualized Volatility for the JPY/$ Exchange Rate, 1995

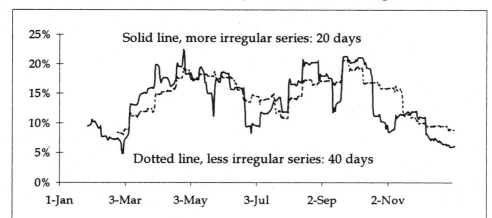

	JPY/$	$/100 JPY	ln of value relatives
Fri-30-Dec-94	99.58	1.0042	....
Mon-2-Jan-95	100.20	0.9980	0.6207%
Tue-3-Jan-95	100.67	0.9933	0.4680%
Wed-4-Jan-95	101.35	0.9867	0.6683%
Thu-5-Jan-95	100.88	0.9913	-0.4648%
Fri-6-Jan-95	101.37	0.9865	0.4895%
Mon-9-Jan-95	100.03	0.9998	-1.3357%
Tue-10-Jan-95	100.03	0.9998	0.0000%
Wed-11-Jan-95	100.09	0.9992	0.0600%
Thu-12-Jan-95	98.67	1.0135	-1.4290%
Fri-13-Jan-95	98.40	1.0163	-0.2689%
		Average	-0.1192%
		Daily standard deviation	0.7650%
		Annualized std	12.3345%

utilized in options pricing. The probability of getting an *up* ball in one trial is intuitively equal to

$$p = \frac{Mu}{Mu + Md}.$$

To keep the trials independent, you must replace the ball after each drawing so as not to alter the ratio Mu/Md. The *drawing with replacement* model is not important when the number of balls is very large when compared with the number of drawings (M much larger than N), and therefore the change in the Mu/Md is minimal and does not affect the outcomes (this has obvious applications in sampling theory). By performing drawings with replacement, we easily get a very large number of possible sequences, such as $\{u, u, d, u, \ldots\}$. All these sequences will have the same probability if and only if $p = (1 - p) = 50\%$. If $p \neq 50\%$ the probability will depend on the number of u-values that distinguish the path and not on the order in which the come about.

2^N = number of all possible paths
$p^S \cdot (1 - p)^{N-S}$ = probability of the paths with S up-balls
$0 \leq S \leq N$ = number of up-balls

Probability Mass Function for the Binomial Distribution

In fact, we are mostly interested in the probability of getting a certain number of u-balls in N steps. This number is conventionally known as *number of successes (S)* and can go from zero (no u-ball is ever drawn) to N, when all the independent random steps yield u-balls. This probability will, of course, equal the probability of the paths characterized by $Nu = S$, times the number of possible (and equiprobable) paths characterized by $Nu = S$. This is usually represented with the following equation.

$$b(S,N,p) = \binom{N}{S} \cdot \underbrace{p^S(1 - p)^{N-S}}_{PATH\ PROB}$$

$$\binom{N}{S} = \frac{N!}{S! \cdot (N - S)!} = \text{number of paths with S successes (up-balls).}$$

The probability of obtaining S successes (up-balls, in our case) in N independent trials is known as the *probability mass function* of the random variable S. The discrete values that S can take are indicated as the *mass point* for the random variable $0 \leq S \leq N$. A four-step binomial process is analyzed in Exhibit 14-6. We can now compute the probabilities for all the possible values of S ($S = 0, 1, 2, \ldots, N$), thereby obtaining a binomial probability mass function such as that shown in Exhibit 14-7. The random variable can take only a finite number of values. The line that connects the dots in the graph is there only to facilitate visualization. If $p = (1 - p)$, the function is symmetric. *A probability mass function is symmetric, with ξ as a point of symmetry if whenever $\xi + a$*

Exhibit 14-6 Binomial Tree, *Pr (Up)* = 50%

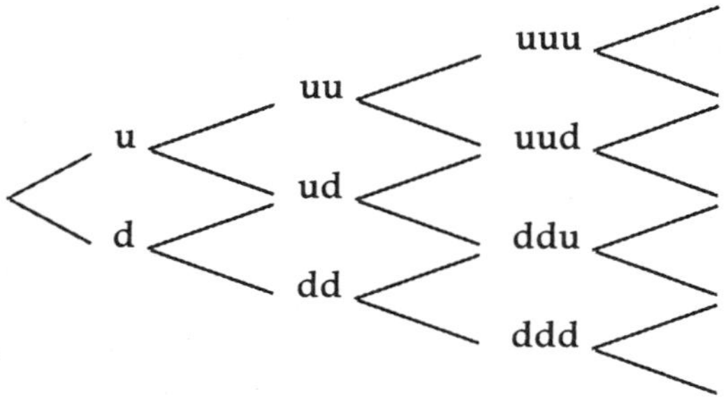

					S	possible paths	$b(S, N, p)$
				uuuu	4	1	0.0625
			uuu				
		uu		uuud	3	4	0.2500
	u		uud				
		ud		uudd	2	6	0.3750
	d		ddu				
		dd		dddu	1	4	0.2500
			ddd				
				dddd	0	1	0.0625
						16	1.0000

Exhibit 14-7 Binomial Distribution, $Pr = 50\%$, Steps $= 14$

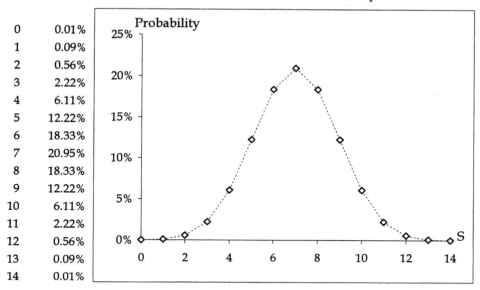

0	0.01%
1	0.09%
2	0.56%
3	2.22%
4	6.11%
5	12.22%
6	18.33%
7	20.95%
8	18.33%
9	12.22%
10	6.11%
11	2.22%
12	0.56%
13	0.09%
14	0.01%

is a possible value of the random variable, so is $\xi - a$; furthermore, $Pr\,(\xi + a) = Pr\,(\xi - a)$. In the exhibit the point of symmetry is $S = 7$. If the shape of the binomial mass function reminds you of the familiar *bell-shaped normal distribution density function*, you are perfectly right. Computing the binomial distribution was quite laborious, and this led to the development of probability functions that could simplify computation while approximating the binomial distribution in a satisfactory way. In fact, the normal distribution was developed with this primary purpose in mind (by De Moivre, a French mathematician, in the first half of the eighteenth century. The *binomial urn* model is credited to Jacob Bernoulli, the great seventeenth-century Swiss mathematician). To-day the binomial distribution is included in all the main PC spreadsheets, not to mention all the available statistical and mathematical packages.

Mean, Variance, and Standard Deviation of the Binomial Distribution

A binomial distribution has a mean, a variance, and a standard deviation (not to mention the higher moments), all of which are related to the value of the random variable S. In one step, the number of successes, up-balls, can be either one or zero; therefore

$$E(S) = p$$

$$\sigma^2(S) = p \cdot (1 - p)^2 + (1 - p) \cdot (0 - p)^2 = (1 - p) \cdot p$$

To extend the results to many steps, just apply the rules for the expected value and variance of a number of independent events:

$E(S) = N \cdot p =$ expected value of S for an N-steps binomial tree
$\text{var} = p(1 - p) =$ variance of a one-step tree

Exhibit 14-8 Binomial Distributions

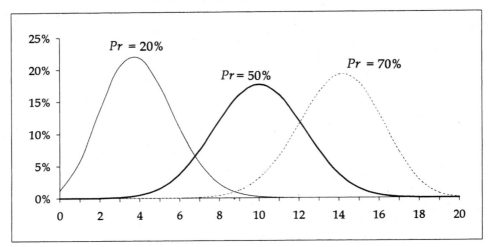

	Pr = 20%	*Pr* = 50%	*Pr* = 70%
E (S)	4	10	14
var (S)	3.20	5.00	4.20
std (S)	1.79	2.24	2.05

$$\sigma^2 = \text{var}(S) = N \cdot p(1 - p) = \text{variance over } N\text{-steps}$$
$$\sigma = std(S) = \sqrt{N \cdot p(1 - p)}$$

From the preceding equations we can easily see that given the number of independent random experiments (N), variance will have a maximum when $p = (1 - p) = 50\%$ (see Exhibit 14-8). The random variable in the binomial distribution can assume only a discreet number of states; therefore the cumulative probability distribution will be a step function measuring the probability of S being lower than $\{1, 2, \ldots, N\}$ (see Exhibit 14-9).

14-4   THE NORMAL DISTRIBUTION

The *normal distribution* was initially developed as an approximation to the binomial distribution, which is difficult to tabulate in a compact format convenient for general use. The normal distribution soon took on a life of its own and is now the cornerstone of an impressive array of scientific and financial applications. The normal distribution is based on the familiar, bell-shaped *normal probability density function* (NDF) for a random variable X that can take all the values on the real line. The tails of the NDF, therefore, are not limited as are those of the binomial probability mass function. Infinitely long tails could appear to be an unwanted feature because no financial variable can take on infinitely large values (not even the consumer price index (CPI) in hyperinflationary economies). The long tails, however, do not represent a problem because the probability of X taking up "unrealistic" values is so small that we can safely ignore it. We speak of a density function and not of a "mass function" because X is continuous and does not take a discrete number of mass points. We have the following equation

Exhibit 14-9 Binomial Probability Distribution, N = 15, p = 50%

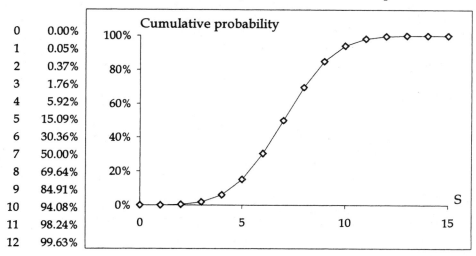

0	0.00%
1	0.05%
2	0.37%
3	1.76%
4	5.92%
5	15.09%
6	30.36%
7	50.00%
8	69.64%
9	84.91%
10	94.08%
11	98.24%
12	99.63%

$$n(x;\,\mu,\,\sigma) \;=\; \frac{1}{\sigma\sqrt{2\pi}}\,\exp\!\left[-\frac{(x-\mu)^2}{2\sigma^2}\right],\ \text{with}\ (-\infty < x < \infty)$$

As you can see, the NDF is expressed in terms of only two parameters, {μ, and σ}. Therefore, when we adopt the normal distribution to model a stochastic process, we just use the desired values {μ, σ} instead of having to compute what parameters will yield the desired expected value and volatility.

Exhibit 14-10 shows that the NDF is clearly symmetric, having μ as a point of symmetry. This symmetry implies that the NDF approximates the binomial distribution more efficiently when the value of p in the binomial is close to 50%. However, the larger n is, the further p can diverge from 50% and still yield a good normal approximation. The values of the NDF *do not* represent the probabilities of the corresponding

Exhibit 14-10 Normal density function, E (K) = 7%, std(K) = 20%

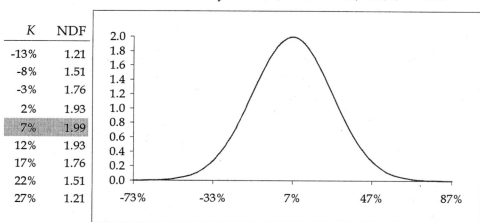

K	NDF
-13%	1.21
-8%	1.51
-3%	1.76
2%	1.93
7%	1.99
12%	1.93
17%	1.76
22%	1.51
27%	1.21

values of x. The random variable X can take all the values on the real line; therefore the probability of a point x is infinitesimally small. The values of $n(x; \mu, \sigma)$ measure the rate of change, the derivative, of the cumulative normal probability distribution $N(x; \mu, \sigma)$. Therefore,

$$N(x; \mu, \sigma) = \Pr(X \leqslant x)$$

$$\frac{d[N(x; \mu, \sigma)]}{dx} = n(x; \mu, \sigma).$$

Another commonly used notation is $N'(x; \mu, \sigma)$. Exhibit 14-10 plots the normal density function relative to possible rates of return (K) of an investment, over a 1yr time horizon. The values of the density function are computed at 5% intervals of the random variable. The table in the exhibit shows the 11 "central" values. The density function is symmetric with the mean $(\mu = 7\%)$ as the point of symmetry.

The area under the bell curve, from $-\infty$ to x, equals the cumulative normal probability distribution. Therefore, for $n(x; \mu, \sigma)$ to be a legitimate probability density function, the area under the whole bell curve must equal 100%. In fact, it is possible to prove that the NDF integrates to 1. You should remember, however, that there is no closed-form integral (no analytic equation) for the normal density function, that is therefore one of the best-known examples of important functions for which we do not have an indefinite integral. Numerical methods to compute the cumulative distribution function are readily available in all spreadsheets and mathematical packages.

$$\int_{-\infty}^{+\infty} n(x; \mu, \sigma)dx = 1$$

The probability of a single point x is infinitesimally small; it is relatively straightforward, however, to compute the probability that X will take a value that falls within a given interval $A < X \leqslant A + h$.

$$\Pr(X \leqslant A + h) - \Pr(X < A) = N(A + h, \mu, \sigma) - N(A, \mu, \sigma).$$

Example. Compute the probability that your investment will have a rate of return of less than -13% or 22% or more over a 1yr horizon (see Exhibit 14-11).

$$\Pr(K < -13\% \,|\, \mu = 7\%, \sigma = 20\%) = N(-13\%: 7\%, 20\%) = 15.866\%$$

$$\Pr(K \geq 22\% \,|\, \mu = 7\%, \sigma = 20\%) = 1 - N(22\%: 7\%, 20\%) = 1 - 77.337\% = 22.663\%$$

Having assigned probabilities to K falling into defined intervals, we can compute its expected value, that must converge to $\mu = 7\%$. As the values of K span the real line, the cumulative expected value will first be negative and then become positive and converge to μ, as in Exhibit 14-12, which plots

$$E(K \,|\, K < k)$$

14-5 NORMAL DISTRIBUTION AND TIME-SERIES VOLATILITY

We saw in Section 14-2 that it is possible to extract mean and volatility from a time series of logs of value relatives. Given these two parameters, we can immediately compute the corresponding normal distribution. We can then check, with adequate

Exhibit 14-11 Probability of *K* Falling into 1% Intervals, such as 6.5%–7.5%

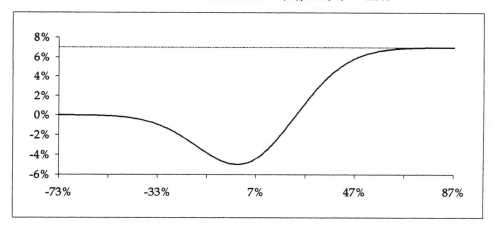

K	Pr
3%	1.96%
4%	1.97%
5%	1.98%
6%	1.99%
7%	1.99%
8%	1.99%
9%	1.98%
10%	1.97%
11%	1.96%

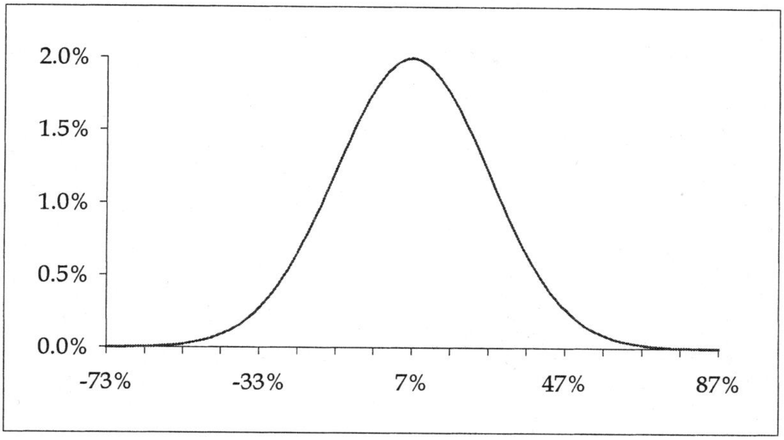

Exhibit 14-12 Cumulative *E* (*K*), std(*K*) = 20%

econometric tools, whether the normal distribution is a good approximation of the real distribution from which we started. A first idea of the goodness of the fit can, however, rely on a simple visual inspection of the plot.

Exhibit 14-14 shows the already examined JPY/$ rate in 1995. To construct the plot, probabilities are referred to in 0.1% daily variation intervals. You can clearly see that the normal distribution provides a very unsatisfactory fit. This result is hardly surprising when you remember how volatility changed throughout the year.

The JPY/$ rate changed from 99.58 to 103.52.

$$\ln\!\left(\frac{103.52}{99.58}\right) = 3.876\%$$

$$\mu(r_D) = \frac{1}{260} \cdot \ln\!\left(\frac{103.52}{99.58}\right) = 0.0149\%$$

$$\sigma(r_D) = 0.8978\%$$

Exhibit 14-13 Normal Cumulative Density Function

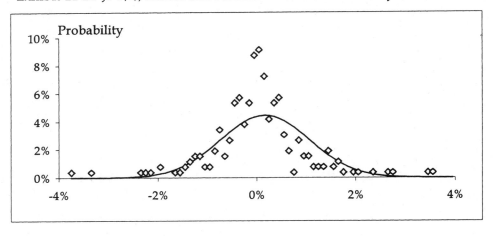

K	NDF
-13%	0.16
-8%	0.23
-3%	0.31
2%	0.40
7%	0.50
12%	0.60
17%	0.69
22%	0.77
27%	0.84

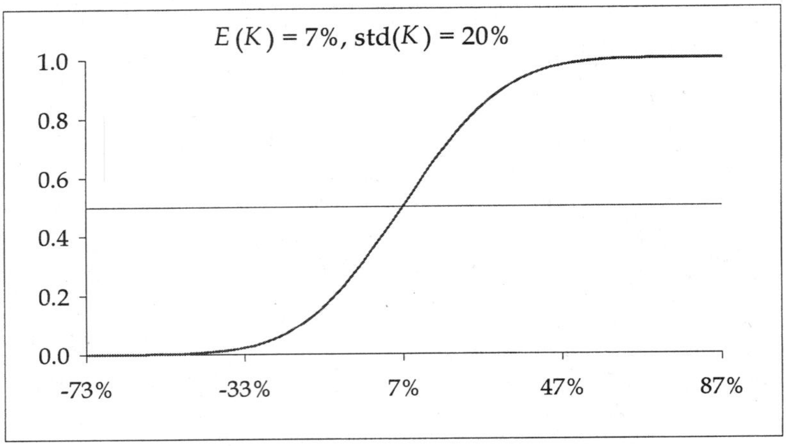

Exhibit 14-14 JPY/$, Actual and Normal Distributions of Daily Variations

14-6 THE STANDARD NORMAL DISTRIBUTION

A standardized normal distribution, known as Z *distribution,* is characterized by $\{\mu = 0, \sigma = 1\}$. This special case of NDF was developed to facilitate numerical computations by tabulating standardized values. The Z distribution is referred to in a number of equations you are likely to come across (including the well-known Black-Scholes options pricing formula), and therefore it makes sense to dedicate some time to examine it from a conceptual point of view. In this book you will not find tables of the cumulative standard distribution because the appropriate computation routine is now available on all major PC spreadsheets. The density equation becomes

$$n(z, 0, 1) = \frac{1}{\sqrt{2\pi}} \exp\left(-\frac{z^2}{2}\right), \text{ for } (-\infty < z < \infty).$$

Exhibit 14-15 shows the Z NDF. Considering that $\{\mu = 0, \sigma = 1\}$, the values on the random variable are in fact expressed in terms of σ; therefore

Exhibit 14-15 Standard Normal Density Function

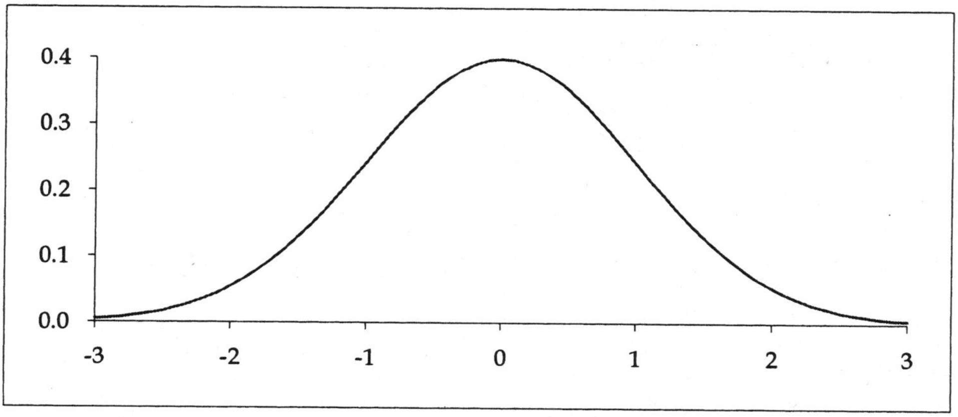

$$z = 2 \Rightarrow z = \mu + 2\sigma$$

Using the Z NDF we can easily compute the values of the standard cumulation distribution, which is usually indicated with the operator $N(\cdot)$. The following well-known values can also be found in general-purpose business documents, such as the annual report of banks:

> To estimate such losses, BAC employs an "earnings-at-risk" (EAR) methodology, which, using a 95 percent confidence interval (that is to say a 2 σ deviation from the mean), employs statistical historical data to measure the loss that would result from an adverse, one day shift in market prices (BankAmerica Corporation, 1994 annual report).

Important Values of $N(\cdot)$

$$\Pr(-\sigma < Z \leq \sigma) = 68.2689\% \quad \Pr(Z > \sigma) = 15.8655\%$$

$$\Pr(-2\sigma < Z \leq 2\sigma) = 95.4500\% \quad \Pr(Z > 2\sigma) = 2.2750\%$$

$$\Pr(-3\sigma < Z \leq 3\sigma) = 99.7300\% \quad \Pr(Z > 3\sigma) = 0.1350\%$$

Let us now deal with the relevant question of how to use the Z distribution when you have to deal with real-life problems where $\{\mu \neq 0, \sigma \neq 1\}$. To do this we must rescale our normal distribution by changing the random variable from X to Z:

$$Z = \frac{X - E(X)}{\sigma(X)} \Rightarrow \{E(Z) = 0, \sigma(Z) = 1\}$$

Let us dwell on this a little more. We can think of the rescaling of the random variable X as consisting of two steps. First, compute the NDF for a new variable:

$$Q = K - E(K) \Rightarrow E(Q) = 0, \sigma(Q) = \sigma(K)$$

The preceding rescaling will not alter the standard deviation (you are only adding a constant to the random variable X). The Q NDF is the same as your original X NDF, except that it will have a mean (point of symmetry) of zero.

Exhibit 14-16 First Step of NDF Rescaling

Q	NDF
-25%	0.91
-20%	1.21
-15%	1.51
-10%	1.76
-5%	1.93
0%	1.99
5%	1.93
10%	1.76
15%	1.51
20%	1.21
25%	0.91

$E(Q) = 0$
$std(Q) = 20\%$

Example, step 1: The probability of X taking a value between -13% and $+7\%$ equals the probability of Q taking a value between -20% and 0% (see Exhibit 14-16).

$$\Pr(-13\% < X \leq 7\%) = \Pr(-13\% - 7\% < Q \leq 7\% - 7\%) = \Pr(-20\% < Q \leq 0\%)$$

The second step of the rescaling consists of dividing Q by $\sigma(X)$. The Z density function will be the same as your Q NDF, except that the values of the random variable are measured in terms of standard deviation from the zero mean (see Exhibit 14-17).

Example, step 2: The probability of K taking a value between -13% and $+7\%$ equals the probability of Z taking a value between -1 and 0. The numerical solution is easily computed using $N(\cdot)$.

$$\Pr(-13\% < X \leq 7\%) = \Pr\left(\frac{-13\% - 7\%}{20\%} < Z \leq \frac{7\% - 7\%}{20\%}\right)$$

$$= \Pr(-1 < Z \leq 0\%) = 34.134\%$$

Exhibit 14-17 Full Rescaling

K	Z	Z-DF
-13%	-100%	24%
-8%	-75%	30%
-3%	-50%	35%
2%	-25%	39%
7%	0%	40%
12%	25%	39%
17%	50%	35%
22%	75%	30%
27%	100%	24%

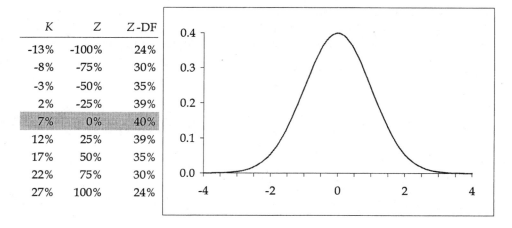

Exhibit 14-18 Symmetry of the Standard Density Function

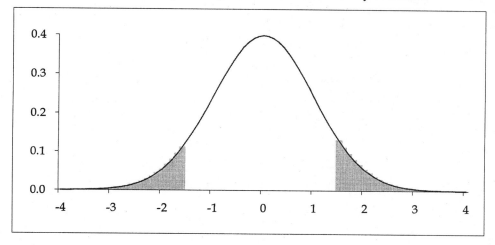

The Truncated Standard Cumulative Distribution

The standard NDF is symmetric, with $\mu = 0$ as the point of symmetry. Therefore the probability of the random variable being greater than a given value z is equal to the probability of the random variable being smaller than $-z$. This property is intuitively evident if you consider Exhibit 14-18, where $z = 1.5$ (i.e., $z = 1.5\ \sigma$).

$$\Pr(X > z) = \Pr(X \le -z)$$

The preceding equation implies some elementary properties of the standard normal distribution, that are often used in algebraic manipulations.

$$\Pr(X \le z) = 1 - \Pr(X > z) = \Pr(X > -z)$$

$$\Pr(X > z) = 1 - \Pr(X \le z) = \Pr(X \le -z)$$

14-7 MATHEMATICAL APPENDIX

Compact Equation for Variance

$\mu = E(x)$.

$$\operatorname{var}(X) = p_1 \cdot [x_1 - \mu]^2 + \ldots + p_N \cdot [x_N - \mu]^2$$
$$= p_1 \cdot [(x_1)^2 - 2\mu \cdot x_1 + \mu^2] + \ldots + p_N \cdot [(x_N)^2 - 2\mu \cdot x_N + \mu^2]$$

$$= E(X^2) + p_1 \cdot [-2\mu \cdot x_1 + \mu^2] + \ldots + p_N \cdot [-2\mu \cdot x_N + \mu^2]$$
$$= E(X^2) - \mu \cdot [p_1 \cdot (2 \cdot x_1 - \mu) + \ldots + p_N(2 \cdot x_N - \mu)]$$
$$= E(X^2) - \mu \cdot (2\mu - \mu)$$
$$= E(X^2) - [E(X)]^2$$

Squared Deviations from the Mean

The sum of the squared deviations from the mean—that is, the variance—is smaller than the sum of the squared deviations from any other number $k \neq E(X)$. Indicate the sum of squared deviations as

$$\phi(k) = p_1 \cdot [x_1 - k]^2 + \ldots + p_N \cdot [x_N - k]^2$$

$$= p_1 \cdot [(x_1)^2 - 2k \cdot x_1 + k^2] + \ldots + p_N \cdot [(x_N)^2 - 2k \cdot x_N + k^2]$$

$$= E(X^2) + p_1 \cdot [-2k \cdot x_1 + k^2] + \ldots + p_N \cdot [-2k \cdot x_N + k^2]$$

$$= E(X^2) - 2k \cdot E(X) + k^2.$$

The minimum of the function will correspond to the point $k = E(X)$, where the first derivative is zero and second derivative is positive.

$$\phi'(k) = -2E(X) + 2k$$

$$\phi''(k) = 2$$

$$-2 \cdot E(X) + 2 \cdot k = 0 \Rightarrow k = E(X)$$

Dividing by $n - 1$ when Computing the Sample Variance

Consider a random sample of size N from a given population. We take the sample mean to be an unbiased estimator for the population mean μ.

$$\bar{X} = \frac{1}{N} \sum_1^N X_J, \text{ where } \bar{X} = \text{sample mean}$$

$$\sum_1^N \frac{(X_J - \mu)^2}{N}, \text{ population variance}$$

We do not know μ and therefore we must use the sample mean, that is $\bar{X}$ instead of μ.

$$\sum_{1}^{N} (X_j - \bar{X})^2 = \sum_{1}^{N} (X_j - \mu + \mu - \bar{X})^2$$

$$= \sum_{1}^{N} [(X_j - \mu) + (\mu - \bar{X})]^2$$

$$= \sum_{1}^{N} [(X_j - \mu)^2 + 2 \cdot (X_j - \mu) \cdot (\mu - \bar{X}) + (\mu - \bar{X})^2]$$

$$= \sum_{1}^{N} (X_j - \mu)^2 + 2 \cdot (\mu - \bar{X}) \cdot \sum_{1}^{N} (X_j - \mu) + N \cdot (\mu - \bar{X})^2$$

$$= \sum_{1}^{N} (X_j - \mu)^2 + 2 \cdot (\mu - \bar{X}) \cdot \left(\sum_{1}^{N} X_j - N \cdot \mu \right) + N \cdot (\mu - \bar{X})^2$$

$$= \sum_{1}^{N} (X_j - \mu)^2 + 2 \cdot (\mu - \bar{X}) \cdot (N \cdot \bar{X} - N \cdot \mu) + N \cdot (\mu - \bar{X})^2$$

$$= \sum_{1}^{N} (X_j - \mu)^2 - 2 \cdot N(\mu - \bar{X}) \cdot (\mu - \bar{X}) + N \cdot (\mu - \bar{X})^2$$

$$= \sum_{1}^{N} (X_j - \mu)^2 - 2 \cdot N(\mu - \bar{X})^2 + N \cdot (\mu - \bar{X})^2$$

$$= \sum_{1}^{N} (X_j - \mu)^2 - N(\mu - \bar{X})^2$$

$$= N \cdot \sigma^2 - N(\mu - \bar{X})^2$$

A well established result in statistics is that the standard deviation of the sample mean [also known as the standard error of the mean] equals the standard deviation of the population divided the square root of the sample size.

$$SE = \sqrt{\frac{\sigma^2}{N}} \Rightarrow E(\mu - \bar{X})^2 = \frac{\sigma^2}{N}$$

$$\sum_{1}^{N} (X_j - \bar{X})^2 = N \cdot \sigma^2 - N \cdot \frac{\sigma^2}{N} = (N - 1) \cdot \sigma^2$$

Dividing by $(N - 1)$ we get

$$\frac{1}{N - 1} \cdot \sum_{1}^{N} (X_j - \bar{X})^2 = \sigma^2$$

Chapter **15**

Stochastic Models

15-1 INTRODUCTION, RANDOM DRAWINGS FROM A BINOMIAL DISTRIBUTION

Binomial trees are often used to model the stochastic behavior of a financial variable, such as stock prices, stock exchange indexes (S&P 500, etc.), foreign exchange (FX) rates, interest rates, and so on. When the result of a random step is up, the variable that we are modeling goes up. Conversely, a down step means that the variable decreases.

We indicate with the word *drift* the expected change in value implied by the tree. Say you want to model the random future behavior of the JPY/$ exchange rate; you may well want to assume that the expected value equals the forward value. The overall result of a series of independent binomial steps is of course random, but the drift can be calculated. Drift is usually measured as annualized exponential yield (R).

The binomial tree must incorporate the desired level of drift and volatility. In Chapters 15 to 18 we shall implicitly assume that both drift and volatility are the same at each node of the binomial tree. The magnitude of the up/down movements at each node, and their probabilities (referred to as *transition probabilities*), determine the volatility at the node, which is often called *local volatility*. If we assume the same drift and the same $\Pr(u)$ at each node, this entails that the volatility will be the same at each node. Therefore we shall use what are known as *constant local volatility trees*.

A *recombining tree* is characterized by the fact that an up step followed by a down step produces the same result as a down step followed by an up step. This entails that the result after n steps will depend only on the number of up steps, exactly as in a binomial distribution. A practical consequence is that recombining trees are a lot simpler to deal with because they have only $N + 1$ end results instead of 2^N. A smallish 24-step nonrecombining tree has already over 16 million possible paths, while the recombining version is limited to 25 (see Exhibit 15-1). There are two widely used approaches to the problem of engineering recombining binomial trees with the desired (constant) level of drift and volatility.

268

Exhibit 15-1 Recombining and Nonrecombining Binomial Trees

1. The method used by Cox, Ross, and Rubinstein allows $p \neq 0.5$. This approach is simple to implement and very much referred to in the financial literature. When p diverges materially from 50%, this procedure can lead to inaccuracies and paradoxical results.
2. The second approach imposes $p = 0.5$, that is, *symmetric transition probabilities*.

Random Drawings from a Binomial Distribution

We may want to generate one random path of a binomial tree. This is a straightforward procedure. In fact, there is an arithmetic process that will generate a random series of numbers, with the desired number of decimal digits, covering uniformly the interval (0,1). This mathematical procedure, which we do not need to examine in this book, is available in all major spreadsheets and in all mathematical and statistical packages.

Things are never as straightforward as we would like them to be. You should be aware of one problem. The random numbers produced by the routine are random only in the sense that they span in a random way the interval on the real line. They are not fully random because, given an initial number (called the *random seed*), the computer will always produce the same identical sequence of uniformly distributed numbers, which for this reason are also indicated as *quasi-random numbers*. To solve this problem, all random-number generators have some routine that will generate the seed using data from the system in a way that will not bias the result (e.g., the time, in millionths of a second, when the random number routine is activated).

Having generated a random number, we decide if this corresponds to an up or a down on the basis of the transition probability (p).

$$RND \leq p \Rightarrow up$$

$$RND = \text{random number}$$

The same series of random numbers will therefore produce different frequencies of ups as a function of the value of p, as shown in Exhibit 15-2.

15-2   THE COX, ROSS, AND RUBINSTEIN (CRR) APPROACH

The use of binomial trees for option pricing is credited to Sharpe (1976) and to Cox, Ross, and Rubinstein (CRR) (1978). The CRR model is based on symmetric proportional changes at each node. The value at the node is therefore multiplied by $u > 1$ in the up step and divided by u in the down step. We therefore have a *multiplicative binomial process* in which the value u is the same for all the nodes of the tree. The

Exhibit 15-2 Random Drawings from a Bernoulli Distribution

Random	30%	40%	50%	60%	70%	80%
0.1057	U	U	U	U	U	U
0.7935	Dw	Dw	Dw	Dw	Dw	U
0.8144	Dw	Dw	Dw	Dw	Dw	Dw
0.1487	U	U	U	U	U	U
0.8611	Dw	Dw	Dw	Dw	Dw	Dw
0.1808	U	U	U	U	U	U
0.0056	U	U	U	U	U	U
0.0503	U	U	U	U	U	U
0.6281	Dw	Dw	Dw	Dw	U	U
0.1664	U	U	U	U	U	U
0.0541	U	U	U	U	U	U
0.5396	Dw	Dw	Dw	U	U	U
0.2768	U	U	U	U	U	U
0.6124	Dw	Dw	Dw	Dw	U	U
0.8037	Dw	Dw	Dw	Dw	Dw	Dw

The first line represents Pr (Up)

Exhibit 15-3 One Node in a CRR Binomial Tree

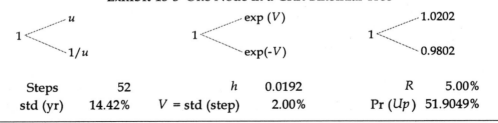

Steps	52	h	0.0192	R	5.00%
std (yr)	14.42%	V = std (step)	2.00%	Pr (Up)	51.9049%

transition probability Pr(u) can be different from 50% but is the same for all nodes; we therefore have constant local volatilities. In Exhibit 15-3 we use weekly steps; therefore $\Delta T = h = 0.0192$.

Let us now determine the control variables (u,p) needed to engineer a tree with the desired drift and volatility. First, it is possible to prove that

$$\ln(u) = \sigma \cdot \sqrt{h} \text{ for } p = 50\%,$$

and that, for values of p that are not too different from 50%

$$\ln(u) \cong \sigma \cdot \sqrt{h}.$$

Given the desired level of annualized std we can therefore easily determine:

$$u = \exp(\sigma \cdot \sqrt{h})$$

Given the desired annualized drift rate R, we can easily determine the correct value of the transitional probabilities:

$$p \cdot u + (1 - p) \cdot \frac{1}{u} = \exp(R \cdot h)$$

$$p = \frac{\exp(R \cdot h) - 1/u}{u - 1/u}$$

Let us recall that because of the convexity of the log function, the preceding tree would display a positive drift when $p = 50\%$. In our example we would have

$$0.5 \times 1.1 + 0.5 \times 0.90909 = 1.0045.$$

The Problem with the CRR Tree

We have already mentioned that in certain cases the CRR construction can lead to inaccuracies and possibly to paradoxical results (negative probabilities). These problems are attributable to the fact that the step-std approximation $\ln(u) \cong \sigma \cdot \sqrt{h}$ can be very inaccurate when p diverges from 50%. This issue, with a proposed solution, is covered in Section 15-6.

A Binomial Tree Example

Let us now consider a simple 12-step binomial tree, volatility = 20%, drift = 6%. The preceding equations will produce the following values.

$$u = \exp\left(20\% \cdot \sqrt{\frac{1}{12}}\right) = 1.0594, \ln(u) = 5.7735\%, \frac{1}{u} = 0.9439.$$

$$p = \frac{\exp\left(\frac{6\%}{12}\right) - 0.9439}{1.0594 - 0.9439} = 52.8956\%$$

With the preceding value of p, the volatility approximation is quite accurate. When you compute the actual volatility using the parameters shown here, you get a value of 19.97%, very close to the target value of 20%. Exhibit 15-4 shows the initial 5 steps of the tree relative to an initial stock value of 100.

Exhibit 15-5 shows the probability mass function for the log yields after the 12 steps. The minimum value is -69.3% (corresponding to 12 down steps). The maximum value is $+69.3\%$ (corresponding to 12 up steps). The 6 up-steps value is zero because the up steps are exactly offset by the down steps.

Notice that the curve looks similar to the familiar bell-shaped normal probability density function. This is a direct consequence of two facts: First, the binomial distribution converges to the continuous normal distribution also when $p \neq 0.5$; second, the payoffs that we have associated with the up steps and the down steps are a simple linear transformation of the random variable. Exhibit 15-6 shows the probability mass function for the values of the actual $ outcomes at the end of the 12-step tree. There are a few important things to notice:

- First, the outcomes are never negative. This is a very useful feature; it would make little sense to have a random process where stocks, FX rates, interest rates, and so on, could take negative values.

Exhibit 15-4 First 5 Steps of a 12-Step Recombining CRR Binomial Tree

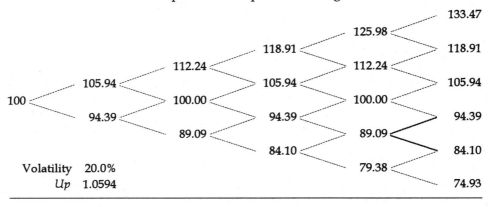

Volatility 20.0%
Up 1.0594

Exhibit 15-5 Probability Mass Function, Steps = 12, sdt = 20%, R = 6%

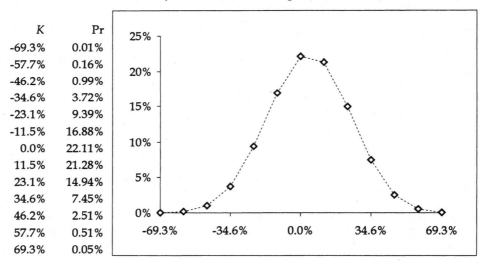

K	Pr
-69.3%	0.01%
-57.7%	0.16%
-46.2%	0.99%
-34.6%	3.72%
-23.1%	9.39%
-11.5%	16.88%
0.0%	22.11%
11.5%	21.28%
23.1%	14.94%
34.6%	7.45%
46.2%	2.51%
57.7%	0.51%
69.3%	0.05%

- Second, the distribution is asymmetric (skewed). Although the short tail is limited by having a minimum value of zero, the long tail can extend to values well in excess of a 100% return. Again, this is a useful feature; in the case of volatile stocks, these returns can certainly be observed (just check the stock price of AOL if you have any doubts).
- Third, the long positive tail means that there are some limitations in the use of this distribution for modeling bond prices. If a bond price rose by 199.93% (the highest outcome in our tree), this would quite probably imply a negative rate of interest. Binomial trees are therefore used to model the stochastic behavior of interest rates, thereby making prices and returns a second level variable (see Chapter 19).
- Fourth, the expected future value is $106.18, which corresponds precisely to our chosen level of drift:

Exhibit 15-6 Probability Mass Function, Steps = 12, std = 20%, R = 6%

FV	Pr	E(FV)
50.02	0.01%	0.01
56.14	0.16%	0.09
63.01	0.99%	0.63
70.72	3.72%	2.63
79.38	9.39%	7.46
89.09	16.88%	15.04
100.00	22.11%	22.11
112.24	21.28%	23.88
125.98	14.94%	18.81
141.40	7.45%	10.54
158.71	2.51%	3.99
178.13	0.51%	0.91
199.93	0.05%	0.10
	100.0%	106.18

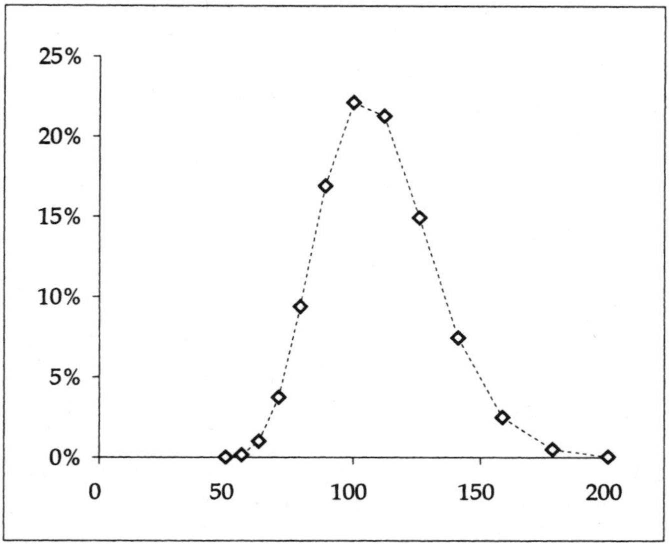

$$\$100 \cdot \exp(6\%) = \$106.18$$

Changing the Number of Steps

A 12-step tree is too coarse for most practical purposes. Increasing the number of steps is quite feasible, but you should note some of the consequences on the parameters of the binomial tree (see Exhibit 15-7).

- The value of u decreases, and the value of p gets closer to 50%; consequently the computed volatility gets even closer to the target value.
- The positive tail grows very fast and becomes quite similar to that of a normal distribution.

Exhibit 15-7 CRR Tree Parameters as a Function of Steps

	12 Steps	52 Steps	260 Steps
Volatility	20%	20%	20%
R	6%	6%	6%
Step drift	0.5000%	0.1154%	0.0231%
Local volatility	5.7735%	2.7735%	1.2403%
Up	1.0594	1.0281	1.0125
Dw	0.9439	0.9726	0.9877
Ln (Up)	5.7735%	2.7735%	1.2403%
Pr	52.8956%	51.3877%	50.6203%
Max $ outcome	199.93	423.01	2,515.11
Min $ outcome	50.02	23.64	3.98

Exhibit 15-8 Probability Mass Function of the $ Outcomes, 24 Steps

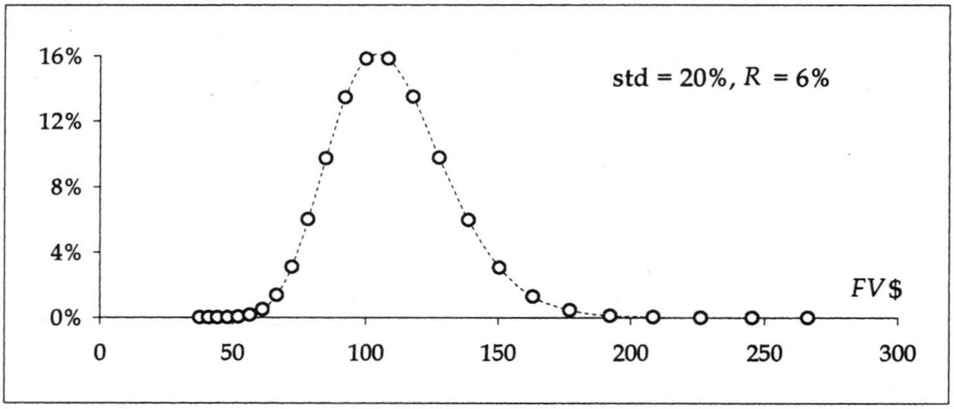

Exhibit 15-8 shows the $-outcome probability mass function for the 24-step case, computed using the same parameters we used for the 12-step case (σ = 20%, drift = 6%). At first sight, the two mass functions appear to be surprisingly different, with the 24-step curve lying well below the 12-step one. The difference, however, is due to the fact that the larger number of possible outcomes means that each outcome is necessarily less probable.

On the other hand, the outcomes are closer to each other, and therefore there are more outcomes spanning a given interval. An intuitive way of measuring this is to compute what percentage of the expected value of the 24-step tree is due to outcomes that are outside the boundaries of the outcomes of the 12-step tree. This value turns out to be quite small: 0.06%. To sum up, increasing the number of steps does not change significantly the probability mass function when the volatility and drift parameters are left unchanged.

15-3 THE SYMMETRIC PROBABILITIES IMPLEMENTATION

With symmetric probabilities we need a new parameter (α) to specify the drift; let us see how.

$$up \rightarrow \exp(\alpha + \sigma \cdot \sqrt{h})$$

$$down \rightarrow \exp(\alpha - \sigma \cdot \sqrt{h})$$

$\sigma \cdot \sqrt{h}$ = local volatility, the parameter α being a constant does not affect variance.

$$\frac{1}{2} \cdot [\exp(\alpha + \sigma\sqrt{h}) + \exp(\alpha - \sigma\sqrt{h})] = \exp(R \cdot h)$$

$$\frac{1}{2} \cdot \exp(\alpha) \cdot [\exp(\sigma\sqrt{h}) + \exp(-\sigma\sqrt{h})] = \exp(R \cdot h)$$

$$\exp(\alpha) = \frac{\exp(R \cdot h)}{\frac{1}{2} \cdot [\exp(\sigma\sqrt{h}) + \exp(-\sigma\sqrt{h})]}$$

Exhibit 15-9 Tree Parameters, with Symmetric Probabilities

	12 Steps	52 Steps	260 Steps
Volatility	20%	20%	20%
R	6%	6%	6%
Step drift	0.5000%	0.1154%	0.0231%
Local volatility	5.7735%	2.7735%	1.2403%
Alpha	0.3334%	0.0769%	0.0154%
Up	1.06297	1.02891	1.01264
Dw	0.94705	0.97339	0.98783
Pr	50%	50%	50%
Max $ outcome	208.10	440.27	2,617.76
Min $ outcome	52.06	24.61	4.14

Exhibit 15-10 Symmetric Probability Implementation

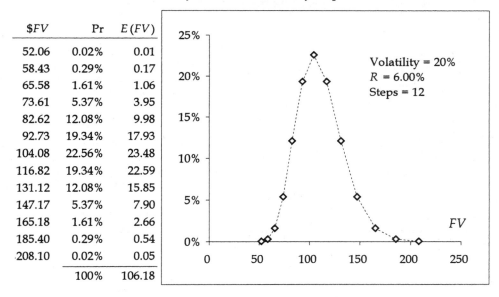

$FV	Pr	E(FV)
52.06	0.02%	0.01
58.43	0.29%	0.17
65.58	1.61%	1.06
73.61	5.37%	3.95
82.62	12.08%	9.98
92.73	19.34%	17.93
104.08	22.56%	23.48
116.82	19.34%	22.59
131.12	12.08%	15.85
147.17	5.37%	7.90
165.18	1.61%	2.66
185.40	0.29%	0.54
208.10	0.02%	0.05
	100%	106.18

Notice that the denominator of the right-hand side of the last equation is the usual concavity correction. For relatively contained levels of local volatility (produced by a tree with an adequate number of steps), we can use the already examined approximation (see Exhibits 15-9 and 15-10).

$$\frac{1}{2} \cdot [\exp(\sigma\sqrt{h}) + \exp(-\sigma\sqrt{h})] \cong \frac{(\sigma\sqrt{h})^2}{2} = \frac{\sigma^2 \cdot h}{2}$$

15-4   RANDOM DRAWINGS FROM A NORMAL DISTRIBUTION

Continuous-time models are mostly based on a stochastic variable that represents a random drawing from a normal probability distribution. Let us see how this works

Exhibit 15-11 Random Drawing from the Standard Normal Distribution

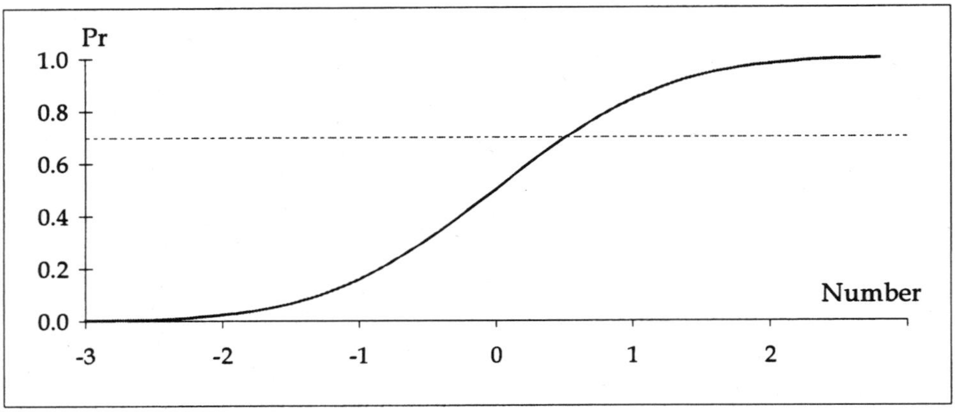

Exhibit 15-12 Random Drawing from the Standard Normal Distribution

Pr	Number	Pr	Number	Pr	Number
0.7789	0.7686	0.7331	0.6222	0.6851	0.4819
0.0752	-1.4382	0.1068	-1.2439	0.5457	0.1147
0.6162	0.2956	0.7192	0.5806	0.1676	-0.9637
0.1370	-1.0937	0.8102	0.8786	0.2645	-0.6295
0.1019	-1.2709	0.1056	-1.2500	0.0235	-1.9869

starting with the standard normal distribution. The problem could appear to be complex but in fact has a rather elegant solution. First, take the cumulative standard distribution. Second, draw a uniformly distributed random number $0 \leq RND < 1$ (see Exhibits 15-11 and 15-12). Third, find what number on the real line has RND as its cumulative probability. This requires finding the inverse function of the cumulative normal distribution; that is,

$$N(\bullet): x \rightarrow \Pr(X \leq x)$$

$$N^{-1}(\bullet): \Pr(X \leq x) \rightarrow x.$$

There is no analytical equation for $N^{-1}(\bullet)$, but the solution can be found with readily available numerical methods. To deal with nonstandard normal distributions, we just multiply the random numbers derived from $N^{-1}(\bullet)$ by the desired level of local volatility, and then we add the required level of local step drift. This process is the reverse of that with which we obtain a Z distribution:

$$Z = \frac{X - E(X)}{\sigma(X)}$$

We can therefore produce the discrete-time approximation of a normal process characterized by

Exhibit 15-13 Binomial and Normal Random Paths

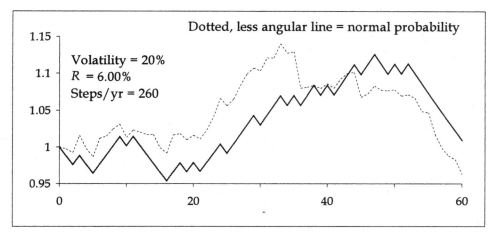

$$\alpha \ = \ drift, \quad \sigma \cdot \sqrt{h} \ = \ local \ volatility.$$

Exhibit 15-13 shows two random paths with daily steps, built with the same drift and volatility and based on the same series of drawings from the uniform distribution $0 \le RND < 1$. One path uses the uniformly distributed random numbers to build a binomial process with symmetric probabilities. The other path uses the random number to draw from the normal distribution.

As you could well expect, the two paths are very much correlated, and the normal distribution implementation differs from the binomial approach because the daily log rates of change can take up a whole variety of values whereas in the binomial approach there is only one possible up value and one down value.

15-5 THE LOGNORMAL DISTRIBUTION

As implied by its name, the lognormal distribution is a probability distribution where the logs of the random variable are normally distributed. Conversely, the normal distribution of a random variable K will generate a lognormal distribution for the random variable $\exp(K)$. The normal distributions that we examined in the previous sections referred to logs of price relatives; therefore S_T/S will be lognormally distributed.

Expected Value of the Lognormal Distribution

The lognormal distribution reflects the following two properties that we examined when we discussed the distribution of price relatives resulting from the binomial distribution of $\ln(S_T/S)$.

1. First, the distribution is asymmetric. S_T/S is always positive, and the right tail stretches out (to infinity in the case of the lognormal density function).
2. Second, the already examined relationship between the log of the expected value and the expected value of the logs holds for the lognormal distribution as well.

$$K \cong \ln\left(\frac{S_T}{S}\right).$$

If K is normally distributed, $K \sim \phi(\mu,\sigma)$, it is possible to prove that

$$\ln\left[E\left(\frac{S_T}{S}\right)\right] = E[K] + \frac{\sigma^2(K)}{2}$$

$$E\left(\frac{S_T}{S}\right) = \exp\left(E(K) + \frac{\sigma^2(K)}{2}\right).$$

Example: Assume that the logs of price relatives are normally distributed as follows:

$$K \sim \phi(\mu = 7\%, \sigma = 20\%)$$

$$E(e^K) = \exp\left[7\% + \frac{(20\%)^2}{2}\right] = \exp(7\% + 2\%) = 1.0942$$

Exhibit 15-14 shows the lognormal density function corresponding to the normal distribution $K \sim \phi(\mu = 7\%, \sigma = 20\%)$. The values tabulated next to the graph show the following:

- The 11 "central" values of K, taken at 1% intervals (e.g., the value $K = 7\%$ refers to the interval $6.5\% \leq K < 7.5\%$)
- The probabilities of K for the 1% intervals
- The corresponding values of $\exp(K)$

If you want the price relatives to have a drift R

$$\mu(K) = R - \frac{\sigma^2(K)}{2}, \text{ where } R \equiv \ln\left[E\left(\frac{FV}{PV}\right)\right].$$

Exhibit 15-14 Lognormal Probabilities for $\exp(K)$

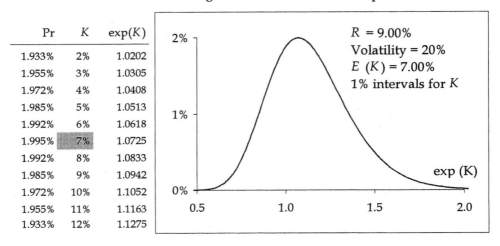

Pr	K	exp(K)
1.933%	2%	1.0202
1.955%	3%	1.0305
1.972%	4%	1.0408
1.985%	5%	1.0513
1.992%	6%	1.0618
1.995%	7%	1.0725
1.992%	8%	1.0833
1.985%	9%	1.0942
1.972%	10%	1.1052
1.955%	11%	1.1163
1.933%	12%	1.1275

R = 9.00%
Volatility = 20%
E (K) = 7.00%
1% intervals for K

Example: You want to use a lognormal distribution to model the future value of a stock (or of a stock index, such as the S&P 500), with an expected return $R = 8\%$ and volatility $\sigma = 20\%$.

$$\mu = \left(8\% - \frac{(20\%)^2}{2}\right) \cdot T = 6\%, \text{ for } T = 1$$

With some algebraic manipulation it is possible to prove that the variance of the outcomes is given by the following equation:

$$\text{var}[\exp(K)] = \exp(2 \cdot \mu + 2 \cdot \sigma^2) - \exp(2 \cdot \mu + \sigma^2).$$

Cumulative Probabilities

Computing the values of the *lognormal cumulative distribution* (to determine the probability of an option expiring out-of-the-money or in-the-money) is a straightforward procedure.

$$\Pr(S_T < X) = \Pr\left[\frac{S_T}{S} < \frac{X}{S}\right].$$

Given the one-to-one mapping between the normal and the lognormal density functions we can write

$$\Pr(S_T < X) = \Pr\left[\ln\left(\frac{S_T}{S}\right) < \ln\left(\frac{X}{S}\right)\right].$$

We can now use the standard normal cumulative distribution function $N(\bullet)$:

$$\Pr(S_T < X) = N\left(\frac{\ln(X/S) - \mu \cdot T}{\sigma \cdot \sqrt{T}}\right).$$

From the preceding equation it follows that

$$\Pr(S_T \geq X) = 1 - N\left(\frac{\ln(X/S) - \mu \cdot T}{\sigma \cdot \sqrt{T}}\right).$$

The symmetry of the standard normal density function entails that we can express the preceding result as

$$\Pr(S_T \geq X) = N\left(-\frac{\ln(X/S) - \mu \cdot T}{\sigma \cdot \sqrt{T}}\right) = N\left(\frac{\ln(S/X) + \mu \cdot T}{\sigma \cdot \sqrt{T}}\right).$$

Example: Compute the lognormal cumulative distribution for $X = 1.6$.

$$K \sim \phi(\mu = 7\%, \sigma = 20\%)$$

$$\Pr(X < 1.6) = N\left(\frac{\ln(1.6) - 7\%}{20\%}\right) = N\left(\frac{47\% - 7\%}{20\%}\right) = N(2) = 97.72\%$$

$$\Pr(X \geq 1.6) = 1 - \Pr(X < 1.6) = N(-2) = 2.275\%$$

Exhibit 15-15 Lognormal Cumulative Distributions of exp(K)

K	Volatility 40%	Volatility 20%
0.80	23.2%	7.1%
0.85	28.1%	12.2%
0.90	33.1%	19.0%
0.95	38.1%	27.2%
1	43.1%	36.3%
1.05	47.9%	45.8%
1.10	52.5%	55.0%
1.15	56.9%	63.6%
1.20	61.1%	71.3%
1.25	64.9%	77.8%
1.30	68.5%	83.2%

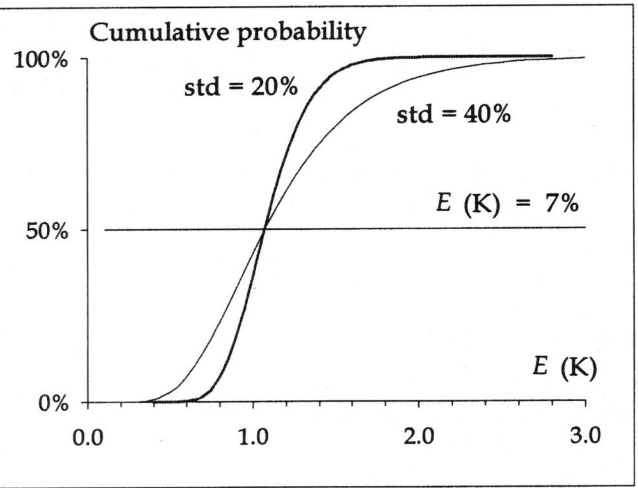

The lognormal cumulative distribution function (CDF) looks somewhat similar to the normal CDF, with the notable exception that the random variable can take only positive values on the real line (see Exhibit 15-15).

Truncated Expected Value of the Lognormal Distribution

The computation of the *truncated expected value*, that is, the expected value corresponding to a portion of the lognormal density function, could be easily carried out with some numerical method. There is, however, an analytical solution. The following equation (which appears also in the Black-Scholes pricing formula) gives the expected value under the right-hand tail of the lognormal density function:

$$E(e^K \mid K \geq X) = \exp\left(\mu(K) + \frac{\sigma^2(K)}{2}\right) \cdot N\left(\frac{\mu(K) + \sigma^2(K) - X}{\sigma(K)}\right).$$

As usual, $N(\bullet)$ represents the operator for the standard normal cumulative distribution function. Indicating with d_1 the value for which we compute $N(\bullet)$, and recalling that

$$E\left(\frac{FV}{PV}\right) = \exp(R) = \exp\left(E(K) + \frac{\sigma^2(K)}{2}\right),$$

we can write the equation as

$$E(e^K \mid K \geq X) = \exp(R) \cdot N(d_1) \equiv E\left(\frac{S_T}{S}\right) \cdot N(d_1).$$

The symbol d_1 is traditionally used because it is commonly adopted in the Black-Scholes equation. From an intuitive point of view, the truncated expected value equals the expected value of the entire distribution exp(R), multiplied by a scaling factor $N(d_1)$.

Exhibit 15-16 Truncated Expected Value of the Lognormal Distribution

fv	E (•) right
0.40	1.0942
0.60	1.0931
0.80	1.0418
1	0.7756
1.20	0.3926
1.40	0.1409
1.60	0.0393
1.80	0.0092
2.00	0.0019

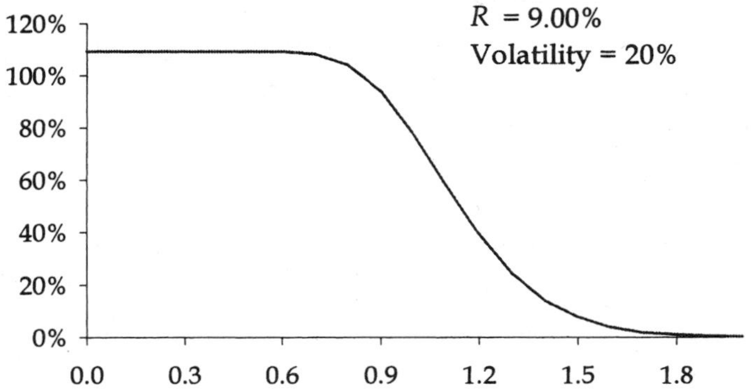

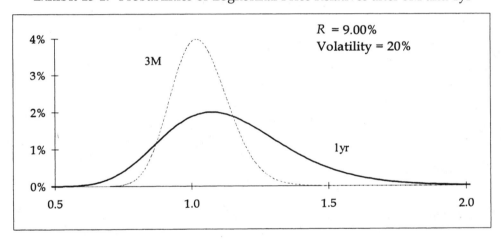

Exhibit 15-17 Probabilities of Lognormal Price Relatives after 3M and 1yr

You can easily check that the scaling factor decreases when X increases, which fits with the intuitive observation that the expected value under the right-hand tail decreases (with limit 0) with the increase of FV/PV. Conversely, the expected value under the left-hand tail increases toward $\exp(R)$. The expected value of the lognormal density function equals $\exp(9\%) = 1.0942$. We can see from the numbers that there is practically no expected value for $X < 0.4$ and for $X > 2$ (see Exhibits 15-16 and 15-17).

15-6 TUNING THE PROBABILITY STRUCTURE OF A CRR BINOMIAL TREE

Take the following CRR binomial step:

$$u = \exp(\lambda)$$

$$\frac{1}{u} = \exp(-\lambda)$$

Exhibit 15-18 Local Volatility in a CRR Tree as a Function of Pr (*Up*)

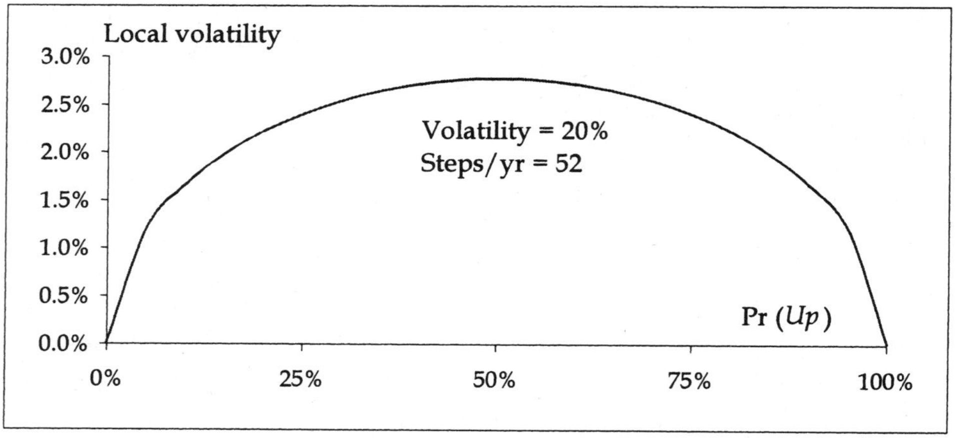

Local volatility

Volatility = 20%
Steps/yr = 52

Pr (*Up*)

$$\text{max (local volatility): } \sigma \cdot \sqrt{h} = \lambda, \text{ for } p = 50\%$$

As p approaches either zero or 100%, volatility falls to zero because the random process degenerates into a deterministic process with one certain outcome, either $\exp(\lambda)$ or $\exp(-\lambda)$ (see Exhibit 15-18). If you define $\{u, d, p\}$ using the CRR equations, you could be using the wrong volatility when the value of p diverges significantly from 50%. If the required σ is low and the target drift is high, the level of p could turn out to be greater than 100%, and this is an obviously absurd result. An example of this problem can be found in Hull (1995), where he points out that for a 10-step tree, a 12% drift coupled with a 1% target σ would require $p = 2.39\%$. After pointing out this problem, Hull suggests an ingenious but irrelevant way to avoid it by using options on futures.

The first straightforward way out of the problem is to use the symmetric probabilities implementation.

If you need a $d = 1/u$ tree, then you can increase the number of steps, and this will cause p to move toward 50%, thereby solving the problem, as shown in Exhibit 15-19. If you need to use a $d = 1/u$ tree, without a very large number of steps and with totally accurate local volatility, it is possible to adjust the parameters to achieve the desired result. The procedure for adjusting p to keep the tree volatility equal to the target level of σ is quite straightforward. First, compute $u, d = 1/u$ in such a way that the step variance will remain unchanged when p diverges from 50%. Using the expected value equation for variance we can write

Exhibit 15-19 CRR Local Volatility and Number of Steps

Steps	Up	Pr(*Up*)	ln(*Up*)	Local vol. realization	Volatility realization
10	1.0159	0.8138	1.5811%	1.2309%	3.8923%
52	1.0070	0.6371	0.6934%	0.6668%	4.8084%
260	1.0031	0.5613	0.3101%	0.3078%	4.9623%

Target Volatility = 5%, R = 8.00%

$$p[\ln(u)]^2 + (1 - p)[-\ln(u)]^2 - [p \cdot \ln(u) - (1 - p) \cdot \ln(u)]^2 = \sigma^2 \cdot \sqrt{\Delta T}$$

$$[\ln(u)]^2 - [2p \cdot \ln(u) - \ln(u)]^2 = \sigma^2 \sqrt{\Delta T}$$

$$4p[\ln(u)]^2 - 4p^2[\ln(u)]^2 = \sigma^2 \sqrt{\Delta T}$$

$$[\ln(u)]^2 = \sigma^2 \sqrt{\Delta T} \, \frac{1}{4p - 4p^2} \Rightarrow u = \exp\left[\sqrt{\frac{\sigma^2 \sqrt{\Delta T}}{4p - 4p^2}}\right].$$

Second, compute the numerical solution of the following equation in p.

$$\ln[p \cdot u + (1 - p)/u] = R \cdot \Delta T$$

Chapter *16*

Binomial Option Pricing: An Introduction

We shall now draw on some of the results obtained in Chapter 15 to examine the binomial option pricing model (BOPM). This will allow us to better understand the well-known Black-Scholes analysis. Under certain not very restrictive assumptions the two models converge and therefore produce the same option price.

The arbitrage-free approach to option pricing was first developed by Fisher Black, Myron Scholes, and Robert Merton and was formalized within the framework of continuous-time finance, adopting the lognormal distribution of stock prices and using the complex mathematical tools of stochastic calculus (both Black and Merton started their academic careers as mathematician-physicists). The simpler-to-understand BOPM was developed a few years later by Sharpe (1976)—another Nobel laureate— and by Cox, Ross, and Rubinstein (1978). The binomial approach is the most straight-forward way to introduce the concepts of risk-neutral pricing and risk-neutralized probabilities (*Martingale probabilities*).

The importance of the BOPM is not purely didactic, however. In fact, the model is very flexible and can be extended in ways that allow pricing and hedging options that are not amenable to the Black-Scholes equation or other closed-form models. The binomial model is also crucially important to an understanding of how options can be replicated (synthetic options) or dynamically hedged. The discrete-time binomial approach is also widely used in pricing options on interest rates.

16-1   ARBITRAGE-FREE OPTION PRICING AND MODELS OF STOCK PRICES

Take the ¥/$ rate. It is an easily observable price; you can stare at its real-time movements on a Bloomberg or Reuters screen. That price is determined by the complex interaction of a multitude of economic agents. Some will think that the current rate is about right. Some will think the ¥ is overpriced and there is money to be made in shorting it. Others will believe is underpriced and that money can be made by holding a long JPY position. Still others don't want to run foreign exchange (FX) risk and will buy or sell currency to cover their trading or investment positions.

Exhibit 16-1 Options and Hedges

Option	Hedge
Short call (call writer)	Long in underlying asset
Long call (call buyer)	Short in underlying asset
Short put (put writer)	Short in underlying asset
Long put (put buyer)	Long in underlying asset

All these different opinions will be formed in a number of different ways—simple seat-of-the-pants hunches; sophisticated FX econometric models; or continuous contact with the market if you work for a market maker. What you will end up doing also depends on the level of risk you can tolerate. And then there is the problem of the different exposures to FX risk. If you have to meet a future ¥ payment, then holding ¥ hedges FX risk. If you will receive JPY payments, then selling the ¥ short will hedge your risk.

Now take the 3M forward ¥/$. The forward rate is determined only by the spot rate and by the riskless money market rates on the $ and the ¥ over the term of the forward. If the covered interest parity were violated, it would be possible to construct a riskless synthetic asset that would yield more than the riskless rate (either in $ or in ¥, at your choice) and therefore would immediately attract market-equilibrating arbitrage. Market participants' views on the ¥/$ rate and on its volatility *do not affect the pricing of the forward relative to the spot.*

The same situation holds for interest rate products (or for equities or stock market indexes for that). Take an intermediate- or long-term bond. If you hedge by selling it forward (or by shorting the relevant exchange-traded future contract), you will be earning the risk-free rate over the term of the forward. An interesting point is that the rate you get by buying and selling forward is completely independent from the maturity of the bond, and therefore from its duration and level of price volatility. If the market recognizes a risk premium on longer bonds, this risk-premium certainly does not affect the return on the synthetic riskless asset.

The big breakthrough in options pricing came from the realization that under certain conditions it is possible to create a synthetic riskless asset (*replicating portfolio*) by combining a long (short) position in an asset—such as a stock—and a short (long) position in the option. This replicating portfolio must yield the riskless rate, and this provides a straightforward answer to the problem of pricing an option given the price of the underlying asset, thereby sidestepping the complications related to risk aversion (risk premia) and to the huge volatility of options prices (see Exhibit 16-1).

The payoff of an option is not a linear function of the price of the underlying asset, and this makes things a lot more complicated than in the simple hedging of a forward contract. You cannot adopt a simple hedge-and-forget strategy. Assume you have written a call on 1,000 Disney shares, strike price $105. You could fully cover the short option by buying 1,000 Disney shares, but this would expose you to the possibility of loss if the share price declines. You are hedged against an up movement but not against a down movement.

To construct the riskless replicating portfolio you must take into account not only the price of the underlying asset but also the volatility of this price, measured with reference to log rates as seen in Chapter 15. Furthermore, the hedge must be *rebalanced*

Exhibit 16-2 Expected Return at Time-0

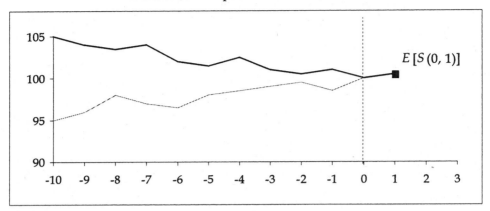

to take into account changes in the market (the most relevant of which is the market price of the underlying asset).

Market Efficiency and Models of Stock Prices

Market efficiency and the random character of stock prices have attracted an impressive amount of high-caliber research given their obvious importance in finance. We shall succinctly cover only a few issues that are directly related to the assumptions underlying the BOPM. For more complete coverage of these issues, see Brealey and Mayers (1996); Sharpe, Alexander, and Bailey (1995); Bodie and Merton (1998); and Chance (1998).

A market is efficient, relative to a given set of information, if it is impossible to make abnormal profits by using this set of information to formulate trading or investing strategies. This in turn implies that the information is fully and immediately reflected in market prices. A widely referred to classification, based on the identification of different information sets, runs as follows:

- *Weak-form efficiency.* Prices at time-0 fully reflect the information contained in the price history up to time-0.
- *Semistrong efficiency.* Prices at time-0 fully reflect all the publicly available information at time-0.
- *Strong-form efficiency.* Prices at time-0 fully reflect all relevant information, both private and publicly available, at time-0.

Most finance professionals (market participants and academics) believe, on the basis of a wide body of empirical evidence, that reasonably liquid and transparent markets are at least weak-form efficient. Price data are readily available in computer-readable format, and abnormal profits are almost impossible to attain by trading on the basis of price history. In turn, this means that if two stocks with comparable levels of riskiness have the same price at a given time T_0, their expected return over a small time interval $T_0 \to T_0 + h$ will be the same irrespective of the price history before T_0 (see Exhibit 16-2).

$$P_A = P_B \Rightarrow E(S_A | T_0 \rightarrow T_0 + h) = E(S_B | T_0 \rightarrow T_0 + h)$$

16-2 THE ONE-STEP BINOMIAL MODEL AND ARBITRAGE-FREE PRICING

Let us start with a one-step binomial tree. This model is so simplified that it cannot be used in the real world. However, like many other elementary models in economics and finance, it will cast some light on important concepts that lie at the foundation of complex applications. You will see that it is possible to get a lot of mileage out of this very simple case. The initial use of a one-step binomial tree is justified by the fact that we can extend the results to a realistic multistep model with a process of backward induction.

One-Step Binomial Tree for a European Call

Consider a European call, expiring in 1 week, on a non-dividend-paying stock. A one-step binomial model therefore implies that we have 52 steps per year. The stock price at time-0 is assumed to be \$100. To simplify notation, we shall often use S whenever this does not generate ambiguity. Let us further assume that, in 1 week's time, the stock will necessarily assume one of the two following values:

$$S_U = \text{Price up}, \ S_D = \text{Price down}$$

$$\ln\left(\frac{S_U}{S_0}\right) > (R \cdot h) > \ln\left(\frac{S_D}{S_0}\right)$$

The preceding inequality expresses a first, somewhat obvious arbitrage-free condition.

- The stock return in the up case must be higher than the riskless yield; otherwise T-bills would dominate the stock, producing a higher return irrespective of the stock performance.
- Conversely, the stock return in the down case must be lower than the riskless rate, otherwise the stock investment would dominate T-bills.

The two possible outcomes for the stock fully determine two values for the call at maturity:

$$C_U = \max[0, S_U - X] = \text{expiry value of the call in the up case}$$

$$C_D = \max[0, S_D - X] = \text{expiry value of the call in the down case}$$

$$S_U > X \Rightarrow C_U > 0$$

$$S_D < X \Rightarrow C_D = 0$$

If the preceding inequalities do not hold, we get the following solutions.

- If $S_U \le X$, the option is bound to expire out-of-the-money; it is therefore worthless and does not need to be hedged.
- If $S_D \ge X$, the option is bound to expire in-the-money and must be hedged with a 1:1 position in the underlying stock.

Exhibit 16-3 One-Step Binomial Tree, Baseline Case

			2.0201	Max(0, S-X)
StepStd	2.00%		102.0201	Su
X	100.00			
S	100.00			
			0	Max(0, S-X)
			98.0199	Sd

We shall now use the Cox, Ross, and Rubenstein (CRR) approach to building the binomial tree.

$$u = \exp(\sigma \cdot \sqrt{h}), \, d = \frac{1}{u} = \exp(-\sigma \cdot \sqrt{h}).$$

We know that the ex-post realized volatility will not coincide with the input volatility whenever Pr(up) $\neq$ 50%. Given a 2% step-std, the volatility error is very small for realistic values of yearly drift. For the moment we shall not specify Pr(up). This implies that we do not specify the expected values of the stock and the call option (see Exhibit 16-3).

Hedge ratio (Δ)

We can now find the quantity of stock (usually indicated with capital delta, Δ) that is needed to hedge one call. Delta will of course be positive if we want to hedge an option we have written, and negative (short position in the stock) if we are hedging an option we have bought. Finding the value of Δ means that we can construct a portfolio (say 0.505 units of stock for each call) that will have the same future value irrespective of whether the stock price goes up or down.

Computing Δ is rather straightforward; we must simply solve one equation with one unknown. What makes this possible is the assumption that we can predict with certainty the values of the two possible outcomes of holding the stock; hence we know the up and down values of the call. If the stochastic process followed by the stock price will not coincide with $\{S_U, S_D\}$, the hedge will not work accurately, and the replicating portfolio will generate either a gain or a loss.

Box 16-1   Hedging a short call option

$\Delta \cdot S_U - C_U = \Delta \cdot S_D - C_D$

given $S_U > X \Rightarrow C_U > 0$ and $S_D < X \Rightarrow C_D = 0$

$$\Delta = \frac{C_U - C_D}{S_U - S_D} = \frac{(S_U - X) - 0}{S_U - S_D}$$

Delta is commonly known as *hedge ratio* because it represents the ratio (*stocks/options*) that will result in a hedged portfolio. Note that Δ equals the ratio of the change in the option price as a function of a small change in the underlying stock price. When we use a continuous-time model, Δ is the partial derivative of the option price as a function of the asset price.

$$\Delta = \partial C / \partial S$$

This interpretation of Δ is straightforward. If a \$1 change in the stock price entails, say, a \$0.505 change in the option price, then it is sufficient to hold \$ 0.505 in stock to hedge one short call option (the \$0.505 gain on the stock will offset the \$0.505 loss on the short option).

Arbitrage-Free Option Pricing

Take the case in which you want to hedge a call option you have written. It is clear that the *long-stock* and *short-option* portfolio will always have an expected present value that is lower than the amount invested to buy the stock:

$$\Delta \cdot S_D < \Delta \cdot S_0$$

$$\Delta \cdot S_U - C_U = \Delta \cdot S_D$$

This loss on the hedged portfolio is the key to arbitrage-free pricing of the option. The call price must be such that the revenue from its sale offsets the loss on the portfolio (see Exhibit 16-4).

$$C_0 = \Delta \cdot S_0 - \frac{\Delta \cdot S_D}{\exp(R \cdot h)} = \Delta \cdot S_0 - \frac{\Delta \cdot S_U - C_U}{\exp(R \cdot h)} = \text{price of a call}$$

Assume a frictionless world where you can borrow at the riskless rate the amount necessary to finance the cost of your replicating portfolio (net of the revenue from the option's sale). The preceding equation can be rearranged to show that the portfolio payout will provide exactly the amount you need to reinbourse your borrowing. We therefore have a *self-financing*, no-arbitrage strategy (see Exhibit 16-5).

$$(\Delta \cdot S_0 - C_0) \cdot \exp(R \cdot h) = \Delta \cdot S_U - C_U = \Delta \cdot S_D$$

A higher level of Δ implies a higher option premium. The loss on the long stock and short option position, which must be compensated by the option premium, equals

$$C_0 = \Delta \cdot [S_0 - S_D \cdot \exp(-R \cdot h)]$$

All other parameters being equal, a higher value of S_0/X implies a higher call price because the higher S_0, the larger the call payoff in the up case:

Exhibit 16-4 Pricing a Call, One Step Binomial Tree

StepStd	2%		2.0201	Max(0, S-X)
R	5.20%		102.0201	Su
X	100			
S	100.00			
Δ	50.50%		0	Max(0, S-X)
C	1.0494		98.0199	Sd

Exhibit 16-5 Pricing a Call Option

	Su	Sd
Borrowed amount	$49.4505	$49.4505
Amount due	-$49.5000	-$49.5000
Long delta stock	$51.5202	$49.5000
Short one call	-$2.0201	$0
Total	$0	$0

Exhibit 16-6 Examples of Call Pricing

StepStd	2%	2.02	Max(0, S-X)	Baseline case
R	5.20%	102.02	Su	At-the-money, $S = X$
X	100			
S	100.00			
Delta	50.50%	0	Max(0, S-X)	
C	1.0494	98.02	Sd	

StepStd	2%	1.52	Max(0, S-X)	Higher Strike price $S < X$
R	5.20%	102.02	Su	Out-of-the-money call
X	100.5			Lower delta
S	100.00			Lower call price
Delta	38.00%	0	Max(0, S-X)	
C	0.7897	98.02	Sd	

StepStd	4%	4.08	Max(0, S-X)	At-the-money, $S = X$
R	5.20%	104.08	Su	Higher volatility
X	100			Higher delta
S	100.00			Higher call price
Delta	51.00%	0	Max(0, S-X)	
C	2.0487	96.08	Sd	

StepStd	2%	2.02	Max(0, S-X)	At-the-money, $S = X$
R	5.20%	102.02	Su	Higher riskless rate
X	100			Higher call price
S	100.00			
Delta	50.50%	0	Max(0, S-X)	
C	1.0494	98.02	Sd	

Exhibit 16-7 Pricing a Call Using Risk-Neutral Probabilities

StepStd	2%			2.0201	Max(0, S-X)
R	5.20%			102.0201	Su
X	100				
S	100.00				
Delta	50.500%			0	Max(0, S-X)
C	1.0494			98.0199	Sd
	Su	Sd	PV [E (*)]		
Pr	52.0011%	47.9989%			
Stock	102.0201	98.0199	100.0000		
C	2.0201	0	1.0494		

$$\Delta = \frac{C_U - C_D}{S_U - S_D} = \frac{S_0 \cdot u - X}{S_0 \cdot u - S_0/u}$$

A higher level of volatility implies a higher option value (S_U is a direct function of volatility). Exhibit 16-6 gives some numerical examples of how the call option price is related to the relevant parameters.

16-3   RISK-NEUTRAL PRICING

We have seen that our hedged portfolio allows us to determine arbitrage-free pricing of the call without reference to the probabilities of the possible outcomes, and therefore without explicit reference to the expected value of the call. This result appears to contrast with the fact that the price of the call should be related to its expected value. Certainly a call should be worth more when it stands a better chance of ending in-the-money. This contradiction is only apparent, however. The probabilities are in fact embedded in the relationship between the stock price and the possible outcomes.

$$S_0 = \frac{Pr(up) \cdot S_U + [1 - Pr(up)] \cdot S_D}{\exp(R \cdot h)}$$

If we use the preceding probabilities, we find that the arbitrage-free price coincides precisely with the expected value of the call (for the mathematical derivation of this equation, see Box 16-2).

$$C_0 = \frac{Pr(up) \cdot C_U + [1 - Pr(up)] \cdot C_D}{\exp(R \cdot h)} = \Delta - \frac{\Delta \cdot S_U - C_U}{\exp(R \cdot h)} = \Delta - \frac{\Delta \cdot S_D - C_D}{\exp(R \cdot h)}$$

The probabilities that we have used are risk-neutral probabilities (martingale probabilities), that is, probabilities that price an asset or a derivative based exclusively on its expected value (discounted at the riskless rate R) without any risk premium (see Exhibit 16-7). In finance it is commonly assumed that assets are priced incorporating some sort of risk premium in the form of a tradeoff between return and risk (such as requiring 100 basis points of extra return, from 6% to 7%, to take on an extra 4% of risk from 11% to 15% standard deviation). This risk-return tradeoff is also fully incorporated in formalized asset-management models where the tradeoff parameter (risk-aversion coefficient) is a control variable utilized by asset managers. The use of risk-neutral probabilities is not in contrast with the commonly held assumptions about risk aversion.

Box 16-2   Expected Value and Arbitrage-free Pricing

Set $S_0 = 1$ and indicate $\Pr(up)$ with p.

$$S_0 = 1 = \frac{p \cdot S_U + (1 - p) \cdot S_D}{\exp(R \cdot h)}$$

$$p \cdot S_U + (1 - p) \cdot S_D = \exp(R \cdot h)$$

$$p = \frac{\exp(R \cdot h) - S_D}{S_U - S_D}$$

The arbitrage-free value of the call derived using the hedge ratio is:

$$C_0 = \Delta - \frac{\Delta \cdot S_U - C_U}{\exp(R \cdot h)} = \Delta - \frac{\Delta \cdot S_D - C_D}{\exp(R \cdot h)}$$

Using the right-hand side of the above equation we can write

$$C_0 = \frac{\Delta \cdot \exp(R \cdot h) - \Delta \cdot S_D + C_D}{\exp(R \cdot h)}.$$

Substituting to its value

$$C_0 = \frac{\dfrac{C_U - C_D}{S_U - S_D} \cdot [\exp(R \cdot h) - S_D] + C_D}{\exp(R \cdot h)}$$

$$C_0 = \frac{p \cdot (C_U - C_D) + C_D}{\exp(R \cdot h)} = \frac{p \cdot C_U + (1 - p) + C_D}{\exp(R \cdot h)}$$

Volatility, Option Value, and Hedge Effectiveness

With forward contracts one can implement fail-safe hedge-and-forget strategies; this cannot be done with options. The option premium is directly related to the level of volatility—in fact, being long (short) an option is known as being long (short) volatility. Therefore, if the volatility outcome turns out to be higher than that used to price the option, the hedge will not function accurately and you will register a loss, if the stock goes either up or down. If the volatility outcome turns out to be lower than expected, the hedged portfolio will generate a gain irrespective of the stock price outcome (see Exhibit 16-8).

16-4   EUROPEAN PUT OPTIONS

The price of a European put can be determined with three different approaches, all of which yield the same result.

Exhibit 16-8 Misjudging Volatility

					103.0455	Su
			Higher		3.0455	Call-up
			realized		48.9925	Outcome
			volatility		(0.5075)	Loss
			StepStd =			
				3.00%	97.0446	Sd
S	100				0	Call-down
X	100				49.0075	Outcome
StepStd	2.00%				(0.4925)	Loss
Su	102.0201					
Sd	98.0199					
Delta	50.50%					
R	5.20%					
Call	1.0494				101.0050	Su
FV of hedge cost	49.5000				1.0050	Call-up
					50.0025	Outcome
			Lower		0.5025	Gain
			realized			
			volatility		99.0050	Sd
			StepStd =		0	Call-down
				1.00%	49.9975	Outcome
					0.4975	Gain

1. Arbitrage-free binomial model
2. Expected value with martingale probabilities
3. Put-call parity

With the arbitrage-free approach we must build a portfolio composed by a short stock position to hedge a short put (delta is therefore negative). The two possible values for the stock fully determine two values for the put at maturity:

$$P_U = \max[0, X - S_U] = \text{expiry value of the put in the up case}$$

$$S_U > X \Rightarrow P_U = 0$$

$$P_D = \max[0, X - S_D] = \text{expiry value of the put in the down case}$$

$$S_D < X \Rightarrow P_D > 0$$

$$\Delta \cdot S_U - P_U = \Delta \cdot S_D - P_D$$

$$\Delta = \frac{P_U - P_D}{S_U - S_D} = \frac{-P_D}{S_U - S_D}, \{-1 < \Delta < 0\}$$

Delta is therefore negative, as expected, and its value falls in the {−1 to 0} interval.

Hedging a short put option implies that you have an initial revenue from the short sale of $\Delta \cdot S_0$ stock. You also have a revenue corresponding to the premium on the put option.

- If the outcome is stock *up*, you will have to buy stock to cover your short while the put option expires out-of-the-money.
- If the outcome is stock *down*, the option will expire in-the-money, and you will have to buy, at the striking price X, one share of stock for each put option you have written. You will then cover your short with delta stock and sell the remainder at the market price $S_D < X$.

The arbitrage-free option price must be such that the initial revenue, invested at the risk-free rate, yields a future value that will cover the cost at maturity.

Box 16-3   Three-way Pricing a Put Option (see Exhibit 16-9)

$-\Delta \cdot S_0 + P_0 =$ initial revenue when you write the delta-hedged put

$-\Delta \cdot S_U =$ negative revenue (cost) at maturity $-$ stock *up*

$X - (1 - \Delta) \cdot S_D = \Delta \cdot S_D + P_D =$ cost at maturity—stock *down*

$P_0 = \dfrac{-\Delta \cdot S_U}{\exp(R \cdot h)} + \Delta \cdot S_0 = \dfrac{\Delta \cdot S_D + P_D}{\exp(R \cdot h)} + \Delta \cdot S_0 =$ arbitrage-free

$P_0 = \dfrac{\Pr(up) \cdot P_U + [1 - \Pr(up)] \cdot P_D}{\exp(R \cdot h)} =$ discounted expected value

$P_0 = X \cdot \exp(-R \cdot h) - S_0 + C_0 =$ put-call parity

---

Alternative Formulation of the One-Step Binomial Model

There is a slightly different way of formulating the one-step BOPM equations that yields exactly the same results (both delta and option price) as the one that we examined earlier in this chapter. You are likely to come across this formulation in other publications or business documents, and therefore it is a good idea to examine it. We shall restrict ourselves, however, to the call option case. This is sufficient to identify the differences between the approaches without belaboring the point.

We defined an arbitrage-free strategy as one that would yield the risk-free rate on a risk-free investment. An arbitrage-free trade can also be defined as a riskless trade that requires no initial investment and will yield a zero net payoff (self-financing no-arbitrage strategy). To be generally applicable, this definition implies a frictionless market where you can borrow and lend at the same riskless rate.

Let us define our replicating portfolio in a way that is consistent with self-financing no-arbitrage strategy. This implies borrowing money at the risk-free rate by issuing a bill to finance the {long stock + short call} portfolio. The net payoff, after reimbursing the bill, must be zero.

$B =$ bills issued, in \$, for each option sold

$$\Delta \cdot S_U - C_U - B \cdot \exp(R \cdot h) = 0$$

$$\Delta \cdot S_D - C_D - B \cdot \exp(R \cdot h) = 0$$

Subtract the second equation from the first to find delta:

Exhibit 16-9 Pricing a European Put: Three Approaches

StepStd	2.00%		0.0000	Max(0, X-S)
R	5.20%		102.0201	Su
X	100			
S	100.00			
Delta	-49.500%		1.9801	Max(0, X-S)
Put	0.9495		98.0199	Sd

	Up	Dw	PV [E (*)]	Risk neutral
Pr	52.0011%	47.9989%		
Stock	102.0201	102.0201	101.9182	
Put	0	1.9801	0.9495	

	PV (X)	99.9000	Put call parity
	Minus S	-100.0000	
	Call	1.0494	
	Put	0.9494	

$$\Delta = \frac{C_U - C_D}{S_U - S_D}$$

Substitute the value of delta in one of the two equations to find B and the call's price.

Chapter *17*

Extending the Binomial Model

17-1 MULTISTEP MODELS

Consider a two-step tree, built using the Cox, Ross, and Rubenstein (CRR) method. The length of each step continues to be 1 week. After two steps, we obtain three possible outcomes (see Exhibit 17-1), where the call's intrinsic value (tangible value) is indicated above the stock prices. One of the three possible values of S_T coincides with S_0. This adds a first element of realism to the model; over the 2-week time horizon, prices do not necessarily move up or down; they can as well remain unchanged (*move sideways* in Wall Street parlance).

To price a 2-week call, we must start at the end of the tree and move backward, one step at a time, to apply the equations that we have examined in the one-step-tree case. At 1 week from maturity we will be in one of the two possible nodes (**A** and **B**):

• If we reach **B**, the option is bound to expire worthless; therefore it must not be hedged and its price is zero.

• If we reach the **A** node, we can apply the same procedure we used for the one-step binomial model to determine both the hedge ratio and the arbitrage-free option price. The fair value of the option is slightly higher than its intrinsic value; this is coherent with the positive time value of call options on non-dividend-paying stock.

At this point we can move back to the origin and determine both Δ_0 and C_0, again using the one-step model equations. The only necessary adjustment is that of using the fair value of the option at nodes **A** and **B** instead of its intrinsic value. The option's value is greater than that obtained with a 1-week model; again, this is coherent with the time-value paradigm—other things being equal, a 2-week call option on a non-dividend-paying stock is worth more than a 1-week option.

Not surprisingly, we can determine the option price using risk-neutral probabilities, getting the same result of arbitrage-free pricing. Exhibit 17-2 provides a self-explanatory numerical example. The two-step model shows clearly that the replicating

Exhibit 17-1 Two-Step Arbitrage-Free Pricing of a Call

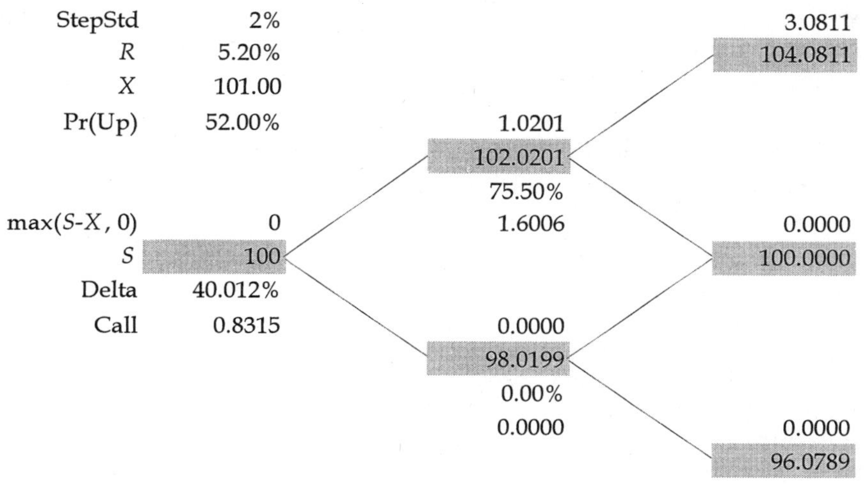

StepStd	2%		3.0811
R	5.20%		104.0811
X	101.00		
Pr(Up)	52.00%	1.0201	
		102.0201	
		75.50%	
max(S-X, 0)	0	1.6006	0.0000
S	100		100.0000
Delta	40.012%		
Call	0.8315	0.0000	
		98.0199	
		0.00%	
		0.0000	0.0000
			96.0789

Exhibit 17-2 Risk-Neutral Pricing of a Call

	Up-Up	Up-Dw	Dw-Dw	E (*)	PV[E (*)]
Prob	0.2704	1.0400	1.0000	.....	.....
S (T)	104.0811	100.0000	96.0789	228.2259	227.7699
C (T)	3.0811	0	0.0000	0.8332	0.8315

portfolio must be rebalanced at each node (*dynamic hedging*); we cannot adopt the simple hedge-and-forget strategies that work with forwards. We shall therefore have one hedging pattern for each of the possible paths taken by the stock price. Irrespective of such patterns, the final value of the portfolio will always equal the *FV*, at the riskless rate *R*, of the cash outlays needed to implement the dynamic hedge (see Exhibit 17-3).

$$\text{Initial outlay} = \Delta_0 \cdot S_0 - C_0; \text{ second outlay} = (\Delta_h - \Delta_0) \cdot S_h$$

Exhibit 17-3 Hedging Dynamics for a Call

Path	Initial outlay	Second outlay	FV of outlays	Payback at mty	Stock at mty	Call at mty
{u, u}	39.1807	36.2013	75.4967	75.4967	78.5777	3.0811
{u, d}	39.1807	36.2013	75.4967	75.4967	75.4967	0
{d, u}	39.1807	-39.2199	0.0000	0	0	0
{d, d}	39.1807	-39.2199	0.0000	0	0	0

Multistep Binomial Tree to Price a Call

Exhibit 17-4 shows a four-step tree to price a 4-week call. You can see that the arbitrage-free approach and the risk-neutral pricing with martingale probabilities lead exactly to the same result, $C_0 = 1.7040$. At each node the fair value of the call will be as follows:

- Zero, when the option is bound to expire worthless
- Greater than the intrinsic value when the option has a chance of expiring in-the-money; this is again coherent with the time-value paradigm.

Note that weekly steps can be somewhat adequate to price an option that expires in 3 months or more (the 13 or more weekly steps will yield a reasonable probability mass function for the log-rates). Weekly steps are far too coarse, however, to manage an options position that requires dynamic hedging to rebalance the replicating portfolio (rebalancing can be needed once a day, and sometimes more often than that).

Because of the risk-neutral approach, you do not need to build the whole binomial tree just to price a plain-vanilla call on a non-dividend-paying stock (or a zero coupon bond). You can in fact simplify the procedure by computing the expected value of the call at maturity using the following equation, which is a straightforward application of the results examined in the last three chapters.

$$C = \exp(-R \cdot h) \cdot \sum_{U=0}^{N} b(U, N, p) \cdot \max[0, \exp(\sigma \cdot \sqrt{h}) \cdot (2U - N) - X]$$

U = number of successes, price-up, in N binomial steps
$b(U, N, p)$ = probability of obtaining U price-up changes

European Puts

European puts can be priced using one of the three possible methods that we have examined for the one-step binomial tree: arbitrage-free replicating portfolio, put-call parity, and risk-neutral pricing (see Exhibit 17-5). A plain-vanilla European put on a non-dividend-paying asset can be priced with the following equation (see Exhibit 17-6):

$$C = \exp(-R \cdot h) \cdot \sum_{U=0}^{N} b(U, N, p) \cdot \max[0, X - \exp(\sigma \cdot \sqrt{h}) \cdot (2U - N)]$$

17-2   EARLY EXERCISE OF AMERICAN PUTS

We have already seen, in Chapter 12, that the time value of a put is not necessarily positive. This entails that under certain conditions, the early exercise of an American put is indeed optimal. Let us see how this works by considering the last step of a binomial tree, at a node that will result in the final value of the stock being lower than the exercise price in the up case as well as in the down case (see Exhibit 17-7). The put is therefore guaranteed to expire in-the-money:

$$S(T - h) \cdot \exp(\sigma - \sqrt{h}) < X$$

The intrinsic value at the node is higher than the risk-neutral price (which is indicated

Exhibit 17-4 Pricing a Call with a Four-Step Tree

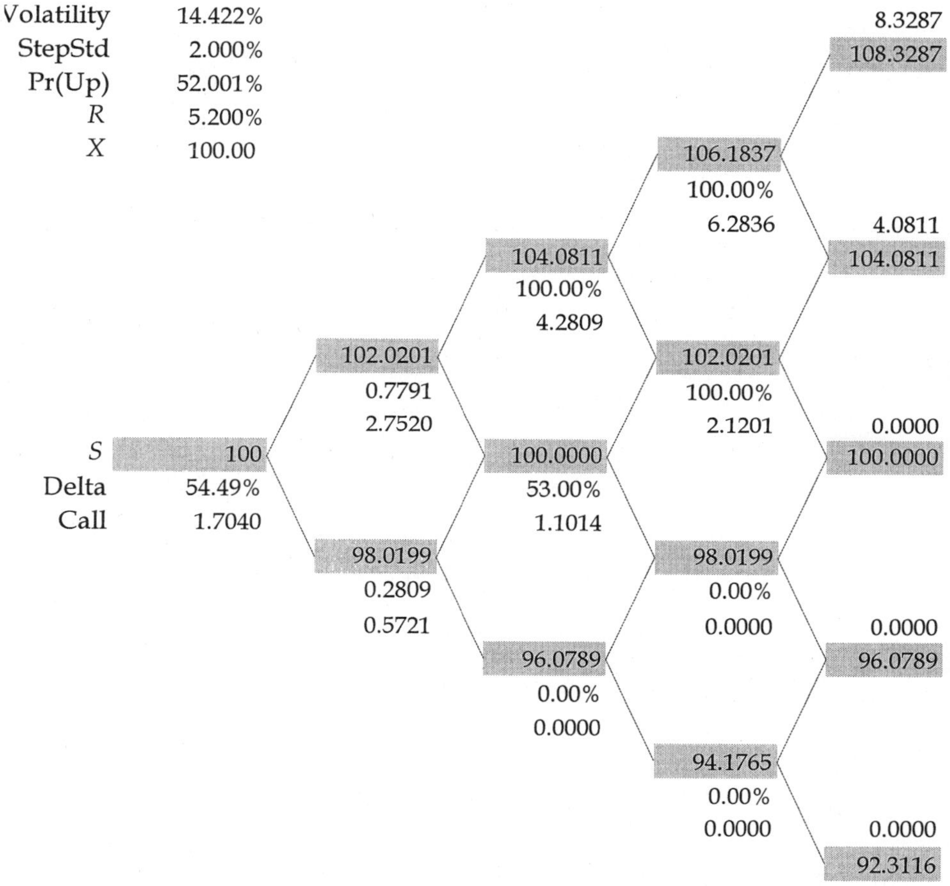

Volatility	14.422%	
StepStd	2.000%	
Pr(Up)	52.001%	
R	5.200%	
X	100.00	

```
                                                              8.3287
                                                            108.3287

                                              106.1837
                                              100.00%
                                              6.2836         4.0811
                              104.0811                      104.0811
                              100.00%
                              4.2809
              102.0201                        102.0201
              0.7791                          100.00%
              2.7520                          2.1201         0.0000
S       100                   100.0000                      100.0000
Delta   54.49%                53.00%
Call    1.7040                1.1014
              98.0199                         98.0199
              0.2809                          0.00%
              0.5721                          0.0000         0.0000
                              96.0789                        96.0789
                              0.00%
                              0.0000
                                              94.1765
                                              0.00%
                                              0.0000         0.0000
                                                             92.3116
```

Pr	$S(T)$	$E[S(T)]$	$C(T)$	$E[C(T)]$
7.31%	108.3287	7.9212	8.3287	0.6090
27.00%	104.0811	28.0996	4.0811	1.1018
37.38%	100.0000	37.3800	0	0.0000
23.00%	96.0789	22.1001	0	0.0000
5.31%	92.3116	4.8998	0	0.0000
100.00%		100.40		1.71
	PV =	100.0000	PV =	1.7040

Exhibit 17-5 Pricing a European Put with a Four-Step Tree

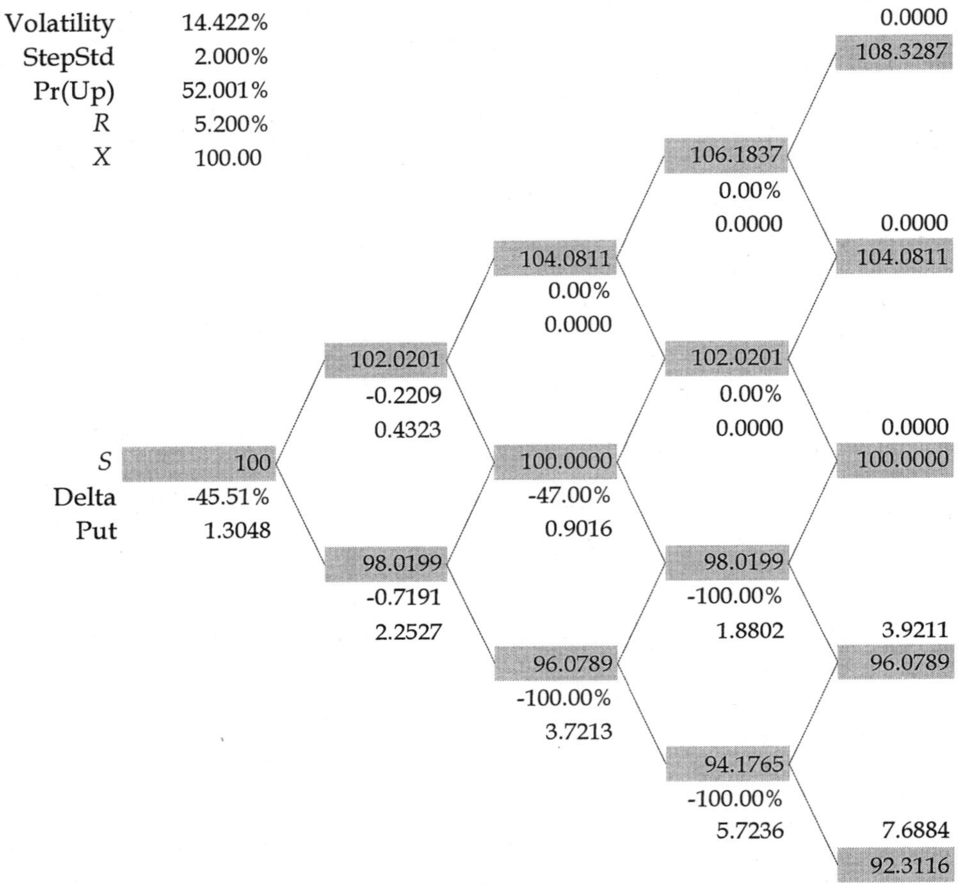

							0.0000
Volatility	14.422%						108.3287
StepStd	2.000%						
Pr(Up)	52.001%					106.1837	
R	5.200%					0.00%	
X	100.00					0.0000	0.0000
					104.0811		104.0811
					0.00%		
					0.0000		
				102.0201		102.0201	
				-0.2209		0.00%	
				0.4323		0.0000	0.0000
S		100			100.0000		100.0000
Delta		-45.51%			-47.00%		
Put		1.3048			0.9016		
				98.0199		98.0199	
				-0.7191		-100.00%	
				2.2527		1.8802	3.9211
					96.0789		96.0789
					-100.00%		
					3.7213		
						94.1765	
						-100.00%	
						5.7236	7.6884
							92.3116

Pr	P(T)	E [P(T)]
7.31%	0.0000	0.0000
27.00%	0.0000	0.0000
37.38%	0.0000	0.0000
23.00%	3.9211	0.9019
5.31%	7.6884	0.4081
100.00%		1.3100
	PV =	1.3048

with EU-put because it coincides with the price of a European put). It is therefore optimal to exercise the option before maturity, and the option price will therefore coincide with its tangible value. The economic intuition underlying this result is that the expected tangible value at maturity is lower than the intrinsic value at the node because of the positive drift in the asset price:

Exhibit 17-6 Risk-Neutral Pricing of European Put and Call

Ups	Pr	$S(T)$	$E[S(T)]$	$E[C(T)]$	$E[P(T)]$
26	0.0000%	168.2028	0.0000	0.00000	0
25	0.0001%	161.6074	0.0002	0.00006	0
24	0.0011%	155.2707	0.0018	0.00063	0
23	0.0085%	149.1825	0.0126	0.00416	0
22	0.0449%	143.3329	0.0643	0.01944	0
21	0.1822%	137.7128	0.2509	0.06871	0
20	0.5886%	132.3130	0.7788	0.19019	0
19	1.5522%	127.1249	1.9732	0.42104	0
18	3.4028%	122.1403	4.1562	0.75338	0
17	6.2818%	117.3511	7.3717	1.08996	0
16	9.8571%	112.7497	11.1139	1.25675	0
15	13.2341%	108.3287	14.3364	1.10223	0
14	15.2695%	104.0811	15.8927	0.62316	0
13	15.1785%	100.0000	15.1785	0	0
12	13.0095%	96.0789	12.4994	0	0.51011
11	9.6066%	92.3116	8.8680	0	0.73859
10	6.0962%	88.6920	5.4069	0	0.68936
9	3.3100%	85.2144	2.8206	0	0.48941
8	1.5276%	81.8731	1.2507	0	0.27691
7	0.5937%	78.6628	0.4670	0	0.12668
6	0.1918%	75.5784	0.1450	0	0.04684
5	0.0506%	72.6149	0.0367	0	0.01385
4	0.0106%	69.7676	0.0074	0	0.00321
3	0.0017%	67.0320	0.0011	0	0.00056
2	0.0002%	64.4036	0.0001	0	0.00007
1	0.0000%	61.8783	0.0000	0	0.00001
0	0.0000%	59.4521	0.0000	0	0.00000
SUM =	100%	.....	102.6341	5.52970	2.89561
PV =	.....	.....	100.0000	5.3878	2.8213
	$S, X = 100$	std = 14.422%	R = 5.20%	$T = 0.5$	$N = 26$

Exhibit 17-7 Early Exercise of American Put

				100.0000
Volatility	14.42%	max $(X-S, 0)$	7.9801	6.0000
StepStd	2%	$S(T-h)$	98.0199	
R	5.20%	Delta	-100%	
Pr (Up)	52.0011%	Put	7.9801	96.0789
X	106.00	European put	7.8742	9.9211

Exhibit 17-8 American Put, CRR Binomial Tree

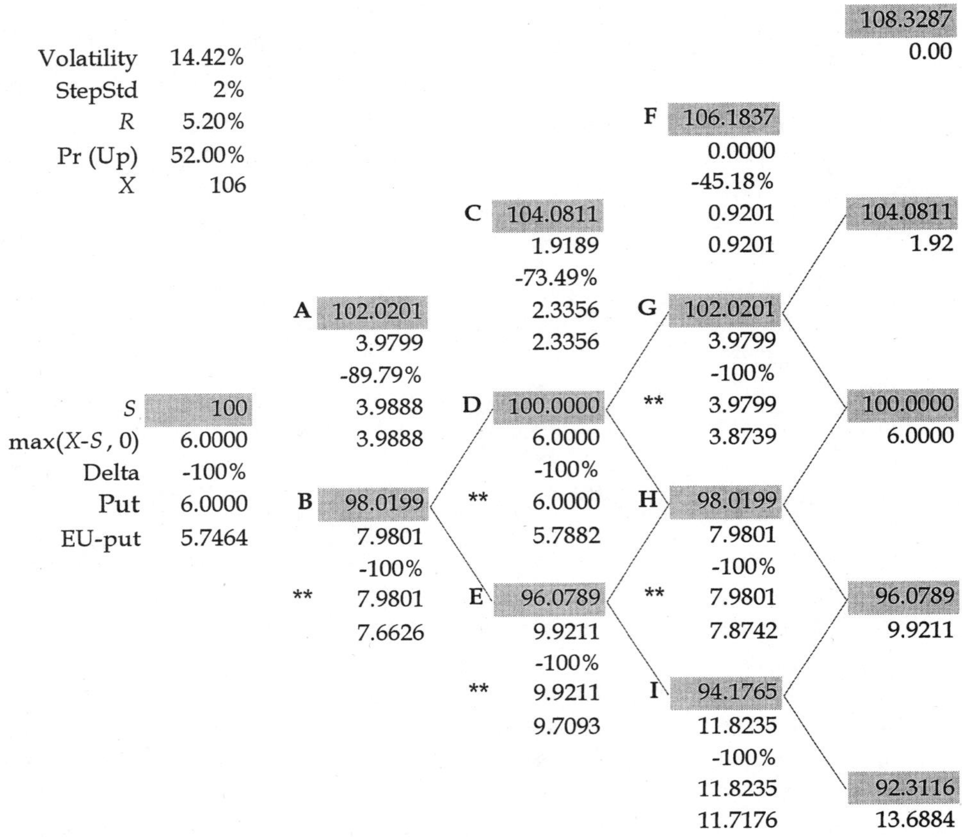

```
                                                                    108.3287
                                                                       0.00
  Volatility  14.42%
  StepStd      2%                              F  106.1837
      R        5.20%                              0.0000
  Pr (Up)     52.00%                             -45.18%
      X        106                                0.9201        104.0811
                                   C  104.0811     0.9201          1.92
                                      1.9189
                                     -73.49%
                    A  102.0201       2.3356    G  102.0201
                       3.9799         2.3356       3.9799
                      -89.79%                     -100%
      S      100       3.9888    D  100.0000  **   3.9799       100.0000
  max(X-S, 0) 6.0000   3.9888       6.0000         6.0000
  Delta     -100%                  -100%
  Put        6.0000  B  98.0199  **  6.0000    H   98.0199
  EU-put     5.7464     7.9801       5.7882        7.9801
                      -100%                       -100%
              **       7.9801   E  96.0789   **    7.9801        96.0789
                       7.6626      9.9211          7.8742         9.9211
                                  -100%
                          **       9.9211    I   94.1765
                                   9.7093        11.8235
                                                 -100%
                                                 11.8235        92.3116
                                                 11.7176        13.6884
```

$$X - S(T - h) > X - S(T - h) \cdot \exp(R \cdot h)$$

The intrinsic value at maturity must also be discounted back to make it directly comparable with the tangible value at time $T - h$.

$$X - S(T - h) > \frac{X - S(T - h) \cdot \exp(R \cdot h)}{\exp(R \cdot h)}$$

To conclude, note that early exercise can also be optimal when you reach a node (such as the initial node in Exhibit 17-8) where the put has a probability of expiring out-of-the-money. At node **F**, the put has a time value and zero tangible value. Move backward to node **C** and the time value decreases because of the asset's positive drift and the discounting. Move again backward to node **A** and the time value becomes quite small ($0.1280 = 4.1168 - 3.9888$). At the origin of the tree, the time-value is slightly negative ($-0.2536 = 5.7464 - 6.0000$).

17-3   DIVIDENDS

Until now we have considered only assets that do not pay dividends or interest; their return is therefore entirely attributable to a positive drift in their value (these assets are sometimes indicated as *zero-leakage* assets). This simplified approach must be extended to take into account stocks that pay dividends, currencies that earn the money-market rate, and bonds or swaps that pay interest.

The Simplest Case: European Put-Call Parity with Defined Dividend

Let us consider a stock that will pay a known dividend on the expiration day of a European call. The ex-dividend date precedes the payment date, and therefore the buyer of the call option will have the right to buy the stock ex-dividend (as a rule, stock options are not *dividend protected*). We can therefore consider the stock as being composed of two assets:

- The expected dividend, which can be treated as a short-term pure discount bond
- An ex-dividend stock

$$S_0 + P - C = \exp(-R \cdot T) \cdot (X + D)$$: put-call parity with defined dividend

It is therefore possible to use a standard option-pricing model (binomial or Black-Scholes), adjusting the exercise price to take into account the dividend (see Exhibit 17-9). Given any outcome $S(T)$ we have the following:

$$C = \max[0, (S_T - D) - X] \equiv \max[0, S_T - (X + D)]$$

$$P = \max[0, X - (S_T - D)] \equiv \max[0, (X + D) - S_T]$$

Exhibit 17-9 Call Pricing with Fixed Dividend = $2

Ups	Pr	S (T)	Dividend	C (T)	E[C(T)]
26	0.0000%	168.2028	2.00	66.2028	0.0000
25	0.0001%	161.6074	2.00	59.6074	0.0001
24	0.0012%	155.2707	2.00	53.2707	0.0006
23	0.0089%	149.1825	2.00	47.1825	0.0042
22	0.0471%	143.3329	2.00	41.3329	0.0195
21	0.1902%	137.7128	2.00	35.7128	0.0679
20	0.6110%	132.3130	2.00	30.3130	0.1852
19	1.6020%	127.1249	2.00	25.1249	0.4025
18	3.4917%	122.1403	2.00	20.1403	0.7032
17	6.4088%	117.3511	2.00	15.3511	0.9838
16	9.9984%	112.7497	2.00	10.7497	1.0748
15	13.3465%	108.3287	2.00	6.3287	0.8447
14	15.3103%	104.0811	2.00	2.0811	0.3186
13	15.1312%	100.0000	2.00	0.0000	0.0000
12	12.8942%	96.0789	2.00	0.0000	0.0000

S, X = $100		*R* = 5.50%	Steps = 26	Sum =	4.6052
Volatility = 14.42%		*T* = 0.5		*PV* =	4.4803

Exhibit 17-10 Call & Put on a Fixed-Rate 7.8% Coupon Bond

Ups	Pr	FV	S (T)	C (T)	P (T)
13	0.227%	105.56	103.61	3.607	0.000
12	1.765%	104.68	102.73	2.733	0.000
11	6.323%	103.82	101.87	1.865	0.000
10	13.843%	102.95	101.00	1.005	0.000
9	20.663%	102.10	100.15	0.152	0.000
8	22.207%	101.26	99.31	0.000	0.694
7	17.679%	100.42	98.47	0.000	1.533
6	10.556%	99.58	97.63	0.000	2.365
5	4.727%	98.76	96.81	0.000	3.190
4	1.568%	97.94	95.99	0.000	4.009
3	0.374%	97.13	95.18	0.000	4.820
2	0.061%	96.33	94.38	0.000	5.625
1	0.006%	95.53	93.58	0.000	6.423
0	0.000%	94.74	92.79	0.000	7.215
Expected value		101.38	99.43	0.345	0.910
PV [E (*)]		100.00	98.08	0.340	0.898

S, X = 100	Volatility = 3%	R = 5.50%	T = 0.25	Steps = 13

This model can be easily adapted to the case where we have a continuous interest accrual, for example, on a coupon bond. Consider the case of an option on a bond carrying a coupon rate of 7.8% while the current riskless rate is 5.5%. The bond will trade at a forward discount. Exhibit 17-10 shows the risk-neutral pricing of a European put and call, both with a strike price of 100 (clean price). The data show clearly that the forward discount must translate into a negative drift in the clean price.

Note that the volatility (a low 3%, which can be appropriate for an intermediate bond) refers to the bond's future value, that is, the invoice price. After deducting the accrued interest, the volatility changes (this is also the case in Exhibit 17-10).

17-4 OPTIONS ON FOREIGN EXCHANGE

A different approach is to assume that the asset does pay a continuous stream of interest or dividends at a constant proportional rate L. This may be somewhat unrealistic for stocks but is a reasonably accurate approximation for foreign exchange (FX). By proportional we mean that the amount of dividend will depend not only on $L \cdot T$ but also on the price of the underlying asset. Think in terms of buying DEM to set up a put-call arbitrage. If you want to have DEM 10 million to deliver in 6 months' time (at the strike price X), it is sufficient to buy the amount that, invested at the riskless rate, will yield the 10 million at time-T:

$$10,000,000 \cdot \exp(-T \cdot R_{DM}) = 9,814,247$$

R_{DM} = riskless rate for the DM (= 3.75%)

Exhibit 17-11 Hedging a 2-week Call on the DEM

								4.0811
								104.0811

				A	
				102.0201	
StepStd	2%			99.93%	
$R	5.50%	max $[0, X - S(T)]$	0	2.0523	0.0000
DMR	3.75%	S	100		100
X	100.00	Delta	51.27%		
Pr (Up)	50.34%	Call	1.0321	**B**	
				98.0199	
				0	
				0	0.0000
					96.0789

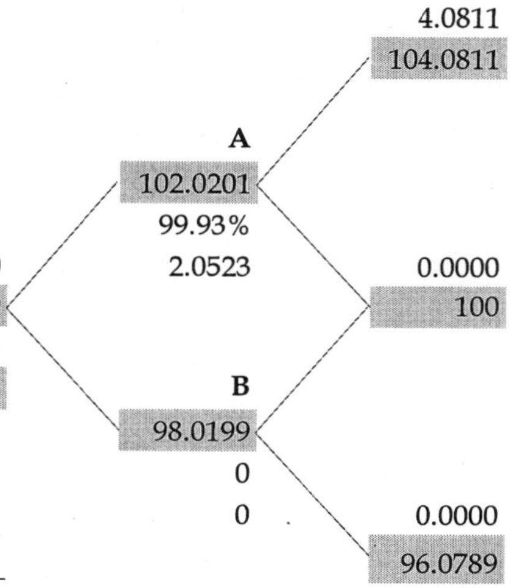

Path	Prob	max $[0, X - S(T)]$	E(*)
{u, u}	25.343%	4.0811	1.0343
{u, d}	49.998%	0	0.0000
{d, d}	24.660%	0	0.0000
	100.00%		1.0321

Whatever the FX rate will be in 6 months' time, the interest component (DEM 185,753) will have a value proportional to the realized FX rate. This entails writing the put-call parity as follows:

Box 17-1   Put-Call Parity with Proportional Dividend

$S_0 \cdot \exp(-T \cdot R_{DEM}) + P - C = X \cdot \exp(-T \cdot R_\$)$

$R_\$$ = riskless rate for the \$ (e.g., 5.50%)

Or, more generally,

$S_0 \cdot \exp(-T \cdot L) + P - C = X \cdot \exp(-T \cdot R)$

For example, consider a simple binomial tree to price a 2-week call to buy DEM at a fixed \$/DEM rate (see Exhibit 17-11). In order not to change the symbology, we shall indicate with S (set at \$100) the price of a given quantity of DEM (e.g., DEM 184 if we use the exchange rate as of 7 April 1998). The underlying asset is therefore a determined amount of DEM instead of, say, one IBM share. It is worth noting that the Philadelphia currency options are for DEM 62,500 per contract. Let us now compute the hedge ratio (Δ). This requires a small adjustment to the usual equation because the amount of DEM purchased to hedge the call will yield interest at 3.75%. Therefore:

$$\Delta S \cdot \exp(\sigma\sqrt{h}) \cdot \exp(h \cdot R_{DEM}) - C_U = \Delta S \cdot \exp(-\sigma\sqrt{h}) \cdot \exp(h \cdot R_{DEM}) - C_D$$

$$\Delta S_U \cdot \exp(h \cdot R_{DEM}) - C_U = \Delta S_D \cdot \exp(h \cdot R_{DEM}) - C_D$$

$$\Delta = \frac{C_U - C_D}{S_U - S_D} \cdot \frac{1}{\exp(h \cdot R_{DEM})}.$$

We can now compute the call value taking into account the interest you receive on the long DEM position. Using the up case we get

$$C = \Delta \cdot S - \frac{\Delta \cdot S_U \cdot \exp(h \cdot R_{DEM}) - C_U}{\exp(h \cdot R_{\$})}.$$

The risk-neutral-probabilities approach continues to hold; therefore you can price the call by computing its discounted expected value. To do so you must compute Pr(up) taking into account that the expected value of holding a DEM interest-bearing asset (riskless bill) is due in part to the expected drift in the asset value (appreciation of the \$/DEM rate) and in part to the interest flow. Therefore the expected drift rate $= R_{\$} - R_{DEM}$. This requires a simple adjustment in the CRR equation we examined in Section 12-3.

$$p \cdot S_U \cdot \exp(h \cdot R_{DEM}) + (1 - p) \cdot S_D \cdot \exp(h \cdot R_{DEM}) = \exp(h \cdot R_{\$})$$

$$p \cdot S_U + (1 - p) \cdot S_D = \exp(h \cdot R_{\$}) \cdot \exp(-h \cdot R_{DEM})$$

$$p = \frac{\exp[(h \cdot (R_{\$} - R_{DEM})] - S_D}{S_U - S_D}$$

You can now use p to compute the equations that we already examined in Section 17-3. Note again that while the expected outcomes at expiration are computed using a net drift rate $= R_{\$} - R_{DEM}$, their present value is computed with $R_{\$}$ (see Exhibit 17-12).

$$C = \exp(-h \cdot R_{\$}) \cdot \sum_{U=0}^{N} b(U, N, p) \cdot \max[0, -X + \exp(\sigma \cdot \sqrt{h}) \cdot (2U - N)]$$

$$P = \exp(-h \cdot R_{\$}) \cdot \sum_{U=0}^{N} b(U, N, p) \cdot \max[0, X - \exp(\sigma \cdot \sqrt{h}) \cdot (2U - N)]$$

17-5   OPTIONS ON FUTURES

Consider a future (or an at-the-market forward). The price of the derivative will be zero because the delivery price (contract price) equals the market's forward price. This entails that the future or the forward does not have an expected drift but only an expected volatility.

To define the put-call parity, consider a portfolio made up of one long future plus one long put and one short call, both with the same exercise price.

Box 17-2   Put-call parity for option on futures

$F_0 + P - C =$ put-call portfolio

$P - C =$ net cost of the put-call portfolio; the future has zero cost

$P - C = \exp(-R \cdot T) \cdot (F_0 - X) =$ put-call parity for the futures option

(Continued)

Exhibit 17-12 Risk-Neutral Pricing of European Put and Call on the DEM

Ups	Pr	$S(T)$	$E[C(T)]$	$E[P(T)]$
26	0.0000%	168.2028	0.0000	0
25	0.0000%	161.6074	0.0000	0
24	0.0006%	155.2707	0.0003	0
23	0.0044%	149.1825	0.0022	0
22	0.0252%	143.3329	0.0109	0
21	0.1093%	137.7128	0.0412	0
20	0.3773%	132.3130	0.1219	0
19	1.0633%	127.1249	0.2884	0
18	2.4910%	122.1403	0.5515	0
17	4.9144%	117.3511	0.8527	0
16	8.2412%	112.7497	1.0507	0
15	11.8245%	108.3287	0.9848	0
14	14.5802%	104.0811	0.5950	0
13	15.4887%	100.0000	0	0
12	14.1873%	96.0789	0	0.5563
11	11.1959%	92.3116	0	0.8608
10	7.5927%	88.6920	0	0.8586
9	4.4057%	85.2144	0	0.6514
8	2.1730%	81.8731	0	0.3939
7	0.9025%	78.6628	0	0.1926
6	0.3116%	75.5784	0	0.0761
5	0.0878%	72.6149	0	0.0240
4	0.0197%	69.7676	0	0.0060
3	0.0034%	67.0320	0	0.0011
2	0.0004%	64.4036	0	0.0001
1	0.0000%	61.8783	0	0.0000
0	0.0000%	59.4521	0	0.0000
	100%	100.8788	4.4997	3.6209
	PV =	98.1425	4.3777	3.5227
	S, X = 100	Vol. = 14.42	$R = 5.50%	DMR = 3.75%

Box 17-2   (Continued)

We have three possible cases:

- $F_T > X$: You pay $F_T - X$ to the buyer of the call and you get $F_T - F_0$ on your futures contract, through the usual mechanism of daily realization of gains and losses. Your net gain (loss) will therefore be $F_0 - X$.
- $F_T = X$: The put and the call expire worthless, and you get $F_0 - X$ on your futures contract. Your net gain (loss) will therefore be $F_0 - X$.
- $F_T < X$: You get $X - F_T$ on your put and $F_T - F_0$ on your futures contract. Your net gain (loss) will therefore be $F_0 - X$.

Exhibit 17-13 Risk-Neutral Pricing of Futures Options

Ups	Pr	F (T)	E [C(T)]	E [P(T)]
26	0.0000%	168.2028	0.0000	0
25	0.0000%	161.6074	0.0000	0
24	0.0004%	155.2707	0.0002	0
23	0.0032%	149.1825	0.0016	0
22	0.0186%	143.3329	0.0081	0
21	0.0834%	137.7128	0.0315	0
20	0.2979%	132.3130	0.0962	0
19	0.8682%	127.1249	0.2355	0
18	2.1037%	122.1403	0.4658	0
17	4.2924%	117.3511	0.7448	0
16	7.4445%	112.7497	0.9491	0
15	11.0471%	108.3287	0.9201	0
14	14.0878%	104.0811	0.5749	0
13	15.4780%	100.0000	0	0.0000
12	14.6627%	96.0789	0	0.5749
11	11.9672%	92.3116	0	0.9201
10	8.3936%	88.6920	0	0.9491
9	5.0372%	85.2144	0	0.7448
8	2.5695%	81.8731	0	0.4658
7	1.1037%	78.6628	0	0.2355
6	0.3941%	75.5784	0	0.0962
5	0.1149%	72.6149	0	0.0315
4	0.0266%	69.7676	0	0.0081
3	0.0047%	67.0320	0	0.0016
2	0.0006%	64.4036	0	0.0002
1	0.0000%	61.8783	0	0.0000
0	0.0000%	59.4521	0	0.0000
	100%	100.0000	4.0278	4.0278
	PV =	97.2875	3.9185	3.9185
	F, X = 100	std = 14.42%	R = 5.50%	T = 0.5

Determining the price of futures options is therefore mostly straightforward. You can use the FX pricing model, setting the rate on the foreign currency to equal the riskless rate $L = R$. This will entail the necessary zero drift (see Exhibit 17-13), where the expected future value of the future equals the value at time-0.

$$E(F_T) = F_0$$

Chapter **18**

The Black-Scholes and Other Option-Pricing Models

In this chapter we shall touch on some relevant topics in option pricing and hedging. Most of the modern advances in continuous-time finance require a relatively advanced mathematical background and therefore cannot be meaningfully covered in this book. They are the playing field of quants and are covered by a truly impressive stream of scientific articles. Advanced books, available in updated editions, are Hull (1997), Duffie (1996), and Merton (1992). A recent introduction to the mathematics of derivative pricing is found in Neftci (1996). The econometrics of finance are covered by Campbell, Lo, and MacKinlay (1997).

18-1 THE BLACK-SCHOLES MODEL

Black, Merton, and Scholes reached their fundamental breakthrough in option pricing in a mathematically sophisticated way, by finding the solution to a stochastic differential equation that describes the dynamic behavior of a hedged stock-call portfolio. Due to this mathematical complexity, a number of books present the Black-Scholes model (BS) without any attempt to give an interpretation of the equation. If we adopt the risk-neutral paradigm, however, it is relatively simple to interpret the BS using only the elementary probability concepts that were covered in Chapters 14 and 15. This helps us in building insight and making sense of the Black-Scholes continuous-time pricing model. The BS model is easy to program because all widely used spreadsheets include a function to compute $N(z)$. Therefore we do not need to consider easier-to-compute approximations to the BS equation or to $N(z)$. We can also avoid producing numerical tables of $N(z)$.

Exhibit 18-1 Payoff of European Options, with Lognormal Stock Prices

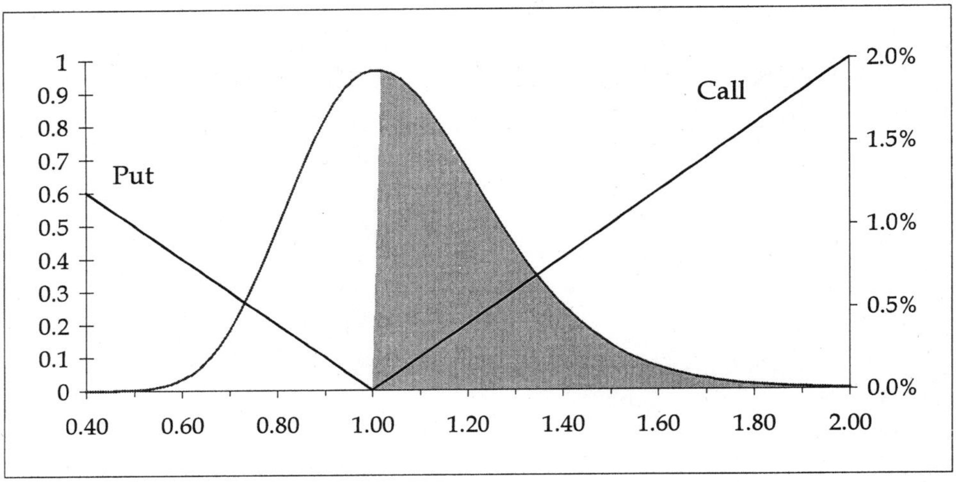

S (0) = $1   X = $1   std (K) = 20%   R = 7%   E (K) = 5%   T = 1

Box 18-1   Black-Scholes for European Calls and Puts

$$C = S \cdot N(d_1) - X \cdot N(d_2) \cdot \exp(-R \cdot T)$$

$$P = -S \cdot N(-d_1) + X \cdot N(-d_2) \cdot \exp(-R \cdot T)$$

$$d_1 = \frac{\ln\left(\frac{S}{X}\right) + \left(R + \frac{\sigma^2}{2}\right) \cdot T}{\sigma\sqrt{T}}$$

$$d_2 = \frac{\ln\left(\frac{S}{X}\right) + \left(R - \frac{\sigma^2}{2}\right) \cdot T}{\sigma\sqrt{T}} = d_1 - \sigma\sqrt{T}$$

where $N(z)$ = standardized normal cumulative distribution, i.e., the probability that a random draw from a standard normal distribution will be less than or equal to z.

Expected Value of European Calls and Puts

Consider Exhibit 18-1. The two straight lines represent the familiar payoff at expiration of a European call and a European put on a non-dividend-paying asset. The payoff values are measured on the left-hand vertical axis. The horizontal axis represents the possible values of the stock at the expiration date of the options S_T. The lognormal probability curve is constructed assuming that

- The stock price at time-0 and the strike are $S = X = \$1.00$.
- The yearly volatility of the exponential rates K is 20%.
- The exponential riskless rate equals 7%.
- Time to maturity equals 1yr.

The annualized expected value of the exponential rates is

$$\mu = R - \frac{1}{2} \sigma^2 = 5\%, \text{ where } R = \frac{1}{T} \cdot \ln \cdot \frac{E(S_T)}{S} = 7\%.$$

The probability values are measured on the right-hand vertical axis and are derived from the lognormal cumulative density function by taking 1% intervals of S_T, for example,

$$\Pr(1.035 \leq S_T < 1.045) = 1.88\%.$$

The expected value at expiration of the call equals the expected value of the right-hand tail (shaded) minus the exercise price multiplied by the probability of the call expiring in-the-money. The expected value of the put equals the expected value of the exercise price minus the expected value at expiration of the lognormal distribution under the left-hand tail.

$$E(C) = E(S_T | S_T \geq X) - X \cdot \Pr(S_T \geq X)$$

$$E(P) = -E(S_T | S_T < X) + X \cdot \Pr(S_T < X)$$

If we subtract the second equation from the first, we obtain an interesting restatement of the put-call parity in terms of expected values.

$$E(C) - E(P) = E(S_T) - X$$

Closed-Form Equation for European Calls

We can now utilize the equations for cumulative probability and truncated expected value to interpret the closed-form solution for the expected value of the European call.

$$E(S_T) = S \cdot \exp(R \cdot T)$$

$$E(C) = S \cdot \exp(R \cdot T) \cdot N\left(\frac{\ln\left(\frac{S}{X}\right) + \left(R + \frac{\sigma^2}{2}\right) \cdot T}{\sigma \cdot \sqrt{T}}\right) - X \cdot N\left(\frac{\ln\left(\frac{S}{X}\right) + \left(R - \frac{\sigma^2}{2}\right) \cdot T}{\sigma \cdot \sqrt{T}}\right)$$

$$= S \cdot \exp(R \cdot T) \cdot N(d_1) - X \cdot N(d_2)$$

Discounting back to time-0, we obtain the BS equation for the European call:

$$C = S \cdot N(d_1) - X \cdot N(d_2) \cdot \exp(-R \cdot T)$$

$N(d_1)$ is the proportion of expected value accounted for by the right-hand tail of the lognormal distribution, while $N(d_2)$ represents the probability under the right-hand tail.

$$d_2 = d_1 - \sigma \cdot \sqrt{T} = \frac{\ln\left(\frac{S}{X}\right) + \left(R + \frac{\sigma^2}{2}\right) \cdot T}{\sigma \cdot \sqrt{T}} - \sigma \cdot \sqrt{T}$$

$$= \frac{\ln\left(\frac{S}{X}\right) + \left(R + \frac{\sigma^2}{2}\right) \cdot T - (\sigma \cdot \sqrt{T})^2}{\sigma \cdot \sqrt{T}} = \frac{\ln\left(\frac{S}{X}\right) + \left(R + \frac{\sigma^2}{2} - \sigma^2\right) \cdot T}{\sigma \cdot \sqrt{T}}$$

$$= \frac{\ln\left(\frac{S}{X}\right) + \left(R - \frac{\sigma^2}{2}\right) \cdot T}{\sigma \cdot \sqrt{T}}$$

Closed-Form Equation for European Puts

The expected value under the left-hand tail of the lognormal distribution equals

$$E(P) = -E(S_T | S_T < X) + X \cdot \Pr(S_T < X)$$

$$E(S_T | S_T < X) = S \cdot \exp(R \cdot T) \cdot [1 - N(d_1)] = S \cdot \exp(R \cdot T) \cdot N(-d_1).$$

The probability of the put expiring in-the-money is

$$\Pr(S_T < X) = 1 - N \cdot (d_2) = N \cdot (-d_2).$$

Therefore,

$$E(P) = S \cdot \exp(R \cdot T) \cdot N(-d_1) + X \cdot N(-d_2).$$

Discounting back to time-0,

$$P = -S \cdot N(-d_1) + \cdot \exp(-R \cdot T)X \cdot N(-d_2).$$

The preceding equation yields the same result that you obtain using the put-call parity.

$$\begin{aligned}
E(P) &= -E(S_T) + X + E(C) \\
&= -S \cdot \exp(R \cdot T) + X + S \cdot \exp(R \cdot T) \cdot N(d_1) - X \cdot N(d_2) \\
&= -S \cdot \exp(R \cdot T) \cdot [1 - N(d_1)] + X \cdot [1 - N(d_2)] \\
&= -S \cdot \exp(R \cdot T) \cdot N(-d_1) + X \cdot N(-d_2)
\end{aligned}$$

Example: Compute the expected value of the put and the call on a stock priced at $100; strike = $100, $\sigma = 20\%$, $R = 5.20\%$, and $T = 0.5$.

$$d_1 = \frac{\ln\left(\frac{100}{100}\right) + \left(5.20\% + \frac{4\%}{2}\right) \cdot 0.5}{20\% \cdot \sqrt{0.5}} = \frac{0 + 0.036}{20\% \times 0.7071} = 0.254558$$

$$d_2 = d_1 - 20\% \cdot \sqrt{0.5} = 0.255458 - 20\% \times 0.7071 = 0.113137$$

$$N(d_1) = 0.600468$$

$$N(d_2) = 0.545039$$

$$C = S \cdot N(d_1) - X \cdot N(d_2) \cdot \exp(-R \cdot T) = 6.941713$$

$$[1 - N(d_1)] = N(-d_1) = 0.399532$$

$$[1 - N(d_2)] = N(-d_2) = 0.454961$$

$$P = -S \cdot N(-d_1) + \exp(-R \cdot T) \cdot X \cdot N(-d_2) = 4.37522$$

18-2 THE GREEK LETTERS

When you manage an options position, you clearly need to know how its value will react to a change in the relevant parameters (stock price, volatility, time to expiration, and risk-free rate). This analysis is usually conducted with reference to the Black-Scholes equation (or other continuous-time finance models) because, in a calculus environment, the rate of change of an option's price with respect to a change in one of the parameters is simply the relevant partial derivative. The delta of a call, that we have already extensively used in binomial pricing models, is therefore defined as $\Delta(C) = \partial C / \partial S$.

Note that the following analysis is only a first introduction. Hedging a complex derivatives portfolio, made up of a large number of options and hedges, is a task fraught with difficulties and uncertainties, as proven by a well-publicized string of derivatives-related losses suffered by corporations, banks, investment managers, and commodities traders.

The most commonly used measures, besides delta, are indicated with the following Greek letters.

• Gamma (Γ) is the derivative of delta with respect to the stock price, that is, to say the second derivative of the option value with respect to the stock price (gamma is a second derivative, like convexity).

• Vega (Λ) is the derivative with respect to the level of volatility. Note that the letter vega (V for volatility) is a misnomer; there is no such Greek letter, and the symbol we have used is in fact a capital lambda. Vega is sometimes referred to as lambda or kappa (K).

• Theta (Θ) is the derivative with respect to time to expiration and measures the rate of time decay of the option's value. Theta is the Greek letter for T.

• Rho (ρ) is the derivative with respect to the riskless rate. Rho is the Greek letter for R.

Due to the difficulty of using and interpreting multidimensional charts, the behavior of the aforementioned partial derivatives is usually represented with a number of straightforward two-dimensional graphs that plot the Greek letters as a function of the key variables affecting their price. We shall follow this approach, starting with delta.

Delta of European Calls and Puts on Non-Dividend-Paying Assets

Delta is the hedge ratio; its values must therefore lie between zero and one. Using the standard BS model for European options, the equations are as follows:

$$\Delta(C) = \frac{\partial C}{\partial S} = N(d_1)$$

$$\Delta(P) = \frac{\partial P}{\partial S} = N(d_1) - 1$$

Exhibit 18-2 European Put and Call Values as a Function of S/X

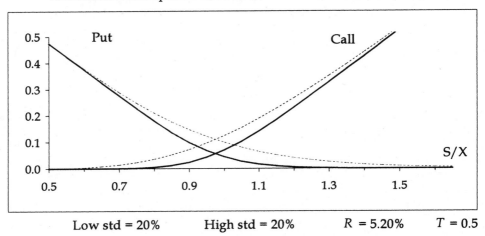

Exhibit 18-2 shows how put and call prices change as a function of S/X, while Exhibit 18-3 plots the corresponding behavior of delta. Volatility is also very important in determining the hedge ratio; we have therefore plotted the option prices and the deltas for two levels of volatility (20% and 40%).

Gamma of European Calls and Puts on Non-Dividend-Paying Assets

The gamma of an option is the derivative of delta with respect to the price of the underlying asset. If we use the standard BS equation we can write the following:

$$\Gamma = \frac{\partial \Delta_C}{\partial S} = \frac{\partial \Delta_P}{\partial S} = \frac{N'(d_1)}{S \cdot \sigma \cdot \sqrt{T}}$$

$$N'(d_1) = \frac{1}{\sqrt{2\pi}} \cdot \exp\left(-\frac{d_1^2}{2}\right) = \text{standard normal density function}$$

Gamma has the same values for puts and calls because the delta functions have the same slope. The gamma adds a quantitative dimension to the visual observation that the delta of an option is very sensitive to changes in the underlying asset price when S/X is close to one. When an option is deep-in-the-money, its gamma is low because the delta will be stable near the 100% hedge level. When the option is far-out-of-the-money, the gamma is low because the delta is close to zero (see Exhibit 18-4).

Vega of European Calls and Puts on Non-Dividend-Paying Assets

The price of a European option will always increase as a consequence of an increase in the volatility of the underlying asset. This increase can be nearly imperceptible, however, when the option trades either deep-in-the-money or far-out-of-the-money. When the value of S/X is close to one, the rate of change of options' values as a function of volatility can be quite pronounced, as shown in Exhibit 18-5.

Exhibit 18-3 Delta of European Options, as a Function of S/X

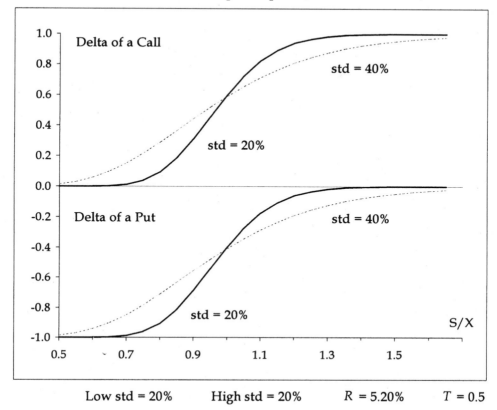

Low std = 20%   High std = 20%   *R* = 5.20%   *T* = 0.5

Exhibit 18-4 Gamma of European Calls and Puts

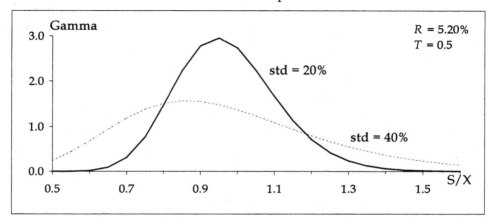

Exhibit 18-5 European Option Values as a Function of Volatility

Std	Call	Put
5%	3.04	0.47
10%	4.25	1.69
15%	5.58	3.02
20%	6.94	4.38
25%	8.31	5.74
30%	9.68	7.12
35%	11.06	8.49
40%	12.43	9.87

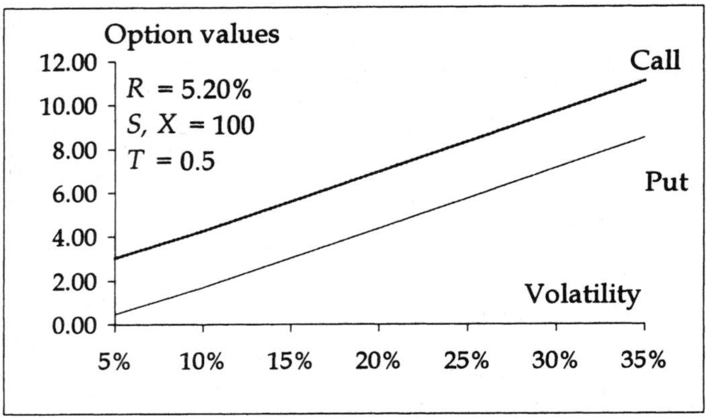

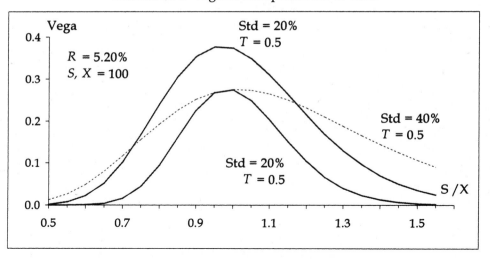

Exhibit 18-6 Vega of European Puts & Calls

Notice that the two functions shown in the exhibit have the same slope for any given value of volatility; therefore gamma will be the same for puts and calls. Mathematically, this is easy to understand by looking at the put-call parity, that shows that the value of the put equals the value of the call plus a parallel shift.

$$P = C + [X \cdot \exp(-R \cdot T) - S]$$

One last note: The effect of volatility changes is clearly higher for longer terms to expiration, because the volatility of the diffusion process is proportional to the square root of T.

$$\Lambda = \frac{\partial C}{\partial \sigma} = \frac{\partial P}{\partial \sigma} = S \cdot \sqrt{T} \cdot N'(d_1)$$

Rho of European Calls and Puts on Non-Dividend-Paying Assets

The value of a call will always increase in response to an increase (e.g., one basis point) in the riskless rate. When the call is far-out-of the-money, C is close to zero and the price increase will be very small. Conversely, when S/X is high and the call is expected to expire in-the-money, the increase in price will be much higher. The value of a put will always decrease when R increases. The absolute value of the price change will be high when the option is deep-in-the-money and low when it is far-out-of-the-money (see Exhibit 18-7.)

$$\rho(C) = X \cdot T \cdot \exp(-R \cdot T) \cdot N(d_2)$$

$$\rho(P) = -X \cdot T \cdot \exp(-R \cdot T) \cdot [1 - N(d_2)] = \rho(C) - X \cdot T \cdot \exp(-R \cdot T)$$

The preceding equation explains why the rho on a put equals that on a call minus a parallel shift. We saw in Chapter 12 that when delta equals one, the time-value of a call coincides with the interest saved by the opportunity of paying the exercise price at expiration. In fact, you can see in Exhibit 18-8 that the rho of the call is equal to the duration of the option.

Theta of European Calls and Puts on Non-Dividend-Paying Assets

The value of European calls on non-dividend-paying assets increases with term to expiration; therefore theta will always be positive. If you want to interpret theta as the rate of time decay, you must change the sign, making it negative.

The value of a European put will usually increase with time to maturity but may very well decrease when early exercise would be optimal, as discussed in Chapter 12. Theta will therefore be negative when S/X is low (see Exhibits 18-9 and 18-10).

$$\Theta(C) = \frac{\partial C}{\partial T} = \frac{S \cdot N'(d_1) \cdot \sigma}{2\sqrt{T}} + R \cdot X \cdot \exp(-R \cdot T) \cdot N(d_2)$$

$$\Theta(P) = \frac{\partial P}{\partial T} = \frac{S \cdot N'(d_1) \cdot \sigma}{2\sqrt{T}} - R \cdot X \cdot \exp(-R \cdot T) \cdot [1 - N(d_2)]$$

$$= \Theta(C) - R \cdot X \cdot \exp(-R \cdot T) = \text{parallel shift.}$$

Exhibit 18-7 Call and Put Prices as a Function of R

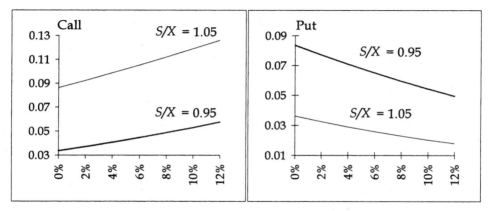

Exhibit 18-8 Rho of Puts and Calls

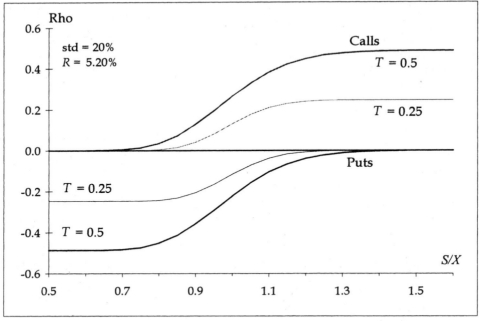

Exhibit 18-9 Value of Calls and Puts as a Function of T
std $= 20\%$, $R = 5.20\%$

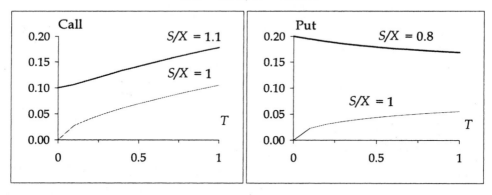

18-3   IMPLIED VOLATILITY; THE VOLATILITY SMILE AND SKEW

Up to now we have always assumed that volatility is an input to option-pricing models. An alternative way of using pricing models is to extract the volatility implied in observed market prices. Consider a European call:

$$C_e = \phi(S, X, \sigma, R, T)$$

This means that

Exhibit 18-10 Theta of Puts and Calls

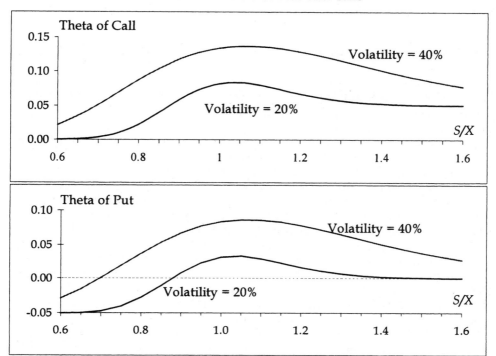

Exhibit 18-11 Computing Implied Volatility

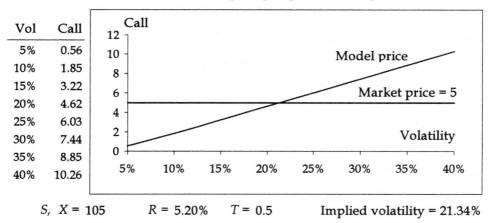

Vol	Call
5%	0.56
10%	1.85
15%	3.22
20%	4.62
25%	6.03
30%	7.44
35%	8.85
40%	10.26

$S,\ X = 105$ $R = 5.20\%$ $T = 0.5$ Implied volatility = 21.34%

$$\sigma = \varphi(C_e, S, X, R, T).$$

It is not possible to define a closed-form solution to determine the implied volatility, but we can compute it with numerical methods. The underlying principle is easy to grasp. We have seen that the price of an option will increase with the level of volatility, as shown in Exhibit 18-11. At this point the numerical procedure will determine the level of volatility corresponding to the intersection between the model's price and the market price.

Volatility Smile and Skew

We should stress that the preceding computation of volatility reflects the option-pricing model you are using, and we have already seen that the basic models we have discussed are based on a series of strong simplifying assumptions. The two assumptions concerning volatility are that the diffusion process of asset prices is lognormal and that volatility is constant. Therefore it should not come as a surprise that implied volatilities, based on market data, reflect a more complex reality.

When we compute implied volatilities, we often come across what is known as the *volatility smile*, shown in Exhibit 18-12, that is, the volatility measured on deep-out-of-the-money or deep-in-the-money options is higher than the volatility measured on at-the-money options. A full discussion of this topic is beyond the scope of this book, but we can intuitively see that the volatility smile is related to the fact that the lognormal assumption can fail to adequately represent the probability of the tails of the distribution of price relatives. If we have what is known as *fat tails*, it is follows that for values of S/X that diverge substantially from one, the option value should be higher. In turn, this higher value entails a higher volatility when solving the equation with a model based on the lognormal distribution. Exhibit 18-13 shows the fat tails phenomenon with reference to the already examined \$/¥ exchange rate. Yet another shape of implied volatility as a function of S/X has been documented in the financial literature—the so called *volatility skew*, shown in Exhibit 18-14, which is very similar to that in Derman, Kamal, Kani, and Lou (1997). This skew in the implied volatility of traded options on the S&P 500 index appeared after the stock market crash of 1987 and is connected to a left skew in the probability distribution of returns. The possible link between the volatility skew and the 1987 crash is well described by Rubinstein (1994): "One is tempted to hypothesize that the stock market crash of October 1987 changed the way market participants viewed index options. Out-of-the-money puts became valued much more highly . . . The market pricing of options since the crash seems to indicate an increasing crash-o-phobia."

Exhibit 18-12 Volatility Smile

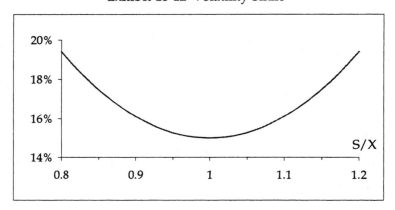

Exhibit 18-13 Fat Tails for the $/JPY Forex Rate (1995)

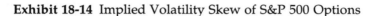

Exhibit 18-14 Implied Volatility Skew of S&P 500 Options

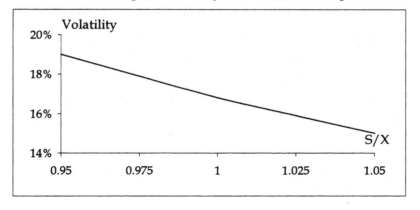

18-4   VARIATIONS ON THE BLACK-SCHOLES EQUATION

As we saw in Section 18-1, the BS model is built on the basis of several restrictive assumptions. Over the years a vast amount of research has gone into relaxing these assumptions, generalizing the results while obtaining an analytical (closed-form) solution. In this section we shall examine two important extensions of the BS, that are both easily tractable from a mathematical point of view and quite relevant to fixed-income analysis: options on foreign exchange (FX) and options of futures. The continuous time results that we shall cover coincide with those that we examined in Chapter 17, within the framework of the binomial option pricing model.

Foreign Exchange Options

FX options can be considered as options where the underlying asset pays a continuous proportional flow of dividends, at a rate L that reflects the riskless rate on the foreign

Exhibit 18-15 Specularity of FX Options

	Call on DEM 180			Put on $ 100	
Spot FX rate	$/DEM	0.5556		DEM/$	1.8000
S(0)	$	100.00		DEM	180.00
X	$	100.00		DEM	180.00
R		5.50%			3.75%
T		0.5			0.5
Adjusted S(0)	$	98.142		DEM	175.12
Volatility		10.00%			10.00%
Option Price	$	3.2045		DEM	5.7680522
				$	3.2045

currency. The ex-dividend (optionable) value of the foreign currency amount under-lying the option is as follows:

$S = Q \cdot FX$ = value of the foreign currency amount underlying the option
$Q^* = Q \cdot \exp(-T \cdot L)$ = ex-dividend amount of foreign currency
$S^* = S \cdot \exp(-T \cdot L)$ = ex-dividend value of the foreign currency amount

while the rates of return will be normally distributed:

$$\ln\left[\frac{S_T}{S \cdot \exp(-T \cdot L)}\right] \sim \phi\left(R - \frac{\sigma^2}{2}, \sigma\right).$$

We can therefore use the standard BS plugging in S^* as the stock value. The specularity of FX transactions entails that a call on DEM against $ is the same thing of a put on $ against DEM. If the call and the put have the same exercise price, they must have the same price, as you can verify examining Exhibit 18-15.

FX Options: The Modified Equations

Plugging in S^* means that we can modify the standard Black Scholes equation, re-casting the result in terms of the forward FX rate.

$$C = S \cdot \exp(-L \cdot T) \cdot N(d_1) - X \cdot N(d_2) \cdot \exp(-R \cdot T)$$

$$C = \exp(-R \cdot T) \cdot \left[\frac{S \cdot \exp(-L \cdot T)}{\exp(-R \cdot T)} \cdot N(d_1) - X \cdot N(d_2)\right]$$

$$C = \exp(-R \cdot T) \cdot [S \cdot \exp(R \cdot T - L \cdot \cdot)(d_1) - X \cdot N(d_2)]$$

We can now use the arbitrage-free forward rate f:

$$f = S \cdot \exp[T \cdot (R - L)]$$

$$C = \exp(-R \cdot T) \cdot [f \cdot N(d_1) - X \cdot N(d_2)]$$

$$P = \exp(-R \cdot T) \cdot [-f \cdot N(d_1) + X \cdot N(d_2)]$$

We can now adjust the value of d_1.

$$d_1 = \frac{\ln\left[\dfrac{S \cdot \exp(-L \cdot T)}{X}\right] + \left(R + \dfrac{\sigma^2}{2}\right)T}{\sigma \cdot \sqrt{T}},$$

where

$$\ln\left[\frac{S \cdot \exp(-L \cdot T)}{X}\right] = \ln\left(\frac{S}{X}\right) - L \cdot T$$

$$d_1 = \frac{\ln\left(\dfrac{S}{X}\right) + R \cdot T - L \cdot T + \dfrac{\sigma^2}{2} \cdot T}{\sigma \cdot \sqrt{T}} = \frac{\ln\left(\dfrac{f}{X}\right) + \dfrac{\sigma^2}{2} \cdot T}{\sigma \cdot \sqrt{T}}$$

$$d_2 = \frac{\ln\left(\dfrac{f}{X}\right) - \dfrac{\sigma^2}{2} \cdot T}{\sigma \cdot \sqrt{T}} = d_1 - \sigma \cdot \sqrt{T}$$

Options on Futures

We have already examined the mechanics of futures options in Section 13-1 and 17-5. The zero expected drift property entails that we can use the FX model setting $L = R$ (the forward rate of a foreign currency against the $ will equal the spot rate when the riskless rates on the two currencies are the same).

$$C = \exp(-R \cdot T) \cdot [F \cdot N(d_1) - X \cdot N(d_2)]$$

$$P = \exp(-R \cdot T) \cdot [-F \cdot N(d_1) + X \cdot N(d_2)]$$

$$d_1 = \frac{\ln\left(\dfrac{F}{X}\right) + \dfrac{\sigma^2}{2} \cdot T}{\sigma \cdot \sqrt{T}}$$

$$d_2 = \frac{\ln\left(\dfrac{F}{X}\right) - \dfrac{\sigma^2}{2} \cdot T}{\sigma \cdot \sqrt{T}} = d_1 - \sigma \cdot \sqrt{T}$$

18-5   MONTE CARLO SIMULATION

A number of problems do not lend themselves to an analytical solution and must be solved using iterative numerical procedures. The two most typical examples we have come across are

- Finding the yield to maturity (*YTM*) of a coupon bond
- Computing the value of the cumulative normal standard distribution N(•)

A characteristic of the aforementioned iterative procedures is that the solution can be computed with the desired level of accuracy and that the result will always be the same when you use the same parameters and precision settings (no matter how many times you compute the *YTM* of a specified coupon bond, you will always get the same result).

Monte Carlo models, which have become quite popular given the impressive growth in the availability of computing power, and represent a completely different class of numeric methods that allow to find satisfactory solutions to problems that would otherwise be thoroughly intractable.

For our purposes, this method consists of building a multistep stochastic model (such as the diffusion process of a stock price or of an FX rate) and, at each node, determining the outcome via a random-number generator. Say the asset price has a 51% probability of taking the UP value at a given node. You use the computer to generate a random number between zero and one. If the random number is lower than 0.51, then the asset price will take the UP value. You then generate another random number to determine the outcome at the second node, and so on, to cover the entire random path.

The process is then repeated a large number of times, each trial being a random sample from a set of possible outcomes. This reliance on a series of random events (number of nodes) (number of trials) explains the origin of the name of this method. Monte Carlo is the capital of the tiny principality of Monaco and is famous worldwide for its casino.

This reliance on random samples means that it is practically impossible for two Monte Carlo estimations to yield the same result. You can improve the level of precision by augmenting the number of trials, but you cannot control it with the same accuracy that is possible with iterative numerical procedures.

This sampling procedure is clearly useful when we must model a process that has such a large number of possible outcomes that exploring them one by one would clearly be unfeasible. This is often the case with diffusion processes; a relatively coarse 26-step binomial tree leads to a staggering number of paths:

$$2^{26} = 67{,}108{,}864$$

The option problems that we have covered up to now could all be solved (with a process of backward induction or with risk-neutral probabilities) taking into account only the possible end values of the binomial tree. Consider now *lockback options,* which have an adjustable strike price equal to the maximum (minimum) price of the underlying asset within the lookback period (see Exhibit 18-16):

- A lookback currency call will give the holder the right to buy the foreign currency at the lowest rate reached over the term of the call (the payoff will therefore be equal to or higher than that of a straight European call with an exercise price equal to the initial exchange rate).
- A lookback currency put will give the holder the right to sell the foreign currency at the highest rate reached over the term of the put (the payoff will therefore be equal to or higher than that of a straight European put with an exercise price equal to the initial exchange rate).

It is clear that the outcome of a lookback option is *path-dependent,* and we cannot compute it considering only the possible end-values of the diffusion process. This option pricing problem can be solved, however, with a Monte Carlo simulation (say

Exhibit 18-16 Random Path for a Currency Option

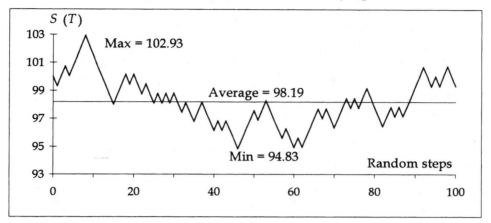

3,000 trials). Each sample path will produce an option payoff, and the arithmetic average of such payoffs will constitute an acceptable approximation of the option price (see Exhibit 18-17).

There are several methods to improve the accuracy and speed of Monte Carlo simulations. One simple way to improve the sampling accuracy is to generate a mirror path for each random path; this will reduce the variance of the simulation by enforcing a simmetic distribution of the outcomes. To control whether the simulation has produced an accurate sampling, you should compute the values of the plain European options (with exercise price equal to the initial price of $100) and compare them with those obtained with the standard binomial model and with the Black-Scholes. Exhibit 18-18 shows the simulation results and the control values for an FX option on $100 worth of DEM, strike = 100, yearly volatility = 10%, $R = 5.50%, DEMR = 3.50%, $T = 0.5$. The binomial trees are computed using 100 steps.

Exhibit 18-17 Random Path and Mirror Path for a Currency Option

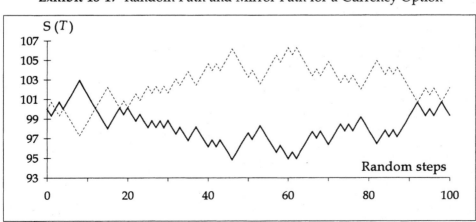

Exhibit 18-18 Simulation Results and Control Values

	Monte Carlo simulations			Binomial tree		Black Scholes
	1st	2nd	3rd	Pr = 0.5	CRR	
European call	3.28	3.22	3.27	3.2808	3.2671	3.2740
European put	2.30	2.25	2.30	2.3031	2.2893	2.2963
Lookback call	5.61	5.54	5.64			
Lookback put	4.84	4.78	4.87			
Asian call	1.36	1.34	1.37			
Asian put	0.00	0.00	0.00			

Modeling the Yield Curve

19-1 INTRODUCTION

The use of stochastic yield-curve models (SYCMs) to price fixed-income assets and derivatives is a somewhat recent development. With the exception of earlier pioneering work in the 1970s, most models were published after the mid 1980s. They come in a variety of flavors, often relatively hard to understand and implement; estimating their parameters usually requires the use of adequate econometric techniques and software. Clearly, some of the more advanced models are mostly of interest to academics conducting advanced research and to financial professionals who develop new methods to structure and price innovative interest-rate derivatives or trading strategies.

To price a European stock call using a binomial model, you will define a one-dimensional vector of possible stock prices at time-T. This vector will reflect the stock's volatility and, under risk-neutral probabilities, its discounted expected value must equal the market price of the stock.

$$S_0 = E[S_T] \cdot \exp(-R \cdot T)$$

When it comes to yield curves, you need to define a two-dimensional matrix of outcomes because each possible realization of the term structure at time-T cannot be expressed with one single number. Assume you want to price, at time-0, a European call, expiring in 1yr, on a noncallable coupon bond with a 10yr maturity. The value of the call at maturity will be contingent on the forward yields spanning a 9yr horizon, from time-1 to time-10.

In spite of this difficulty, we cannot just ignore stochastic yield models as if they were a mere mathematical extension of well-known concepts. Finance professionals should have some basic knowledge of what SYCMs are about, given the central role that they play in a number of real-life applications. We shall therefore concentrate on some of the basic issues addressed by a few important and relatively straightforward models that have been widely used in real life. These are the one-factor arbitrage-free models pioneered by Ho and Lee (1986); Kopprash et al. (1987, also known as the Salomon Brothers model); and Black, Derman, and Toy (1990, usually referred to as the BDT).

This approach should allow you to get a good grasp of the problems that must be solved for the implementation of an operational SYCM and will shed some more light on arbitrage-free stochastic processes. Readers who want to gain a good knowledge of a larger number of interest yield models will find a rigorous, mathematically demanding analysis in Rebonato (1996).

Why Use Stochastic Spot Yield–Curve Models?

We know that stock prices are a function of a large number of macro- and microvariables, such as economic cycle, level of interest yields, foreign exchange (FX) movements, corporate earnings, productivity gains, degree of national and international competition, corporate governance, and so on.

Stock analysts make it their profession to determine how this multitude of factors will influence the stock market performance of different corporations, industries, and countries. To be sure, investigations into the factors that determine stock returns are not limited to the practitioners' world; witness the recent series of pathbreaking articles by Fama and French.

When it comes to price derivatives that have stocks as their underlying asset, the usual approach is to assume that the stock price reflects, with all the inevitable uncertainties, all the usable information. The option is then priced relative to the stock (you will remember that delta is expressed in fractions of stock). This entails that all stocks are assumed to have the same expected return—that is, the riskless yield under risk-neutral probability measure. Stocks can, of course, have different levels of expected volatility; volatility, however, is an input to option-pricing equations and numerical methods.

For a number of purposes, such as pricing a short-term option on a standard bond future, we can consider the underlying asset as if it were a share of stock (the futures price automatically corrects for the accrual of interest). This simple approach is inadequate in most cases, however.

- First, the lognormal assumption does not work that well for fixed-income instruments. With volatile stocks, we can reasonably assume that very large changes in value will have a low probability of occurrence, but can happen. Plenty of stocks have doubled or halved in value in a few months. When it comes to bonds also a very large drop in yields cannot increase the price above the sum of the cash flows. For a 10yr, 6.50% coupon bond, the maximum price is $165, and this corresponds to a zero yield to maturity (*YTM*). For the same 10yr bond, a drop in price from par to $50 would entail a *YTM* of over 17%.
- Second, we must often price options that mature in many years' time (think of a callable bond). This entails that the fixed-income instrument will have a shorter duration when the option expires and will therefore be less sensitive to yield movements. Barring insolvency, the bond will be priced at par at maturity. This effect is illustrated in Exhibit 19-1. The stochastic path of a bond price is therefore

Exhibit 19-1 Price of a Coupon Bond—Brownian Bridge 5yr, 8% Eurobond

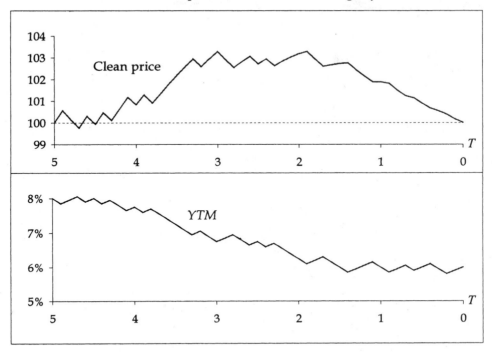

anchored, like a bridge, to the initial value and to its redemption value at maturity. This explains why a bond price is said to follow a Brownian bridge stochastic process, reverting to a known terminal value.

- Third, in many cases you need to price, in a coherent way, options on a number of fixed-income securities that are characterized not only by different terms to maturity, but also by different cash flow patterns (zeros, coupon bonds, amortizing bonds and swaps, etc.). If you want to assign reasonable volatilities you must, by necessity, compute the different durations, or better still, the different key rate durations.

- Fourth, a number of standard option-pricing models assume that the riskless yield remains unchanged over the life of the option. In the case of short-term stock options, this is a relatively harmless assumption. When it comes to fixed-income products, it does not make much sense to assume a constant riskless yield when the price of the security is assumed to be volatile precisely because yields can change.

- Fifth, the volatility of a bond relative to that of its *YTM* increases with duration. On the other hand, the volatility of long yields is usually lower than the volatility of short yields. This entails that in determining the random process followed by a bond's price, we must take into account both the yield volatility and the duration of the security. It is therefore clear that if you want to use prices instead of yields in the stochastic process, you end up using yields, albeit in an implicit way. In fact, the volatility of bond prices can be expressed in terms of both yields and prices, and the two volatility measures are linked by well-defined functions.

There is one bit of widely used terminology that we should examine before concluding this introductory section; that is the traditional distinction between *arbitrage-free* yield-curve-fitting models and *equilibrium models*. You should be aware, however, that this distinction is slowly fading away because a new generation of arbitrage-free equilibrium models is being built.

Arbitrage-free models are somewhat analogous to the Black-Scholes (BS) approach. They take the yield curve as a given in the same way that the BS treats stock prices as an exogenous variable. The next step is to define an arbitrage-free stochastic process for yields. The SYCM should therefore price correctly both interest-rates options and options-free bonds in the same way the BS prices correctly the underlying asset, in the limiting case of a call with zero strike price $X = 0$. Arbitrage-free models must therefore be fitted (calibrated) to reflect the spot yield curve. The purpose of this approach was clearly stated in the 1986 article by Ho and Lee:

> We take the term structure as given and derive the feasible subsequent term structure movements. These movements must satisfy certain constraints to ensure that they are consistent with an equilibrium framework. Specifically, the movements cannot permit arbitrage profit opportunities. . . . The main advantage of our approach is that it enables us to utilize the full information of the term structure to price contingent claims. Further, when our model is used to price a straight bond . . . the theoretical price is assured to be that determined by the observed term structure.

Equilibrium models were developed earlier than the arbitrage-free variety (see Vasicek [1977] and Cox and Ingersoll [1985]). These models endogenize the evolution of the term structure, based on assumptions that can be econometrically tested, such as mean reversion and risk premia for holding longer-maturity bonds. The term structure produced by equilibrium models is internally free from arbitrage, that is, arbitrage-free within the model's term structure. Equilibrium models are analogous to all those econometric models that aim at providing forecasts of the future evolution of economic variables.

The forward yield curve is, however, a representation of market-determined future yields. It is usually the case that the forward yield curve that is an output of equilibrium models does not coincide with the market-determined forward yield curve. The equilibrium output yield curve is therefore internally arbitrage-free but nonconsistent with arbitrage-free prices in the open market.

This certainly creates a big problem if you want to use equilibrium models to price fixed-income securities and derivatives for trading purposes. The discrepancy between the market and the model's output entails that (1) either you would never trade because you would price securities and derivatives away from the market, or, more dangerously, that (2) everybody will trade with you because your prices are such as to allow arbitrage. The problem would be a lot less important if you were an active asset manager taking positions with a view of doing better than the market.

19-2   ARBITRAGE-FREE PRICING

When modeling the spot yield curve, we must do it in such a way as to avoid arbitrage. Let us start with a simplified scenario where we consider only 1yr and 2yr zeros. The 1yr forward yield, $fR(1,2)$, is computed taking into account that the 1yr bond allows to lock in the 1-year return. The forward yield therefore depends on both the 1yr and the 2yr yields, as shown in Exhibit 19-2.

Exhibit 19-2 Spot and Forward Yields

R (0, 2)	R (0, 1)	R (1, 2)	B (1, 2)	B (0, 2)
	6.50%	5.50%	94.65	88.6920
6.00%	6.00%	6.00%	94.18	88.6920
	5.50%	6.50%	93.71	88.6920

Let us briefly recall the forward yield equation. The condition that the 1-year horizon return on the 2-year zero must equal the yield on the 1-year zero can be expressed as follows:

$$\exp[R(0,1)] = \frac{\exp[-f\,R(1,2)]}{\exp[-2\cdot R(0,2)]} = \exp[-f\,R(1,2) + 2\cdot R(0,2)].$$

Take the logs and rearrange to get:

$$f\,R(1,2) = 2\cdot R(0,2) - R(0,1).$$

The forward yield equation can also be rearranged to show that the *PV* of the forward price of the 2yr zero (computed with the spot 1yr yield) must equal the spot price of the 2yr zero (see Exhibit 19-2):

$$\exp[-2\cdot R(0,2)] = \exp[-f\,R(1,2) - R(0,1)]$$

$$B(0,2) = \exp[-R(0,1)]\cdot f\,B(1,2)$$

$$B(t,T) = PV \text{ at time-}t \text{ of the unit zero with mty } T$$

Binomial Process and Convexity Correction

To keep things as simple as possible, let us use a one-step binomial tree with yearly steps. Within this setting, a stochastic model of the yield curve entails modeling the value of the 1yr yield 1 year forward. Risk-neutral probabilities entail that the expected return on the 1yr and the 2yr zeros must be the same over the first-year time horizon.

$$\exp[R(0,1)] = \frac{E[B(1,2)]}{B(0,2)} \text{ local expectations hypothesis.}$$

With an equiprobable binomial tree, Pr(up) = 50%, we can write the preceding equation as follows:

$$\exp[R(0,1)] = \frac{1}{2}\cdot\frac{\exp[-R_U(1,2)] + \exp[-R_D(1,2)]}{\exp[-R(0,2)]}$$

In turn, this means that because of the convexity of the present value function, the expected value of the future 1yr yield must be higher than the 1yr yield, 1 year forward.

Exhibit 19-3 Convexity Correction, Constant Basis Point Volatility

	T-0		T-1	T-2
B (0, 2) =	88.6920	ƒB (1, 2) =	93.9883	100.00
R (0, 1) =	5.8000%	ƒR (1, 2) =	6.2000%	

```
                                    93.0484 ---------------------- 100.00
                                    7.2050%
            88.6920 <
                                    94.9281 ---------------------- 100.00
                                    5.2050%
```

	E (B) =	93.9883	100.00
	E (R) =	6.2050%	

$$E[R(1, 2)] > f\ R(1, 2)$$

The forward yield gives a no-arbitrage forward price within a deterministic model. When we introduce volatility, the arbitrage-free constraint on the expected forward price entails an expected future yield that does not coincide with the forward yield. Luckily, correcting for convexity is a rather simple procedure. Assume that the 1yr yield follows a simple stochastic process, such as the following:

$$R_D(1, 2) = R_U(1, 2) - 2 \cdot \sigma_{bp} \cdot \sqrt{h}$$

The volatility of the process outlined here is expressed with reference to the future value of the 1yr rate and is therefore expressed in basis points, hence the name basis point (bp) volatility (see Exhibit 19-3). The preceding equation is simple to prove; see the Mathematical Appendix. You can now find, with numerical methods, the up value that satisfies the local expectations hypothesis.

$$88.6920 = \exp(-5.8\%) \cdot \frac{1}{2} \cdot (93.0484 + 94.9281)$$

You will also notice that because of the convexity correction, the expected value of the one-year rate is slightly higher than the 1-year forward rate.

$$\frac{1}{2} \cdot (7.2050\% + 5.2050\%) > 6.20\%$$

A better stochastic process can be obtained assuming that the short-term yield changes are proportional to the level of yields, with a yearly volatility σ that leads to

$$R_U(1, 2) = R_0(0, 1) \cdot \exp[(\sigma \cdot \sqrt{h}) + \mu],$$

$$R_D(1, 2) = R_0(0, 1) \cdot \exp[-(\sigma \cdot \sqrt{h}) + \mu].$$

To compute the convexity correction we can use the following property (see the Mathematical Appendix):

$$\sigma\sqrt{h} = \frac{1}{2} \cdot \ln\left[\frac{R_U(1, 2)}{R_D(1, 2)}\right], \text{ therefore}$$

$$\ln[R_D(1, 2)] = \ln[R_U(1, 2)] - 2 \cdot \sigma\sqrt{h}.$$

It is therefore straightforward to determine the down yield as a function of the up value and of the desired volatility.

$$R_D(1, 2) = \exp\{\ln[R_U(1, 2)] - 2 \cdot \sigma\sqrt{h}\}$$

$$R_D(1, 2) = \frac{R_U(1, 2)}{\exp(2 \cdot \sigma\sqrt{h})}$$

Given the desired level of volatility, we can compute numerically the up yield that will satisfy the local expectations hypothesis (see Exhibit 19-4). The model is extremely coarse and cannot be used for real-life applications, but we can use it to price both the options and the zero itself (the price of the zero will be the price of a call with $X = 0$).

$$C = \exp[-R(0, 1)] \cdot \frac{1}{2} \cdot [\max(0, P_U - X) + \max(0, P_D - X)]$$

$$P = \exp[-R(0, 1)] \cdot \frac{1}{2} \cdot [\max(0, -P_U + X) + \max(0, -P_D + X)]$$

Exhibit 19-4 Convexity Correction with Proportional Yield Volatility

	T-0	T-1		T-2
B (0, 2) =	88.6920	f B (1, 2) =	93.9883	100.00
R (0, 1) =	5.8000%	f R (1, 2) =	6.2000%	
		92.8368		100.00
		7.4327%		
	88.6920			
		95.1398		100.00
STD=	20.00%	4.9823%		
		E (B) =	93.9883	100.00
		E (R) =	6.2075%	

$$C = 0.9436 \cdot \frac{1}{2} \cdot [\$0.856 + 0] = \$0.404 \quad \{X = \$94.00\}$$

$$P = 0.9436 \cdot \frac{1}{2} \cdot [0 + \$0.880] = \$0.415 \quad \{X = \$94.00\}$$

You can easily verify that the put-call parity holds:

$$\underbrace{\$88.692 + \$0.415 - \$0.404}_{S + P - C} = 0.9436 \times \$94.00 \quad \{X = \$94.00\}$$

$$C = 0.9436 \cdot \frac{1}{2} \cdot [\$94.856 + \$93.120] = \$88.692 \quad \{X = 0\}$$

The 1yr yield-diffusion process could be made more realistic by increasing the number of steps to get a more credible range of outcomes; see Exhibit 19-5 for an example based on a four-step binomial process. This sort of process could be used to price single-maturity instruments such as caplets and floorlets. From a computational point of view, this model is easy to solve. First, you determine the step-volatility:

$$\sigma\sqrt{h} = 20\% \sqrt{0.25} = 10\%.$$

Next, you express all the values of the yield vector as a function of the top yield and of step volatility:

$$0.074323 = \frac{0.090778}{\exp(2 \cdot \sigma\sqrt{h})}, \quad 0.060850 = \frac{0.074323}{\exp(2 \cdot \sigma\sqrt{h})}, \cdots$$

Exhibit 19-5 Convexity Correction with Proportional Yd Volatility

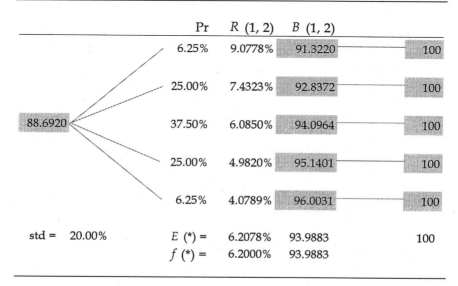

	Pr	R (1, 2)	B (1, 2)	
	6.25%	9.0778%	91.3220	100
	25.00%	7.4323%	92.8372	100
88.6920	37.50%	6.0850%	94.0964	100
	25.00%	4.9820%	95.1401	100
	6.25%	4.0789%	96.0031	100
std = 20.00%	E (*) =	6.2078%	93.9883	100
	f (*) =	6.2000%	93.9883	

At this point you can use the binomial probabilities' vector and the yields' vector to determine, with numerical methods, which value of the top yield will satisfy the equation

$$B(0, 2) = \exp[-R(0, 1)] \cdot E[B(1, 2)].$$

19-3   THE PROBLEM WITH SPOT YIELDS CORRELATION

Let us now extend the analysis, assuming that we have zeros covering more than two yearly maturities. The yield curve that we shall use is summarized in Exhibit 19-6. The 1-year forward yields are computed with the following equation:

$$\exp[f\, R(T-1, T)] = \frac{\exp[T \cdot R(0, T)]}{\exp[(T-1) \cdot R(0, T-1)]}$$

$$f\, R(T-1, T) = T \cdot R(0, T) - (T-1) \cdot R(0, T-1)$$

Difficulties in Modeling Spot Yields

Say we want to price a European call, maturity 1yr, on a 4yr coupon bond (which will have a maturity of 3 years when the option expires). We now need the stochastic process for the full 3yr term structure, 1 year forward.

Let us assume, for simplicity, that the proportional volatilities of the different spot yields are all equal to 15%. Let us further assume that the changes in the spot yields are not correlated. Put more loosely, the probability of the 2yr spot yield going up or down is not influenced by the movement in the 1yr yield. The result of this one-step binomial process, with convexity correction, is shown in Exhibit 19-7. Having determined the possible future values of the {1yr, . . . , 4yr} spot yields, we could try to use them to price interest-rate options and fixed-income securities. In practice, we cannot use a spot-rate process because the zero-correlation assumption does not make economic sense and leads to inconsistent results. Let us first briefly examine the problems with this approach and then examine how we can obtain a reasonable process by modeling short forward rates.

- First, a massive amount of statistical evidence indicates that spot rates are far from being uncorrelated. In fact, movements in the short-term yield "explain" most of the movements of the other spot yields.

Exhibit 19-6 Spot and Forward Yield Curves

T	R (0, T)	B (0, T)	1yr Fwrds
0			
1	5.80%	94.36	5.80%
2	6.00%	88.69	6.20%
3	6.20%	83.03	6.60%
4	6.40%	77.41	7.00%
5	6.60%	71.89	7.40%

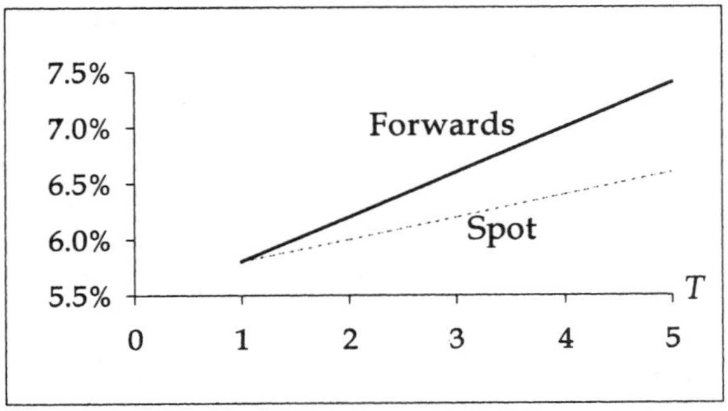

Exhibit 19-7 One-step Binomial Process for Several Spot Yields

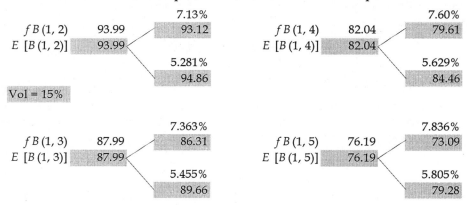

• Second, if we consider spot rates for more than two periods, we can easily get absurd results. Exhibit 19-8 shows how the spot-yields process implicitly determines a forward-yields diffusion. Limiting ourselves to the first two spot yields (1 and 2 years, respectively) generates four possible 1yr forwards.

Take the UD case in Exhibit 19-8, which entails that, in 1 year's time, you would get a 1yr forward of 7.13% and a 2yr forward of 3.78%. This is certainly not a realistic outcome. Another improbable outcome is DU, which entails

$$R(1,2) = 5.28\% \text{ and } R(2,3) = 9.45\%.$$

When you consider the interplay of longer spot rates, you easily get absurd results. Take the 4 and the 5yr spot yields. The UD case entails that the future value of the 3yr zero will be lower than that of the 4yr zero, thereby defining a negative 1yr forward rate.

$$[R_U (1,4) \text{ and } R_D (1,5)] \Rightarrow R(4,5) < 0$$

Exhibit 19-8 Uncorrelated Forward Yields

	R (1, 2)	R (1, 3)	R (2, 3)
U U	7.13%	7.36%	7.60%
U D	7.13%	5.45%	3.78%
D U	5.28%	7.36%	9.45%
D D	5.28%	5.45%	5.63%

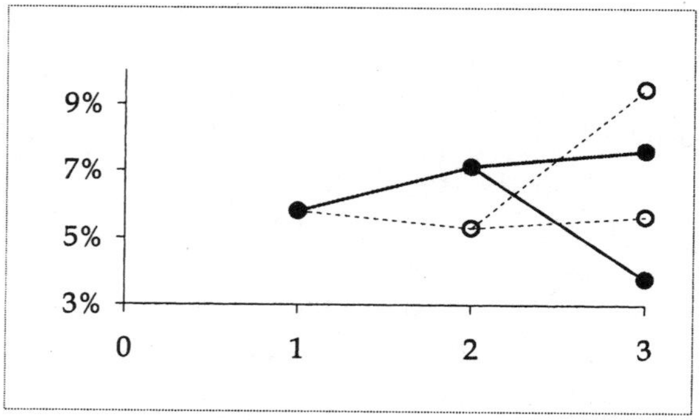

The problem with defining a stochastic process in terms of spot yields clearly lies in the fact that the term spot structure we want to model must produce a consistent structure of forward yields. *In fact, it turns out that it is much simpler to define a credible stochastic model for forward yields and to obtain the needed spot yields as a result.*

19-4 THE HO AND LEE ONE-FACTOR MODEL

The pioneering work by Ho and Lee (1986) took the approach of modeling the one-period rate and deriving the spot rates for {2, 3, . . . periods} from the forward structure. This is known as a *one-factor* model because, by construction, the one-period yield is the only source of volatility, and therefore all the variability of the term structure is driven by the short yield changes. In other words, all the spot rates are fully correlated to the short rate. This approach is therefore the complete opposite of modeling uncorrelated spot yields.

The Ho and Lee is based on an equal-probability tree and on the assumption of constant bp volatility at each of the nodes. The first step can be summarized as follows:

$$\begin{cases} R_U\ (1,2) = R(0,1) + \eta + \mu_1 \\ R_D\ (1,2) = R(0,1) - \eta + \mu_1 \end{cases}$$

$\eta = \sigma \cdot \sqrt{h}$
μ_1 = drift term

At this point we can easily compute the value of the up rate, which will price the 2yr zero correctly. If we assume the bp standard deviation to be 1%, we obtain the same result as in Exhibit 19-3, and this defines the value of the drift term.

$$\begin{cases} R_U\ (1,2) = R(0,1) + \eta + \mu_1 = 5.8\% + 1\% + 0.406\% = 7.206\% \\ R_D\ (1,2) = R(0,1) - \eta + \mu_1 = 5.8\% - 1\% + 0.406\% = 5.206\% \end{cases}$$

Having determined the two values of $R(1,2)$, we can now proceed to compute the three possible values of $R(2,3)$. The procedure for doing this is relatively straightforward.

Express the possible yield values in terms of the top yield; the local volatility remains unchanged while the drift term is recalculated. It is easy to see that this volatility structure produces a recombining binomial tree.

$$\begin{cases} R_{UU}\ (2,3) = R(0,1) + 2 \cdot \eta + \mu_1 + \mu_2 \\ R_{UD}\ (2,3) = R_{UU}\ (2,3) - 2 \cdot \eta \\ R_{DD}\ (2,3) = R_{UU}\ (2,3) - 4 \cdot \eta \end{cases}$$

Express the possible values of $B(2,3)$ in terms of the aforementioned rates.

$$\begin{cases} B_{DD}\ (2,3) = 100 \cdot \exp[-R_{UU}\ (2,3)] \\ B_{UD}\ (2,3) = 100 \cdot \exp[-R_{UU}\ (2,3) + 2 \cdot \eta] \\ B_{UU}\ (2,3) = 100 \cdot \exp[-R_{UU}\ (2,3) + 4 \cdot \eta] \end{cases}$$

We can now discount the expected values of $B(2,3)$ back to time-1. This however must be done using the two (already determined) values of $R(1,2)$, as shown in Exhibit 19-9.

$$\begin{cases} B_D\ (1,3) = \exp[-7.205\%] \cdot \dfrac{1}{2} \cdot [B_{DD}\ (2,3) + B_{UD}\ (2,3)] \\[2mm] B_D\ (1,3) = \exp[-7.205\%] \cdot \dfrac{1}{2} \cdot [B_{UU}\ (2,3) + B_{UD}\ (2,3)] \end{cases}$$

Exhibit 19-9 Structure of the Ho and Lee Model, Flat Yield Curve, std (bp) = 1%

						0.125		
B (0, 1)	94.176					91.352	----	100
B (0, 2)	88.692			*0.25*		9.045%		
B (0, 3)	83.527			85.163				
B (0, 4)	78.663		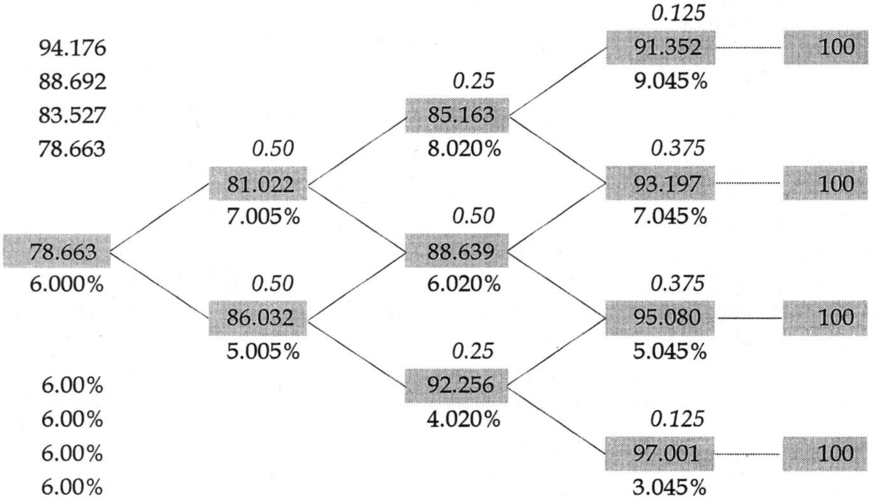 *0.50*	8.020%		*0.375*		
		81.022				93.197	----	100
		7.005%		*0.50*		7.045%		
	78.663			88.639				
	6.000%	*0.50*		6.020%		*0.375*		
		86.032				95.080	----	100
		5.005%		*0.25*		5.045%		
R (0, 1)	6.00%			92.256				
R (0, 2)	6.00%			4.020%		*0.125*		
R (0, 3)	6.00%					97.001	----	100
R (0, 4)	6.00%					3.045%		

E (R)	6.005%	6.020%	6.045%
var(R)	0.010%	0.020%	0.030%
std(R)	1.00%	1.41%	1.73%
E(B)	83.527	88.674	94.148
f B	83.527	88.692	94.176

The final step is to discount back to time-0, using the 1yr spot rate. This discounted value must equal the price of a 3yr zero. It is clear that the present value of the complex discounting procedure is a function of the top value of $R(2,3)$, which we can find with an iterative numerical procedure. Notice that after the first binomial step, the expected value of the zeros is slightly different from the forward value; this is again due to the convexity correction because the different $B(2,3)$ values are discounted back to time-0 using different rates.

$$E[B(2,3)] \neq f\,B\,(2,3)$$

You can extend the model just by repeating the process that was used for the second step. This procedure tends to be computationally heavy because at each step, the yield vector and the price vector become one element longer. Furthermore, the discounting process of the $B(T - h, T)$ values goes through the branches of a more and more complex tree.

To build a more realistic process, you must obviously use smaller time intervals. In real-life applications you will probably be modeling quarterly or monthly yields when pricing a derivative that extends several years into the future. A monthly rate model to cover 30yr maturities is a rather massive 360-step tree. When these models were first proposed, this did create a computational problem, and a number of adjustments were implemented to deal with processing time and memory limitations. Today, most of these computational bottlenecks have been overcome by the dazzling performance of workstations.

Exhibit 19-10 European Options on 1yr Zero, Option mty = 2yr, std (bp) = 1%

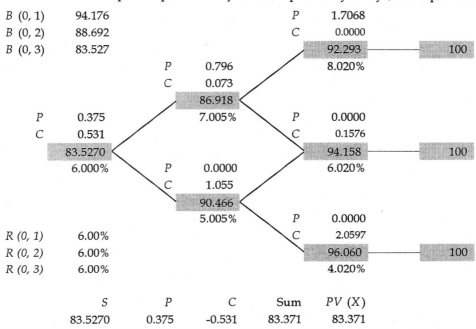

B (0, 1)	94.176
B (0, 2)	88.692
B (0, 3)	83.527

| P | 1.7068 |
| C | 0.0000 |

92.293 ———— 100
8.020%

| P | 0.796 |
| C | 0.073 |

86.918
7.005%

| P | 0.375 |
| C | 0.531 |

83.5270
6.000%

| P | 0.0000 |
| C | 0.1576 |

94.158 ———— 100
6.020%

| P | 0.0000 |
| C | 1.055 |

90.466
5.005%

| P | 0.0000 |
| C | 2.0597 |

96.060 ———— 100
4.020%

R (0, 1)	6.00%
R (0, 2)	6.00%
R (0, 3)	6.00%

S	P	C	Sum	PV (X)
83.5270	0.375	-0.531	83.371	83.371

Exhibit 19-10 shows how to use the HL tree to price European put and call options, 2yr maturity, on the 3yr zero (which will be a 1yr zero at exercise time). You are therefore pricing 1yr caplets and floorlets. You can easily check for yourself that by setting $X = 0$ you will be pricing the 3yr zero. When you have the same exercise price for the put and the call, the put/call parity must hold, as shown in the last row of the exhibit. The HL model can be easily extended to cover the real-life case of a nonflat yield curve. Exhibit 19-11 shows the calculations relative to our three-step tree.

19-5 THE BLACK, DERMAN, AND TOY ONE-FACTOR MODEL

The Ho and Lee pioneering approach had some shortcomings that prompted further developments in the arbitrage-free approach:

- Local volatilities remain constant throughout time, and we know that this hypothesis is in general not supported by adequate statistical evidence.
- Working with bp volatilities is not considered realistic; in fact, volatilities appear to be proportional to the yield level.
- Constant bp volatility can also produce negative yields, which isn't an acceptable result.

A first remedy to these limitations was provided by the BDT, which became very popular in the financial industry because it is a relatively straightforward model and allows a realistic fitting of the observed term structure of both yields and volatilities.

Exhibit 19-11 Structure of the Ho and Lee Model, Upwards Sloping Spot Yield Curve, std (bp) = 1%

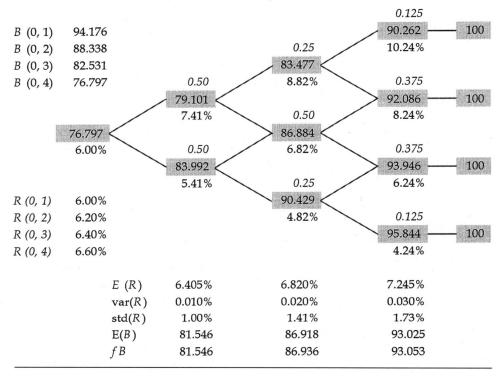

B (0, 1)	94.176
B (0, 2)	88.338
B (0, 3)	82.531
B (0, 4)	76.797

R (0, 1)	6.00%
R (0, 2)	6.20%
R (0, 3)	6.40%
R (0, 4)	6.60%

E (R)	6.405%	6.820%	7.245%
var(R)	0.010%	0.020%	0.030%
std(R)	1.00%	1.41%	1.73%
E(B)	81.546	86.918	93.025
f B	81.546	86.936	93.053

It is based on the familiar lognormal process for the short yield, which means that it cannot lead to negative yields. The lognormal stochastic process also implies that changes in yields tend to be proportional to the level of yields, a common-sense characteristic that fits with available empirical evidence.

The model produces a recombining binomial tree, which is much simpler to interpret and to compute than the nonrecombining variety (an earlier model, the "original Salomon Brothers model," developed by the U.S. bond powerhouse, led to nonrecombining trees; see Tuckman, 1995).

A Very Simple BDT Binomial Tree

Let us start with a binomial representation of a process where yields change lognormally. We shall model the 1yr yield—which is the one factor in the model—assuming a flat yield curve and coarse yearly steps in the tree. After 1 year we get the familiar up and down nodes

$$R_U (1,2) = R(0,1) \cdot \exp(\mu_1 + \sigma \cdot \sqrt{h})$$
$$R_D (1,2) = R(0,1) \cdot \exp(\mu_1 - \sigma \cdot \sqrt{h})$$

Pr(up) = 50%

It is easy to prove (see Mathematical Appendix) that

Exhibit 19-12 Basic Structure of the Black, Derman, Toy Model Volatility of 1yr Forward Rate = 15%

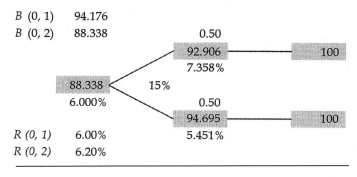

B (0, 1)	94.176	
B (0, 2)	88.338	

R (0, 1)   6.00%
R (0, 2)   6.20%

Exhibit 19-13 BDT Model with Upwards Sloping Spot Yield Curve and Non-Stationary Local Volatilities

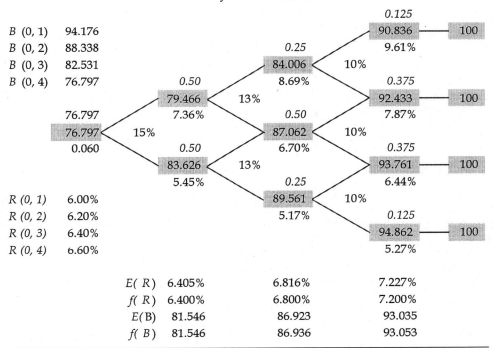

B (0, 1)	94.176
B (0, 2)	88.338
B (0, 3)	82.531
B (0, 4)	76.797

R (0, 1)	6.00%
R (0, 2)	6.20%
R (0, 3)	6.40%
R (0, 4)	6.60%

E(R)	6.405%	6.816%	7.227%
f(R)	6.400%	6.800%	7.200%
E(B)	81.546	86.923	93.035
f(B)	81.546	86.936	93.053

$$\sigma \cdot \sqrt{h} = \frac{1}{2} \cdot \ln\!\left(\frac{R_U}{R_D}\right)$$

$$2 \cdot \sigma \cdot \sqrt{h} = \ln(R_U) - \ln(R_D)$$

$$R_D = \exp[\ln(R_U) - 2 \cdot \sigma \cdot \sqrt{h}]$$

Exhibit 19-14 BDT Model, Pricing European Put and Call on 4yr zero, Options'
Expiration = 2yr

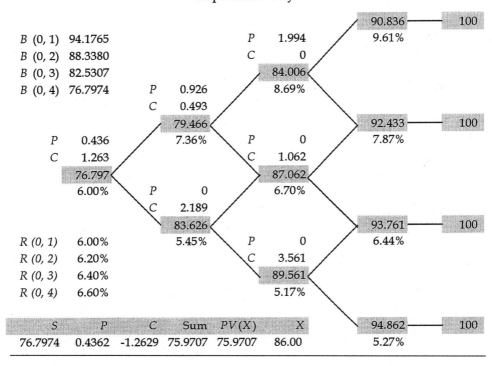

	S	P	C	Sum	PV(X)	X
	76.7974	0.4362	-1.2629	75.9707	75.9707	86.00

$$R_D = R_U \cdot \exp(-2 \cdot \sigma \cdot \sqrt{h})$$

At this point we can determine with numerical methods the value of $[R_U(1,2)]$, which
will correctly price the 2yr zero (see Exhibits 19-12, 19-13, and 19-14). Using the BDT
to price European puts and calls is relatively straightforward. We have already examined the case of options on $B(2,3)$ within the context of the HL model. Exhibit
19-14 shows how to use the BDT tree to price European put and call on the 4yr zero,
expiration date in 2 years (when the zero will be a 2yr zero).

19-6   MATHEMATICAL APPENDIX

Take a random process that can have only two equiprobable outcomes $\{u > d > 0\}$.

$$E(X_2) = \frac{1}{2}(u + d).$$

$$\text{var}(X_2) = \frac{1}{2} \cdot (u^2 + d^2) - \left[\frac{1}{2} \cdot (u + d)\right]^2$$

$$= \frac{1}{2} \cdot (u^2 + d^2) - \frac{1}{4} \cdot u^2 - \frac{1}{2} \cdot u \cdot d - \frac{1}{4} \cdot d^2$$

$$= \frac{1}{4} \cdot u^2 - \frac{1}{2} \cdot u \cdot d + \frac{1}{4} \cdot d^2$$

$$= \left(\frac{1}{2} \cdot u - \frac{1}{2} \cdot d \right)^2$$

$$\sigma = \frac{1}{2} \cdot (u - d)$$

This can be easily adapted to the case in which we measure volatility relative to the log rates.

$$\sigma = \frac{1}{2} \cdot [\ln(u) - \ln(d)] = \frac{1}{2} \cdot \ln\left(\frac{u}{d}\right)$$

Selected Bibliography

Arditti, F. D. *Derivatives.* Boston: Harvard Business School Press, 1996.

BankAmerica Corporation. 1994 annual report.

Bernstein, P. L. *Against the Goods: The Remarkable History of Risk.* New York: John Wiley & Sons, 1996.

Bernstein, P. L., and A. Damodoran, ed. *Investment Management.* New York: John Wiley & Sons, 1998.

BIS (Bank for International Settlements). *Central Bank Survey of Foreign Exchange and Derivatives Market Activity—1995.* Basle, February 1996.

BIS (Bank for International Settlements). *International Banking and Financial Market Developments.* Basle, Various issues.

Black, F., E. Derman, and W. Toy. "A One-Factor Model of Interest Rates and Its Applications to Treasury Bonds Options." *Financial Analysts Journal,* January–February 1990, pp. 33–39.

Black, F., and M. Scholes. "The Pricing of Options and Corporate Liabilities." *Journal of Political Economy* 81 (1973): 637–54.

Bodie, Z., and R. C. Merton. *Finance.* Upper Saddle River, N.J.: Prentice Hall, 1998.

Brealey, R. A., and S. C. Myers. *Principles of Corporate Finance,* 5th ed. New York: McGraw-Hill, 1996.

Brown, R. H., and S. M. Schaefer. "Term Structure of Real Interest Rates and The Cox, Ingersoll and Ross Model." *Journal of Financial Economics* 35 (1994) 3–42.

Burrough, B., and J. Helyar. *Barbarians at the Gate: The Fall of RJR Nabisco.* New York: Harper & Row, 1990.

Campbell, J. Y., A. W. Lo, and A. G. MacKinlay. *The Econometrics of Financial Markets.* Princeton, N.J.: Princeton University Press, 1994.

Chance, D. M. *An Introduction to Derivatives,* 4th ed. Fort Worth: Dryden Press, 1998.

Chew, L. *Managing Derivative Risk: The Use and Abuse of Leverage.* New York: John Wiley & Sons, 1996.

Cooper, I. A., and A. Mello. "Default Risk of Swaps." In *Advanced Topics in Risk Management,* ed. R. Schwartz and C. Smith. Englewood Cliffs, N.J.: Prentice-Hall, 1993.

Copeland, T., T. Koller, and J. Murrin. *Valuation: Measuring and Managing the Value of Companies.* New York: John Wiley & Sons, 1991.

Cox, J., S. Ross, and M. Rubinstein. "Option Pricing: A Simplified Approach." *Journal of Financial Economics* November 17 (1978): 229–63.

Cox, J. and M. Rubinstein. *Options Markets.* Englewood Cliffs, N.J.: Prentice-Hall, 1985.

Crawford, G., and B. Sen. *Derivatives for Decision Makers.* New York: John Wiley & Sons, 1996.

Damodaran, A. *Investment Valuation.* New York: John Wiley & Sons, 1996.

Derman, E., I. Kani, and J. Zou. "The Local Volatility Surface." *Financial Analysts Journal,* 52 July–August (1996).

Dornbush, R., and S. Fischer. *Macroeconomics,* 6th ed. New York: McGraw-Hill, 1994.

Duffie, D. *Futures Markets.* Englewood Cliffs, N.J.: Prentice Hall, 1989.

Duffie, D. *Dynamic Asset Pricing Theory.* Princeton, N.J.: Princeton University Press, 1996.

Edwards, F. R., and C. W. Ma. *Futures and Options.* New York: McGraw-Hill, 1992.

Edwards, C. L. "Open Market Operations in the 1990s." *Federal Reserve Bulletin,* November 1997, 859–74.

Elton, E. J., and M. J. Gruber. *Modern Portfolio Theory and Investment Analysis,* 5th ed. New York: John Wiley & Sons, 1995.

Fabozzi, F. J. *Bond Markets, Analysis, and Strategies,* 3rd ed. N.J.: Prentice-Hall, 1996.

Fabozzi, F.J., and G. Fong. *Advanced Fixed Income Portfolio Management.* Chicago: Probus, 1994.

Fama, E. F. "The Information in the Term Structure." *Journal of Financial Economics* 13 (1984): 509–521.

Fama, E. F., and K. French. "Business Conditions and Expected Returns on Stocks and Bonds." *Journal of Financial Economics* 25 (1989): 23–49.

Fama, E. F. and K. French. "The Cross-section of Expected Stock Returns." *Journal of Finance* 47 (1992): 427–67.

Fama, E. F., and K. French. "Size and Book-to-Market Factors in Earning and Returns." *Journal of Finance* 50 (1995): 131–55.

Fama, E. F., and K. French. "Common Risk Factors in the Returns on Stocks and Bonds." *Journal of Financial Economics* 33 (1993): 3–56.

Fama, E. F., and K. French. "Multifactor Explanations of Asset Pricing Anomalies." *Journal of Finance* 51 (1996a): 55–84.

Fama, E. F., and K. French. "The CAPM Is Wanted, Dead or Alive." *Journal of Finance* 51 (1996b): 1947–58.

Federal Reserve Bank of Richmond. *Instruments of the Money Market,* 7th ed., ed. T.Q. Cook and R. K. LaRoche. Richmond, Va. Federal Reserve Bank of Richmond, 1993.

Feynman, R. P. *The Character of Physical Law.* New York: Penguin, 1992.

French, K. "A Comparison of Futures and Forward Prices." *Journal of Financial Economics* November (1983): 311–42.

French, K., and R. Roll. "Stock Return Variances: The Arrival of Information and the Reaction of Traders." *Journal of Financial Economics* 17 (1986): 5–26.

Galitz, L. *Financial Engineering,* rev. ed. London: *Financial Times.* Pitman, 1995.

Garbade, K. D. *Fixed Income Analytics.* Cambridge, Mass.: MIT Press, 1996.

Gastineau, G. L., and M. P. Kritzman. *Dictionary of Financial Risk Management.* Frank J. Fabozzi, 1996.

Grabbe, J. O. *International Financial Markets.* New York: Elsevier Science, 1996.

Haugen, R. A. *Modern Investment Theory,* 3d ed. Englewood Cliffs, N.J.: Prentice-Hall, 1993.

Ho, T. S. Y., and S. B. Lee "Term Structure Movements and Pricing Interest Rate Contingent Claims." *Journal of Finance* 41 December (1986): 1011–29.

Ho, T. S. Y. *Strategic Fixed Income Investment.* Homewood, Ill.: Dow Jones–Irving, 1990.

Ho, T. S. Y. "Key Rate Durations: Measures of Interest Rate Risk." *Journal of Fixed Income* 2 (1992): 29–44.

Homer, S., and M. L. Leibowitz. *Inside the Yield Book.* New York: Prentice-Hall and New York Institute of Finance, 1972.

Hull, J. C. *Introduction to Futures and Options Markets,* 2d ed. Englewood Cliffs, N.J.: Prentice-Hall, 1995.

Hull, J. C. *Options, Futures and other Derivatives,* 3d ed. Englewood Cliffs, N.J.: Prentice-Hall, 1997.

Ingersoll, J. E. *Theory of Financial Decision Making.* Savage, Md.: Rowman and Littlefield, 1987.

International Securities Markets Association. *Formulae for Yield and Other Calculations,* 2d ed. 1992.

Jarrow, R. A. *Modeling Fixed Income Securities and Interest Rate Options.* New York: McGraw-Hill, 1996.

Jarrow, R. A., and S. M. Turnbull. *Derivative Securities.* Cincinnati: South-Western College Publishing, 1996.

Jorion, P. *Big Bets Gone Bad*. San Diego: Academic Press, 1995.

Kopprash, R. et al. *Effective Duration and the Pricing of Callable Bonds*. Salomon Brothers, 1987.

Krugman, P. *Currencies and Crises*. Cambridge, Mass.: MIT Press, 1992.

Krugman, P. *Peddling Prosperity, Economic Sense and Nonsense in the Age of Diminished Expectations*. New York: W. W. Norton, 1994.

Levich, R. M. *International Financial Markets*. Boston: Irwin McGraw-Hill, 1998.

Litzenberger, R. H. "Swaps: Plain and Fanciful." *Journal of Finance* 47 (1992): 831–50.

Macaulay, F. *Some Theoretical Problems Suggested by the Movements of Interest Rates, Bond Yields, and Stock Prices in the United States since 1856*. New York: National Bureau of Economic Research, 1938.

Malkiel, B. G. *A Random Walk Down Wall Street*, 6th ed. New York: W. W. Norton, 1996.

Markowitz, H. M. *Portfolio Selection: Efficient Diversification of Investments*. New York: John Wiley & Sons, 1959.

Marshall, J. F., and K. R. Kapner. *Understanding Swaps*. New York: John Wiley & Sons, 1993.

Mayle, J. *Standard Securities Calculation Methods*, 3d ed. New York: Securities Industry Association, 1993.

McMillan, L. G. *McMillan on Options*. New York: John Wiley & Sons, 1996.

Merton, R. C. "Theory of Rational Option Pricing." *Bell Journal of Economics and Management Science* 4 (1973): 141–83.

Merton, R. C. *Continuous-Time Finance*, rev. ed. Cambridge, Mass.: Blackwell, 1992.

Mishkin, F. S. *Financial Markets, Institutions, and Money*. New York: HarperCollins, 1995.

Neftci, S. N. *An Introduction to the Mathematics of Financial Derivatives*. San Diego: Academic Press, 1996.

Peters, E. *Chaos and Order in the Capital Markets*, 2d ed. New York: John Wiley & Sons, 1996.

Price, J. A. M., and S. K. Henderson. *Currency and Interest Rate Swaps*, 2d ed. London: Butterworths, 1988.

Rebonato, R. Interest Rate Option Models. New York: John Wiley & Sons, Inc., 1996.

Ross, S. "The Arbitrage Theory of Capital Asset Pricing." *Journal of Economic Theory* 13 (1976): 341–360.

Rubinstein, M. "Implied Binomial Trees." *Journal of Finance* 49 (1994): 771–818.

Salomon Brothers. 1994 annual report.

Sandford, C. S. *Financial Markets in 2020*. New York: Bankers Trust Company, 1993.

Saunders, A., and I. Walter. *Universal Banking in the United States*. Oxford: Oxford University Press, 1994.

Sercu, P., and R. Uppal. *International Financial Markets and the Firm*. Cincinnati: South-Western College Publishing, 1995.

Shaefer, S. M. "The Problem with Redemption Yields." *Financial Analysts Journal* July–August (1977): 59–67.

Sharpe, W. *Investments*. Englewood Cliffs, N.J.: Prentice-Hall, 1976.

Sharpe, W., G. Alexander, and J. Bailey. *Investments*, 5th ed. Englewood Cliffs, N.J.: Prentice-Hall, 1995.

Smith, R. C., and I. Walter. *Global Financial Services*. The Institutional Investor Series in Finance. New York: Harper and Row, 1990.

Smith, R. C. *Comeback: The Restoration of American Banking Power in the New World Economy*. Boston: Harvard Business School Press, 1993.

Solnik, B. *International Investments*, 4th ed. Reading, Mass.: Addison-Wesley, 2000.

Soros, G. *Soros on Soros: Staying Ahead of the Curve*. New York: John Wiley and Sons, 1995.

Stigum, M. *The Repo and Reverse Markets*. Homewood, Ill.: Dow Jones-Irving, 1989.

Stigum, M. *The Money Market*, 3rd ed. Homewood, Ill.: Dow Jones-Irving, 1990.

Sundaresan, S. *Fixed Income Securities and their Derivatives*. Cincinnati: South-Western College Publishing, 1997.

Taleb, N. *Dynamic Hedging: Managing Vanilla and Exotic Options*. New York: John Wiley & Sons, 1997.

The Economist. "The Myth of the Powerless State." 7 October 1995.

The Economist. "International Banking Survey." 27 April 1996.

Tuckman, B. *Fixed Income Securities: Tools for Today's Markets.* New York: John Wiley & Sons, 1995.

Ungar, E. *Swap Literacy: A Comprehensible Guide.* Princeton, N.J.: The Bloomberg Press, 1996.

Vasicek, O. "An Equilibrium Characterization of the Term Structure." *Journal of Financial Economics* 5 (1977): 177–88.

Walmsley, J. *The New Financial Instruments,* New York: John Wiley & Sons, 1988.

Walmsley, J. *New Financial Instruments,* 2nd ed. New York: John Wiley & Sons, 1998.

Yawitz, J. B. *Convexity: An Introduction.* New York: Goldman Sachs, 1986.

Index